CONCISE ENCYCLOPEDIA of Knowledge

CONCISE ENCYCLOPEDIA of Knowledge

edited by
Michael Dempsey

GRAFTON BOOKS
A Division of the Collins Publishing Group

LONDON GLASGOW
TORONTO SYDNEY AUCKLAND

For Inky, Christopher and Paul

Grafton Books
A Division of the Collins Publishing Group
8 Grafton Street, London W1X 3LA

Published by Grafton Books 1986

British Library Cataloguing in Publication Data

Concise encyclopedia.—(Concise dictionaries)
1. Children's encyclopedias and dictionaries
I. Dempsey, Michael W. II. Series
032 AG5

ISBN 0-246-12822-4

Typeset by V & M Graphics Ltd, Aylesbury, Bucks
Printed in Great Britain by
Hazell Watson & Viney Ltd, Aylesbury

Introduction

The CONCISE ENCYCLOPEDIA has articles on all kinds of topics, arranged in alphabetical order. This enables you to find information quickly and easily. Many articles contain cross-references to other articles that tell you more about the subject. These are indicated by SMALL CAPITALS.

In addition there is information presented in charts (including a detailed chronology of history) and many illustrations. All the statistics in the book are the latest available. For cities, two population figures are given where appropriate: one for the city itself and one that includes the suburbs (metropolitan area).

There are maps of major geographical regions and countries, close to the articles they illustrate. The key to their colouring and symbols is below.

- Grasslands
- Forests
- Mountains
- Deserts
- Polar conditions

- ■ Cities with more than 1,000,000 people
- ● Cities with more than 250,000 people
- • Towns
- □ Country capital
- ▲ High peak, above sea level
- ▼ Depth, below sea level

Obviously you will not find all you need to know about a subject in this encyclopedia. But you will find it invaluable at home or at school – and easy to carry between the two.

A

Aachen City in West Germany, situated on boundary with Netherlands and Belgium. Founded by Romans in first century AD on site of natural springs. Site of the tomb of Charlemagne. Pop: 244,000.

Aardvark A thickset burrowing mammal of southern Africa. Known also as the earthpig, it is the sole member of the order *Tubulidentata*. It licks up termites with its long, sticky tongue.

Aardvark

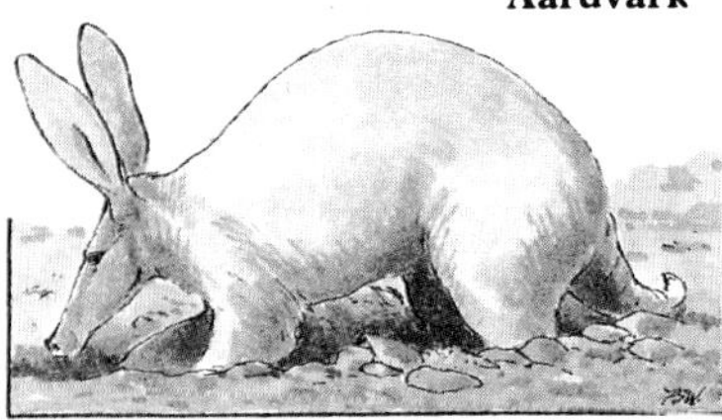

Abacus A simple calculating machine used for hundreds of years in many parts of the world. It consists of rows of beads strung on wires. Beads on the first wire count as ones, those on the second wire count as tens, on the third wire they count as hundreds, and so on. The abacus is still used in Eastern countries such as China and Japan.

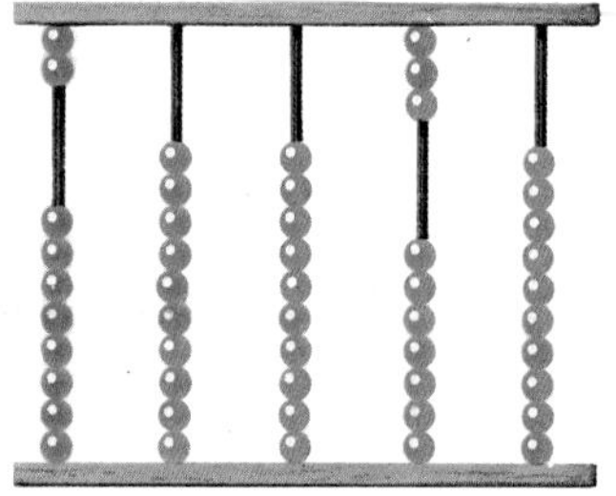

By moving beads to and fro on an abacus all arithmetical processes can be carried out.

Aborigine Term used for the original – aboriginal – inhabitants of a country or region. Used particularly for Australian aborigines.

Abraham Biblical figure regarded as the father of the Hebrews and the founder of Judaism. According to the Old Testament he received God's promise that his people would inherit the land of Canaan.

Absolute zero The lowest possible temperature that can theoretically be obtained: –273.16°C. At this point the molecules of a substance would cease to move and the substance would have no heat. In experiments scientists have come to within one-millionth of a degree of absolute zero.

The absolute scale is based upon absolute zero. In this scale the melting point of ice becomes 273.16°K (degrees Kelvin, after Lord Kelvin) and the boiling point of water 373.16°K.

Acacia Large group of trees belonging to the pea family, sometimes called mimosas. Many, including the wattle, have bright yellow flowers. They grow in warm countries.

Acceleration The word acceleration is normally used to mean an increase in speed. To the scientist it means much more than this: it means the rate of change of velocity, and this involves changes in direction as well as speed. If you are walking towards north and then turn left, you have accelerated in a westerly direction.

Accelerator, particle Machine used to study the structure of ATOMS. The tiny particles from which atoms are made are accelerated to very high speeds and then made to strike a target. Atoms in the target may be split apart by the collision and the results photographed. During acceleration, the particles travel along a straight or circular tube that may be several kilometres long.

Achilles In Greek legend a hero of the Trojan War who slew Hector. He died when the only vulnerable spot on his body, his heel, was wounded by PARIS.

Acid Acids are a group of chemicals that are known for their sour taste. Some acids, such as sulphuric acid, hydrochloric acid, and nitric acid, are very strong and can corrode even the strongest metals. Other acids are harmless. Citric acid gives oranges and lemons their sharp taste. There is acetic acid in vinegar. All acids turn a special kind of paper called litmus paper from blue to red.

Acoustics The study of sound. An acoustics engineer designing a concert hall has to control the way sound is reflected and absorbed by walls, roof, and even people. If the sound is reflected too much, echoes may be set up. If it is absorbed too much, the sound will die away too quickly.

Adam, Robert (1728–92) Famous Scottish-born architect who, together with his brother **James** (1730–94), imitated the classical style, paying as much attention to the interior decoration and furniture of a house as to its exterior.

Adder Also called the common viper, this poisonous snake is about 65 cm long and is characterized by the dark zig-zag markings along its grey or brown back. Adders give birth to live young.

Adelaide Major port and capital city of South Australia, situated on R. Torrens. Pop: 953,000 (met area).

Adonis In Greek legend, a beautiful youth loved by Aphrodite. When he was killed by a boar, she persuaded the gods to allow him to return from Hades and live on Earth for six months of each year.

Aeneas In Greek legend, the leading Trojan to escape from Troy. His many adventures, including shipwreck, his love affair with Queen Dido of Carthage, and eventual arrival at the site of the future city of Rome, are recounted in Virgil's *Aeneid*.

Aerodynamics The study of air moving around solid objects. Aerodynamics sometimes deals with air moving against an object, like the wind filling the sails of a boat or flowing around a bridge or a building. Sometimes it deals with an object moving through air, such as a car or a plane. An important part of aerodynamics is streamlining – shaping an object so that air flows smoothly around it.

Aerosol An aerosol is a gas which has solid or liquid particles in it. Natural aerosols include clouds, fog and smoke. Paints and other products are packaged in aerosol cans. When a button is pressed, liquified gas shoots out at high pressure, carrying the paint or other product with it as a fine spray.

Aesop (6th century BC) Greek slave popularly believed to be the author or collector of many Greek fables.

Afghanistan Mountainous, landlocked state of SW Asia. The cultivated land is confined to the fertile valleys and plains where most people are subsistence farmers. Wheat is the staple crop, and sheep and goats the most important domestic animals. Area: 648,000 km^2; Pop: 14,448,000; Cap: Kabul.

Africa A continent separated from Europe by the Strait of Gibraltar and from Asia by the Suez Canal. The land is mostly a high, rolling plateau with steep slopes leading down to narrow coastal plains. The northern part is taken up by the largest desert in the world – the Sahara. Africa contains some of the poorest countries in the world. Area: 30,319,000 km^2; Pop: 513,000,000. See map on pages 8 and 9.

Wind tunnel tests are used to improve the streamlining of high-speed vehicles.

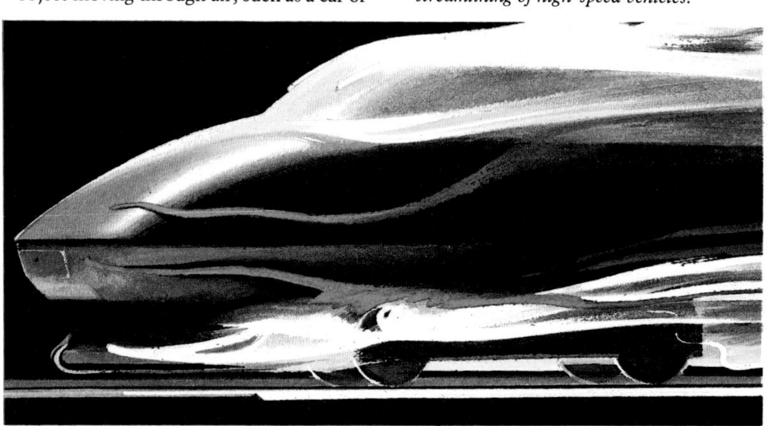

Africa (Map)

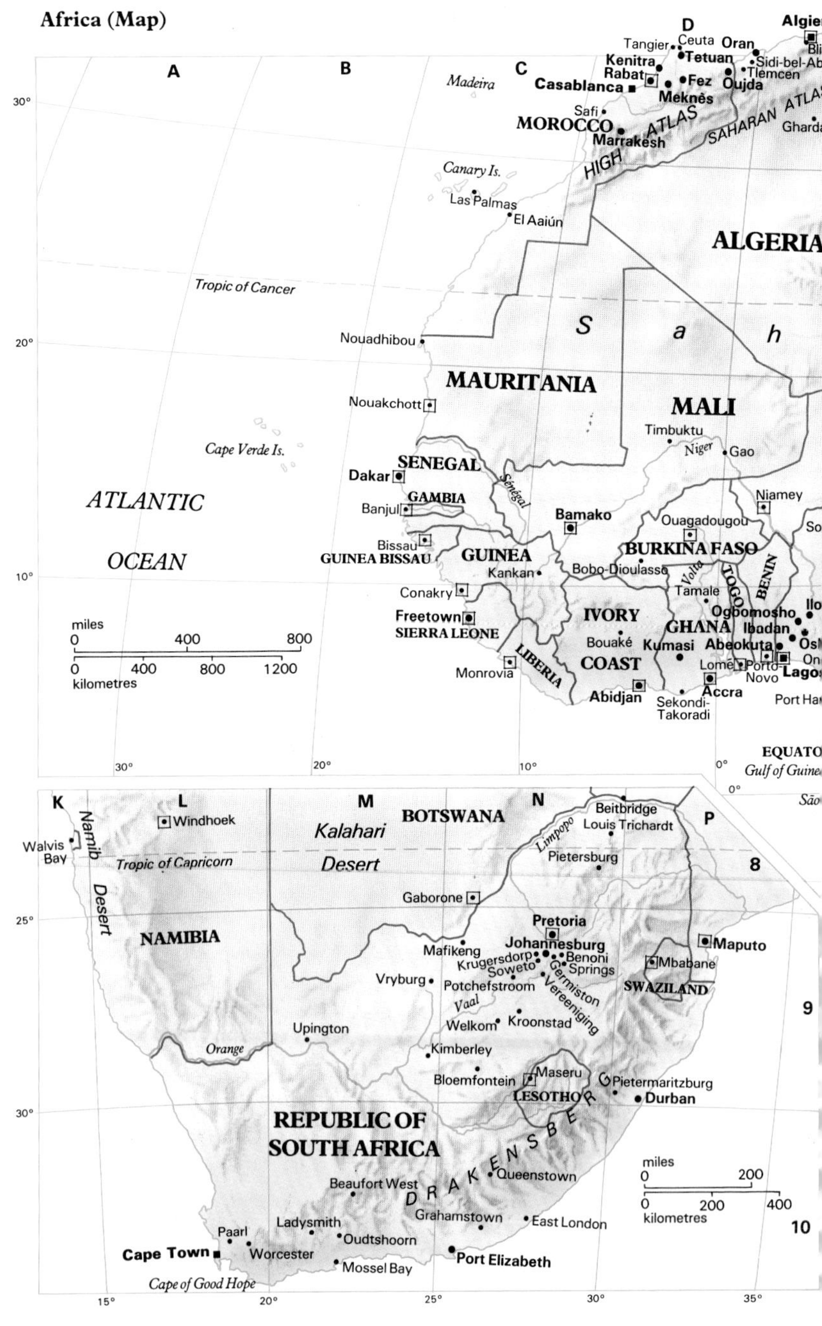

A
B
C
D
Madeira
Tangier
Ceuta
Oran
Tetuan
Kenitra
Rabat
Casablanca
Fez
Meknês
Oujda
Tlemcen
Safi
MOROCCO
Marrakesh
HIGH ATLAS
SAHARAN ATLAS
Canary Is.
Las Palmas
El Aaiún
ALGERIA
Tropic of Cancer
Nouadhibou
MAURITANIA
Nouakchott
MALI
Timbuktu
Niger
Gao
Cape Verde Is.
SENEGAL
Dakar
GAMBIA
Banjul
Sénégal
Bamako
Niamey
Ouagadougou
ATLANTIC
OCEAN
Bissau
GUINEA BISSAU
GUINEA
BURKINA FASO
Kankan
Bobo-Dioulasso
Volta
TOGO
BENIN
Conakry
Tamale
Freetown
SIERRA LEONE
IVORY COAST
Ogbomosho
Ibadan
Abeokuta
GHANA
Bouaké
Kumasi
Lomé
Porto-Novo
Lagos
Monrovia
LIBERIA
Abidjan
Accra
Sekondi-Takoradi
miles
0
400
800
0
400
800
1200
kilometres
EQUATO
Gulf of Guine
30°
20°
10°
0°
K
L
M
N
P
Windhoek
Walvis Bay
Namib Desert
Tropic of Capricorn
Kalahari Desert
BOTSWANA
Beitbridge
Louis Trichardt
Limpopo
Pietersburg
8
Gaborone
Pretoria
NAMIBIA
Mafikeng
Johannesburg
Krugersdorp
Soweto
Benoni
Springs
Germiston
Vereeniging
Maputo
Mbabane
SWAZILAND
Vryburg
Potchefstroom
Vaal
Welkom
Kroonstad
9
Upington
Orange
Kimberley
Bloemfontein
Maseru
LESOTHO
Pietermaritzburg
Durban
REPUBLIC OF SOUTH AFRICA
DRAKENSBERG
Queenstown
Beaufort West
Grahamstown
East London
Ladysmith
Paarl
Oudtshoorn
Worcester
Cape Town
Mossel Bay
Port Elizabeth
Cape of Good Hope
miles
0
200
0
200
400
kilometres
10
25°
30°
15°
20°
25°
30°
35°

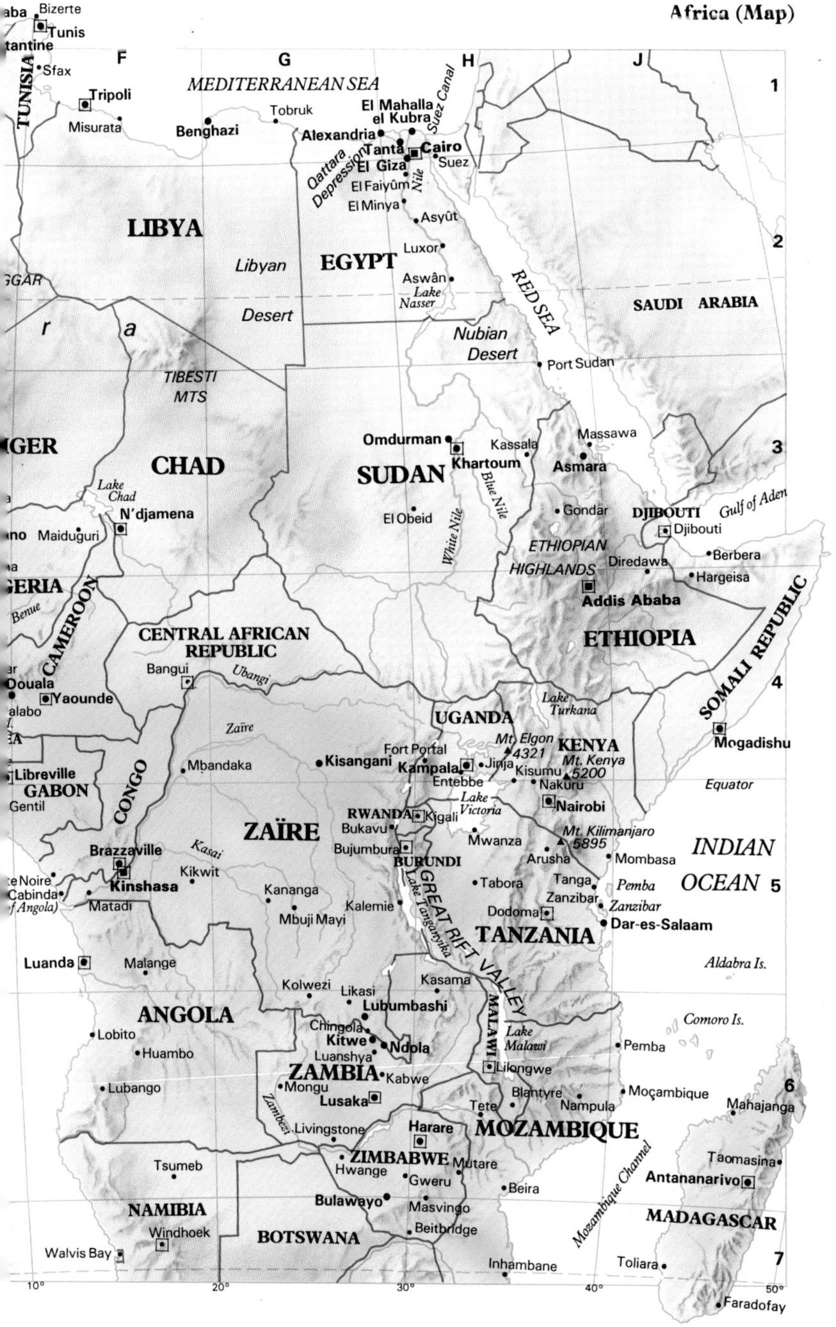

F G H J

1 2 3 4 5 6 7

MEDITERRANEAN SEA
TUNISIA
Bizerte
Tunis
Sfax
Tripoli
Misurata
Benghazi
Tobruk
El Mahalla el Kubra
Suez Canal
Alexandria
Tanta
Cairo
Suez
Qattara Depression
El Giza
El Faiyûm
Nile
El Minya
Asyût
LIBYA
Libyan Desert
EGYPT
Luxor
Aswân
Lake Nasser
RED SEA
SAUDI ARABIA
Nubian Desert
Port Sudan
TIBESTI MTS
CHAD
Lake Chad
N'djamena
Maiduguri
Omdurman
Khartoum
Kassala
Massawa
Asmara
SUDAN
Blue Nile
White Nile
El Obeid
Gondar
DJIBOUTI
Djibouti
Gulf of Aden
ETHIOPIAN HIGHLANDS
Diredawa
Berbera
Hargeisa
Addis Ababa
ETHIOPIA
SOMALI REPUBLIC
Benue
CAMEROON
CENTRAL AFRICAN REPUBLIC
Bangui
Ubangi
Douala
Yaounde
Lake Turkana
UGANDA
Zaïre
Mt. Elgon 4321
KENYA
Mt. Kenya 5200
Mogadishu
Fort Portal
Mbandaka
Kisangani
Kampala
Jinja
Kisumu
Nakuru
Entebbe
Equator
Libreville
GABON
Gentil
CONGO
Lake Victoria
Nairobi
RWANDA
Kigali
ZAÏRE
Bukavu
Mwanza
Mt. Kilimanjaro 5895
Kasai
Bujumbura
Arusha
Mombasa
INDIAN OCEAN
Brazzaville
BURUNDI
Kinshasa
Kikwit
Tabora
Tanga
Pemba
Cabinda
Matadi
Kananga
Lake Tanganyika
GREAT RIFT VALLEY
Kalemie
Zanzibar
Mbuji Mayi
Dodoma
Dar-es-Salaam
TANZANIA
Luanda
Malange
Aldabra Is.
Kolwezi
Likasi
Kasama
Lubumbashi
ANGOLA
MALAWI
Comoro Is.
Lobito
Chingola
Kitwe
Ndola
Lake Malawi
Pemba
Huambo
Luanshya
ZAMBIA
Kabwe
Lilongwe
Lubango
Mongu
Lusaka
Blantyre
Moçambique
Mahajanga
Zambezi
Tete
Nampula
Livingstone
Harare
MOZAMBIQUE
Mozambique Channel
Tsumeb
ZIMBABWE
Hwange
Mutare
Toamasina
Gweru
Antananarivo
Beira
NAMIBIA
Bulawayo
Masvingo
MADAGASCAR
Windhoek
Beitbridge
BOTSWANA
Walvis Bay
Inhambane
Toliara
Faradofay

10° 20° 30° 40° 50°

Agamemnon In Greek legend, the leader of the Greek armies during the Trojan War. On his return home he was killed by his wife Clytemnestra.

Agaric Any member of a large group of toadstools characterized by radiating gills beneath the cap. The group includes the edible field mushroom as well as poisonous types such as the 'fairy tale' fly agaric and the death cap.

Agricola, Gnaeus Julius (AD *c* 37–93) Brilliant Roman general and statesman who came to Britain to complete its conquest and was governor for seven years.

Air A colourless mixture of gases that surrounds the Earth and is vital to all

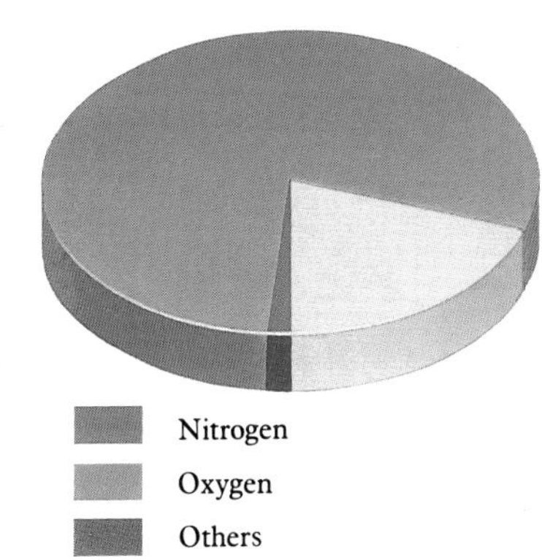

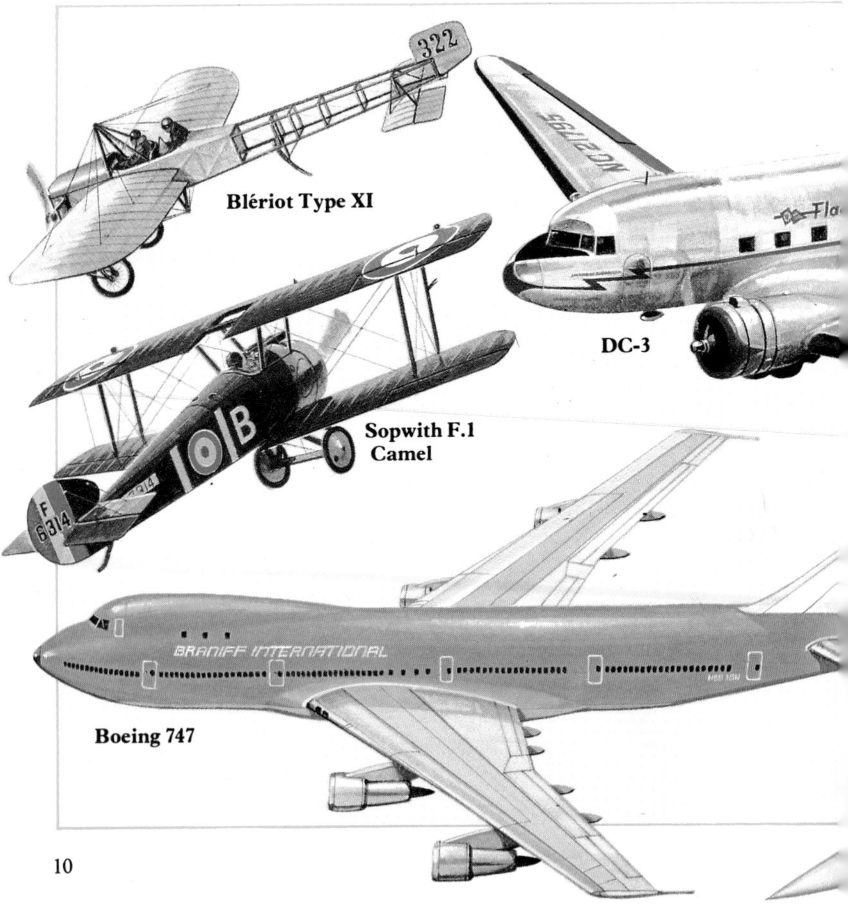

Blériot Type XI

DC-3

Sopwith F.1 Camel

Boeing 747

living things. Air consists mainly of nitrogen (78 per cent) and oxygen (21 per cent). Air also holds some water in very fine particles called vapour. The humidity of the air is the amount of water vapour it contains.

Aircraft Machines which fly by making use of buoyancy, or of aerodynamic forces. AIRSHIPS, HELICOPTERS, gliders and aeroplanes are all aircraft.

Aeroplanes fly using the 'lift' produced by air flowing over specially shaped wings (aerofoils). These are curved at the top and almost flat underneath. Air passing over the wing travels faster than air passing under the wing because it has farther to go. This creates lower pressure above the wing than beneath it, and the resulting 'suction' lifts the wing and the plane. The thrust needed to push the aeroplane through the air comes either from a propeller or from a GAS TURBINE (jet) engine.

The first sustained 'heavier-than-air' machine flight was made on 17 December, 1903 by the American Orville Wright in a flimsy machine designed by himself and his brother Wilbur. Developments in design were rapid, especially during the two World Wars. In 1952 the first jetliner entered service. It heralded a boom in air travel, now catered for by wide-bodied and 'jumbo' jets. The first commercial supersonic airliner, Concorde, was put into service in 1976.

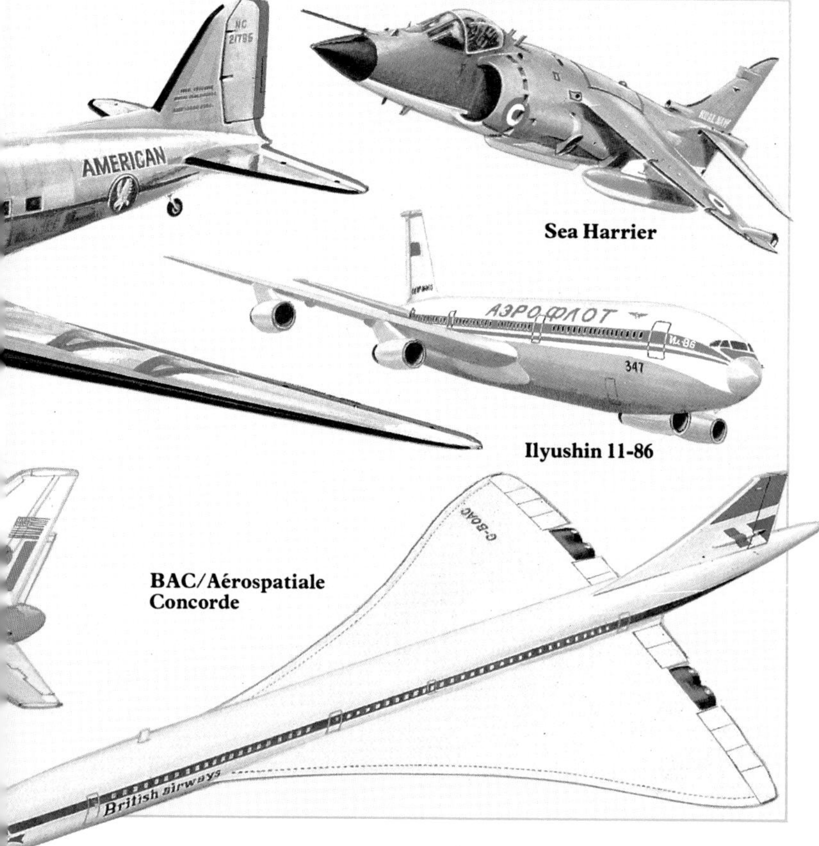

Sea Harrier

Ilyushin 11-86

BAC/Aérospatiale Concorde

Airships were used by Germany to bomb London in World War I, with little success.

Airship A lighter-than-air craft powered by an engine or engines, that can be steered. The German Zeppelin airships were used during and after World War I. But when the British *R101* crashed in 1930, followed by the destruction by fire of the Zeppelin *Hindenburg* in 1937, airship construction virtually ended. Modern airships are lifted by non-inflammable helium gas instead of the dangerous hydrogen of the past.

Ajax In Greek legend a giant and one of the heroes of the Trojan War. He quarrelled with Odysseus over the armour of the dead warrior Achilles. When the armour was awarded to Odysseus Ajax went mad with rage and later killed himself with his own sword.

Alaska The USA's largest state was named Seward's Folly after the US Secretary of State William Seward bought it from Russia for $7.2 million in 1867. Gold was discovered in 1896 and minerals, especially oil, now dominate the booming economy. Area: 1,518,800 km²; Pop: 402,000; Cap: Juneau.

Albania A small mountainous country on the Adriatic Sea. Albania is the poorest country in Europe despite considerable mineral resources. After World War II a communist government was established. Area: 28,700 km²; Pop: 2,900,000; Cap: Tiranë.

Albatross Large black and white sea birds of the southern oceans, famed for their flying ability. The largest species, the wandering albatross, has a wingspan of more than four metres.

Albino An animal that lacks skin pigments, resulting in a pure white individual.

Alchemy A mixture of science and magic that was popular in the Middle Ages. It centred around attempts to find the Philosopher's Stone, which would change ordinary metals into gold and make human beings immortal. It was from the work of the alchemists that the modern science of chemistry developed.

Alcohol The name given to a group of chemical substances, also called ethanol and ethyl alcohol. Alcohols are widely used in industry, particularly in dissolving organic chemicals.

Intoxicating alcoholic drinks are made by a process called FERMENTATION. Wine is made by fermenting fruit juices. Beer is produced by fermenting grain. The fermented liquid can be *distilled* to make spirits such as whisky and gin.

Alexander the Great (356–323 BC) Son of Philip II of Macedon. Became king in 336 BC. In 334 he began a series of victorious campaigns including the defeat of the Persian Empire of Darius III (331 BC) and the conquest of lands as far east as India. When his armies refused to go any further Alexander turned back. At Babylon he caught a fever and died. Subsequently his great empire crumbled.

Egyptian coin showing the head of Alexander the Great.

Alfred the Great (AD 849–899) King of Wessex from AD 871. He was defeated many times by the Danes and was forced to pay Danegeld to them. In AD 878 he fled to the Somerset fens where the burning of the cakes is supposed to have taken place. He finally defeated the Danes at Edington and divided England with them. An able administrator, he promoted the spread of education and built many ships.

Algae A group of simple plants, most of which live in water, others in damp places on land. About 25,000 different kinds are known, some green, some brown and some red. Many are single-celled, and too small to be seen without a microscope. Others are large SEAWEEDS.

Algebra A brance of mathematics in which letters and symbols are used to represent quantities. For example, the formula for the area of a circle is $a = \pi r^2$. In this formula a stands for area and r is the radius of the circle. π is the Greek letter *pi*, a constant equal to approximately 3.1416.

Algeria Second largest country in Africa but almost 90% of the land is desert. Most people live in the narrow coastal plain bordering the Mediterranean, where cereal crops, citrus fruits and grapes are grown. Southwards the land rises to the Atlas Mts then falls away to the Sahara Desert. Few people live in the Sahara but this region is Algeria's chief source of wealth, for it contains large deposits of oil and natural gas. Area: 2,382,000 km^2; Pop: 21,351,000; Cap: Algiers.

Alkali Alkalis are soluble BASES – substances which combine with or neutralize acids to form salts. Caustic soda and potash are alkalis. They form a solution in water that has a bitter taste. They are used to make soaps. Household ammonia is also an alkali.

Allergy A usually irritating response to certain substances, for example pollen causing sneezing or certain foods causing a rash.

Alligator Large swamp-dwelling reptiles of the crocodile family. One kind lives in southern N America, another in China. The alligator has tough knobbly skin, a huge mouth set with sharp teeth, and eyes on top of its head. These allow it to see its prey while remaining largely submerged in the water.

Alloy A mixture of two or more metals. When metals are mixed, the resulting alloy is often quite different from the original pure metals. For example, copper is soft and quite weak, but when zinc is added to it to make brass, or tin is added to make bronze, the result in both cases is a hard, strong metal.

Almond A deciduous tree of south-western Asia which has been grown elsewhere for many hundreds of years. It belongs to the rose family. There are several varieties of almond. Some are grown for their nuts, others for their pretty pink blossom.

Alphabet Group of letters, or signs, which stand for sounds and are used to write down a language. The Greek alphabet had 24 letters, the Roman alphabet 26. Our alphabet comes from the Roman. Other alphabets used today include the Russian, Japanese, Hebrew and Arabic.

Alps Mountain range in S central Europe, stretching in a great arc from the south of France through Switzerland and Italy to Austria. Contains some of Europe's highest peaks including Mont Blanc (4807 metres).

Aluminium Lightweight, corrosion-resistant metal which conducts electricity well.

Aluminium alloys combine strength with lightness and are widely used in the construction of vehicles, ships and aeroplanes. Metal is refined from one ore – bauxite – in a process requiring huge amounts of electrical energy. Chem. symbol Al.

Amazon Largest river in South America and the world (by volume), flowing from the Andes through Peru and Brazil to the Atlantic coast. It drains the biggest area of tropical rain forest in the world. It is navigable as far as Iquitos in Peru, 3700 km from the sea. Length: 6500 km.

Amazons In Greek legend a tribe of warlike women who fought against the Greeks in the Trojan War. One of the Labours of Heracles (Hercules) was to retrieve the girdle of their queen Hippolyte.

Amber Hard substance formed from the resin of pine trees that lived millions of years ago. Some lumps of amber contain the remains of prehistoric insects that were trapped by the sticky substance. The finest amber is used for jewellery.

American Indians The original inhabitants of North and South America came from Asia. They crossed the narrow Bering Strait to Alaska during the Great Ice Age and gradually spread throughout the continents. In Central and S America civilizations such as the Mayas, Aztecs and Incas emerged before the arrival of the Europeans. In N America the Indians lived in tribes that hunted, gathered or fished. Today most N American Indians live on crowded reservations.

American Revolution (1775–83) The war in which 13 colonies of North America gained independence from Britain. The colonists hated paying taxes to the British government when they had no representatives in parliament. At first they wanted only changes in the law, but after war broke out, the colonies issued their Declaration of Independence. The British troops were defeated and the commander of the colonial forces, George WASHINGTON, became first president of the United States of America.

Amoeba Microscopic protozoan (single-celled organism) made of jelly-like cytoplasm. Amoebae move and feed by pushing out false feet called *pseudopodia*.

Map of the Indian Nations in 1880. Inset: Sitting Bull, the famous Indian warrior who led the Sioux at the battle of Little Bighorn (1878) in which General Custer and his troops perished.

They reproduce by division.

Amphibian A cold-blooded animal belonging to the vertebrate class *Amphibia* which contains FROGS, TOADS and NEWTS. They live in or by water or return there to breed. They metamorphose from egg to tadpole to adult. SALAMANDERS and caecilians are also amphibians.

Amsterdam Port and capital city of the Netherlands, connected by canal to North Sea. An historic commercial centre, constructed on numerous small islands divided by canals. Pop: 729,000.

Amundsen, Roald (1872–1928) Norwegian explorer. First to negotiate the Northwest Passage (1903–06) and first to reach the South Pole (1911), a month before his English rival Robert Scott. He died while on a rescue mission to a crashed airship in the Arctic.

Anaconda Largest S American constricting snake which grows up to 10 metres long and lives near water. It is olive green with black rings or spots. It eats birds and small mammals.

Anaemia Shortage of red blood cells and consequently haemoglobin which makes the skin look pale and causes lack of energy.

Anaesthetics Drugs used in medicine that cause loss of feeling and so eliminate pain. There are two types: local anaesthetics that work on a restricted area of the body, and general anaesthetics that act on the entire body.

Anatomy Study of the structure of plants and animals, internal and external, and often involving dissection.

Anchovy Small marine fish, only 14 cm long, related to the herring.

Andersen, Hans Christian (1805–75) Danish author, poet and novelist. After years of poverty he gained recognition with his fairy tales. Among the best known are *The Ugly Duckling*, *The Red Shoes* and *The Little Mermaid*.

Andes Mountain system in South America, running along the Pacific coast for the entire length of the continent. Source of many rivers including the Amazon. Highest peak is Ancohuma (7014 metres). The range is rich in minerals.

Andorra Small principality located in the Pyrenees between France and Spain. Created by a treaty in 1278, the co-princes are now the Spanish Bishop of Urgel and the President of France.

Andromeda In Greek legend the daughter of Cepheus and Cassiopeia. To appease Poseidon, who had been angered by the claim that she was more beautiful than the Nereids, Andromeda was chained to a rock to be devoured by a sea monster. She was rescued by Perseus and later married him.

Anemone Several species of flowering plant related to the buttercup and often known as windflowers.

Angel Falls Waterfall on the Caroni River, SE Venezuela. Highest falls in the world. Longest drop: 807m; Total height: 980m.

Angelico, Fra (1387–1455) Italian painter and monk. Many of his frescoes can be found in Rome and Florence.

Anglerfish A bottom-living fish with an enormous head and huge jaws. A long fin-ray on the top of its head lures other fishes into its jaws.

Anglo-Saxons Ancestors of the English people. The Anglo-Saxons were tribes from Germany – Angles, Saxons, and Jutes – who invaded England in the 5th century and drove the Celtic Britons out of the English lowlands. They established several kingdoms, such as Northumbria, Mercia and Wessex, and became Christians. The Saxon kings of Wessex united England for the first time in the 10th century.

Angola Republic on the coast of W Africa. Savanna covers much of the land but there are forests in the north and semi-desert in the south. Most of the people are subsistence farmers or cattle herders. Angola gained its independence in 1975 after more than four centuries of Portuguese rule. The communist government is supported by Cuban troops. Area: 1,247,000 km^2; Pop: 7,741,000; Cap: Luanda.

Animal A member of the animal kingdom (rather than the plant kingdom) which comprises organisms which move about freely and feed on plants (or other animals). Animals are classified into numerous groups from vertebrates to single-celled protozoa, according to their phylum, class, order, family, genus and species.

Annelid Member of a group of soft-bodied worms with long, distinctly ringed or segmented bodies. The group includes EARTHWORMS, bristleworms and LEECHES.

Ant About 15,000 species of social insect, related to bees and wasps. In a typical ant colony, the queen lays eggs which are tended by numerous wingless females called workers. In some species, there are large workers called soldiers to defend the nest. None of the workers lays eggs. Every year some of the eggs produce new queens and winged males, which mate during a 'wedding flight' from the nest.

Antarctica An ice-shrouded continent larger than Europe surrounding the South Pole. Few plants can survive the harsh climate and animals such as penguins depend upon the sea for their food. The only human inhabitants are scientists at a number of permanent stations. Area: 13,209,000 km^2.

Anteater Mammals of the order *Edentata*. The giant anteater lives in S America. It has a long bushy tail and long thin snout. It rips open ant nests with its claws and licks up the insects with its whiplike tongue. It is also called an antbear.

Antelope Large group of mostly African ruminants with hoofs and horns. The horns are unbranched but very varied in shape. They are rarely used in defence; antelopes run from their enemies and seek safety in herds. There are many different kinds ranging from the cow-sized eland to the dog-sized dik-dik. Other species include the sable, the kudu, the SPRINGBOK, the GAZELLE and the GNU.

Antibiotics Substances which destroy or inhibit the growth of disease-causing micro-organisms. Most are derived from fungi. Penicillin was the first to be discovered, in 1928 by Sir Alexander Fleming, though it took another 12 years before the drug was fully developed and ready for use.

Antibody A substance produced by the body to fight infection by harmful bacteria or viruses, and to immunize a person against future attack. Antibodies are produced by certain white blood cells.

Antigen A foreign substance in the body, usually associated with a bacterium or virus, that results in the production of antibodies.

Anubis In ancient Egyptian myth, the god who led the dead to judgement. He is depicted with the head of a jackal.

Ape The four mammals most closely related to humans are the apes: the CHIMPANZEE, GORILLA, ORANG-UTAN and GIBBON. The largest at nearly two metres tall is the gorilla. Like the others it is a forest dweller feeding mainly on fruit and leaves. None of the apes has a tail.

Aphid A group of tiny insects including greenfly and blackfly. Aphids are bugs, and are also known as plant lice. They are serious pests as they deform plants by sucking their sap. They also spread plant diseases.

Aphrodite Greek goddess of love, fertility and beauty. The daughter of Zeus and mother of Eros, she is said to have sprung from the foam of the sea. (Roman equivalent Venus.)

Apollo Greek and Roman god of light, the arts, medicine and prophecy, and second only to Zeus in importance.

Apollo programme This was the American man-on-the-moon programme. A total of 12 astronauts landed on the Moon between July 1969 and December 1972. The astronauts were launched into space in the three-man Apollo command module. Two astronauts later transferred to the lunar module to make the Moon landing.

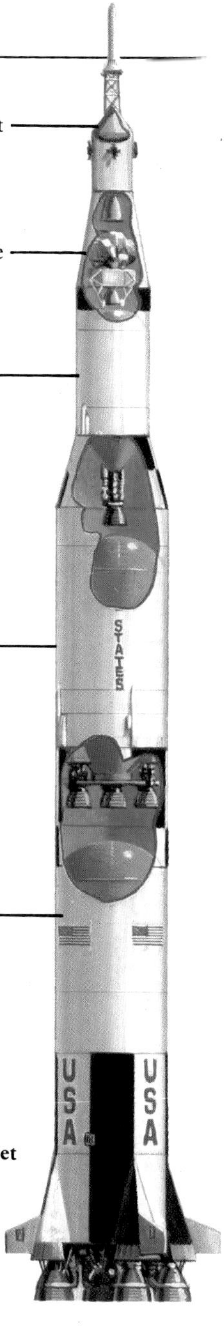

crew compartment

lunar module

3rd stage

2nd stage

1st stage

Saturn V moon rocket

Apostles Early followers of Jesus Christ, particularly those twelve disciples chosen by him, including Simon Peter, James and John, Matthew and Judas Iscariot.

Appalachian Mountains Mountain range in the USA, running from Maine to Alabama, parallel to the Atlantic coast. Highest peak is Mount Mitchell (2037 metres).

Apple The most widely eaten of all fruits, thousands of different varieties of apple are grown all over the world. The apple tree is a member of the rose family.

Arabs Descendants of the original inhabitants of Arabia who have spread with their culture, language and religion (Islam) throughout western Asia and N Africa. Today most are town-dwellers though some – the Bedouin – still pursue a nomadic life in the desert.

Arachnid Group of arthropods containing the SPIDERS, harvestmen, SCORPIONS and mites. Arachnids are most readily distinguished from insects by their four pairs of walking legs (an insect has three pairs).

Archaeology The study of the past. Archaeologists study objects such as graves, remains of buildings and bits of broken pottery, in order to find out about life in the past. These objects have often been buried for hundreds of years and must be carefully excavated. Archaeologists can discover facts about people who lived in prehistoric times.

Archaeopteryx Prehistoric bird that lived during the Jurassic period. Descended from the dinosaurs, it had teeth and claws on its wings. Although it had feathers, it was probably a weak flyer.

Archaeopteryx

Archimedes (*c* 287–*c* 212 BC) Greek mathematician, engineer and physicist. He is remembered for the Archimedean screw (a device for raising water) and for his principle of buoyancy (Archimedes' principle).

Architecture Architecture is the science of building; an architect produces the plans from which a builder works.

Most civilizations and ages in history have had their own distinctive styles of architecture. The ancient Greeks raised elegant marble columns, while the Romans invented the arch and the vaulted roof. The castles and Christian cathedrals of the Middle Ages at first followed the Roman style, but later buildings have the pointed arches and soaring spires known as Gothic. Renaissance architects returned to the 'classical' simplicity of Greece and Rome, but by the 1600s a more elaborate, decorated style called Baroque had appeared.

Modern architecture has its own style, using new materials such as plastic, reinforced concrete and steel, as well as traditional stone and brick. The typical building of today is the tall skyscraper.

Arctic Northern polar region composed of the Arctic Ocean and the surrounding lands of North America, Asia and Scandinavia. Due to the tilt of the Earth's axis, there is at least one day each year in the Arctic when the Sun does not set, and another day when the Sun does not rise. The number of such days increases towards the North Pole which has six months continuous day followed by six months continuous night.

Ares Greek god of war. The son of Zeus and Hera, he supported the Trojans in the Trojan War. (Roman equivalent Mars.)

Argentina Second largest nation in S America. Argentina is a major farming nation and agricultural products account for almost 90% of its exports. The main crops are wheat, maize, linseed, sugar and cotton. Cattle raising is concentrated on the pampas and sheep rearing on the windy plains of Patagonia in the south. Area: 2,766,000 km^2; Pop: 30,228,000; Cap: Buenos Aires.

Argon The most abundant of the inert gases in the atmosphere. Used in gas-filled light bulbs, in gas discharge tubes (where it produces a blue glow) and in arc-welding. Chem. symbol A.

Argonauts In Greek legend, the band of heroes who accompanied Jason in the search for the Golden Fleece.

Aristophanes (450–385 BC) One of the greatest Greek playwrights and poets. His writings are full of good-natured ridicule of the people and customs of his time.

Aristotle (384–322 BC) Greek philosopher who was a pupil of Plato and tutored the young Alexander of Macedon. He founded the famous Lyceum school at Athens and wrote on a wide range of subjects: metaphysics, ethics, politics, logic and literature.

Arithmetic A branch of mathematics that deals with counting and calculating, using numbers. The four main operations in arithmetic are addition, subtraction, multiplication, and division.

Armada, Spanish (1588) A great fleet sent by King Philip II of Spain to conquer England. With the help of the weather and using fireships (burning hulks set to drift into the enemy), the English navy was able to prevent the Spanish ships picking up soldiers in the Netherlands, as planned. Chased by the English, the Spaniards retreated around the north of Britain. Only 67 ships out of 130 reached home safely.

Armadillo Several kinds of mammals with bony armour-plating on their backs. They live in S and C America and in the southern United States. They burrow in the ground and eat insects. Some are able to roll up into a ball.

Armour Protective clothing, usually metal, worn to prevent injury in battle. Most fighting men have worn some kind of armour since ancient times. The most elaborate was worn by medieval knights, who even rode armoured horses. Guns and explosives made armour less useful, but soldiers still wear helmets today, and modern warships and tanks have armour plating.

Army Military organization for fighting on land. The earliest armies in history were raised in ancient Egypt and Assyria. Later, the Greeks and Romans had formidable armies of soldiers trained to fight on foot (infantry) and on horseback (cavalry). Cavalry remained the 'shock troops' of armies until modern times, and the soldier's main weapons for thousands of years were the bow, spear and sword.

With the invention of GUNPOWDER

(known in Europe by the 1400s) came artillery, and by World War I (1914–1918) guns, bombs and tanks were such deadly weapons that armies numbering millions of men were unable to advance from their defensive trenches. Modern armies have tanks, rockets and air support and can move at great speed. The world's largest army is China's, followed by the USSR, USA and Vietnam.

Arsenic Metallic element whose compounds are very poisonous. Chem. symbol As.

Art Work created by an artist. Although 'art' is often used as another word for painting, it also describes other creative activities such as architecture, drama, literature, music and sculpture. This group of subjects is often called 'the arts'.

Artemis Greek goddess of the moon and night, twin sister of Apollo. Also a virgin, a hunter, a protector of women and the goddess of wild nature. (Roman equivalent Diana.)

Arthropod Member of the phylum Arthropoda which includes arachnids, insects, crustaceans, centipedes and millipedes. Arthropods outnumber all other animal species.

Arthur (*c* AD 600) A legendary king whose seat was supposedly at the fabled Camelot where he presided over the Knights of the Round Table.

Ash Deciduous trees up to 40 metres high, belonging to the olive family. Their winged seeds hang in bunches called keys. The timber is highly prized.

Asia The largest and most populous continent, occupying 30 per cent of the world's total land area and containing 60 per cent of the total population. Its many different types of land include the cold wastes of Siberia in the north, the waterless Gobi desert of Central Asia, the mighty Himalaya Mountains enclosing India, and the hot, wet forests and islands of the Southeast.

Most of Asia's people are farmers, and rice is the main crop of the wetter regions. Many of the countries are very poor with few industries. The great exception is Japan, one of the world's leading industrial nations. Area: 44,387,000 km^2; Pop: 2,757,383,000. See map on pages 20 and 21.

The Spanish Armada was harried up the Channel by English ships. These were smaller but faster than the Spaniards, and their guns had a longer range.

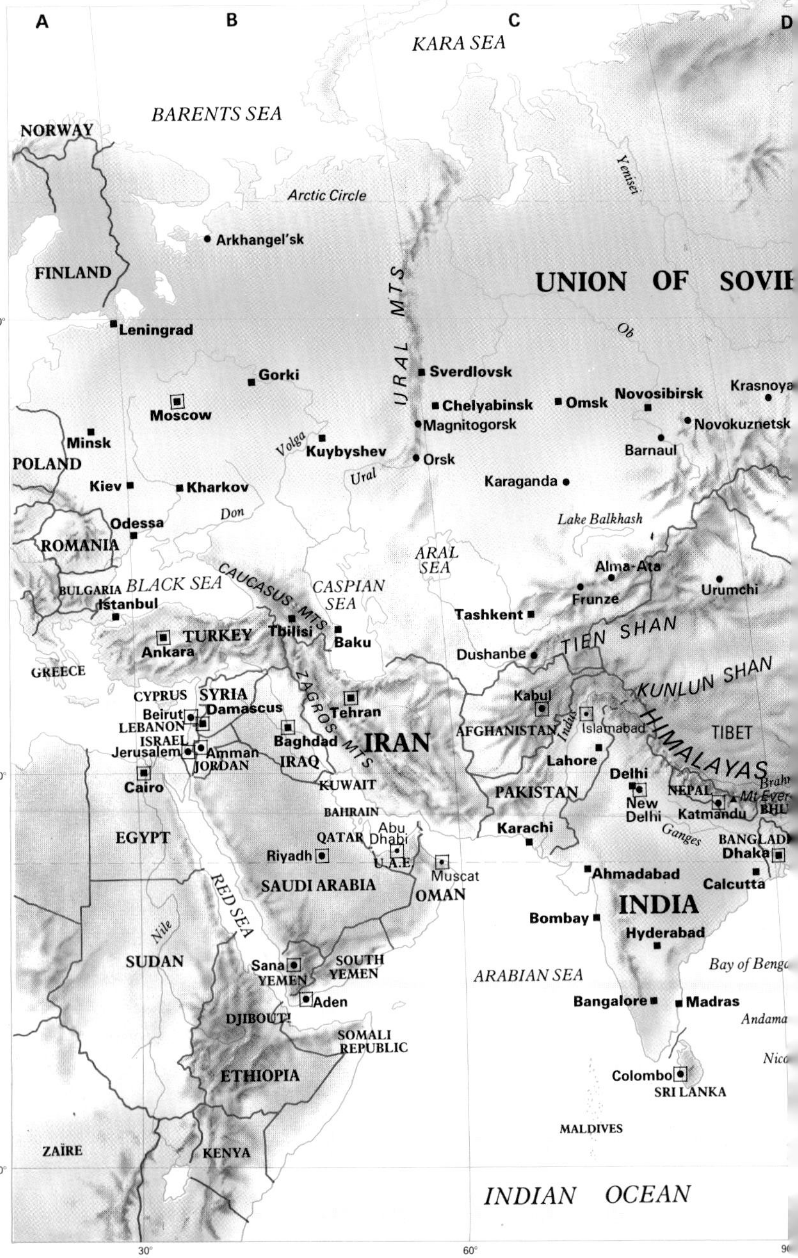

Asia (Map)

A B C D

KARA SEA
BARENTS SEA
NORWAY
Arctic Circle
Yenisei
Arkhangel'sk
FINLAND
URAL MTS
UNION OF SOVI
60°
Leningrad
Ob
Gorki
Sverdlovsk
Moscow
Chelyabinsk
Omsk
Novosibirsk
Krasnoya
Magnitogorsk
Novokuznetsk
Minsk
Volga
Kuybyshev
Barnaul
POLAND
Orsk
Ural
Kiev
Kharkov
Karaganda
Don
Odessa
Lake Balkhash
ROMANIA
ARAL SEA
CAUCASUS MTS
Alma-Ata
BULGARIA
BLACK SEA
CASPIAN SEA
Urumchi
Frunze
Istanbul
Tbilisi
Tashkent
Baku
TURKEY
Ankara
TIEN SHAN
Dushanbe
GREECE
ZAGROS MTS
KUNLUN SHAN
CYPRUS
SYRIA
Kabul
Beirut
Damascus
Tehran
LEBANON
Indus
Islamabad
ISRAEL
Baghdad
IRAN
AFGHANISTAN
HIMALAYAS
TIBET
Jerusalem
Amman
JORDAN
Lahore
IRAQ
30°
Cairo
KUWAIT
Delhi
Brahm
PAKISTAN
NEPAL
Mt Ever
New Delhi
BAHRAIN
Katmandu
BHU
EGYPT
Abu Dhabi
Karachi
QATAR
Ganges
BANGLAD
Riyadh
U.A.E.
Dhaka
Muscat
RED SEA
Ahmadabad
SAUDI ARABIA
Calcutta
OMAN
INDIA
Nile
Bombay
Hyderabad
SUDAN
Sana
SOUTH YEMEN
YEMEN
ARABIAN SEA
Bay of Beng
Aden
Bangalore
Madras
DJIBOUTI
Andama
SOMALI REPUBLIC
Nico
ETHIOPIA
Colombo
SRI LANKA
MALDIVES
ZAÏRE
KENYA
0°
INDIAN OCEAN
30°
60°
90

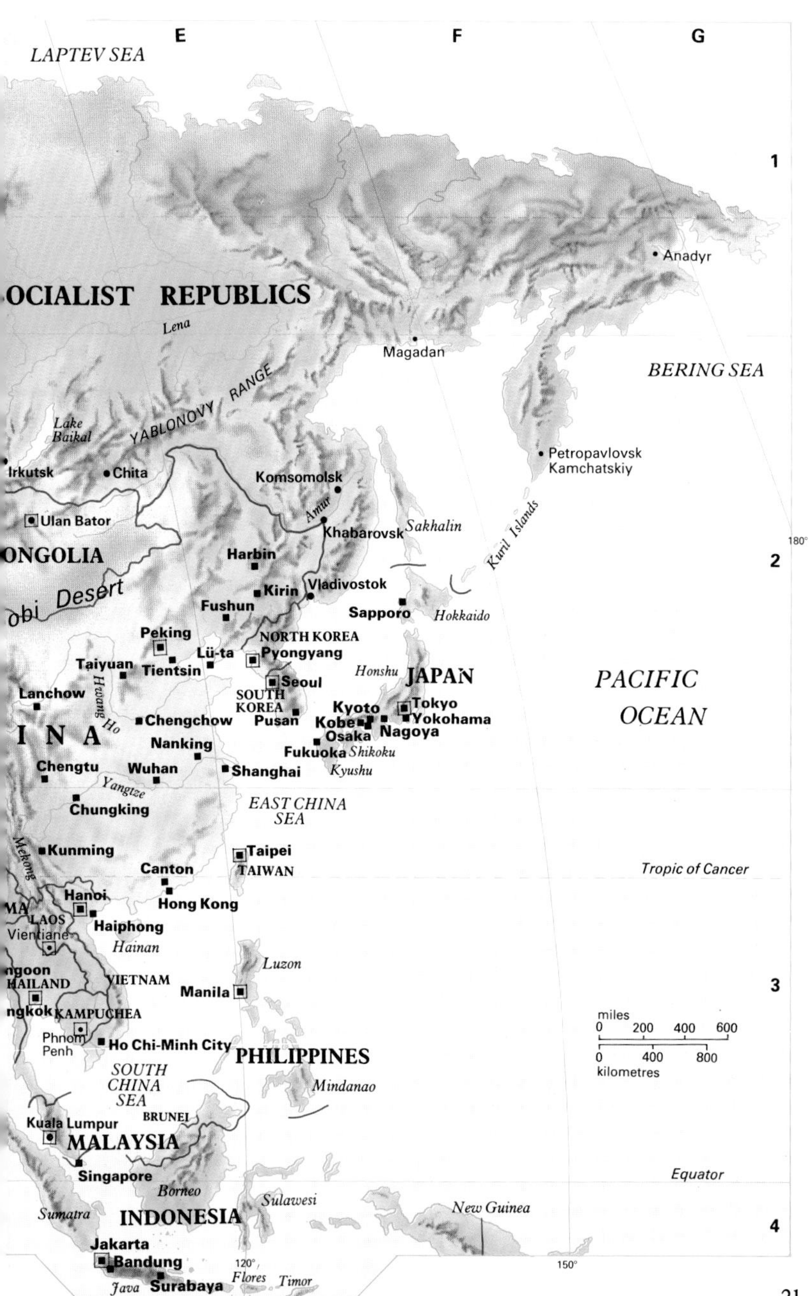
E
F
G
LAPTEV SEA
1
Anadyr
OCIALIST REPUBLICS
Lena
Magadan
BERING SEA
YABLONOVY RANGE
Lake Baikal
Petropavlovsk Kamchatskiy
Irkutsk
Chita
Komsomolsk
Amur
Ulan Bator
Kuril Islands
Khabarovsk
Sakhalin
180°
ONGOLIA
Harbin
2
Kirin
Vladivostok
obi Desert
Fushun
Sapporo
Hokkaido
Peking
NORTH KOREA
Lü-ta
Pyongyang
Taiyuan
Tientsin
Honshu
JAPAN
PACIFIC OCEAN
Seoul
Hwang Ho
Lanchow
SOUTH KOREA
Kyoto
Tokyo
Chengchow
Pusan
Kobe
Yokohama
I N A
Osaka
Nagoya
Nanking
Fukuoka
Shikoku
Chengtu
Wuhan
Shanghai
Kyushu
Yangtze
Chungking
EAST CHINA SEA
Mekong
Kunming
Taipei
Canton
TAIWAN
Tropic of Cancer
Hanoi
Hong Kong
MA
LAOS
Haiphong
Vientiane
Hainan
Luzon
ngoon
HAILAND
VIETNAM
Manila
3
miles
0 200 400 600
ngkok
KAMPUCHEA
Phnom Penh
Ho Chi-Minh City
PHILIPPINES
0 400 800
kilometres
SOUTH CHINA SEA
Mindanao
Kuala Lumpur
BRUNEI
MALAYSIA
Singapore
Equator
Borneo
Sulawesi
New Guinea
Sumatra
INDONESIA
4
Jakarta
Bandung
120°
150°
Flores
Timor
Java
Surabaya

Asp Several types of small poisonous snake including the Egyptian cobra.

Assassin Originally a member of a Muslim secret society, trained to murder their enemies. The word is now used to describe a murderer, particularly one who kills for political motives. The original assassins got their name from the drug hashish. They were destroyed by the MONGOLS in the 13th century.

Association football Popularly known as soccer, the most widely played team game in the world. A rough-and-ready football was played in the Middle Ages. In the 19th century it was taken up by English schools, dividing into Association football and RUGBY FOOTBALL (in which the ball could be handled). Today soccer is played in almost every country. The principal competition for national teams is the World Cup, held every four years. There are 11 players in a soccer team, with one or two substitutes normally allowed. Play is for two halves of 45 minutes each.

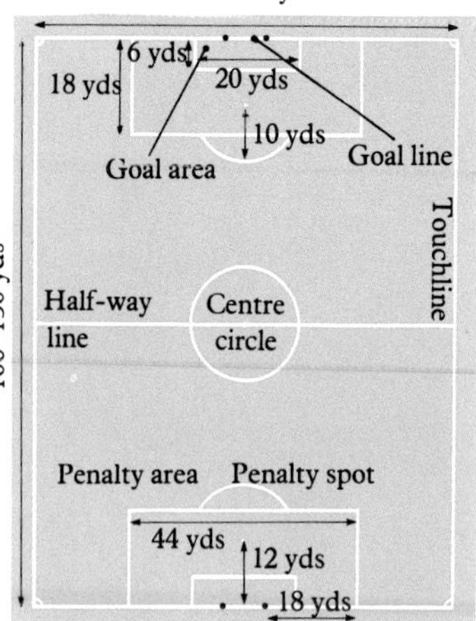

Association football (soccer) pitch

Assyrians An ancient people of the Middle East. From their homeland in northern Mesopotamia, the Assyrians created a powerful empire between the 19th and 7th centuries BC. With slave labour, they built large and splendid citadels. They brought together many ancient cultures of Mesopotamia, and used a form of writing which has been preserved on clay tablets.

Asteroids A swarm of rubble circling the Sun between the orbits of Mars and Jupiter. Asteroids range in size from small boulders to Ceres, 950 km in diameter. They may be material left over from the formation of the planets or debris from a former planet that broke up.

Astrology The study of the movement of the heavenly bodies and their influence on people and their affairs. Though astrology is no longer regarded as a science, its practice in ancient times paved the way for astronomy.

Astronomy The study of the Sun, planets and other heavenly bodies. The astronomer's most important instrument is the TELESCOPE since he is studying objects not miles but LIGHT-YEARS away. His laboratory is called an OBSERVATORY.

Athene Greek goddess of war and wisdom. She is supposed to have sprung fully grown from the forehead of her father Zeus. (Roman equivalent Minerva.)

Athens Capital city of Greece. A cultural, religious and industrial centre. It is an historic city, centre of the ancient Greek civilization, and home of Socrates, Plato and Aristotle. Athens is famous for its ancient remains, especially the Parthenon on the Acropolis, and is a popular tourist centre. Pop: 862,000.

Athletics Sport involving track and field events of various kinds, some dating back to ancient Greece and the first OLYMPIC GAMES. Track events include sprinting (short-distance) and long-distance running, HURDLING, relays, and the Marathon run of 26 miles 385 yards. Field events include long, high and triple jumping, and throwing events, such as the discus, hammer, javelin and shot-putting. The world's strongest athletics nations are the United States, the USSR and East Germany.

Atlantic Ocean Second largest ocean in the world, bordered by Europe and Africa in the east and North and South America in the west. A massive subterranean ridge runs N–S through the middle of the ocean and rises above sea-level in places. Area: 82,000,000 km^2.

Atlas In Greek legend a Titan who warred against Zeus and was condemned to bear the heavens on his shoulders.

Atmosphere Thin envelope of air that is held by gravity to the surface of the spinning Earth. As well as supplying the gases vital to plant and animal life the atmosphere acts as a shield during the day, protecting the Earth from much of the Sun's fierce heat and dangerous ultra-violet radiation. By night it serves as a blanket, preventing too much heat escaping to space. Without the atmosphere, temperatures would rise to 80°C during the day and fall to −140°C at night.

Although invisible, air has weight. The entire atmosphere weighs more than 5000 million million tonnes. At sea-level, the pressure of the air is 1 kg per cm^2 (1013 millibars) but it decreases rapidly with height.

Atom Everything in the universe is made of very, very tiny particles called atoms. If the atoms in something are packed tightly together, that something is a solid. If the atoms are not so tightly packed, that something is a liquid. And if the atoms move about a great deal, we have a gas, like air.

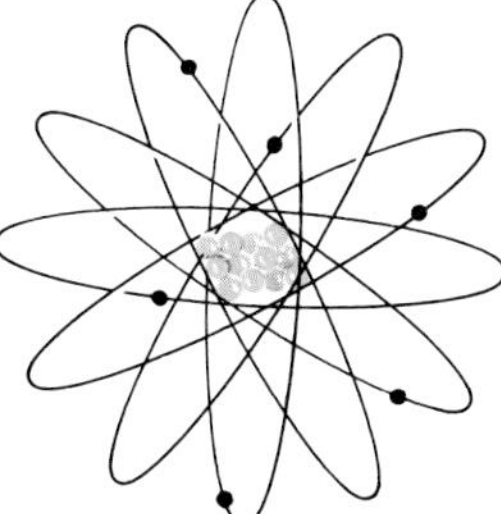

Carbon atom

Atoms themselves are made up of even smaller particles called protons, electrons and neutrons. Protons and neutrons are in the centre of atoms, called the nucleus. Electrons, which have a negative electric charge, orbit the nucleus. Protons have a positive charge; neutrons have no charge. The simplest atom is that of the light gas hydrogen. It has just one electron orbiting one proton. Other atoms are much more complicated. The carbon atom, for example, has a nucleus consisting of six protons and six neutrons, around which spin six electrons.

Diagram of the atmosphere. Weather is confined to the lowest level, the troposphere (from 8–18 km thick). The stratosphere contains a layer of ozone gas which prevents most of the Sun's harmful ultra-violet rays from reaching the Earth's surface. Glowing lights, or aurorae, caused by radiation from the Sun occur in the rarefied (thin) air of the ionosphere.

Attila (406–453) King of the HUNS who with his barbarian hordes laid waste many fine European cities. Defeated for the first time by the Roman general Aetius in Gaul, he sacked a number of Italian cities before famine and pestilence drove him back across the Alps.

Auckland Port and largest city in North Island, New Zealand. Capital from 1840 to 1865. Major commercial and industrial centre and principal port. Pop: 806,000 (met area).

Augustus, Gaius Octavianus (63 BC–AD 14) The first Roman Emperor. Adopted heir of JULIUS CAESAR, he originally ruled jointly with Mark Antony and Lepidus, but by 30 BC he had become master of Rome. Given many titles by the Senate, including imperator (general) and augustus (revered), he brought peace and stability to the Roman Empire after a century of civil wars.

Auk Group of black and white sea-birds including the little auk, PUFFIN, GUILLEMOT and RAZORBILL. Auks nest on sea cliffs and spend most of their time at sea, catching fish. The flightless great auk became extinct in the 1840s.

Austen, Jane (1775–1817) English novelist. Daughter of a clergyman, she led a quiet, unassuming life, yet wrote six of the finest novels in English literature: *Sense and Sensibility*, *Pride and Prejudice*, *Mansfield Park*, *Emma*, *Northanger Abbey* and *Persuasion*. Her novels are famed for their satirical humour.

Australia An island continent larger than Europe (excluding the USSR) but with less than 5% of the population. This is largely because of the nature of the climate: two-thirds of the land is desert or semi-desert. Over 50% of the people live in the four largest cities and most of the remainder live in the fertile south-eastern region and along the narrow eastern coastal plain.

Australia is a major farming nation. It produces almost one-third of the world's wool and is the third largest exporter of wheat. Other important agricultural products include meat, dairy produce and sugar-cane. Mining is another major source of wealth with large deposits of bauxite, iron ore, lead, zinc, coal, copper, off-shore oil and 20% of the Western world's known uranium reserves. Industry is becoming increasingly important, with steel, aluminium, vehicles and textiles being the chief manufactures.

In 1901 the former colonies of New South Wales, Queensland, South Australia, Tasmania, Victoria and Western Australia joined together to form the independent Commonwealth of Australia. Today, Australia is one of the world's most prosperous nations. Area: 7,686,000 km^2; Pop: 15,462,000; Cap: Canberra. See map on pages 26 and 27.

Austria Mountainous republic in central Europe. Present-day Austria is the remnant of the multi-national Hapsburg Empire that until its defeat in World War I embraced much of central and south-eastern Europe. It is now a buffer state between the Eastern and Western blocs and maintains a strict policy of neutrality. Area: 83,800 km^2; Pop: 7,544,000; Cap: Vienna.

Automation The control by machine of any process, such as manufacturing, traffic control, piloting aircraft, or updating bank balances.

Automobile In 1885 Karl Benz in Germany introduced the first practical automobile, a three-wheeled vehicle with a petrol engine. The following year his fellow countryman, Gottlieb Daimler, built the first four-wheeled motor vehicle. The following list details some of the milestones in automobile development.

1892 Diesel engine (Rudolf Diesel, Germany)
1895 Pneumatic tyres (Michelin brothers, France)
1901 Assembly-line production (Ransom Olds, USA)
1906 Silver Ghost (C.S. Rolls and Henry Royce, Britain)
1908 Model T Ford ('Tin Lizzie'), first 'people's car' (Henry Ford, USA)
1911 Electric starter (Cadillac, USA)
1920 Hydraulic brakes (Duesenberg, USA)
1928 Synchromesh gears (Cadillac, USA)
1938 The Volkswagen 'Beetle' (designed by Ferdinand Porsche, Germany)
1939 Automatic transmission (Oldsmobile, USA)
1948 Radial-ply tyres (Michelin, France); Tubeless tyres (Goodrich, USA)
1950 Disc brakes (Dunlop, Britain)
1955 Self-levelling hydropneumatic suspension (Citroen, France)
1957 Rotary petrol engine (Felix Wankel, Germany)
1959 Transverse engine, front-wheel drive Mini (Alex Issigoni, BMC, Britain)
1980 Instant sealing safety tyres (Dunlop, Britain)

1886 Daimler

1895 Panhard-Levassor

1915 Model T Ford

1907 Rolls-Royce Silver Ghost

1953 Volkswagen 'Beetle'

1959 BMC Mini

1977 BMW 733i saloon

B
C
D
E
A
INDONESIA
Sumba
Timor
10°
Melville I.
TIMOR SEA
Darwin
ARNHEM LAND
Katherine
Wyndham
Birdum
15°
KIMBERLEY PLATEAU
Derby
Hall's Creek
Broome
BARKLY
Tennant Creek
Great Sandy Desert
NORTHERN TERRITORY
Port Hedland
20°
Dampier
AUSTRALIA
HAMERSLEY RANGE
MACDONNELL RANGE
Mount Newman
Tropic of Capricorn
Alice Springs
Simpson Desert
BARLEE RANGE
Gibson Desert
Ayers Rock 867
Carnarvon
25°
MUSGRAVE RANGES
WESTERN AUSTRALIA
Mount Magnet
Great Victoria Desert
SOUTH AUSTRALIA
Geraldton
Nullarbor Plain
30°
Kalgoorlie
Moora
Coolgardie
Eucla
Ceduna
Port Augus
Northam
Perth
Fremantle
Mandurah
Narrogin
Esperance
Great Australian Bight
Eyre Pen.
Bunbury
Port Lincoln
Spencer Gulf
Augusta
Albany
Kangaroo I.
35°
INDIAN OCEAN
40°
miles
0
200
400
0
200
400
600
kilometres
115°
120°
125°
130°
135°

G
H
J
K
L
1
2
3
4
5
6
7
8
9
10
11
N
O
M
PAPUA NEW GUINEA
Cape York
Solomon Islands
GREAT BARRIER REEF
CORAL SEA
Cooktown
Cairns
Normanton
GREAT DIVIDING RANGE
Townsville
Bowen
Hughenden
Mackay
Winton
Great Artesian Basin
Barcaldine
Rockhampton
QUEENSLAND
Bundaberg
Maryborough
Charleville
Toowoomba
Brisbane
Goondiwindi
Gold Coast
Lismore
Bourke
R. Darling
Narrabri
Grafton
Nyngan
Tamworth
Broken Hill
Port Macquarie
NEW SOUTH WALES
Dubbo
Taree
Orange
Newcastle
Katoomba
Sydney
R. Murray
Wagga Wagga
Wollongong
Canberra
VICTORIA
Albury
Wangaratta
Bendigo
Mt Kosciusko 2230
Ballarat
Melbourne
Geelong
Morwell
King I.
Bass Strait
Flinders I.
Devonport
Launceston
Mt Ossa 1617
TASMANIA
Hobart
145°
150°
155°
160°
165°
170°
175°
35°
40°
45°
Kaitaia
Whangarei
North I.
Auckland
Waihi
Hamilton
Tauranga
Rotorua
Opotiki
Waitara
Taupo
New Plymouth
Lake Taupo
Gisborne
Mt Egmont 2518
2797
Napier
Wanganui
TASMAN SEA
Palmerston North
Levin
Cook Strait
Masterton
Nelson
Wellington
Westport
Blenheim
NEW ZEALAND
Greymouth
South I.
SOUTHERN ALPS
SOUTH PACIFIC OCEAN
Mt Cook 3764
Christchurch
Timaru
Wanaka
Alexandra
Dunedin
Gore
Balclutha
Invercargill
Stewart I.
miles
0
100
200
300
0
100
200
300
400
kilometres

B

Baboon Old World monkeys which live in large tribes of up to 100 individuals led by a large male. The males are fierce fighters. They have dog-like faces and short tails.

Babylon An ancient town on the River Euphrates, south of Baghdad. It was the centre of a powerful kingdom between the 20th and 6th centuries BC. The city was famous for its ziggurat (a stepped pyramid) and its Hanging Gardens, which were one of the Seven Wonders of the ancient world. Most of the city which has been excavated by archaeologists was built in the reign of Nebuchadnezzar II in the 6th century BC.

Bach, Johann Sebastian (1685–1750) German composer, organist and choirmaster. Primarily wrote church music, particularly for the organ. His works include more than 200 cantatas, 3 passions, 5 masses, 29 concertos, and 48 preludes and fugues.

Bacon, Francis (1561–1626) English philosopher and statesman. Author of *Essays* and *Novum Organum*.

Bacteria Single-celled organisms usually classed as plants and visible only through a microscope. Millions of bacteria are on everything we touch, including our own skin. They play an important part in breaking down dead matter. Bacteria multiply at an enormous rate. Some cause disease, while others are useful in medicine.

Baden-Powell, Lord Robert (1857–1941) Founder of Boy Scout movement (1908) and the Girl Guides (1910). Also famous for his brilliant defence of Mafeking during the Boer War.

Badger Thickset carnivore with coarse greyish fur and a white head with broad black stripes. The animal builds a large maze of tunnels, called a set, where it lives with its family, coming out at night to feed.

Badminton Rackets game invented in the late 19th century at Badminton House, the home of the English Duke of Beaufort. Badminton is played on an indoor court. The players (two in singles, four in doubles) use stringed rackets to hit a shuttlecock. This is made of cork into which are stuck plastic feathers (originally goose feathers). In badminton, a player can only score a point on his or her own service. The first to collect 15 points wins the game.

Baghdad Capital city of Iraq, on R Tigris. Important for textile and tobacco products. Founded in 762 AD, it rapidly became a major cultural and commercial centre. Pop: 3,206,000.

Bahamas Group of low-lying islands in the Atlantic south-east of Florida. There are about 700 islands, of which less than 40 are inhabited. Wide, sandy beaches and a warm climate have made tourism the Bahamas' chief industry. It is also a major banking centre. Area: 13,933 km²; Pop: 228,000; Cap: Nassau (on New Providence I.).

Bahrain Island in the Arabian Gulf 25 km off the coast of Saudi Arabia. Site of the first oil discovery in the Arabian peninsula in 1932. Today, Bahrain has one of the Middle East's major oil refineries. Area: 621 km²; Pop: 411,000; Cap: Manama.

Baird, John Logie (1888–1946) Scottish inventor who developed the first true television in 1926.

Bald eagle N American fish eagle and national bird and emblem of United States.

Balearic Islands Group of islands belonging to Spain in the Mediterranean. They include Majorca, Minorca, Ibiza and Formentera. The islands are a major tourist resort.

Ballet Dramatic entertainment combining dancing, music, scenery and costume, created by a choreographer. Ballet began at the French court in the mid 1600s. The five classical positions of feet, arms and body were established in the 18th century. In the 19th century dancers began to go *en pointe* (up on their toes) but there was little more innovation. At the beginning of this century the impresario DIAGHILEV revitalised the ballet in Paris (Ballets Russes) and choreographers like Georges Balanchine, Frederick Ashton and Isadora Duncan carried on from him. Today Martha Graham, working in the United States, and others elsewhere produce more innovative works but people still flock to see the classics: *Giselle, Coppélia, Nutcracker, Swan Lake, La Fille mal Gardée*, amongst others.

Balloon A balloon is a bag of light material filled with air or other gas. Balloons can only drift in the wind. The first manned balloon was a hot-air craft. It took off in

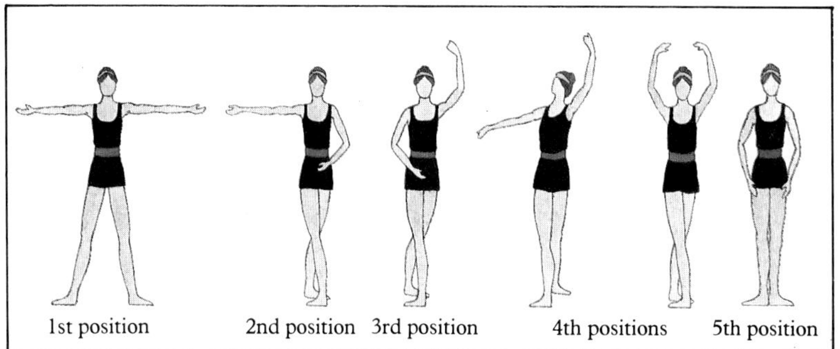

The five positions are the foundations of ballet. Each gives perfect balance.

1783 and was built by the French brothers Montgolfier. In the same year, the first gas-filled balloon took off. It was filled with hydrogen. In the 1800s balloons were used for observation. Today, balloons equipped with scientific instruments are sent up to the upper atmosphere to radio back information. Hot-air ballooning has become a popular sport.

Balzac, Honoré de (1799–1850) French novelist who wrote over 80 novels including *Le Père Goriot* and *La Cousine Bette*.

Bamboo Giant plants of the grass family, with some kinds growing to nearly 40 metres at a tremendous rate. Bamboo grows in tropical areas and is used in building and in the construction of boats. The plants rarely flower, some only every 30 years. But all the plants of one species flower together and then die.

Banana Large tropical plant with nutritious fruit widely grown in C America and the West Indies. Each plant bears one crop of bananas and then dies back.

Bangkok Port and capital of Thailand. Its royal palace, floating market and several hundred Buddhist temples make it a popular tourist centre. Pop: 4,702,000.

Bangladesh One of the poorest nations in the world, Bangladesh is about the size of England and Wales but has more than twice as many people. Nearly all the land is composed of the fertile flood plains of the Ganges and Brahmaputra Rivers and their swampy delta. More than 75% of the people farm the land and the staple crop is rice. But even the best harvests do not provide enough food and food is the major import. Area: 144,000 km^2; Pop: 99,000,000. Cap: Dhaka.

Barbados A small, densely populated Caribbean island with an economy based on sugar-cane and tourism. Formerly a British colony, it became independent in 1966. Area: 430 km^2; Pop: 254,000.

Barcelona Major port and industrial city in Spain. Tourist centre with wide avenues and historic buildings. Pop: 1,745,000.

Barium Soft, silvery metal which is very reactive and is found in nature only as a compound. Barium sulphate is opaque to X-rays and is the vital ingredient of the 'barium meal' used by radiologists to make a patient's alimentary canal show up more clearly in X-ray pictures. Chem. symbol Ba.

Bark The outer covering of trees and woody plants. The surface layer is made of dead corky tissue and protects the inner living layers. See **Cork**.

Barley The first cereal to be cultivated, barley is still an important crop. It is used for animal food and malted for brewing and distilling.

Barnacle Crustaceans that attach themselves to rocks, ships' bottoms and sometimes other animals. They are protected by chalky plates which open underwater to allow the animal to trap food.

Barometer An instrument for measuring atmospheric pressure. The mercury barometer consists of a column of mercury in a glass tube, up-ended in a trough of mercury. The height of the mercury in the tube depends upon the pressure of the air acting on the mercury in the trough. The aneroid barometer contains a metal capsule out of which most of the air has been drawn, its sides held apart by a spring. The pressure of the air on the capsule sides is used to move a pointer over a dial.

Barrie, J(ames) M(atthew) (1860–1937) Scottish dramatist whose play *Peter Pan* has delighted children for decades. Also author of novels including *Quality Street*.

Bartók, Béla (1881–1945) Hungarian composer, much of whose work is based on the folk music of his native country. Among his works are six string quartets, piano and violin concertos, orchestral music, including the *Concerto for Orchestra*, a ballet and one opera: *Bluebeard's Castle*.

Base A substance that reacts chemically with an acid to form a salt and water. Bases are the opposite of acids in that they turn red litmus paper blue.

Baseball National game of United States, similar to the older English game of rounders. Baseball began in the 1830s and since the early 1900s has been the most popular US sport. There are nine players on each side. The pitch is known as the 'diamond', and runs are scored by the batter striking the ball thrown by the pitcher and completing a run around the four 'bases'. The chief US baseball event is the World Series play-off between the winners of the National and American Leagues. Baseball is also played in Japan, Australia and parts of Latin America.

Basketball American game usually played indoors between two teams. Each team may have up to 12 players, but only five may be on court at one time. At each end of the court is a basket or net, just over 3 metres off the ground and projecting from a backboard. The object of the game is to score by throwing the ball so that it drops into the basket. Two points are awarded for each score, with one point for a score made from a free throw. Basketball is now played in over 140 countries.

Bass Name given to several types of fish, both marine and freshwater. The common sea-bass is a predatory fish which lives in small shoals off rocky shores. It grows up to 80 cm long.

Bat The only mammal truly capable of flight. The wings are large folds of skin stretched across the animal's long fingers and attached to its limbs and body. Bats are nocturnal creatures with extremely poor vision. They navigate by echo location. In temperate climates they hibernate during the winter, generally hanging upside-down in a dark, sheltered place.

Common long-eared bat

Battery Batteries make electricity from chemicals inside them. Dry batteries, or primary CELLS, such as those used in torches, make electricity for only a limited time. Others, such as car batteries, are secondary cells. They can be recharged when they run down. This is done by passing an electric current through the battery. Car batteries usually have six cells connected in series, each cell giving 2 volts. The whole battery therefore gives about 12 volts.

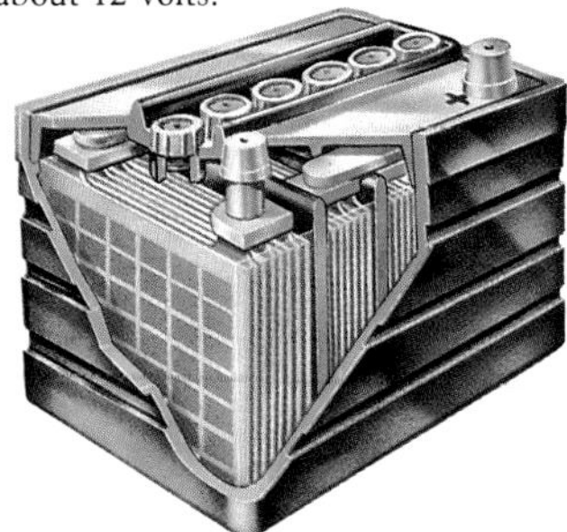

Plates of lead and lead dioxide, surrounded by sulphuric acid, generate electricity in a car battery.

Bean Plants of pea family which produce nutritious seeds and pods, themselves called beans. Important source of protein for animals and humans. Types include kidney, lima, soya, mung, haricot and runner beans.

Bear Large shaggy mammals with powerful limbs and claws. American bears include the brown bears (among them the largest of all, the Kodiak), the black bears, and the fierce grizzly bears. Asian bears include the black Himalayan bear, the slow-moving sloth bears and the smallest bear of all, the Malayan sun bear. The spectacled bear lives in S America and the POLAR BEAR in the Arctic.

Most bears sleep through the winter and give birth to their cubs in the winter den. The cubs stay with their mother for up to three years, learning how to gather berries and nuts as well as to hunt and fish.

Bearings Parts of machines which support turning shafts. They are designed to let shafts rotate with as little friction as possible. This increases the efficiency of the machine. Ball bearings and roller bearings are the most common types.

Beatles, The Britain's most successful 'pop' group ever, comprising John Lennon, Paul McCartney, George Harrison and Ringo Starr. At the height of their fame during the 1960s their new image and highly original songs caught the imagination of youth the world over.

Beaver N America and Europe's largest rodent, over 80 cm long. After many years of being hunted, European beavers are now found only in Scandinavia. Beavers have a large flat tail and webbed back feet. They live in holes in the river bank, or build dams to create pools in which to build a home, called a lodge.

Bee A group of insects related to ants and wasps. Some bees, including honey bees, are highly social. They live in colonies with an egg-laying queen, infertile female workers to gather food and tend the young, and males (drones) to mate with new queens. Bumble bees are also social though not so organized. Solitary bees include the mining bee which nests in the ground, the carpenter bee which nests in wood and the leaf-cutter bee which makes a nest from leaves. Bees can sting but are not aggressive. They feed on nectar and pollen from flowers.

Beech Large, strong deciduous tree growing up to 30 metres tall. The fruit, known as beechmast, consists of a hairy green husk which dries and splits open to release one or two shiny brown triangular nuts. Some beeches have purple leaves and are called copper beeches.

Beethoven, Ludwig van (1770–1827) Great German composer of orchestral, choral and chamber music. He began as a solo pianist in Vienna but growing deafness cut short his career as a virtuoso. His major works include nine great symphonies, a violin concerto, many piano concertos and sonatas, and the opera *Fidelio*.

Cross section of a beaver lodge, showing the underwater entrance and the snug living quarters.

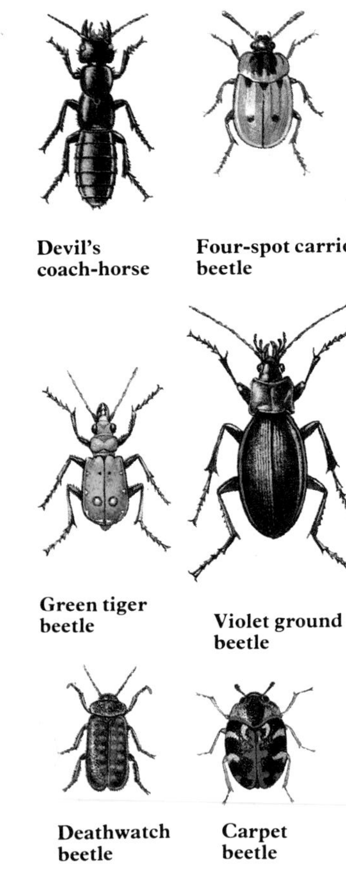
Devil's coach-horse

Four-spot carrion beetle

Green tiger beetle

Violet ground beetle

Deathwatch beetle

Carpet beetle

Sacred scarab beetle

Beetle Widespread group of insects, recognized by their hard wing-covers. Although they can fly, most beetles are ground-dwellers, and many are burrowers. They eat almost anything, including other insects and a variety of plant food, as well as carrion and dung. Many beetle larvae are pests, damaging plants and trees. There are about 330,000 species of beetle, making up the insect group Coleoptera.

Beirut Port and capital city of Lebanon. Founded by the Phoenicians, it rose to become a leading financial and commercial centre and one of the most fashionable cities of the Middle East. In recent years, however, Beirut has become a battleground for rival Muslim and Christian forces. Pop: 939,000.

Belfast Port and capital of Northern Ireland. Major industrial and commercial centre with one of the largest shipbuilding yards in UK. Scene of much conflict since the late 1960s. Pop: 298,000.

Belgium A small, densely populated and highly industrialized kingdom in western Europe. Belgium is a bi-lingual country with Dutch-speaking Flemish people in the north and French-speaking Walloons in the south. Area: 31,000 km^2; Pop: 9,872,000; Cap: Brussels.

Belgrade Port and capital of Yugoslavia, on R. Danube. Industrial and cultural centre. The city has had a turbulent history and was badly damaged in World War II. Pop: 1,455,000.

Belize A small country on the Caribbean coast of Central America. The climate is warm and moist and tropical plantation crops, such as bananas and sugar-cane, are the chief exports. Area: 23,000 km^2; Pop: 153,000; Cap: Belmopen.

Bell, Alexander Graham (1847–1922) Scottish-born American scientist who invented the telephone and organized the Bell Telephone Co. in 1877.

Bellerophon In Greek legend a hero who captured and rode the winged horse PEGASUS.

Bellini, Giovanni (*c* 1430–1516) Venetian painter whose pupils included Titian and Tintoretto. His most famous works include *Circumcision, Feast of the Gods* and *Blood of the Redeemer*.

Benin Formerly called Dahomey, Benin is a small, poor and densely populated communist republic in western Africa. Some 80% of the population is concerned with farming; maize, rice and manioc are the staple crops. Palm oil, raw cotton and coffee are the major exports. Area: 113,000 km²; Pop: 3,894,000; Cap: Porto-Novo.

Berlin Capital of East Germany and enclave of West Germany. Severely bombed during World War II, the city was subsequently divided into four zones, East Berlin being occupied by the Russians and the rest by French, British and American forces. Friction between the two sides led to the construction of the notorious Berlin Wall in 1961. Pop: West Berlin 1,081,000, East Berlin 1,188,000.

Berlioz, Hector (1803–1869) French composer and pioneer of Romanticism in music. Compositions include the symphonies *Romeo et Juliet* and *Symphonie fantastique*, the operas *The Trojans* (usually performed in two parts) and *The Damnation of Faust*, a great Requiem and many songs.

Bermuda Group of islands in the W Atlantic Ocean 930 km from the US coast. Sandy beaches and a pleasant climate have led to a large tourist industry. Bermuda has been a British dependency since 1620. Area: 53 km²; Pop: 55,000; Cap: Hamilton.

Bethlehem Town in W Jordan, 10 km SW of Jerusalem. Believed to be birthplace of Jesus.

Bible Holy book of Christians and Jews. It is in two parts. The Old Testament, originally written in Hebrew, tells of the creation of the Earth by God and the story of the Israelites, whose prophets foretold the coming of the Messiah. The New Testament (sacred only to Christians) tells of the life, work, and death of JESUS, and the early spread of CHRISTIANITY.

Bicycle A two-wheeled vehicle powered by the rider's legs. The early bicycles were propelled by the rider's feet on the ground. Later, in 1865, pedals were invented. Then came the 'pennyfarthing', which had an enormous front wheel turned by pedals and a small rear wheel. Today's bicycle has a chain-driven rear wheel, ball bearings, tyres filled with air, and gears.

Binary code In the binary arithmetic system only two numbers are used, 0 and 1. This system is ideal for computers because the machine only has to recognize the difference between a big electrical current and a small current – a big current is 1, a small current, 0.

Biochemistry Study of the chemical processes that take place inside plants and animals.

Biology Study of all living things, including their structure, chemical activity, habits, distribution and origin.

Birch A group of slender, deciduous trees growing in northern lands. They have thin, white, peeling bark, small leaves and durable wood.

Bird A warm-blooded vertebrate with wings. Its body is covered in feathers and it has a beak and no teeth. Birds reflect some of their reptilian ancestry in that they have scaly legs and feet and lay eggs. Most are well adapted for flight, with large flight muscles attached to a broad breast bone, and light bones, many of which are hollow. There are several flightless species.

Bird of Paradise Spectacular family of birds from New Guinea and N Australia. The males have a dazzling variety of brightly coloured plumage and elongated tail feathers. The females are duller.

Birmingham Major industrial centre and second largest city in Britain. It became important during the Industrial Revolution, when it was the base of scientists and industrialists including Watt, Priestley and Wedgewood. Pop: 1,007,000.

Bismarck, Otto von (1815–1898) Skilful Prussian statesman. Known as the Iron Chancellor he created the German Empire and was Chancellor of Germany 1871–90. He used the Schleswig-Holstein dispute to defeat the Austrians and provoked the Franco-Prussian War (1870–71). He unified Germany with William I as emperor, and under his control industry and commerce prospered.

Bison The massive wild cattle – buffalo – of N America that once roamed the plains in vast herds. The smaller European bison, the wisent, is now rare.

Bittern A heron-like bird of reeds and marshes, with brown, speckled plumage. When still, with its bill pointed skywards, it is hard to spot among the reeds.

Bivalve Member of a group of aquatic molluscs whose shells consist of two hinged valves. The group includes mussels, clams and oysters.

Bizet, Georges (1838–75) French composer and pianist whose *Carmen* is one of the most popular operas. Other compositions include the opera *The Pearl Fishers* and the orchestral suite (No. 1) from '*L'Arlésienne*'.

Blackbird Common bird of thrush family. The male is all black with bright yellow beak; the female is a dull brown with a slightly mottled breast and a dull beak. Blackbirds are fine songsters.

Black Death A form of the disease known as plague, which swept through Asia and Europe in the 14th century. Plague was carried by fleas on rats, and was very infectious. About one-third of the population of England died of it between 1347 and 1350, and it came back every few years until the end of the 15th century.

Black hole A region in space where gravity is so strong that nothing can escape, not even light. Black holes may result from the collapse of a giant star or supernova. Matter falling into a black hole is sucked into oblivion.

Black Sea Sea in E Europe and SW USSR, bordered by Turkey, Bulgaria, Romania and the USSR. Fed by Danube, Don, Bug, Dniester and Dnieper Rivers. Area: 460,000 km^2.

Black widow Venomous S American spider. It is shiny black with a red diamond on its underside. The female's extremely painful bite is not deadly to humans, though it is to the male spider whom she often consumes after mating.

Blake, William (1757–1827) English poet, artist and mystic. Poems include *Songs of Innocence* and *Songs of Experience*.

Blood A red substance pumped by the heart through a network of blood vessels to all parts of the body. The blood is the body's transport and defence system. It carries oxygen from the lungs, digested food and any waste material. It also carries chemical messengers called hormones. Blood consists of a fluid called plasma and two types of blood cell – red and white corpuscles. The red ones contain a substance called haemoglobin which carries oxygen from the lungs. The white ones help to protect the body from infection and disease.

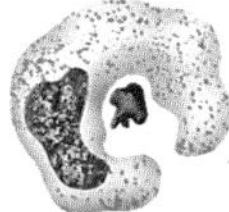

Red corpuscles (left) are disc-shaped. Phagocytes (right) are white blood cells that engulf, or eat, bacteria.

Boa Large non-poisonous snakes of tropical America that kill their prey by squeezing and use their teeth only for defence. Their jaws can stretch to swallow animals bigger than their heads and they can live for months without food.

Boadicea (Boudicca) (AD ?–62) Queen of the Iceni, a tribe of Britons in eastern England. She rose against the invading Romans but was defeated in AD 61 and the following year poisoned herself.

Boar, wild Wild pig once common in Britain and nothern Europe. It is still found in southern and central Europe, North Africa and Asia.

Wild boar

Boccaccio, Giovanni (1313–75) Italian author and poet, best known for his bawdy work *Decameron*.

Boer War Popular name for the South African War of 1899–1902. The Boers ('farmers') were descendants of Dutch settlers in South Africa. They opposed the expansion of British power in the region, and conflict grew until war broke out between the British and the two Boer republics of the Transvaal and Orange Free State. The Boers were excellent guerrilla fighters against the superior British power, but eventually they accepted British rule in return for a promise of self-government in the future.

Bolivar, Simon (1783–1830) Known as 'the liberator', he led the fight for freedom from Spanish rule in Venezuela, Colombia, Ecuador, Peru and Bolivia. Though defeated in 1812 and 1815 he finally overcame the Spanish at Ayacucho. Bolivia is named after him.

Bolivia Mountainous, landlocked republic in S America. More than half the people are subsistence farmers, the staple crops being maize and potatoes. Cash crops include sugar-cane and coffee. Bolivia's chief wealth lies in its minerals. It is the world's second largest producer of tin. Lead, zinc, copper, iron and many other ores are also mined on the high plateau. Large oil and gas deposits have been discovered. Area: 1,098,000 km²; Pop: 6,000,000; Caps: Sucre (legal) and La Paz (admin).

Bombay India's largest port and textile centre, formerly HQ of British East India Company (1668–1858). Pop: 5,971,000.

Bonaparte See **Napoleon I**.

Bone A hard, strong material that forms the framework of the body, the skeleton. The bones fit together to allow a wide range of movements. They are cushioned from one another by a pad of softer material called cartilage. Attached to the bones by straps, or tendons, are the muscles. These cause the bones to move at points called joints. Ligaments, made up of an elastic substance, hold the bones firmly in place at the joints.

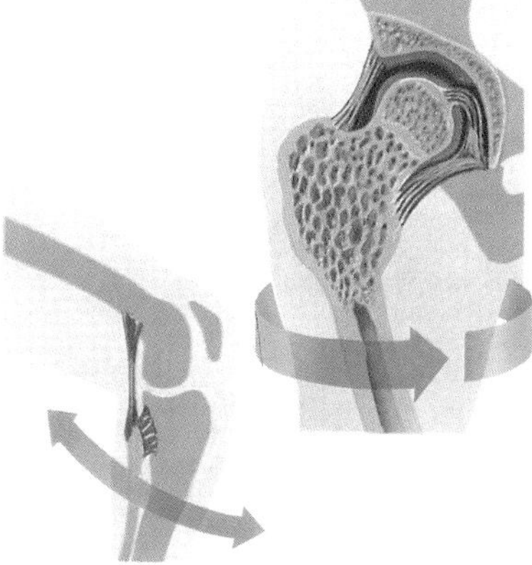

The knee joint (left) is a hinge joint: it can move only to and fro. The hip joint (right) is a ball and socket joint: it can move in many directions.

Bonn Capital of West Germany, situated on the R. Rhine. Birthplace of Beethoven. Pop: 288,000.

Booth, William (1829–1912) English evangelist and founder of Salvation Army (1878).

Borgia Powerful Spanish-Italian family. Among its members were the Popes Callistus III (Alfonso, 1455–58) and Alexander VI (Rodrigo, 1492–1503). **Cesare Borgia** (1476–1507) was a leading figure of the Renaissance and a ruthless general who unsuccessfully attempted to conquer central Italy. His sister **Lucrezia** (1480–1519) was a great patroness of the arts and famed for her beauty.

Borodin, Alexander (1833–87) Russian composer (and professor of chemistry). His works include the opera *Prince Igor* (finished by Rimsky-Korsakov) and two symphonies.

Boron A semi-metallic element whose best known compound is borax, a crystalline salt with uses ranging from antiseptics to food preservation. Boron is used in the control rods of nuclear reactors because it absorbs electrons readily. Chem. symbol B.

Boston Port and capital of Massachusetts, USA. Commercial centre of New England. Site of BOSTON TEA PARTY in 1773. Pop: 563,000.

Boston Tea Party An incident leading to the American Revolution. On 16 December 1773, some rebellious colonists (disguised as Indians) threw 342 chests of tea into Boston harbour. The tea was taxed, and the colonists objected to the tax because it was passed by a parliament in which they had no representatives.

Botany The study of plants.

Botany Bay An historic site in New South Wales, Australia, first discovered in 1770 by an expedition led by Captain James Cook. Cook and his chief scientist, Sir Joseph Banks, called it Botany Bay because they collected so many plants there. The first Australian settlers landed at Botany Bay in 1788, but they soon moved north to what is now Sydney.

Botha, Louis (1862–1919) South African soldier and statesman who fought against the British in the Boer War. He was prime minister of the Union of South Africa from 1910–19. During World War I he captured German South-West Africa.

Botswana An independent land-locked republic in southern Africa about the size of France. Much of the land is scrubland suitable only for cattle ranching. Formerly the British Protectorate of Bechuanaland, Botswana gained its independence in 1966. Area: 600,000 km²; Pop: 1,033,000; Cap: Gaborone.

Botticelli, Sandro (1447–1510) Florentine painter, mostly religious and classical subjects. Most famous works are *The Birth of Venus* and *Primavera*.

Boudicca See Boadicea.

Bower bird Several kinds of small birds of Australia and New Guinea, some with remarkable courtship behaviour. To attract a mate, the male builds a bower, strews it with bright feathers, flowers or shells, and dances to win her attention.

Bowls Game played indoors or on a grass area known as a 'green'. The players roll heavy balls known as 'woods' towards a smaller white ball or 'jack', the object being to place your ball as near to the jack as possible.

Ten-pin bowling, popular in the United States and in other countries, is a game similar to skittles.

Boxing Combat sport in which the contestants fight inside a square 'ring'. They wear gloves and may strike blows only with the clenched fist and only at certain parts of the body (the head and torso). The ancient Greeks and Romans boxed, and during the 18th century bare-fist 'prize-fighting' became popular in England. In the 19th century the 'Queensberry rules' were introduced to make boxing less brutal.

Boyle, Robert (1627–1691) English physicist. Boyle's Law states that the volume of a gas at a given temperature varies inversely according to the pressure, i.e. if the volume doubles, then the pressure halves and *vice versa*.

Brahms, Johannes (1833–97) German composer. Works include more than 200 songs, concertos for the violin and piano, four great symphonies as well as choral music.

Braille, Louis (1809–52) Frenchman who, blind himself, invented a system of reading and writing for the blind.

Brain The control centre of the body, receiving messages and giving out instructions to all parts of the body by way of nerves. Together with the spinal cord it makes up the central nervous system. Various parts of the brain are concerned with different mental activities or control different parts of the body. The sides, top and front of the brain, called the cerebral hemispheres or cerebrum, are concerned with thinking and conscious control of the body. At the back of the brain lies the cerebellum, concerned with unconscious body control such as heart beat.

Brasilia Capital of Brazil. Modern city, inaugurated in 1960 and purpose-built to serve as nation's new capital. Pop: 1,177,000.

Brazil The fifth largest country in the world, Brazil occupies almost half the area of South America. In the north the densely forested basin of the R. Amazon covers half the country. Much of the rest is composed of plateaux and highlands. Until recently, the economy was firmly based on agriculture. But great strides have been made in the last decade to industrialize the country, with massive HEP schemes providing the power for industries ranging from steelmaking to plastics. Industrial products now account for more than 50% of the exports. Area: 8,512,000 km^2; Pop: 134,380,000; Cap: Brasilia.

Bread Most widely manufactured food, a baked dough of flour, water and, usually, yeast to raise it. Baked since Egyptian times, bread comes in a variety of shapes and sizes, the most ubiquitous being the enriched white sliced loaf.

Bridge Something that allows traffic to pass over a river, valley, road or other obstacle. The three main types of bridge are the beam, the arch and the suspension. Beam bridges are made of strong girders that stretch from one side to the other. Sometimes the middle of the bridge rests on supports. Arch bridges may have one or more arches. Sydney harbour bridge is an arch bridge. Suspension bridges hang from very strong steel cables passing over towers at either end. The ends of the cables are firmly fixed in the ground.

Brisbane Port and capital city of Queensland, Australia. The city was founded as a penal colony in the 1820s and developed into an important industrial and commercial centre. Pop: 1,087,000 (met area).

Bristol Port and admin centre of Avon, England, on R. Avon. Commercial and cultural centre with university and cathedral. Formerly important for aircraft industry. Pop: 388,000.

British Isles Group of islands off NW Europe comprising the political divisions of Eire and the United Kingdom.

Britten, Benjamin (1913–76) English composer. Best known for his vocal, choral and operatic works. Operas include *Peter Grimes*, *Billy Budd* and *The Turn of the Screw*.

Bromine Reddish, foul-smelling liquid element whose vapour irritates the eyes and nose. It unites readily with many other elements to form bromides. One of the most important is the light-sensitive silver bromide used in photographic emulsions. Chem. symbol Br.

Brontë, Charlotte (1816–55) English novelist. One of three daughters of an Anglican clergyman. In order to get their work published they used male pseudonyms. Charlotte wrote *Jane Eyre*, *Shirley*, *Villette* and *The Professor*. Her sister **Emily** (1818–48) wrote *Wuthering Heights* and **Anne** (1820–49) wrote *Agnes Gray* and *The Tenant of Wildfell Hall*.

Brontosaurus Huge herbivorous dinosaur of the Jurassic period, some 21 metres long and weighing 30 tonnes. Also called Apatosaurus and Atlantosaurus.

Bronze Age The prehistoric period when people learned to make tools out of metal. They mainly used copper to start with, but bronze (an alloy of copper and tin) was soon found to be easier to cast and stronger. In the Middle East, the Bronze Age began before 3000 BC, but in Britain it did not begin until about 1800 BC. It lasted until the Iron Age.

Browning, Robert (1812–99) English poet known for the long poem *The Ring and the Book* and earlier poetry. His wife, **Elizabeth Barrett Browning** (1806–61) was also a poet.

Bruce, Robert (1274–1329) Scottish hero who took part in the revolt against Edward I. He later led the revolt himself and eventually defeated the English at Bannockburn in 1314. This victory secured Scottish independence.

Bruckner, Anton (1824–96) Austrian composer whose works include a string quartet, nine symphonies, and a number of masses.

Brueghel, Pieter (1525–1570) Flemish painter who is famed for his brightly coloured landscapes and peasant scenes. His sons, **Jan** (1568–1625) and **Pieter the Younger** (1564–1638), were also painters.

Brunei A small oil-rich nation on the north coast of Borneo. Many people are farmers, with rice being the chief crop, and most have a high standard of living due to the nation's oil revenues. Area: 5800 km^2; Pop: 214,000; Cap: Bandar Seri Begawan.

Brunel, Isambard Kingdom (1806–1859) English engineer who helped his father, **Marc Isambard Brunel** (1769–1849), to build the Rotherhithe tunnel under the Thames. He designed and constructed the Great Western Railway as well as the steamships *Great Western*, *Great Britain* and *Great Eastern*. He also built numerous bridges.

Brussels Port and capital of Belgium on R. Senne. Served as the centre of the Belgian revolution of 1830. Now the admin centre of the EEC. Pop: 1,042,000.

Bucharest Capital of Romania, on R. Dimbovita. Prominent industrial centre. Pop: 1,960,000.

Budapest Capital of Hungary on R. Danube. Originally separate towns of Obuda and Buda on the right bank and Pest on the left bank which were united in 1873. Pop: 2,082,000.

Buddhism Religion practised mostly in the East by followers of Buddha who believe that sufferings result from desire and only the extinguishing of desire brings peace. The Noble Eightfold Path to that enlightened peace (*nirvana*) is by right belief, aspiration, speech, conduct, occupation, effort, thought and meditation.

Buddhists believe that special ways of sitting help them to meditate.

Budgerigar Small Australian green and yellow parakeet that lives wild in flocks. Many domestic varieties have been bred and are popular as caged pets.

Buenos Aires Capital, commercial centre and leading port of Argentina, on estuary of Rio de la Plata. Pop: 2,973,000.

Buffalo Bill (William Frederick Cody, 1846–1917) US cavalry scout who gained fame for his Wild West show which successfully toured America for many years.

Bug True bugs are insects which look rather like beetles, but unlike beetles do not have jaws. Their mouths are 'beaks' used to pierce plants and suck up their juices. Bugs live on and under water as well as on land, and some, such as APHIDS and leafhoppers, are pests.

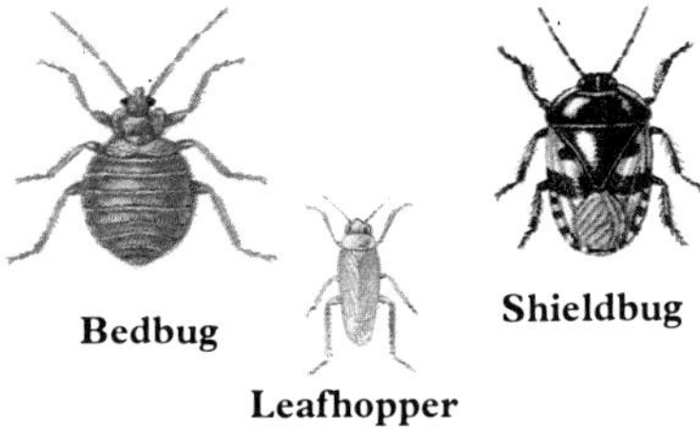

Bulb Underground reproductive organ and food store of certain plants consisting of a short stem surrounded by thick fleshy leaves. Tulips and onions are both bulbs.

Bulgaria A communist republic of south-eastern Europe bordering the Black Sea. Until the mid-20th century Bulgaria was one of Europe's more backward countries. Then, with Soviet aid, the country was industrialized and the farms mechanized. The staple crops are wheat and maize. Cultivation of tobacco, a traditional Bulgarian crop, has also been expanded. Engineering is the chief industry with machinery accounting for two-thirds of Bulgarian exports. Area: 111,000 km^2; Pop: 8,696,000; Cap: Sofia.

Bullfinch A beautiful bird, disliked by fruit-growers because it eats the buds of fruit trees. Both sexes have black caps and the male has a bright red breast. Bullfinches live in Europe, N America and Asia.

Bunting A family of seed-eating birds that look similar to finches, with stout bills for cracking open seeds and nuts. They include the corn and reed buntings and the YELLOWHAMMER.

Yellowhammers

Bunyan, John (1628–88) Nonconformist preacher and author of *Pilgrim's Progress*. He spent long periods in prison for his outspoken evangelistic views.

Buoyancy The ability of an object to float in water. This depends on the density of the object. Wood will float in water because it is less dense than water. A metal ship floats for the same reason: the amount of water displaced by a ship is heavier (denser) than the ship itself.

Burkina Faso (Upper Volta) Country in W Africa, landlocked, but with rivers flowing south into Ghana. This high, dry country is bordered by the Sahara Desert and has a small, unreliable rainfall. The people live by keeping livestock and farming, but drought frequently forces them to leave their lands. Area: 274,179 km^2; Pop: 6,733,000; Cap: Ouagadougou.

Burma Nation in SE Asia. The central part of Burma is a fertile plain drained by the Irrawaddy R. Most of the people work on the land, with rice being the staple crop and the leading export. Sugar-cane, tobacco, and oil-seeds are other economically important crops. Extensive hardwood forests produce Burma's other leading export – teak. Area: 677,000 km^2; Pop: 35,000,000; Cap: Rangoon.

Burns, Robert (1759–1796) Scottish poet whose tender and humorous poems include *Tam O'Shanter, Auld Lang Syne* and *My Love is like a Red, Red Rose*.

Burundi One of the poorest nations in the world, Burundi lies in the heart of Africa. More than 80% of the people lead primitive farming lives, but the land is densely populated and the soil is poor. Area: 28,000 km²; Pop: 4,663,000; Cap: Bujumbura.

Bushman Among the oldest people of Africa, but now greatly reduced in numbers, the Bushmen are nomadic hunters who live in family groups in the Kalahari Desert. They have their own language, customs and rituals.

Butter Food made by churning milk fat. Used in cooking and as a spread for bread. It takes 10 litres of milk to make one kilo of butter.

Buttercup Several species of flowering plant characterized by their waxy, yellow, five-petalled flowers. They have poisonous juices and are avoided by grazing animals.

Butterfly Among the most beautiful of insects, butterflies are generally more colourful than their close relatives, the MOTHS. Both insects have large wings and feed on flowers. After mating, the female butterfly lays eggs which hatch into larvae called caterpillars. The caterpillar feeds on plants and eventually turns into a chrysalis or pupa, inside which it changes into the adult insect or imago. Most butterflies have short adult lives, but a few species can live through the winter in a state of hibernation.

Buzzard A large, hawk-like bird of prey with broad wings. It soars high in the sky, preferring wooded and hilly country. Buzzards feed on rabbits, mice and other small animals.

Byron, Lord (George Gordon Byron, 1788–1824) English romantic poet and satirist who left England in 1816 to travel in Europe. He died of a fever in Greece. His long romantic poems include *Childe Harold's Pilgrimage* and *Don Juan*.

Byzantine Empire A medieval Christian empire in the Middle East. In AD 395 the Emperor Constantine divided the Roman Empire in two, with a new eastern capital at Constantinople (now Istanbul). A distinctive culture developed in Byzantium during the next two or three centuries. The Byzantine, or Eastern, Empire became divided from the rest of the Christian world, and was influenced by the Arabs and other neighbours. It far outlasted the Roman Empire in the West, and did not finally disappear until the Turks captured Constantinople in 1453.

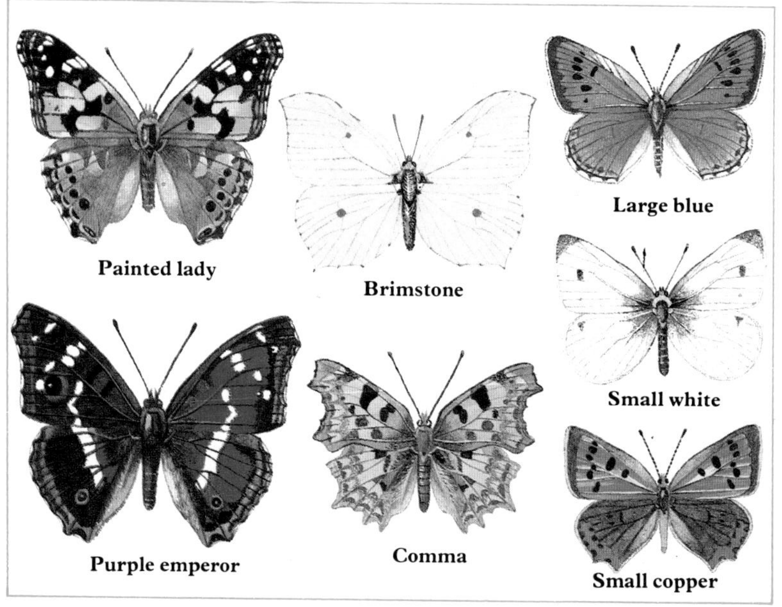

C

Cabot, John (1425–*c* 1500) Italian explorer who settled in England. Supported by Henry VII he sailed westwards in 1497 in search of the riches of the Far East. He discovered what he believed to be Asia but was in fact Newfoundland and Nova Scotia.

Cactus A family of plants that live in dry places, mostly in the United States and Mexico. Adapted to desert life, the stems can store water and the roots spread out to catch any rain. Prickly spines protect the plants from thirsty animals. The giant saguaro cactus grows up to 15 metres tall. Smaller species are often cultivated as house plants.

Caddis fly Flying insects which look similar to moths. They spend their larval stage in water, often building themselves cases of stones, shell fragments and vegetable matter. Inside the case, the larva is well hidden and protected from predators.

Cadmium Metallic element widely used as a corrosion-resistant plating on other metals and in copper alloys for making electric cables. Chem. symbol Cd.

Cairo Capital of Egypt, at the head of Nile delta. Africa's largest city with a famous Muslim university founded in 972 and many fine mosques. Pop: 6,824,000.

Calcium Highly reactive metallic element which does not occur in the pure form in nature, though its compounds make up a large part of the Earth's crust. They include marble, chalk and limestone (all calcium carbonate) among many others. Chem. symbol Ca.

Calculus A branch of mathematics which deals with changing quantities. In *differential calculus*, the rate of change is calculated. The speed of something, for example, is found by calculating the rate at which the object's distance from a given point changes with time. *Integral calculus* is the reverse of differential calculus. It calculates the quantity from its rate of change.

Calcutta Port and capital of West Bengal state in NE India. Largest city in India. Site of 'Black Hole of Calcutta' guard-house in which 123 Britons were killed in 1756. Pop: 3,149,000.

Calendar A system of reckoning and organizing time in days, months and years. The Romans invented the calendar we use today but it did not quite match the solar year – the time taken for the Earth to orbit the Sun. By the late sixteenth century it was 10 days out. In 1582 Pope Gregory XIII removed 10 days from the calendar and made minor adjustments that keep it accurate to about 25 seconds per year.

California Most populous state of USA, located on the Pacific coast. The value of goods produced in California is greater than in any other US state. Area: 411,000 km^2; Pop: 23,668,000.

Calvin, John (1509–64) French religious reformer who broke with the Catholic Church in 1533. He settled in Geneva where he established a centre to preach his austere brand of Protestantism.

Camel Hoofed mammal related to the llama. The Arabian camel, or dromedary, has one hump, the Bactrian camel of Asia two humps. Fat stored in the humps helps camels survive in deserts.

Arabian camel

Camera An instrument for taking photographs. When we take a photograph, light rays from the object we are photographing enter a light-tight container through a small hole when a shutter opens for a fraction of a second. The light rays form an image of the object on a strip of light-sensitive film. The film is treated with chemicals (developed), then the developed film is printed onto a special kind of paper.

The focus and aperture of the lens, and exposure time, can all be automatically adjusted by some modern cameras.

Light passing through the lens of a camera forms an inverted image on the film.

Cameroon A republic of central Africa bordering the Gulf of Guinea. Cameroon is becoming an increasingly prosperous nation. Though less than 5% of the land is cultivated, plantation crops including cocoa, coffee, peanuts, tea, bananas and cotton are important exports. There are large bauxite deposits and the building of HEP stations has made Cameroon the leading aluminium producer in Africa. It is also an oil exporting nation. Area: 475,000 km²; Pop: 9,507,000; Cap: Yaoundé.

Canada Second largest country in the world, Canada is a rich nation with a wealth of natural resources. One is the fertile soil of the southern plains which have made Canada the world's second largest exporter of wheat. Farther west lie the great cattle ranches. To the north of the farming regions there are huge coniferous forests. Lumber, pulp and newsprint are major exports. Minerals include petroleum and natural gas, copper, nickel, lead and zinc. The leading manufactures are steel, paper and aluminium.

The settlement of Canada was pioneered by the French but Anglo-French wars resulted in the colony coming under British rule in 1763. In 1931 Canada became an independent member of the Commonwealth. Area: 9,975,000 km²; Pop: 25,142,000; Cap: Ottawa.

Canaletto, Antonio (1697–1768) Italian painter who is famed for his Venetian scenes. In the mid-1700s he also painted many London scenes including views of the Thames and Richmond.

Canals Man-made waterways for the movement of barges, ships, and sometimes for irrigation. Before the coming of the railways, canals were the most important means of transporting goods. Unlike roads, canals can only go up or down hill by means of *locks*. Locks are watertight chambers with gates at each end. Water can be pumped into and out of locks to raise or lower a vessel.

Canary Islands Group of islands in Atlantic Ocean, off NW coast of Africa, belonging to Spain. The group includes Tenerife, Gran Canaria, La Palma and Lanzarote. The islands are a noted tourist centre. Pop: 1,170,000.

Canberra Capital of Australia, situated in Australian Capital Territory. The town has grown rapidly since being chosen as capital in 1908. The majority of the working inhabitants are employed by the government. Pop: 246,000 (met area).

Cancer An abnormal and uncontrollable growth of the cells, usually resulting in a tumour. Where the growth is restricted and does not spread to other parts of the body the tumour is said to be benign. One in which cancer cells break away and infect other healthy areas is said to be malignant. Leukaemia is a form of cancer of the blood.

Canute (*c* 994–1035) A wise and firm ruler who became king of England in 1016, of Denmark in 1018 and of Norway in 1028. During his reign peace and order were restored to England and he gave new authority to the Church. He married Emma, widow of King Ethelred II.

Cape Canaveral The main site used by the United States for space launches. Located in eastern Florida, it was known as Cape Kennedy from 1963–1973.

Capercaillie This bird is the largest member of the grouse family. Capercaillies live in northern pine forests. The male is black or dark grey and displays before the brown-feathered female by fanning out his tail and uttering a variety of strange squawks and screeches.

Cape Town Seaport and capital of Cape Province and legislative capital of South Africa situated on Table Bay on the SW coast. The area was settled in 1652 by the Dutch East India Company. Pop: 1,490,000 (met area).

Capybara Largest of the rodents, measuring up to 1.2 metres in length and weighing up to 200 kg, the capybara resembles a huge guinea pig. It lives by rivers in S America and is a strong swimmer.

Caracas Capital city of Venezuela. Centre of resistance to Spanish control from 1811–21. Modern city with oil and sugar refining. Pop: 2,476,000.

Carbohydrate One of the three main kinds of foods that are essential to the body. The others are PROTEIN and FAT. Carbohydrates such as sugar and starch are made up of carbon, hydrogen, and oxygen. They are made during photosynthesis in green plants.

A selection of foods rich in carbohydrates. They provide energy quickly but if eaten to excess lead to fatness.

Carbon Non-metallic element which is present in all living things. Carbon atoms form a larger number of compounds than all other elements put together, and the study of these compounds is the basis of organic chemistry. In the pure state, carbon appears in nature in two forms – as the soft, flaky graphite used to make pencil 'leads' and as the hard, brittle diamond, the hardest of all known substances. Chem. symbol C.

Carbon dioxide A colourless gas which is present in the atmosphere in various quantities. It is formed when a carbon-containing substance, such as wood or coal, is burnt. It is also breathed out by animals. Plants use carbon dioxide when they make food by photosynthesis. Chem. symbol CO_2.

Carbon monoxide Colourless, poisonous gas with no taste or smell. It is formed when there is insufficient air for carbon-containing substances to be completely burnt. Car exhaust fumes, for instance, contain carbon monoxide. Chem. symbol CO.

Carburettor The part of an internal combustion engine that mixes the petrol vapour with air in the correct proportions for combustion in the cylinders.

Card games Games played with printed cards. An English pack of cards has four 'suits' (hearts, spades, diamonds and clubs), numbered from one (ace) to ten, Jack, Queen, King. Where playing cards were invented is not known but it was probably in Asia. Cards reached Europe in the Middle Ages, the first pack probably being the Tarot (which has 78 cards). There are many card games, which often involve gambling. Among the most popular today are bridge, cribbage, poker, rummy and whist. Most card games need up to four players, but patience can be played by a single player.

Cardiff Port and capital of Wales, situated in South Glamorgan, at the mouth of the R. Taff on the Bristol Channel. Major coal-shipping port, grain importer, and iron and steel centre. Pop: 274,000.

Caribbean Sea Part of the Atlantic Ocean, the Caribbean Sea is bounded by the West Indies, Central America and northern South America.

Caribou Brownish-grey deer of N America standing up to 1.5 metres at the shoulder. Both sexes bear antlers. Caribou spend their summers grazing on the TUNDRA. In winter they move south to the shelter of the forest. The European reindeer is a semi-domesticated form of the caribou.

Carnivore Any meat-eating animal. More specifically, a term applied to any member of the mammalian order Carnivora which includes the foxes, cats and badgers.

Carp A family of fishes that includes many familiar freshwater species, among them the roach, dace, chub, minnow, carp and goldfish. They have no teeth in their jaws, but have teeth in the back of the throat with which they grind up their food.

Carroll, Lewis (Charles Lutwidge Dodgson, 1832–98) English writer and mathematician whose most famous works are *Alice's Adventures in Wonderland* and *Through the Looking Glass*. These grew from stories that he told to the children of Dean Liddell (Alice was one of them).

Carthage An ancient city in North Africa, near modern Tunis. Carthage was a great power in the western Mediterranean in the 3rd century BC, when it was challenged by the rising young republic of Rome. The contest between them, known as the Punic Wars, contained many great exploits such as the invasion of Italy across the Alps in 219 BC by the Carthaginian general HANNIBAL. Carthage finally lost, however, and the city was destroyed by the Romans in 146 BC.

Cartier, Jacques (1491–1557) French explorer and navigator. Born at St Malo he was the first to explore the Gulf of St Lawrence and discovered the St Lawrence River.

Cartilaginous fish Fishes with skeletons of cartilage (gristle) instead of bone, such as sharks, rays and skates.

Caspian Sea Salt lake situated between Europe and Asia, in USSR and Iran. The world's largest inland body of water. It lies 28 metres below sea level and is believed to be shrinking. Area: 420,000 km^2.

Cassandra In Greek legend the daughter of Priam and Hecuba. She was given the gift of prophecy by Apollo, but when he failed to win her he decreed that no-one should ever believe her prophecies.

Cassowary Large flightless bird related to the emu. It lives in New Guinea and N Australia.

Castle A military stronghold which was also usually the home of a great noble or ruler. Stone castles were built in Europe during the Middle Ages. Besides towers and battlements, they were guarded by a moat and, later, a sliding iron door called a portcullis. In the 15th century, gunpowder and cannon made it much easier to attack a castle. Except for some coastal forts, no castles have been built with a serious military purpose since then.

Cat Any member of the carnivorous cat family which includes the LION, LEOPARD, CHEETAH, TIGER, WILD CAT and domestic cat.

Domestic cats are divided into short-haired and long-haired types. Among the former are Oriental cats including: Siamese, Burmese, Abyssinians and the tailless Manx cat. Long-haired (Persian) cats are prized for their beautiful coats but are more difficult to keep as pets.

Blue British Shorthair

Brown Tabby Shorthair

American Wirehair

Burmese

Persians

Angora cat

Catalyst A substance that speeds up a chemical reaction but is not itself changed in the process. Catalysts are widely used in the chemical industry.

Caterpillar Larval stage of certain insects, particularly moths and butterflies. As they grow, caterpillars moult several times before they are ready to pupate.

Catfish A group of about 2000 species of fish. Catfishes have no scales but all have long barbels on the mouth.

Cathedrals Christian churches important as the seat of a bishop and, often, for their size and fine architecture. A cathedral is the principal church of a diocese. The great cathedrals of the Middle Ages are among the most impressive European buildings. Some took hundreds of years to complete. Examples are Cologne (Germany), Chartres (France), and Canterbury (England).

Catherine the Great (1729–96) German by birth, she married the future Tsar Peter III of Russia in 1744. She was declared Empress Catherine II of Russia in 1762 after the murder of her incompetent husband. Despite initial efforts to introduce sweeping reforms, the French revolution and the domestic unrest turned her into a reactionary. Her reign saw the strengthening of the power of the nobility and the expansion of Russia.

Cathode-ray tube A glass tube which has had the air sucked out of it and in which cathode rays (streams of electrons) are produced. A beam of electrons produced at one end of the tube is made to strike a screen at the other end. This screen is coated with chemicals which glow when struck by the electrons. When the electron beam is deflected back and forth, it traces an image on the screen. The screen of a television set is the end of a cathode-ray tube. These tubes are also used in RADAR and as OSCILLOSCOPES.

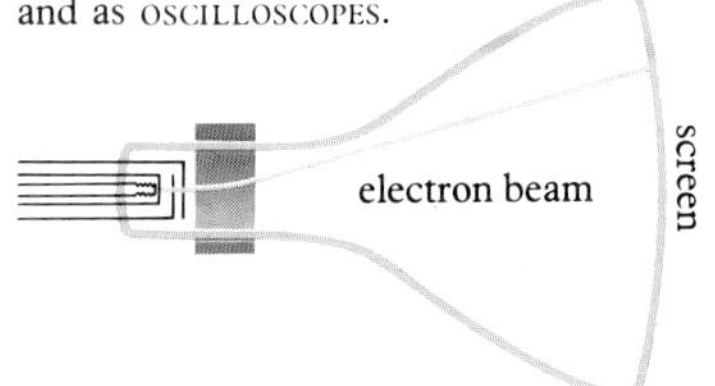

Diagram of a cathode-ray tube, showing the electron beam which scans the phosphor-coated screen.

Cattle Domestic cattle belong to the ox family along with their wild relatives the bison and buffalo. They are important farm animals from which we get beef, milk, butter, cream and cheese, as well as leather. All cattle are ruminants. They have stomachs with four sections. Food can be stored in one part and returned to the mouth to be chewed as cud.

Aberdeen-Angus, Brahman and Hereford are beef breeds. Friesian, Jersey and Guernsey are dairy breeds. Redpolls and Shorthorns are bred for milk and meat. India has the largest population of cattle, followed by the United States.

Caucasus Mountain range in USSR, situated between the Black and Caspian Seas. Contains a number of glaciers and Europe's highest peak, Mt Elbrus (5633 metres).

Cavendish, Henry (1731–1810) English scientist. He investigated the properties of hydrogen and carbon dioxide, and conducted research into the mass and density of the Earth.

Caxton, William (1422–1491) The first English printer. He set up his own press at Westminster in 1476. Amongst the works printed by him were the *Canterbury Tales* by Chaucer, *Le Morte D'Arthur* by Malory and *Aesop's Fables*.

Cedar Coniferous trees related to pines. The elegant cedar of Lebanon grows up to 40 metres tall and may live for thousands of years. Other kinds of cedar are the deodar, Atlas and Cyprus cedar. The red and white cedars of N America are not true cedars.

Cell, biological The tiny units from which all living things are made. A typical cell consists of a cell wall containing a fluid and various tiny particles which together are called the protoplasm. Towards the centre of the cell is the nucleus. This contains the chromosomes which carry all the cell's 'information'.

Cell, electric A device that produces electricity from chemicals. In its simplest form, an electric cell consists of two different electrical conductors in a solution that also conducts electricity, called the electrolyte. The conductors can be zinc and copper or, as in modern dry batteries, a carbon rod in a zinc outer case. These are called primary cells and cannot be recharged. The car BATTERY is a rechargable secondary cell.

Cellulose Substance (carbohydrate) found in most plants, forming the main element of cell walls. Its fibrous nature makes it an important raw material in the textile industry.

Celts A prehistoric people who spread over much of western Europe during the Iron Age. They had iron weapons earlier than others, which gave them an advantage in war. The Celts were a number of different, though related, peoples or tribes. They never formed states or kingdoms, but they had a rich culture. They built towns of some size in France. Today, the Celtic tradition is strong in places such as Brittany, Wales and Scotland, where local people regard the Celts as direct ancestors.

Centaurs In Greek legend half-man, half-horse beings who lived on Mount Pelion in Thessaly.

Centipede Group of arthropods that have between 15 and 177 pairs of legs. The first pair form poisonous fangs. Centipedes live in damp places, under stones or in houses, hunting other small invertebrates at night.

Central African Republic Landlocked country in central Africa with few resources and a small population. Coffee, cotton and peanuts are the only cash crops. Diamonds are the chief export, though uranium is also mined. Area: 622,935 km^2; Pop: 2,890,000; Cap: Bangui.

Cephalopod Member of a group of marine molluscs containing squids, octopuses and cuttlefish. Unlike other molluscs, cephalopods have a distinct head surrounded by suckered tentacles and the shell (when present) is internal. The animals move by a form of jet water-propulsion.

Ceramics Pottery of all kinds, including china, porcelain and earthenware. All these are made of clay mixed with water and baked (fired) in a hot oven (kiln) to harden it. The Chinese were the first to make fine ceramics, several thousand years ago. The best china is called porcelain. Earthenware is coarser. To make round shapes, the potter throws a lump of wet clay onto a disc which is kept spinning as the potter moulds the clay into shape. Most ceramics have a shiny surface called a glaze. This is painted on before the clay is fired.

Cerberus In Greek legend a three-headed dog who guarded the gates of Hades. His capture was one of the Labours of Heracles (Hercules).

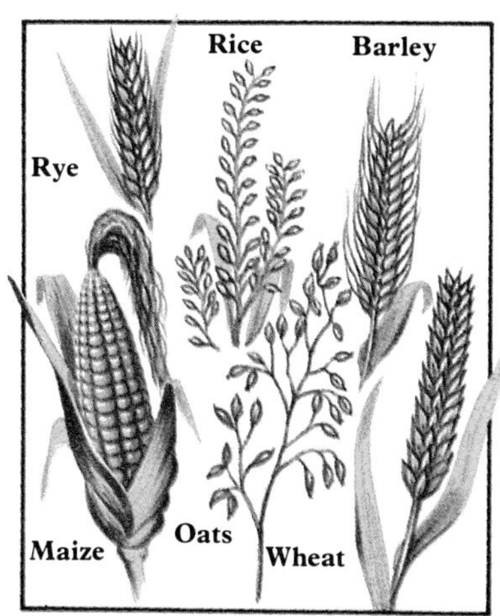

Cereals Plants of the grass family cultivated for their seeds (grain). The most important crop is RICE which is the staple diet of Asia. WHEAT is the most important in Europe and America, being made into flour, bread and breakfast foods. Millet, BARLEY, oats, rye and sorghum are grown for human and animal consumption.

Cervantes (Saavedra), Miguel de (1547–1616) Foremost Spanish novelist, soldier and adventurer. He fought at the Battle of Lepanto, spent five years as a slave in Algiers and wrote the humorous classic *Don Quixote de la Mancha*.

Cézanne, Paul (1839–1906) French impressionist painter who specialized in portraits and landscapes.

Chad Large, landlocked country in N central Africa and one of the poorest nations in the world. Most people raise crops, particularly millet, for their own families, or are nomadic herdsmen. Area: 1,283,901 km^2; Pop: 5,116,000; Cap: N'Djamena.

Chaffinch A common but striking bird of European woodlands and gardens. The wings and tail are black with white bars and the male has a pink face and underparts with a blue crown.

Chalk A pure form of limestone composed largely of the remains of tiny marine creatures. Some of the most famous chalk deposits are those forming the 'white' cliffs of Dover, England.

Chameleon Lizards (mostly African) renowned for their ability to change colour to match their surroundings. They have long gripping tails and immensely long tongues which shoot out to catch insects.

Chamois

Chamois Small, agile mountain ruminant which lives in small flocks in Europe and W Asia. It looks like a goat but is related to the antelopes.

Champlain, Samuel de (1567–1635) French navigator and explorer who founded the French colony of Quebec in 1608. He also discovered the lake that bears his name.

Channel Islands Group of islands in the English Channel off NW coast of France. The islands belong to the British Crown but are self-governing. The main islands are Guernsey, Jersey, Sark and Alderney. Dairy and market garden produce are the chief exports. Pop: 125,000.

Chaplin, Charlie (Sir Charles Spencer 1889–1977) Famous comedian of silent films. His baggy trousers and bowler hat endeared him to millions all over the world. His best known films include *The Gold Rush, The Great Dictator, Modern Times* and *Limelight*.

Chariot A two-wheeled vehicle drawn by one, two or more horses. The ancient chariot was a small, open-backed cart used mainly in war. Some peoples, such as the Celts, fixed knives to the hubs of the wheels. Chariot races were a popular sport in the Roman and Byzantine Empires.

Charlemagne (Charles I, AD 742–814) Son of Pepin, he became king of the Franks in 771 and subsequently ruled Italy, Gaul and large areas of Germany and Spain. Crowned Holy Roman Emperor in 800 for having restored Leo III to the papal see, he controlled his immense empire through an efficient administrative system. He encouraged reform of the Church and was a great patron of learning.

Charles I (1600–1649) King of England, Scotland and Ireland from 1625. His marriage to the Catholic Henrietta Maria was very unpopular and foreign ventures led by his favourite the Duke of Buckingham were costly failures. Kept

The Ancient Chinese built fine chariots drawn by trotting horses.

short of money by the Puritan parliament he was forced to rely on ancient methods of taxation which resulted in the revolt of parliament and the Civil War in which he was ultimately defeated. Tried for treason, Charles was executed in 1649.

Charles II (1630–85) King of England, Scotland and Ireland from 1660. A Roman Catholic at heart he had to accept the laws passed by parliament enforcing religious conformity. His eventful reign saw the Plague and The Great Fire of London. Known as the Merry Monarch he had several illegitimate children but was succeeded by his unpopular brother, James II.

Charon In Greek legend the boatman of Hades who ferried the dead across the Styx.

Chaucer, Geoffrey (*c* 1340–1400) English poet and diplomat. His works include the *Parliament of Fowls, Troilus and Criseyde* and *Canterbury Tales*.

Cheetah Fastest of all land animals, the cheetah, a long-legged member of the cat family, is capable of speeds of 110 km/h in short bursts. It lives on open plains from southern Africa to India.

Chekhov, Anton (1860–1904) Russian dramatist and writer of short stories. His plays include *The Cherry Orchard, Uncle Vanya* and *The Seagull*.

Chemical formulae A chemist knows a molecule of water as H_2O. This is a chemical formula meaning that the water molecule contains two atoms of hydrogen (H_2) and one of oxygen (O).

Chemical industry An industry which includes a vast number of different manufacturing processes. Acids such as sulphuric acid, and alkalis such as caustic soda are examples of useful chemicals which can be used to produce more complex chemical substances. The oil and coal industries produce chemicals used as raw materials to make such things as plastics, detergents and synthetic fibres. Other important parts of the chemical industry produce fertilizers, insecticides and drugs.

Chemical reactions Chemical processes involving two or more substances. These processes result in chemical changes in the substances. If a piece of wood is burned, this is a chemical reaction. The wood turns to ash, and heat and light are given off. This burning is the joining together of the wood with oxygen from the air.

Chemistry The study of the make-up and properties of substances and how they work together. There are two main branches of chemistry – organic and inorganic. Organic chemistry deals with compounds of the element carbon. These compounds are in all living matter. Inorganic chemistry is concerned with the compounds of all other elements.

Cherry The cherry tree is a member of the rose family. As well as the wild cherry there are cultivated varieties producing fruit of varying sweetness and colour. Some trees are cultivated for their blossom.

Chess Game for two players, each using 16 pieces on a board of 64 squares. Chess may have originated in India. It was popular throughout W Europe by the 13th century.

Chestnut A deciduous tree of the beech family, also known as the Spanish chestnut. The fruit consists of a spiky husk containing two or three shiny brown nuts that are commonly eaten. The tree is unrelated to the horse chestnut.

Chicago Second largest city in USA on the shores of L. Michigan in Illinois. Major industrial and commercial centre with the largest railway yards in the world and one of the busiest airports. Pop: 3,005,000 (met area: 7,104,000).

Chile Over 4000 km long but never more than 400 km wide Chile is a country in South America bordering the Pacific Ocean. Only the central region is suitable for agriculture and this is where 90% of the people live. Chile is rich in minerals and is one of the leading producers of copper in the world. Area: 756,900 km^2; Pop: 11,700,000; Cap: Santiago.

Chimpanzee A large African ape (and our closest animal relative). It lives in forests in Africa in small family groups, eating fruit and leaves and revealing considerable intelligence. Even in the wild chimps are capable of using simple tools. See picture on page 16.

China The third largest country in the world with by far the greatest number of people – almost 25% of the world total. Eastern China is composed of fertile lowlands drained by many large rivers including the Hwang Ho, the Yangtze Kiang and the Si Kiang. Westwards the land rises to plateaux and mountains which take up 80% of the country. Rice is the chief cereal crop in the south, wheat and millet in the north. Mineral resources include huge coal deposits, petroleum and natural gas, iron ore and tungsten. The leading manufactures are steel, machinery, chemicals and textiles. Petroleum is now a major export. One of the world's earliest civilizations grew up in the river valleys of China, and periods of foreign rule changed the culture little. Communist rule was established over the entire mainland in 1949 after a long and bitter civil war. Area: 9,596,220 km^2; Pop: 1,031 million. Cap: Peking (Beijing).

Chip See **Silicon chip**

Chipmunk N American (and Asian) ground squirrel which lives in underground burrows. It eats nuts and berries and can store them in pouches in its cheeks.

Chlorine Poisonous yellowy-green gas that attacks the eyes, throat and lungs. First poison gas to be used in warfare (World War I). Its compounds (chlorides) have important industrial uses as bleaches and disinfectants. Chem. symbol Cl.

Chlorophyll Green substance or pigment in most plants. The plant uses it to trap the energy in sunlight during PHOTOSYNTHESIS.

Cholera Acutely infectious bacterial disease, contracted from food or water contaminated with human faeces. Prevalent in countries where proper sanitation is not available.

Chopin, Frédéric (1810–49) Polish-born pianist and composer. From 1831 he lived in Paris and nearly all his work was composed for solo piano. While his mazurkas and polonaises reveal his strong feelings of Polish nationalism he also wrote two piano concertos, numerous studies and nocturnes. For a time he lived with the novelist George Sand.

Christianity Religion with the greatest worldwide following, based on the life and teachings of JESUS CHRIST. Christians believe that Jesus was the Messiah (saviour) prophesied in the Old Testament, who died to save mankind. The early Christians were persecuted but the religion spread, became institutionalized and eventually split into numerous Churches and sects of varying beliefs. See also **Protestantism; Roman Catholicism.**

Early Christians were persecuted by the Romans. Many were 'fed to the lions'.

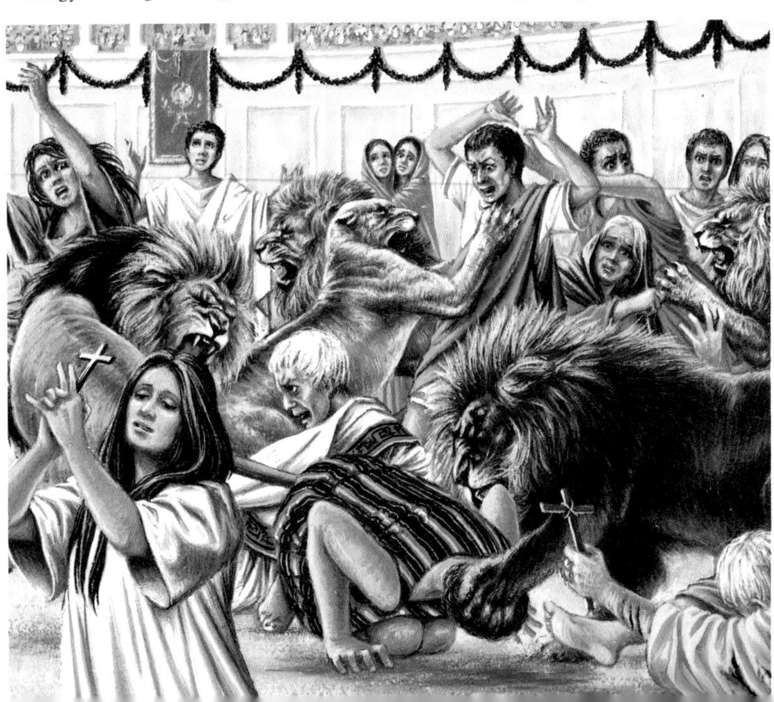

Christmas (December 25th) One of the most important festivals of the Christian Church, it celebrates the birth of Jesus. Christmas is also a time for family gatherings and traditionally for present-giving.

Chromium Hard, corrosion-resistant metal widely used to give a shiny plating to other metals. Industrially important in the production of various chrome steels, such as stainless steel. Chem. symbol Cr.

Chromosome Tiny bodies within the nucleus of a cell that carry all the information required by the cell to function and reproduce efficiently. The information is in the form of a code, contained in a complex substance called DNA. Most chromosomes exist in pairs, each of a pair carrying almost identical information. The human cell contains 23 pairs.

Chrysalis Pupa or resting stage of butterflies, moths and some other insects.

Chrysanthemum Members of the daisy family of plants, cultivated for their extravagant blossoms. They flower in the autumn.

Churchill, Winston Spencer (1874–1965) Statesman, soldier and writer. Elected member of parliament in 1900 he was First Lord of the Admiralty from 1911–15. He was Chancellor of the Exchequer from 1924–29 and became Prime Minister of a coalition government in 1940, leading Britain through World War II. Prime Minister again in 1951 he retired in 1955. He wrote *The History of the English Speaking Peoples* and was awarded the Nobel Prize for literature in 1953. He was knighted in the same year.

Winston Churchill

Cicada Bugs commonly found in warm countries, which 'sing' by vibrating small membranes called tymbals.

Cicero, Marcus Tullius (106–43 BC) Foremost of Roman orators he became consul in 63 BC. He supported the murder of Julius Caesar but was himself put to death for having denounced Mark Antony.

Cinema The art of making films, or the building in which films are shown. Ways of taking photographs in rapid sequence were developed in the 1870s, and celluloid film strips in 1889. By the 1890s 'moving pictures' were given public showings and became so popular that a new industry grew up, centred on HOLLYWOOD, USA, to keep pace with public demand. Early films were silent. It was not until 1927 that the first 'talkie' appeared.

Circe In Greek legend a temptress who turned Odysseus' companions into swine.

Circus an entertainment held in a circular arena, or 'ring'. The charioteers of ancient Rome raced horses round the track of the Circus Maximus. Modern circuses began in the 1700s with Astley's show in London. Today the typical show features clowns, jugglers, acrobats and sometimes performing animals. Shows may be given in a large tent, the 'Big Top', under the direction of a ringmaster.

Citrus fruits The fruits of citrus trees include ORANGES, lemons, limes, grapefruits, tangerines and many others. The berries have tough oily skins and soft juicy flesh. They contain citric acid which tastes like lemon juice and ascorbic acid (Vitamin C). They are important health-giving foods and are widely cultivated both in America and the Mediterranean. Oranges are the largest crop.

Civil rights Rights which in a free country are held to be everyone's – such as freedom of speech or freedom from racial discrimination. In the United States, the civil rights movement struggled to improve the lives and opportunities of black people. The most famous civil rights leader was Martin Luther King Jr. Civil rights are threatened in any country with a harsh government.

Civil service Organization which carries out the day-to-day business of running a country. Various departments and ministries make up the civil service - examples are defence, foreign affairs, law and order, health, agriculture, transport and so on. The government of the day decides on policy and civil servants carry it out.

Civil War, American The contest between North and South in the United States, 1861–65. The North was industrial while the South was agricultural; Southerners had slaves but Northerners did not. These differences came to a head when an anti-slavery campaigner, Abraham Lincoln, was elected president and seven (later eleven) Southern states left the Union.

The war was fought to prevent the Union breaking up. The North (the Union) had most of the advantages, but at first the South (the Confederate states) had better generals and soldiers. With Union victories at Vicksburg and Gettysburg (1863), the tide turned in favour of the North. After four years of war in which about 700,000 people died, the Confederate hero, General Robert E. Lee, surrendered to the Union commander, General Ulysses S. Grant, at Appomattox (9 April 1865). Slavery was abolished, and the rebel states returned to the Union.

Civil War, English (1642–46 and 1648) The struggle between the forces of King Charles I (Cavaliers) and of Parliament (Roundheads), over who should have the greater power in government. At first the Royalist forces did well, but Parliament held London and the South-east and, after Oliver Cromwell created the New Model Army, the Royalists were decisively defeated at Marston Moor (1644) and Naseby (1645). The fighting ceased in 1646 with the surrender of the King, but flared up again in 1648 after his escape. He was finally recaptured and beheaded in 1649, after which Britain became a republic under Oliver Cromwell.

Oliver Cromwell and his New Model army at Marston Moor (1644).

Clam A bivalve mollusc. Over 12,000 species are known, in both sea and fresh water. Most lie buried in the mud of shallow water, burrowing with their powerful 'foot'.

Clay A soft, 'plastic' rock made of very fine particles. When heated and dried clay becomes very hard. It has been used for centuries in brick-making. Kaolin, a form of clay, turns white when heated and is used in making porcelain.

Cleopatra (69–30 BC) A brilliant, ambitious and alluring woman who became joint sovereign of Egypt with her brother Ptolemy XII in 51 BC. Supported by Julius Caesar she led a successful revolt and ruled with her younger brother Ptolemy XIII from 48 BC. She was Caesar's mistress until his murder in 44 BC and later the mistress of Mark Antony. After Antony and Cleopatra were defeated at the Battle of Actium in 31 BC they fled and she committed suicide with an asp bite the following year.

Climate The average weather pattern of a particular region. Temperature and rainfall are the main climatic factors. Temperatures generally decrease steadily away from the equator, though they also decrease with height. Rainfall varies more widely: it depends partly on distance from the sea and partly on the direction of the prevailing wind. Climates near the equator are much the same all year round. Away from the equator the changing seasons become more and more marked.

Clive, Robert (1725–74) English soldier whose victory at the Battle of Plassey firmly established British power in India. Twice governor of Bengal, he amassed a great fortune. Returning to England, Clive was accused of corruption and, although acquitted, he later committed suicide.

Clocks Devices for telling the time. Ancient peoples used water-clocks, candle-clocks, sand glasses and sun dials to measure the passage of time. During the Middle Ages, mechanical clocks driven by weights came into use. The making of *clockworks* – the intricate mechanisms inside clocks – became a highly skilled craft. In the 1600s pendulum clocks made time-keeping more accurate. Today's quartz clocks are kept to time by a vibrating crystal, while the most precise atomic clocks are so accurate that they should lose less than a second in 300 years!

Cloud A mass of small water droplets or ice crystals formed by the condensation of water vapour in rising and cooling air. Clouds fall into two main types: cumuliform, or 'heap' clouds, and stratus, or 'layer' clouds. Cumuliform clouds are produced by strong rising air currents. They range from fair-weather cumulus resembling small puffs of cotton-wool to the towering, anvil-headed cumulonimbus thundercloud. Stratiform clouds are grey blankets which may stretch unbroken across the sky. See picture on next page.

CLIMATES AND VEGETATION

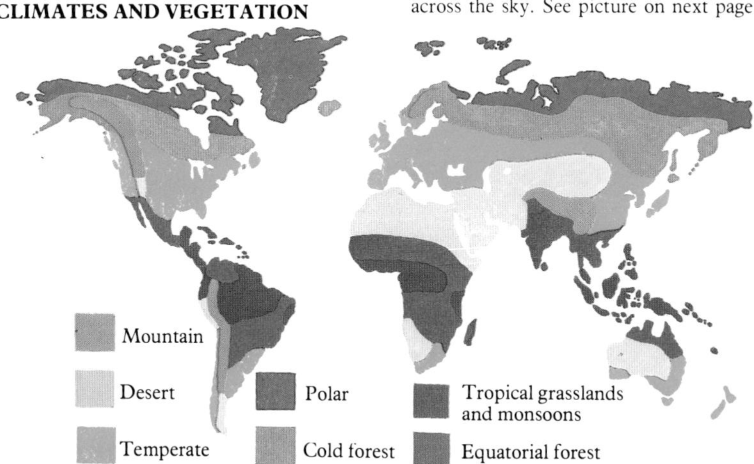

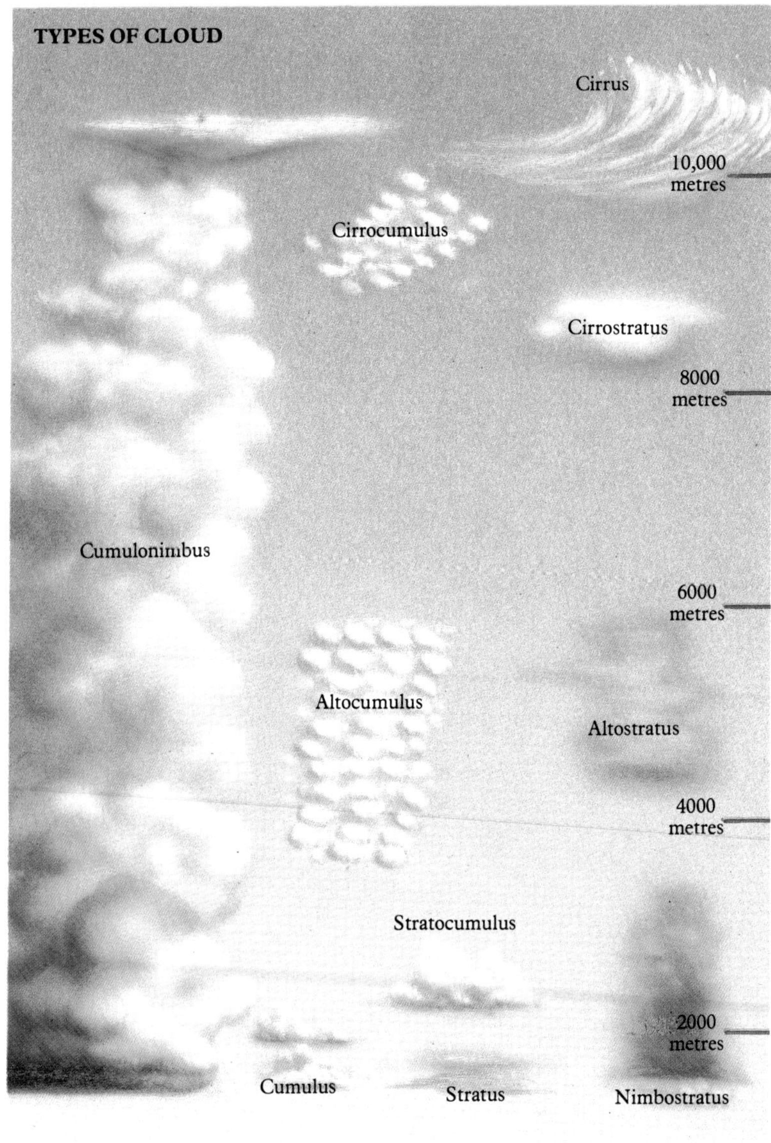
TYPES OF CLOUD
Cirrus
10,000 metres
Cirrocumulus
Cirrostratus
8000 metres
Cumulonimbus
6000 metres
Altocumulus
Altostratus
4000 metres
Stratocumulus
2000 metres
Cumulus
Stratus
Nimbostratus

Clubmoss A small group of flowerless green plants that look similar to mosses though they are more closely related to the ferns.

Coal A valuable fossil fuel found in layers, or seams, under the ground. It is called a fossil fuel because it was made millions of years ago from dead plants. Products obtained from coal include coke, plastics, dyes and explosives.

Cobalt Metal widely used in high temperature and magnetic alloys. Chem. symbol Co.

Cobra Poisonous hooded snakes from Africa and Asia. The snakes either bite or spit venom at their victims. The bite is deadly and the venom directed at the eyes can cause blindness. Cobras are deaf so they cannot be 'charmed' by music as many people claim. The snake is merely wary of the charmer. Even the king cobra which reaches 5.5 metres in length will rarely attack a person.

Cocaine Substance obtained from the leaves of the coca shrub. Formerly used as a local anaesthetic, it is a dangerous, habit-forming drug.

Cockatoo Members of the parrot family characterized by their crest of head feathers and loud screech. In the wild they live in flocks and feed on fruit, seeds and nuts, causing considerable damage in orchards and farms. They live in Australia, New Guinea and the Pacific islands. Their plumage is mostly white.

Cockle Several species of bivalve mollusc with heart-shaped and often ribbed shells. Cockles have a long 'foot' with which to burrow into sand or mud on the sea bed.

Cockroach One of the most widespread and hard-to-destroy insect pests. Most species live in hot countries. In cooler places, they seek warmth often in kitchens and restaurants.

Cocoa Powder made from the beans of the cacao tree and used to make chocolate. The trees grow in S America and W Africa.

Coconut The coconut is the fruit of the coconut palm, a tropical tree that stands up to 30 metres high. Inside the hard coconut shell is the seed which yields oil; the hairy husk fibre is used to make matting; the wood is used in building and the tree's leaves for roofing.

Cod One of the most important food fishes. Nearly 20 species are found in the N Atlantic and N Pacific. The group also

Coal is formed from the remains of woody plants that grew in swampy forests many millions of years ago. As the plants died and sank in the mud they were slowly pressed into coal.

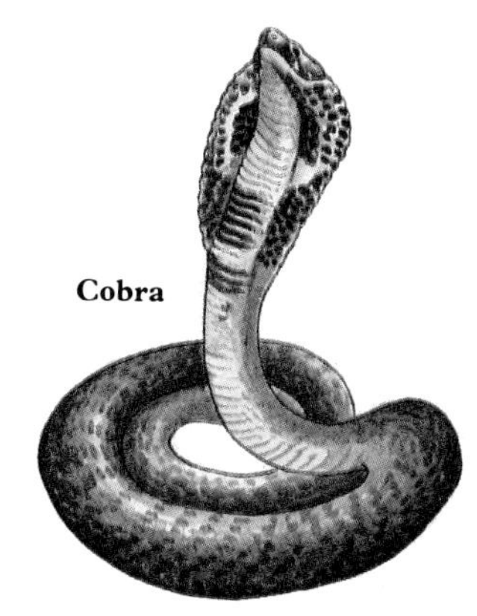

Cobra

contains the lings, hake and rocklings.

Coelenterate Member of a group of aquatic invertebrates which includes JELLYFISHES, HYDRA, CORALS and SEA ANEMONES.

Coffee Beverage made from the seeds of a small evergreen tree native to Ethiopia. The seeds, or 'beans', are roasted to develop the flavour and then ground. Brazil is the leading coffee-producing nation.

Coleridge, Samuel Taylor (1772–1834) English poet and friend of Wordsworth. His poems include *The Ancient Mariner, Kubla Khan* and *Christabel*.

Cologne City in West Germany, situated on W bank of R. Rhine. Cologne was the first German city to be bombed in World War II. Most of the city was destroyed but the impressive cathedral remained virtually intact. Pop: 977,000.

Colombia Republic in NW South America with coastlines on both the Pacific Ocean and the Caribbean Sea. Colombia is the world's second largest producer of coffee which accounts for 50% of the nation's exports. Mineral resources include rich deposits of petroleum and coal. Gold, platinum and emeralds are also mined. Area: 1,138,825 km^2; Pop: 28,900,000; Cap: Bogotá.

Colorado beetle An insect pest which can destroy potato crops. The beetle is about 10 mm long and striped black and yellow. It is native to N America but has spread to Europe where it does great damage.

Colorado beetle

Colosseum An ancient building in Rome. It is an amphitheatre, or stadium, which was built in the 1st century AD. The entertainments of the ancient Romans, which included gladiator fights and chariot races, were held there. Nearly 200 metres wide, it could hold 50,000 seated spectators on marble benches. The impressive ruins are still to be seen.

Colour An object appears to have a certain colour because its surface reflects light of that colour. White light, or sunlight, is a mixture of all colours. A red flower is red because it takes in all the other colours and throws back only red. A white flower gives back to our eyes all the colours of light. Our eyes are most sensitive to the *primary* colours – red, blue, and green. Other colours are combinations of these.

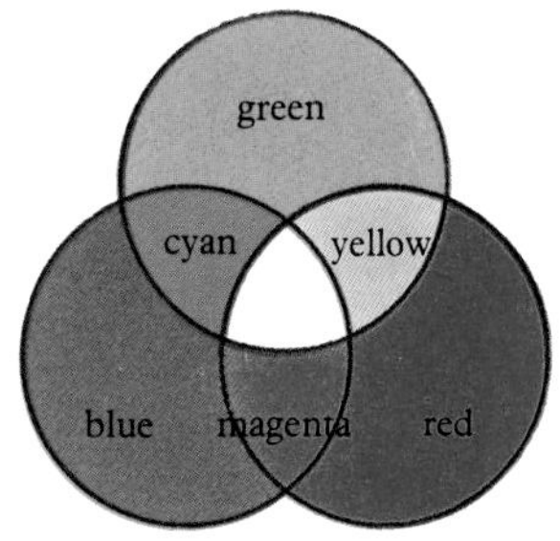

Some results of mixing blue, green and red light. Equal amounts of all three make white, the colour of sunlight.

Mixing paints is different. Any colour of paint can be obtained by using yellow, blue and red.

Columbus, Christopher (*c* 1451–1508) Genoese explorer who was supported by Ferdinand and Isabella of Spain in his search for a new passage to China. He discovered instead the New World in 1492. He made three further expeditions discovering many West Indian islands but his final journey was a failure and he died in poverty.

Combustion This is another word for burning, a chemical reaction that produces heat and light. Substances combine with oxygen when they burn. Combustion is a form of oxidation.

Comet A frozen ball of gas and dust which circles the Sun in a long looping orbit. As a comet approaches the Sun it begins to glow; gas and dust are released to form a tail stretching millions of kilometres through space. Halley's comet is the most famous. First recorded in 240 BC, it returns every 75 or 76 years, most recently in late 1985 and early 1986.

Commonwealth of Nations Formerly the British Commonwealth, a group of more than 40 countries linked in a loose, friendly association. Commonwealth leaders meet regularly to discuss world affairs and Commonwealth athletes take part in the Commonwealth Games. There are various aid programmes, and arts and science exchanges between members. Queen Elizabeth II is head of the Commonwealth.

Communism Political theory put forward in the mid 1800s by Karl Marx and Friedrich Engels, and later developed by Lenin in the USSR and by Mao Tse-tung in China. The basic idea of Communism is that property and the means of production are held in common, so factories, farms, railways and shops are state controlled and collectively worked. The first country to have a Communist government was Russia, after the 1917 Revolution.

Compass An instrument for finding the way. A magnetic compass always points to the Earth's magnetic poles. These are close to the North and South Poles. Most compasses consist of an arrow-shaped piece of magnetized metal balanced on the point of a short rod. The rod sticks up from the compass card. A compass needle always points north and south because the Earth itself is a large magnet and one magnet always affects another (see **Magnetism**).

Composite flower Flower made up of many tiny flowers called florets, each with its own reproductive parts - carpels and anthers. Dandelions and daisies both have composite flowers.

Compound A substance made up of two or more elements in definite proportions. Compounds are formed when elements join together and make a new substance which is completely different from the elements it contains. For example, hydrogen and oxygen gases combine together to make the compound water.

Computer An electronic device which accepts data (information), works on the data as instructed, and gives out the results of its calculations. Computers can work out problems very quickly. They can also store vast amounts of information. With improvements in the SILICON CHIP, computers are becoming much smaller and faster. Scientists are now trying to give them an artificial intelligence.

Concrete A hard, strong building material made of cement, sand, gravel and water. Reinforced concrete has steel rods built into it to give greater strength. When concrete is first mixed it is a paste which can be moulded into any shape. It soon sets rock-hard. Millions of tonnes of concrete are used each year in structures ranging from dams to door-steps.

Condensation The process by which vapour turns to a liquid. The condensation of water vapour in the atmosphere produces clouds, rain and snow. At ground level it produces fog, dew and frost.

The effects of condensation at ground level.

Confederate states The 11 Southern states which tried to form a separate nation from the United States during the CIVIL WAR. They adopted a constitution (1861) which was closely modelled on the US constitution, and elected Jefferson Davis president. The capital was Richmond, Virginia. The Confederate states were not recognized as an independent nation by other countries, and they were defeated in 1865.

Confucius (*c* 551–479 BC) Chinese reformer and philosopher. Living in an age when tyranny and cruelty abounded in China he preached justice, moderation and love of man's fellow man. The *Analects* is a record of his sayings.

Congo Republic in W central Africa straddling the equator with a short Atlantic coastline. Much of the country consists of densely forested lowlands drained by the R. Zaïre and its tributaries. Coffee, cocoa and sugar cane are important cash crops and along with hardwoods form the chief exports. Minerals include off-shore oilfields and valuable potash deposits. Area: 342,000 km^2; Pop: 1,745,000; Cap: Brazzaville.

Congress The law-making assembly or PARLIAMENT of the United States. Congress has two elected houses, the Senate and the House of Representatives. The President is not a member of Congress; the laws proposed by the President and government have to be passed by votes in Congress. The first US Congress was the Continental Congress of 1774 in Philadelphia. A second Congress issued the historic Declaration of Independence in 1776.

Conifer Member of a group of trees which bear their seeds in cones. Conifers are gymnosperms, and they include such trees as PINES, FIRS and CEDARS.

Conservation The preservation of the natural environment to maintain its beauty and prevent the destruction of plants and animals.

Constable, John (1776–1837) British landscape painter. His works include *The Hay Wain, The Cornfield* and *Valley Farm.*

Constellations On a clear, dark night about 2000 stars are visible to the naked eye. Ancient astronomers divided the sky into star patterns, or constellations, a tradition which is continued today. The constellations are named after legendary

NORTHERN HEMISPHERE CONSTELLATIONS
1 Cetus **2** Pisces **3** Aries **4** Triangulum **5** Andromeda **6** Pegasus **7** Lacerta **8** Cygnus **9** Equuleus **10** Delphinus **11** Aquila **12** Sagitta **13** Lyra **14** Draco **15** Hercules **16** Ophiuchus **17** Serpens **18** Corona Borealis **19** Boötes **20** Coma Berenices **21** Virgo **22** Canes Venatici **23** The Little Bear **24** Cepheus **25** Cassiopeia **26** Camelopardus **27** The Great Bear **28** Leo Minor **29** Leo **30** Lynx **31** Cancer **32** Hydra **33** The Little Dog **34** Gemini **35** Orion **36** Taurus **37** Auriga **38** Perseus

SOUTHERN HEMISPHERE CONSTELLATIONS
1 Capricornus **2** Aquarius **3** Pisces **4** Grus **5** Tucana **6** Phoenix **7** Sculptor **8** Cetus **9** Fornax **10** Eridanus **11** Lepus **12** Orion **13** Monoceros **14** Canis Major **15** Columba **16** Doradus **17** Pictor **18** Volans **19** Carina **20** Puppis **21** Pyxis **22** Vela **23** Leo **24** Crater **25** Hydra **26** Corvus **27** Virgo **28** Libra **29** Ophiuchus **30** The Serpent **31** Aquila **32** Sagittarius **33** Corona Australis **34** Scorpio **35** Lupus **36** Centaurus **37** The Southern Triangle **38** Ara **39** Indus **40** Pavo **41** Apus **42** Octans **43** Chamaeleon **44** Musca **45** The Southern Cross (Crux) **46** Hydrus

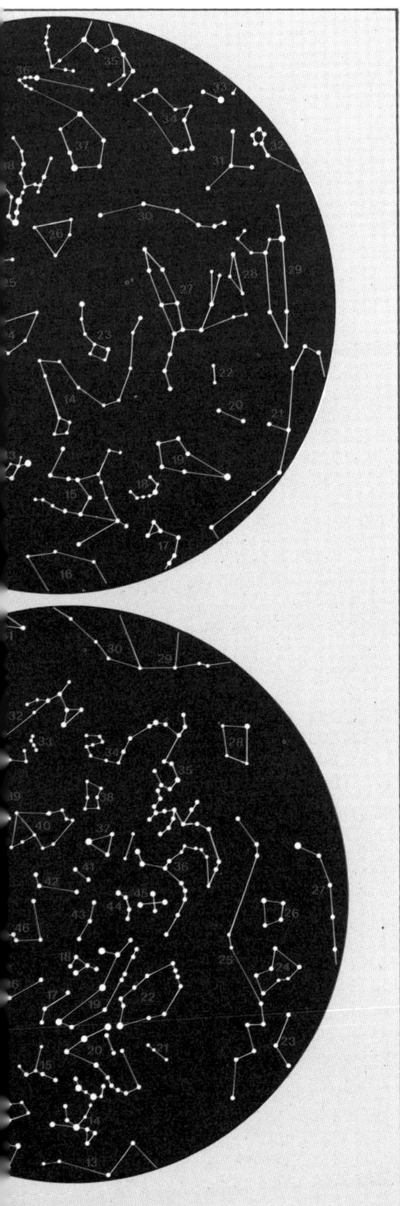

figures and animals, although it is often difficult to see the resemblance. Some constellations are visible only from the northern or southern hemisphere.

Continents The great land masses of the world. Each rests on a 'plate' or series of plates which make up the crust of the Earth like pieces of a jigsaw. Scientists believe the continents have 'drifted' to their present positions over millions of years as the plates have been moved by convection currents inside the Earth. See TECTONIC PLATES.

Cook, James (1728–79) English navigator who explored and charted the coasts of eastern Australia and New Zealand and the Pacific coast of N America. He was killed by Hawaiian natives.

Cook, Mt Mountain in the Southern Alps of South Island, New Zealand. Highest peak in country. Height: 3764 metres.

Copenhagen Port and capital city of Denmark, situated on the E coast of Zealand. It has large shipyards, and is an important cultural and manufacturing centre. Pop: 1,209,000 (met area).

Copernicus, Nicolas (1473–1543) Polish astronomer who proclaimed that the Sun is at the centre of the Solar system with the Earth revolving around it.

Copper Reddish-brown metal which is an excellent conductor of electricity and heat. Widely used in electrical equipment, boilers and electroplating. Its numerous alloys include bronze (with tin), brass (with zinc) and cupro-nickel (with nickel). Chem. symbol Cu.

Coral Sea creatures that live either singly or in colonies. Corals are coelenterates. Their bodies are polyps, encased in chalky cups or skeletons. The base of the polyp is attached to a solid surface and around the mouth is a ring of tentacles used for catching food. In tropical waters, corals form huge reefs and even islands, called atolls.

Cork Light, springy substance obtained from the bark of the cork oak tree. It is virtually non-absorbent and can be compressed, qualities which make it ideal for bottle stopping. It is also used to cover floors and for shoe soles.

Corm Underground food store of certain plants, e.g. crocus, consisting of a short swollen stem. The corm bears buds and is capable of vegetative reproduction.

Cormorant A large sea bird also seen in

river estuaries. It is black, with short legs and a rather snake-like head. The bill is hooked for catching fish.

Corrosion The eating away of metals by water, air or chemicals such as acids. The rusting of iron and steel is the most common kind of corrosion. It is caused by oxygen in the air attacking the metal in the presence of moisture. Corrosion can be prevented by paint or other surface coating.

Corsica Large island in the Mediterranean and part of France. It has had a turbulent past, conquered by numerous powers, including the Romans and the Vandals. The island is a popular resort. Birthplace of Napoleon Bonaparte. Pop: 270,000.

Cortes, Hernando (1485–1547) Spanish conquistador. With only 550 men he crushed the Aztec civilization of Montezuma in Mexico between 1519 and 1521 and was appointed governor in 1523. In 1541 he took part in an unsuccessful expedition to Algiers with Charles V of Spain. He died in virtual obscurity.

Cosmic rays High energy radiation, mostly in the form of charged particles that strike the Earth from outer space. Scientists are not sure where cosmic rays come from, although some seem to come from the Sun.

Cossacks Famous fighters and horsemen from southern and eastern Russia. They fought as mercenaries for the tsars in exchange for privileges and a degree of independence. They fought against the Bolsheviks and consequently lost their special status, though they served courageously in World War II.

Costa Rica Central American republic with coastlines on both the Caribbean Sea and Pacific Ocean. The forested coastal plains are separated by central highlands and plateaux where most of the people live. Coffee and bananas are the chief cash crops and major exports. Area: 50,000 km^2; Pop: 2,600,000; Cap: San José.

Cotton The most important natural fibre, cotton is made from the fluffy, white seed hairs of cotton plants, and has been cultivated, spun and woven since prehistoric times. The seeds are used for oil and cattle food. It was the basis of a major textile industry in Britain in the 19th century. This has declined, but cotton is still widely grown and manufactured in United States, USSR, China and India.

Cotyledon Leaf inside a seed which, in many cases, grows to form part of the young plant. Flowering plants are grouped according to whether their seeds contain one cotyledon (the MONOCOTYLEDONS) or two (DICOTYLEDONS).

Coyote Wild N American relative of the dog, sometimes called the prairie wolf. It preys on small rodents and occasionally sheep. It has an eerie howl.

Coypu Large South American rodent that grows up to 60 cm long. Coypus were once bred for their fur (nutria) but many escaped and set up colonies in Europe and N America. They have large heads, webbed feet and a long hairless tail. They live in river banks, doing considerable damage by burrowing, and are expert swimmers.

Crab Crustacean with five pairs of jointed legs and a broad, flat cover or carapace protecting the body. The eyes are on movable stalks and the first pair of legs usually ends in grasping claws which the crab uses to catch prey. Most crabs live in the sea but a few are found in fresh water and some on land.

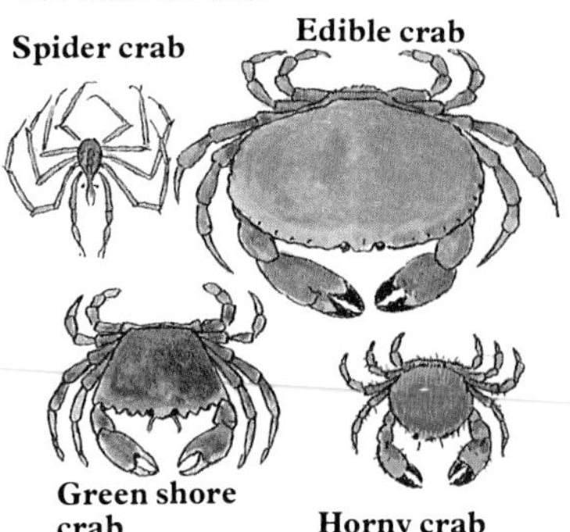

Crane Wading birds with long necks and long legs. The whooping crane is known for its loud call and the crowned crane for its beautiful head feathers. Elegant birds, cranes often rest on one leg with their heads laid on their backs.

Crane-fly Large mosquito-like insect, also known as daddy-long-legs. Crane-flies have thin bodies with spindly legs and fly rather clumsily. The larvae of many species are known as leatherjackets.

Cranmer, Thomas (1489–1556) Theologian and priest who supported Henry

VIII's divorce from Catherine of Aragon and was rewarded with the Archbishopric of Canterbury. A leading figure in the Reformation of the Church, he was burned at the stake, when Catholic Mary I came to power.

Crete Island in E Mediterranean. Largest of the Greek islands, it was the centre of the Ancient Minoan civilization.

Cricket Insects similar to grasshoppers but with much longer antennae. Male crickets sing to the females by rubbing together their wing-cases.

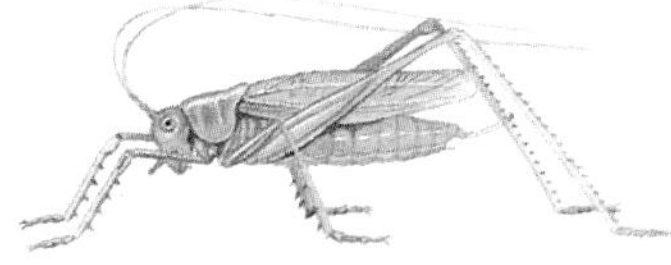

Bush cricket

Cricket (sport) Bat and ball game which began in England and has spread to other Commonwealth countries, and also to Pakistan and South Africa. A 'gentleman's game' in the 18th century, cricket is (after soccer) England's national game. Cricket internationals, called Test matches, last five days. There are also three-day and one-day matches. Each team has 11 players; one side fields, while the other bats, two players at a time going to the wicket.

Crimean War (1853–56) A war in which Britain and France supported Turkey against Russia. It broke out after the Turks refused to allow the Russians to act as 'protectors' of Christians living in the Turkish empire, but a deeper cause was Britain's fear of an expanding Russia. French and British troops landed in the Crimean peninsula, fought several battles (at great cost) and captured Sebastopol before the Russians agreed to a peace. The work of Florence NIGHTINGALE in the Crimea led to great improvements in nursing.

Crocodile Large scaly reptiles related to ALLIGATORS. They bask in rivers and swamps in tropical Africa and Asia. Fearsome predators able to kill a man, some grow to more than six metres long. The Nile crocodile is the largest.

Croesus (?–*c* 547 BC) The last king of Lydia, he acquired immense wealth through trade. He conquered parts of western Asia Minor but was defeated by Cyrus the Great of Persia (546 BC).

Cro-Magnon man Name given to a group of cave-dwellers who lived in Europe during the Old Stone Age, over 10,000 years ago. They used tools and weapons made of flint or bone and got their food by hunting wild animals and gathering wild plants. On the walls of their caves they painted marvellous pictures of the animals they hunted.

Cromwell, Oliver (1599–1658) English soldier and statesman who assumed control of the anti-Royalist forces after the outbreak of the Civil War, demanded the execution of Charles I and declared England a republic. In 1653 he established a Protectorate and ruled as Lord Protector, refusing the crown in 1657. His government was marked by intolerance and cruelty in Ireland.

Cronos In Greek legend a Titan, god of agriculture and harvests and father of Zeus. (Roman equivalent Saturn.)

Crossbill A bird belonging to the finch family that gets its name from its unusual beak, the lower part of which crosses to the left of the upper part. With this beak the bird can extract seeds from the fir cones on which it feeds. The male is predominantly red, the female yellowy-brown.

Crossbill

Crow Family of mainly black birds which includes the RAVEN, ROOK, JACKDAW, JAY and MAPGIE. They are active and aggressive, with harsh, noisy voices. They eat almost anything, including grain and vast quantities of caterpillars and other insects. The common or carrion crow is about 50 cm long.

Crusades Military expeditions or wars with a religious purpose, especially those expeditions that set out from Europe in the Middle Ages to capture Jerusalem and the Holy Land from Muslim rule. They involved many kings and noblemen. The First Crusade (1095–99), begun by the

Christians fight Muslims during one of many unsuccessful Crusades.

Pope, captured Jerusalem and set up Christian states in the Middle East. The recapture of Christian territory by the Muslims led to further Crusades, but these were less successful. By the end of the 13th century, the Holy Land was once more firmly in Muslim hands.

Crustacean Member of a group of largely aquatic arthropods including crabs, shrimps, barnacles, woodlice and countless smaller creatures. Crustaceans have an external skeleton (exoskeleton) which may be thin and transparent, as in the case of tiny marine animals, or thick and tough, as in the 'shell' of a crab. Most breathe through GILLS.

Crystal A solid that has become solidified in a definite geometric shape. Most substances are made up of tiny crystals. If you look at sugar through a magnifying glass you will see that it is made up of crystals with flat sides. Salt grains are tiny cubes, and all salt crystals are built in the same way. Common salt is made up of two different kinds of atoms - sodium and chlorine. It is because the sodium and chlorine atoms are arranged in cube patterns that all salt grains are little cubes.

A solid which is not made up of crystals is said to be *amorphous*.

Cuba Island republic in the Caribbean Sea largely composed of rolling hills and fertile valleys. The warm climate is ideal for cash crops such as sugar, which accounts for more than 75% of the exports, together with tobacco, coffee, bananas and cotton. Mineral resources include some of the largest deposits of nickel in the world. In 1959, following a rebellion, Cuba became a communist state. Area: 115,000 km^2; Pop: 9,995,000; Cap: Havana.

Cuckoo Large grey bird that is often heard and seldom seen. The familiar 'cuckoo' call of the male heralds the spring. The birds winter in southern Africa and spend April to August in Europe. The female lays her eggs in the nests of other birds, one egg in each nest, removing one of the existing eggs as she does so. When hatched the young cuckoo gets rid of any other chicks or eggs. The foster parents, often much smaller than the cuckoo, have to work very hard to satisfy the alien chick's enormous appetite.

Cuckoo chick and foster parent.

Curie, Marie (1867–1934) Gifted scientist who, together with her husband Pierre, discovered radium. They shared the Nobel Prize for physics in 1903. Marie also received the Nobel Prize for chemistry in 1911. Her daughter Irène Joliot-Curie and her husband Frederic Joliot were awarded the Nobel Prize for chemistry in 1935 for their discovery of artificial radioactivity.

Curlew A wading bird of moors and marshes. It uses its long downward-curving bill to dig for insects and other small creatures in the mud.

Cuttlefish A group of cephalopod molluscs related to the squids, with a chalky inner shell or 'cuttle-bone'. Cuttlefish have streamlined bodies, up to 1.5 metres long. At the head end are eight arms and two long tentacles, all bearing suckers and used to seize prey.

Cybernetics The study of the control systems of both people and machines, and how information is given to control systems. If a rocket is flying too slowly, a message is given automatically to the rocket's control centre to increase the rocket's speed. If your heart is beating too slowly, a signal is given to your brain's control centre and your heartbeat is speeded up. Cybernetics covers all automatic control devices, including relays, selectors, computers, and robots. By using cybernetics, machines can perform tasks without the aid of human operators.

Cyclone Any revolving storm. In temperate latitudes cyclones are known as DEPRESSIONS. TROPICAL CYCLONES are far more fierce. They are known as hurricanes or typhoons.

Cyclopes In Greek legend race of one-eyed giants who lived in Sicily. They forged a thunderbolt for Zeus which enabled him to win a battle against the Titans.

Cypress A group of coniferous trees found in cooler parts of the northern hemisphere and on mountains in warmer lands. They have overlapping, scale-like leaves and small, woody cones.

Cyprus Island republic in E Mediterranean off Turkish coast. Two mountain ranges, the Kyrenia Range in the N and the Olympic Mts in the S, are separated by a wide fertile plain. Cyprus gained its independence in 1960, but strife between the Greek and Turkish inhabitants eventually led to the present partition of the country. Area: 9250 km^2; Pop: 661,000; Cap: Nicosia.

Czechoslovakia Republic in central Europe historically divided into three regions – Bohemia, Moravia and Slovakia. Although farming is important, particularly in the plains and valleys, Czechoslovakia is a highly industrialized nation producing iron and steel, armaments, automobiles, machinery, textiles and chemicals. Czechoslovakia came into being in 1918 at the end of World War I. It was liberated by the Russians in 1944 and a communist state was established in 1948. Area: 127,900 km^2; Pop: 15,500,000; Cap: Prague.

D

Daedalus In Greek legend an architect and sculptor who built the labyrinth for the MINOTAUR, and wings for himself and his son Icarus. They flew from Crete to Sicily but Icarus ventured too close to the Sun; the wax holding the wings together melted and he dropped into the sea.

Da Gama, Vasco (*c* 1460–1524) Portuguese navigator who was the first to sail to India from Europe around the Cape of Good Hope (1497–98).

Daguerre, Louis (1789–1851) French painter and pioneer of photography. He discovered the 'daguerreotype' photographic process.

Daimler, Gottlieb (1834–1900) German inventor who improved the internal combustion engine, built the first motorcycle, and founded the Daimler Motor Company.

Dairy farming Dairying is the rearing of cattle for milk, butter, cheese and other milk (dairy) products. Cows are specially bred to give high daily milk yields of almost 10 litres. The best dairy farmlands are those in cool temperate regions where the rainfall is sufficient to produce ample grass. Examples include western and central Europe, New Zealand and parts of the United States.

Dali, Salvador (b 1904) Spanish surrealist artist. His work usually depicts strange unconnected images as though from a dream-world.

Dallas City in Texas, USA. Major centre for petroleum production and scene of President Kennedy's assassination in 1963. Pop: 845,000.

Dalton, John (1766–1844) English chemist who put forward the theory that all matter is composed of indestructible atoms and that atoms of the same element are identical.

Dam A thick wall of concrete, rock or earth built across a river to hold back water. Dams can be used to store water for irrigation, to provide a water supply for towns, or to let water fall through turbines which generate electricity.

Damascus Capital of Syria, on R. Barada. Reputed to be the oldest city in the world. Damascus contains over 200 mosques. Pop: 1,156,000.

Dandelion A widespread flowering plant

related to the daisy. Its leafless stems support solitary, bright yellow flower-heads. The fruits are topped by feathery white 'parachutes' which form the familiar dandelion clock.

Dante (Alighieri 1265–1321) Italy's greatest poet. His most famous work, the *Divine Comedy*, portrays a vision of hell, purgatory and paradise. In 1302 he was exiled from Florence and thereafter led a wandering life.

Danube Second largest river in Europe, flowing from the Black Forest in Germany to the Black Sea. It forms part of the boundaries between Czechoslovakia and Hungary, and Romania and the USSR. It also flows through Austria and Yugoslavia. The river is an historic trade route, linked by canal to the Rhine and Oder. Length: 2850 km.

Dardanelles Strait connecting the Sea of Marmara with the Aegean Sea, between European and Asian Turkey. Scene of an unsuccessful Allied campaign during World War I (1915).

Dark Ages The period of European history between the time of the Roman Empire and the height of medieval civilization, roughly from the 5th to the 10th century. The Dark Ages are only 'dark' because less is known about them than about many other historic periods.

Darwin Port and capital of Northern Territory, Australia. Devastated in 1974 by a cyclone, the city has since been rebuilt. Pop: 42,000 (met area).

Darwin, Charles Robert (1809–82) English naturalist. After a voyage around the world on the *Beagle* he spent 20 years collecting evidence for his theory of evolution. This appeared in 1859 in his *Origin of Species* and caused bitter controversy.

Charles Darwin

Date palm Tree grown in N Africa and the Middle East and more recently in the USA. Grows to between 10 and 30 metres in height and yields as many as 200 sweet, highly nutritious dates.

David (?–*c* 970 BC) A great warrior and wise ruler of the Jews. As a boy he slew the giant Goliath with a mere sling.

David, Jacques Louis (1748–1825) French painter who was the founder of the Classical School in France. Though an ardent republican, he was court painter to Louis XVI and later Napoleon.

Davy, Sir Humphry (1778–1829) English physicist and chemist who invented the safety lamp used by miners (Davy lamp). He proved that chlorine is an element and used ELECTROLYSIS to isolate potassium, barium, magnesium, strontium and sodium.

Day The time taken for the Earth to spin once on its axis. This varies slightly when measured by the position of the Sun in the sky, but the mean or average solar day is 24 hours.

D-Day The day on which the Allied forces in the Second World War invaded Normandy, 6 June 1944. D-day was the beginning of a campaign which ended with the surrender of Germany, almost one year later.

Dead Sea Salt lake bordered by Israel and Jordan. About 800 km long and 15 km wide, it lies 395 metres below the level of the Mediterranean and has a very high mineral and salt content.

Debussy, Claude (1862–1918) French composer best known for his piano music. Among his many other compositions are the orchestral suites *L'Après-midi d'un Faune* and *La Mer*, and the opera *Pelléas et Mélisande*.

Decorations Awards, usually medals, given for bravery in war or outstanding achievement in peacetime. Examples of military decorations are the Victoria Cross (British), Croix de Guerre (French) and Congressional Medal of Honor (United States). The George Cross (British) is awarded for bravery by a civilian, while decorations such as the Order of the British Empire (OBE) are given to people for service in various fields including sport, local government, industry etc.

Victoria Cross | Legion of Honour | Congressional Medal of Honor | George Cross | Golden Star

Deer Hoofed mammals which, like cows, graze and chew the cud. The males have bony, usually branched antlers which are shed and regrown every year. Only in CARIBOU and reindeer do the females have antlers. The largest deer is the ELK of northern Europe and Asia and its counterpart the moose of N America. Others include the red deer, fallow deer and roe deer of Europe, the wapiti and white-tailed deer of N America and the muntjacs, sika and axis deer of Asia.

Defoe, Daniel (1660–1731) English author who wrote *Robinson Crusoe*. He openly criticised the government of the day and his *Shortest Way with Dissenters* landed him in gaol. Other works include the novels *Moll Flanders* and *Roxana*, many poems and countless political pamphlets.

Degas, Edgar (1834–1917) French impressionist painter, best known for his paintings of ballet dancers.

de Gaulle, Charles (1890–1970) French statesman and general. During World War II he led the Free French forces from England. He was president of France 1945–46 and was re-elected president in 1958 under a new constitution. He is remembered for ending the war in Algeria (1962), for withdrawing France from NATO and for building a French nuclear force.

Delacroix, Eugène (1798–1863) French romantic painter of historical and literary subjects, amongst them *Massacre of Chios* and the *Barricade*.

Delhi Capital of India, on the Jumna R. The city has two parts: the modern city of New Delhi, the commercial and government centre, and Old Delhi, the old walled city containing the Red Fort (1052) and the 17th century palace of Shah Jahan, built when the city was capital of the Mogul Empire. Pop: 3,288,000.

Delius, Frederick (1862–1934) English composer of German descent who spent most of his life in France. Among his most popular orchestral works are *Brigg Fair* and *On Hearing the First Cuckoo in Spring*.

Demeter Greek goddess of agriculture. Grief-stricken when her daughter, Persephone, was abducted by HADES (Pluto) to the underworld, she caused all the fruits and crops of the Earth to wither. Zeus intervened and decreed that Persephone should spend one-third of the year with her husband Hades and two-thirds with her mother, during which time Demeter was happy and saw to the growth of all crops. (Roman equivalent Ceres.)

Democracy 'Democracy' is Greek for 'government by the people'. In a democracy, the people elect representatives to PARLIAMENT at regular intervals to make the laws of the country.

Denmark Kingdom in NW Europe consisting of the peninsula of Jutland and a number of islands, the largest being Zealand and Funen. The country is low-lying and rolling, the highest point being only 173 metres above sea level. The land is intensively farmed and Denmark specializes in dairying and pig-farming. There are few mineral resources, and light industries, such as electronic equipment, textile and furniture manufacturing, have been developed. Area: 43,000 km^2; Pop: 5,112,000; Cap: Copenhagen.

Density The amount of mass (matter) in a substance for each unit of its volume. Density is calculated by dividing a body's mass by its volume. In the metric system, density is measured in grams per cubic centimetre or kilograms per cubic metre.

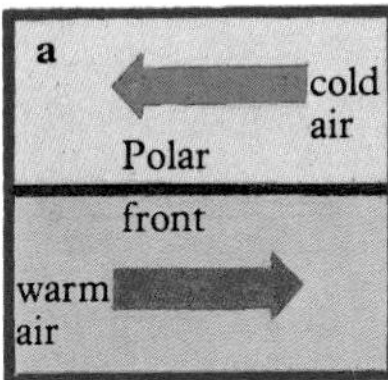

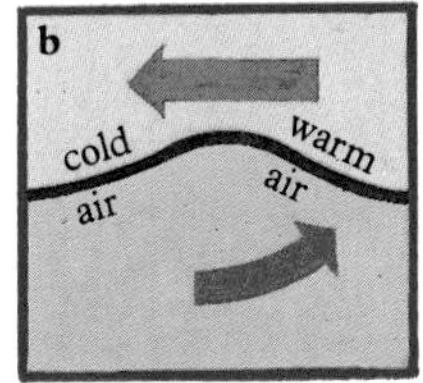

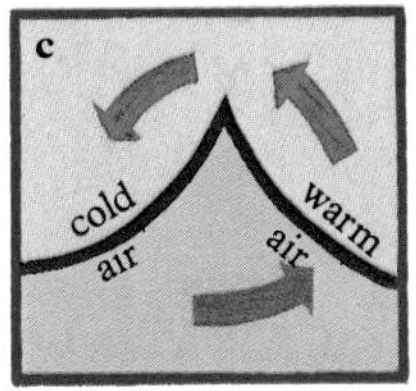

Depression In meteorology a region of low pressure associated with stormy, unsettled weather. Depressions form along the polar FRONT where cold polar air meets warmer air from the subtropics (**a**). Waves develop in the front (**b**); the cold, dense air wraps around the warm, low-pressure air and the whole system begins to rotate (**c**). Clouds and rain occur along the fronts where the air masses meet.

Descartes, René (1596–1650) French philosopher, mathematician and soldier. His system of philosophy is summed up in his own phrase *Cogito, ergo sum* (I think, therefore I am).

Desert Any large area of land that receives less than 250 mm of rain per year. Deserts may be hot, e.g. Sahara, temperate, e.g. Gobi, or cold, e.g. Antarctica. In all, deserts cover 20 per cent of the world's land surface. Largest is the Sahara, reaching across N Africa from the Atlantic to the Red Sea. Driest is the Atacama desert in S America where many years may pass without a drop of rain.

Detroit Port and city in Michigan, USA, situated on Detroit R. Centre of Ford motor car industry. Pop: 1,203,000 (4,353,000 met area).

Dew Water droplets formed by the condensation of water vapour in air chilled by contact with the cold ground.

Dewar, James (1842–1923) British physicist and chemist. He liquified hydrogen and invented the vacuum flask. With the aid of Sir Frederick Abel he invented the explosive cordite.

Dew point The temperature at which air is saturated and can hold no more water in the form of vapour. If the air is cooled below this temperature, the excess water

The strange landscapes of hot deserts are largely the work of wind erosion.

vapour condenses to water droplets, forming clouds, fog, dew and frost.

Diaghilev, Sergei Pavlovich (1872–1929) Russian ballet impresario who founded the Ballet Russe in Paris in 1908, introducing such great dancers as Pavlova and Nijinsky.

Diamond A crystalline form of pure carbon, the hardest substance known and a highly prized gemstone. South Africa is the world's leading diamond producer.

Dias, Bartolomeu (*c* 1450–1500) Portuguese navigator who was the first European to round the Cape of Good Hope (1487–88).

Diatom A group of single-celled or colonial algae found in both fresh and salt water. Diatoms have a hard silicon 'shell' that can often look beautiful under a microscope.

Dickens, Charles (1812–70) English novelist who began his career as a journalist. His works vividly portray life in 19th century England with its great social evils, often blending sentiment with humorous caricature. His 15 much-loved novels include *The Pickwick Papers*, *David Copperfield*, *Great Expectations* and *Bleak House*.

Dicotyledon By far the larger of the two groups of flowering plants, including such common plants as the rose and the oak. Dicotyledons have seeds containing two seed leaves, or COTYLEDONS, which act as a food store and often form the first leaves after germination.

Dido In classical legend the founder and Queen of Carthage.

Diesel engine A type of internal combustion engine that is similar to the petrol engine. It burns heavy oil instead of petrol. The air/oil mixture is compressed in the cylinders and ignites without the need for sparks from spark plugs. The diesel engine is widely used in trucks, buses and railway locomotives.

Digestion The process by which large food particles are broken down into smaller units which can then be absorbed into the body through the gut wall. It involves the food being attacked by special chemicals called enzymes. Different enzymes work on different types of food. Some break down starchy foods, some proteins, and others fats. In humans, most digestion takes place in the stomach and the small intestine. Waste material passes out of the body through the anus.

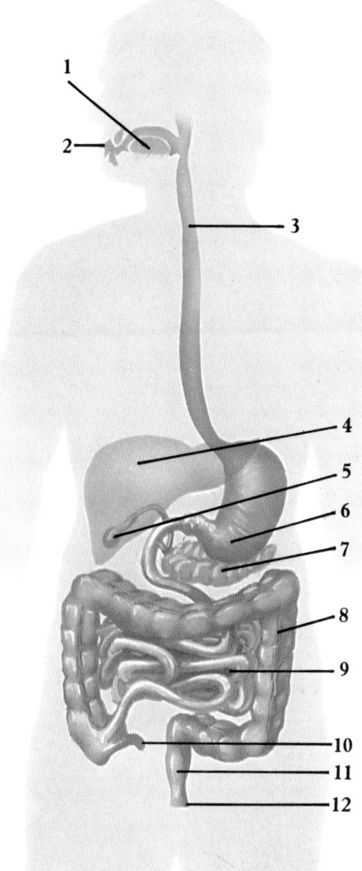

The alimentary, or food, canal extends down through the body from mouth to anus.
Key to labels:
1 tongue
2 mouth and teeth
3 oesophagus
4 liver
5 gall bladder
6 stomach
7 pancreas
8 large intestine
9 small intestine
10 appendix
11 rectum
12 anus.

Dinosaurs Extinct reptiles that lived during the Mesozoic Era. The name means 'terrible lizard' and some of them were fearsome. The carnivorous TYRANNOSAURUS rex was six metres tall and had huge gaping jaws. Most of the carnivores were, however, smaller and relied on speed to catch their prey.

Few would have attacked an 85-tonne BRONTOSAURUS or 26-metre-long Diplodocus. These lumbering plant-eaters were protected by their vast bulk. Many of the smaller plant-eaters, with neither size nor speed for protection, were armoured like tanks. STEGOSAURUS had a row of bony plates on its back and a spiked tail. Triceratops, a horned dinosaur, could charge its enemies like a rhinoceros.

The dinosaurs ruled the Earth for some 140 million years and then suddenly disappeared, probably because of a sudden climatic change, with temperatures too low for cold-blooded animals to survive.

Diode A diode is a device that allows an

electric current to flow in one direction and not the other. Diodes used to be thermionic valves, but these have now been largely replaced by semiconductors. A semiconductor diode is usually made from a thin slice of silicon crystal. Each side of the slice has a different material added to it to give the sides different properties. One side is called n-type material, the other p-type. Between the n-type and p-type materials is a p-n junction. When the n-type side is made positive by an alternating current, a current flows through the semiconductor. When the voltage is reversed, the p-n junction forms a barrier and no current flows. Diodes are used extensively in all kinds of electronic circuits.

Dionysus Greek god of wine, fertility and vegetation. (Roman equivalent Bacchus.)

Dipper A bird of streams and rivers, also called the water-ousel. It has dark brown feathers, with a white breast, and hops in a characteristic bobbing fashion about the pebbles in a stream, catching water insects and other small creatures.

Disease Illness caused by a harmful bacterium or virus infecting the body. Most serious diseases can now be treated with drugs and, in certain parts of the world, many once-common diseases, such as smallpox and typhoid, have been eliminated.

Disney, Walt (1901–66) American cartoonist who created Mickey Mouse and Donald Duck. He is perhaps best known for his *Snow White and the Seven Dwarfs* which was the first full-length animated cartoon film. Others include *Pinocchio*, *Bambi*, *Dumbo* and *Fantasia*.

Disraeli, Benjamin (1804–81) British statesman, novelist and life-long rival of Gladstone. He was elected to parliament in 1837 and was twice Prime Minister (Conservative): 1868 and 1874–1880. He acquired a controlling share in the Suez Canal for Britain and had Queen Victoria crowned Empress of India (1876).

Distillation Distilling is a way of separating or purifying liquids by heating them to boiling point and then cooling the vapour so that it becomes a liquid again. Strong alcoholic drinks are made by distilling weaker alcoholic solutions to remove much of the water from them. By condensing steam we obtain *distilled water*. It contains almost no impurities.

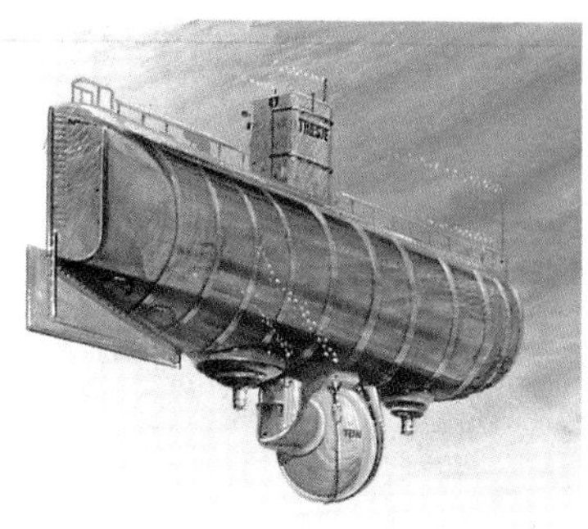

Diving machines such as bathyscaphes can plumb the ocean deeps.

Diving When a diver descends into the water, he or she must be supplied with air. A deep-sea diver who has to remain under water for a long period can be supplied with air through a flexible pipe from the surface. The skin-diver uses a self-contained aqualung apparatus. Air comes from compressed air tanks strapped to his back. This air is fed through a valve system to the diver's face mask.

If a diver has been fairly deep down and rises to the surface too quickly, he is liable to experience an attack of the 'bends'. This is a serious form of cramp caused by nitrogen bubbles leaving the blood.

Djibouti Republic in NE Africa which owes its existence to the port of Djibouti near the southern entrance to the Red Sea. The country is barren and has no mineral resources. Area: 22,000 km^2; Pop: 289,000; Cap: port of Djibouti.

DNA (deoxyribonucleic acid) A complex material carried by the chromosomes inside a cell nucleus. It bears all the information required by a cell in the form of a code. Each piece of information is called a gene, and the code is commonly referred to as the genetic code. When a particular protein is required by a cell, a section of the DNA is copied and used as a template for building it. During growth or reproduction, when a cell is about to divide, all the DNA is copied so that the new cell receives a complete set.

Dodo An extinct, turkey-sized, flightless bird that lived in Mauritius. It was hunted to death by European sailors in the 17th century.

DOGS
Kerry blue terrier
Corgi
Cavalier King Charles spaniel
Beagle
Afghan hound
Chow chow
Basset hound
Golden retriever

Dog Domestic carnivores developed from wolves into an array of breeds classified (in Britain) as hounds, gundogs, utility, working and toys. Dogs which are neither thoroughbred nor crossbred are known as mongrels.

Dogfish Any of several species of small shark. The lesser spotted dogfish is the most common. It grows up to 1 metre long and is covered in brown spots. Also known as the rock salmon or rough hound.

Dolphin Group of toothed whales with a pronounced beak. The common dolphin is the best known. In the wild it roams the oceans in schools; in captivity it is a playful natural acrobat, intelligent and with a friendly disposition towards people.

Domesday Book A book of records made in 1085–87 by order of King William I of England (the Conqueror). William wanted the survey done to make sure that he was receiving all the taxes due to the royal government. The Domesday Book is full of facts about land ownership and farming at that time.

Dominican Republic Caribbean state occupying the eastern two-thirds of the mountainous island of Hispaniola. Most of the people are farmers and the standard of living is low. The chief cash crop is sugar and sugar refining is the chief industry. Area: 49,000 km^2; Pop: 6,400,000; Cap: Santo Domingo.

Donkey Small domesticated relative of the horse, descended from the wild ass of N Africa, which makes a gentle pet and patient beast of burden.

Doppler effect The apparent change in frequency of sound or light caused by motion. For example, the sound of a racing-car engine seems higher when the car approaches and lower after it has passed. The actual pitch of the sound remains constant, of course. It is only the movement of the car in relation to the listener that causes the apparent change in pitch (frequency). Astronomers use the Doppler effect to study the speed of stars. They do this by measuring the apparent change in the frequency of a star's light waves caused by its motion.

Dormouse A small rodent that looks similar to a mouse but behaves more like a squirrel. Dormice have long, often bushy tails and are good climbers. They are active at night and hibernate for several months during the winter.

Dostoyevsky, Feodor (1821–81) Russian novelist and revolutionary who spent many years in the labour camps of Siberia and was once condemned to death. His great novels include *Crime and Punishment*, *The Idiot* and *The Brothers Karamazov*.

Doyle, Arthur Conan (1859–1930) British writer who originally trained to be a doctor. Creator of the famous Sherlock Holmes stories.

Dragonfly Insects that are among the most efficient aerial hunters. Dragonflies catch other insects on the wing, usually near or over water. They can fly forwards or backwards and can also hover in mid air. They have excellent eyesight and many species are brightly coloured. The dragonfly nymph lives under water and is an equally fierce predator.

Drake, Francis (*c* 1540–96) English seaman and adventurer. He sailed round the world in the *Golden Hind* (1577–80) and in 1587 destroyed the Spanish fleet at Cadiz. In 1588 he took a leading part in the destruction of the Spanish Armada.

Drama Performance of dance, acting, mime and music, first known in ancient Greece. Greek plays (tragedies or comedies) were written in poetry and performed in large open-air theatres. In the Middle Ages Bible stories were acted out as plays, called miracle and mystery plays, performed in church or on carts wheeled round the streets. Morality plays were dramas in which good and evil characters were shown, to teach a moral or lesson. The greatest English dramatist was William SHAKESPEARE. No modern playwright has surpassed his work.

Drugs Chemicals used by doctors to treat mental and physical disorders. There are various types having different effects. For example, antibiotics (e.g. penicillin) are used to fight infection, amphetamines are used as anti-depressants, and barbiturates as sedatives and in sleeping pills. Many of these drugs are habit-forming and, if taken without proper medical supervision, may lead to addiction, and serious damage to health. See also NARCOTICS.

Dublin Capital and port of Irish Republic at mouth of R. Liffey. Cultural and commercial centre with large brewing and food processing industries. Pop: 566,000.

Duck A group of birds found worldwide, always close to water. There are two main groups of ducks: those which feed on the

surface of the water (the dabbling ducks) and the diving ducks. Dabbling ducks, which can often be seen up-ended, feeding on water plants, include the MALLARD, SHOVELER and TEAL. Diving ducks include the EIDER, merganser and pochard.

Duckbill See **Platypus**.

Dugong Seal-like mammals that live along the tropical coasts of the Indian Ocean. Some 2.5 metres long, they paddle leisurely through the swampy water using their flippers and rudder-like tails. They feed on water weeds. Often known as sea-cows.

Dumas, Alexandre (1802–70) French novelist who with the help of assistants wrote hundreds of adventure novels. Among the most famous are *The Count of Monte Cristo* and *The Three Musketeers*.

Dunant, Jean Henry (1828–1910) Swiss humanitarian who founded the Red Cross. After a long period of poverty he was 'rediscovered' and awarded the Nobel Peace Prize in 1901.

Dürer, Albrecht (1471–1528) German engraver and painter famed for his drawings and copper engravings. His best-known works include *The Knight*, *St Jerome in his Study* and *Melancholia*.

Dvorak, Antonin (1841–1904) Czech composer and conductor. His works include the symphony *From the New World*, *The Slavonic Dances* and the opera *Rusalka*.

Dyes Nearly all the dyes used today are synthetic, made from products distilled from coal tar – the aniline dyes. Aniline dyes are cheaper, brighter, and faster than the earlier natural dyes such as madder (red) and indigo (blue).

E

Eagle Large, broad-winged birds of prey. All are superb fliers with keen eyesight, powerful talons and hooked, flesh-tearing beaks. They include the harpy eagle of S America, the crowned and martial eagles of southern Africa, the BALD EAGLE of N America and the golden eagle which inhabits mountainous areas throughout most of the northern hemisphere.

Ear Organ in mammals concerned with hearing and balance. There are three main parts: the outer ear consisting of the ear lobe and the passage leading to the ear-drum; the middle ear which contains three tiny bones transmitting vibrations from the ear-drum; and the inner ear which contains the sense organs of hearing and balance.

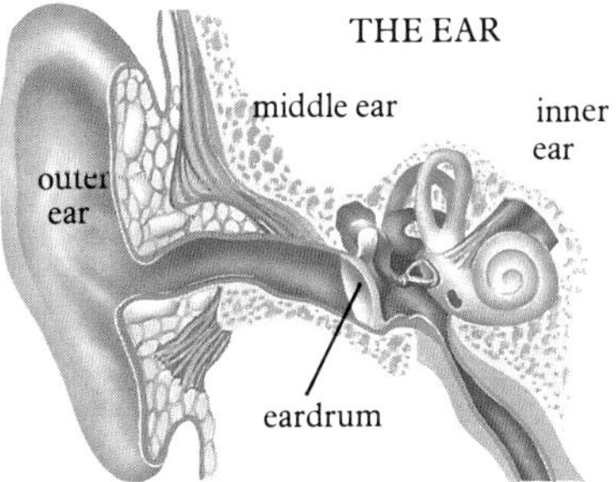

Earth One of the smaller planets of the Solar system, measuring 12,757 km across the equator, and third in line from the Sun at an average distance of 149,600,000 km. The Earth rotates on its axis once a day and orbits the Sun once a year, its tilted axis producing the SEASONS. The crust of the Earth, rarely more than 50 km thick, overlies a mantle of dense, partly molten rock surrounding a core composed of nickel and iron.

Earth history The Earth was formed, along with the other planets in the Solar system, about 4,500 million years ago, and the earliest known rocks date from about 4,000 million years ago. A record of the Earth's history is preserved in the layers of rock that have been formed at various times and the remains of plants and animals (FOSSILS) they contain. See also chart on pages 182 and 183.

THE STRUCTURE OF THE EARTH

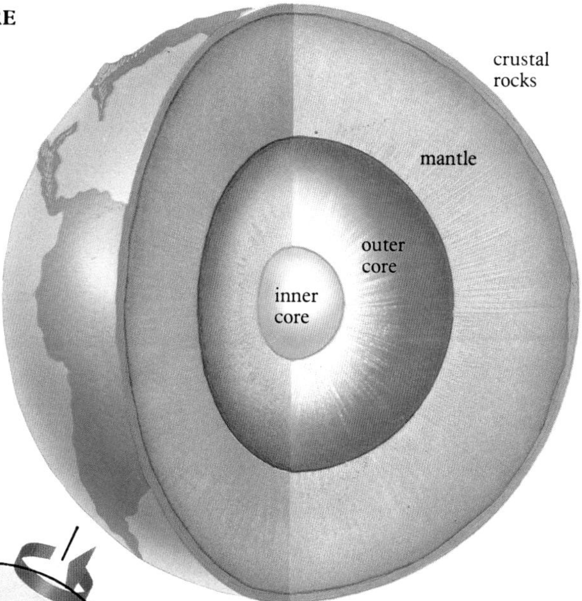

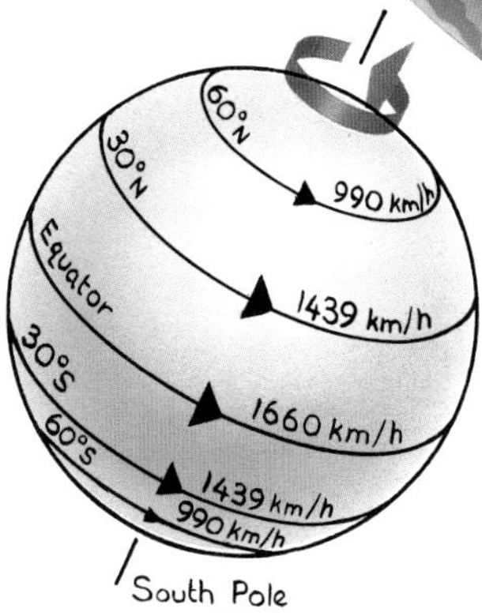

The speed of the Earth's rotation varies with latitude from 1660 km/h at the equator to zero at the poles.

Earthquake Shock waves travelling through the ground as a result of volcanic explosions or the movement of crustal rocks. Weaknesses in the crustal rocks often occur where mountain ranges have been recently created. One of the most famous is the San Andreas fault in California. The movement of rocks along this fault partially demolished San Francisco in 1906.

Earthworm A large group of about 2500 species of annelid worm that burrow in the ground. Earthworms eat their way through the soil, leaving behind unwanted remains as 'casts'. By doing this they help to drain the soil and supply it with air.

Earwig Insects with pincers on their rear end (the pincers are curved in the male, straight in the female). Some earwigs can fly, but rarely do so, usually hiding away in dark places during daylight. At night they come out to scavenge on dead insects and plant matter.

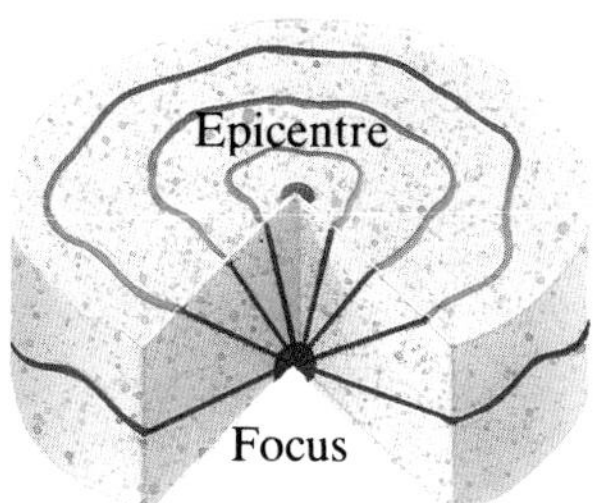

Shock waves travel out from the focus, or origin, of an earthquake. The epicentre is the point on the ground above the focus.

Easter One of the most important festivals of the Christian Church when Jesus's death and rising from the dead are remembered. Easter falls in March or April.

Easter Island Volcanic island in S Pacific Ocean, situated 3800 km off coast of Chile, to which it belongs. Easter I. is famous for its ancient large stone statues.

Echidna Also known as the spiny anteater, this egg-laying mammal (monotreme) resembles a hedgehog. It lives in Australia and New Guinea and feeds almost entirely on termites.

Echinoderm Marine invertebrates with radially symmetrical bodies – i.e. the limbs and organs are arranged regularly around a central point. The group includes the SEA URCHINS, STARFISHES, sea cucumbers and brittlestars. Echinoderms have no central brain nor even a distinct head.

Echo A sound that is heard again as it is reflected off something. Sound waves travel at a known, fixed speed, so they can be used to find out how far away something is. From the time delay between the original sound and the returning echo, it is possible to calculate the distance of the reflecting object. Ships' sonar uses this principle to find the depth of the sea. Radar uses echoes from radio signals.

Eclipse An event that occurs when the Earth and Moon move into each other's shadow. When the Moon passes in front of the Sun, a dramatic solar eclipse can be seen in those regions where the Moon's shadow falls on Earth. When the Earth passes between the Sun and the Moon, a lunar eclipse occurs.

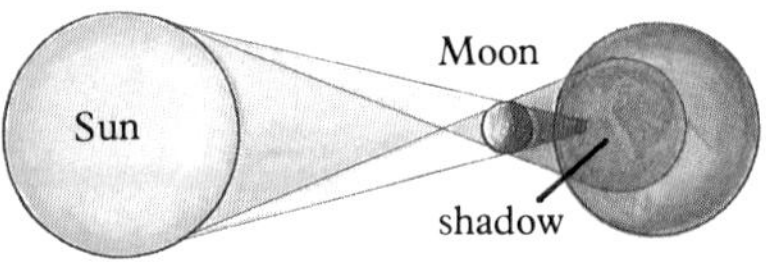

A solar eclipse

Ecology Study of the relationships between plants and animals and their environment, including how organisms interact with each other and with their surroundings.

Ecuador Republic in South America situated on the equator. Two ranges of the Andes run in a N-S direction through the country. They enclose fertile, temperate plains where many of the people live, despite frequent earthquakes. Ecuador has valuable petroleum reserves, and oil revenues account for two-thirds of the nation's foreign earnings. Area: 284,000 km^2; Pop: 8,648,000; Cap: Quito.

Edinburgh Capital of Scotland on Firth of Forth. Seat of the Scottish throne during the 15th and 16th centuries. Among many fine buildings are Holyrood Palace and the castle which crowns the rocky outcrop on which the historic city is built. Famed for its annual arts festival. Pop: 436,000.

Edison, Thomas Alva (1847–1931) American inventor who held over 1300 patents. Among his inventions were the phonograph, the transmitter and receiver for the automatic telegraph, the electric light bulb and the first electricity generating station in the world.

Edward III (1312–77) King of England from 1327. He began the Hundred Years War with France in 1337 and together with his son, Edward the Black Prince, took an active part in it. During his reign England (and most of Europe) was ravaged by the Black Death which decimated the population and caused great social unrest.

Eel A long slim fish that migrates from fresh water to the sea to breed. The male grows up to 50 cm long, the female up to a metre. Eels spawn in the Sargasso Sea in the western Atlantic Ocean. The leaf-like larvae drift across the Atlantic to Europe where the eels may live in rivers for 10 years or more before returning to the sea.

Egypt Country in N Africa, bordered by the Mediterranean and Red Seas. It has a hot climate, and away from the fertile valley of the R. Nile, the land is mostly desert. Crops include cotton, sugar-cane, dates, fruit and vegetables grown on irrigated fields. Most people live along the banks of the Nile, whose waters have been harnessed by the Aswân Dam to give electricity for industry. Tourism is important with many visitors coming to admire the pyramids and other ancient wonders. Area: 1,001,710 km^2; Pop: 47,049,000; Cap: Cairo.

Egypt, Ancient One of the great civilizations of the ancient world founded on the banks of the River Nile over 6000 years ago. Ancient Egypt was a monarchy, with strict laws and customs which hardly changed during many centuries. Its

history is divided into kingdoms and dynasties, beginning about 3000 BC and ending with the conquest by Alexander the Great in 330 BC.

Egypt, both ancient and modern, is 'the gift of the Nile', for the river is virtually the sole source of water. Inset: The pharaoh Akhenaton and his beautiful wife Nefertiti.

Eider Duck which spends its time at sea and which is famed for the softness of its feathers or down. The male common eider is black and white, the female is brown.

Eiffel Tower Huge wrought-iron tower in Paris. Some 400 metres high, it was designed by Alexandre Gustave Eiffel and built in 1889 when it was the tallest structure in the world.

Einstein, Albert (1879–1955) German-born mathematician and physicist whose theory of relativity proved to be the greatest scientific advance since Newton's theory of gravitation. He was awarded the Nobel Physics Prize in 1921.

Elasticity The property of a material that makes it go back to its original shape after it has been pushed or pulled out of shape. All solids are elastic to some degree. Even a steel object dropped on the floor will bounce up a small way because the force of impact squeezes the steel and the floor slightly out of shape. Unless the force of impact is too great, both the steel and the floor will return to their original shape.

Elder Deciduous shrub or small tree bearing clusters of white flowers and juicy black berries that are frequently used for making wine.

El Dorado Legendary South American kingdom of immense wealth, sought but never found by numerous Spanish and English explorers, including Sir Walter RALEIGH.

Electric circuit Before an electric current can flow, there must be a complete loop called a circuit. Electrons flow in a conductor when 'pressure' (voltage) is

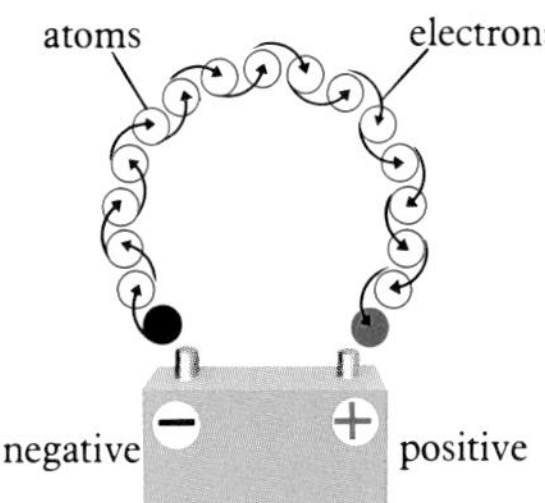

An electric circuit showing the flow of electrons from atom to atom.

applied to them, the source of pressure being a battery or generator. The electricity in a battery will not make a light bulb glow until the bulb and battery are joined by wires through which electricity can flow. This is a circuit.

Electricity Electricity is electrons in motion. Electrons are tiny negatively charged particles that are normally bound in orbits around the positive nuclei (centres) of atoms. But electrons can be detached from their atoms and made to flow along a wire as an electric current. To make this happen, 'pressure' must be applied to them. The source of electric pressure can be a battery or a generator. The term for electrical pressure is *voltage*.

Materials are divided into three kinds by their electrical properties: *conductors* are materials that let currents flow easily (they are usually metals); *insulators* are materials such as plastic and rubber in which currents cannot flow; and *semi-conductors* are materials that let a current flow with difficulty. Transistors are made from semiconductors such as silicon.

Electric motor A machine that turns electricity into movement by making a shaft rotate. It is the opposite of an electric generator, which turns movement (powered by, for example, water, coal or oil) into electricity.

Electrolysis A process in which an electric current is passed through a liquid, causing a chemical reaction to take place. If the liquid is a solution that contains a metal, the current passing through the liquid breaks down the solution and the metal is removed. Electrolysis is important in industry. Aluminium is produced by this means, and items such as cutlery are *electroplated* by electrolysis.

Electromagnet Electricity is closely related to magnetism. An electromagnet is an example of this relationship. When an electric current is passed through a wire, a magnetic field is set up round the wire. This magnetic field can be made much stronger by winding the wire round an iron bar to make an electromagnet. Small electromagnets are used in telephones and electric bells. Powerful electromagnets are used for picking up iron and steel scrap and in electric motors.

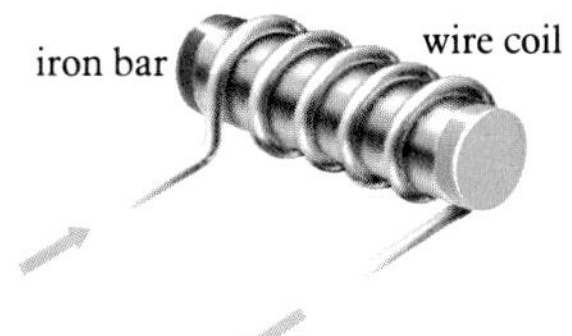

An electromagnet. The current-carrying wire turns the iron bar into a magnet.

Electromagnetic radiation LIGHT waves, RADIO waves, ULTRA-VIOLET waves and INFRA-RED waves (heat) are all forms of electromagnetic radiation. The only difference between them is that they have different wavelengths. Light waves are much shorter than radio waves – they have a higher frequency. Other forms of electromagnetic radiation are COSMIC RAYS, gamma rays, and X-RAYS. These have shorter wavelengths than ultra-violet waves.

The Sun and other stars give off electromagnetic radiation of many kinds, but the Earth's atmosphere stops many of these reaching us.

Electronics The branch of science that deals with the accurate control of electric currents. Radios, television sets, computers, tape-recorders, radars, X-ray machines, and pocket calculators are all electronic devices. The transistor and the silicon chip are at the heart of most electronic circuits.

Electron microscope An ordinary microscope can be used to see objects as small as a thousandth of a millimetre across. But it cannot show anything smaller because of the wavelength of visible light. To see even smaller objects, the electron microscope is used. It employs beams of electrons instead of light and can let us see things that are only one ten-thousandth of a micrometre across (a micrometre is a millionth of a metre).

Element A chemical element is a substance that cannot be broken down chemically into simpler substances. All chemical substances are either elements or COMPOUNDS. Compounds are combinations of two or more elements. Each element has ATOMS containing a certain fixed number of protons (the element's atomic number). Elements with atomic numbers from 1 to 92 occur naturally. Some 14 other elements can be made artificially by bombarding substances with high-speed atomic particles.

THE ELEMENTS

Element	*Symbol*	*Discovered*			
Carbon	(C)	Ancient	Bromine	(Br)	1826
Copper	(Cu)	Ancient	Thorium	(Th)	1828
Gold	(Au)	Ancient	Vanadium	(V)	1830
Iron	(Fe)	Ancient	Lanthanum	(La)	1839
Lead	(Pb)	Ancient	Erbium	(Er)	1843
Mercury	(Hg)	Ancient	Terbium	(Tb)	1843
Silver	(Ag)	Ancient	Ruthenium	(Ru)	1845
Sulphur	(S)	Ancient	Caesium	(Cs)	1860
Tin	(Sn)	Ancient	Rubidium	(Rb)	1861
Zinc	(Zn)	Ancient	Thallium	(Tl)	1861
Arsenic	(As)	Medieval	Indium	(In)	1863
Bismuth	(Bi)	Medieval	Gallium	(Ga)	1875
Antimony	(Sb)	Medieval	Holmium	(Ho)	1878
Phosphorus	(P)	1669	Ytterbium	(Yb)	1878
Cobalt	(Co)	1735	Samarium	(Sm)	1879
Platinum	(Pt)	1735	Scandium	(Sc)	1879
Nickel	(Ni)	1751	Thulium	(Tm)	1879
Hydrogen	(H)	1766	Neodymium	(Nd)	1885
Fluorine	(F)	1771	Praseodymium	(Pr)	1885
Nitrogen	(N)	1772	Dysprosium	(Dy)	1886
Chlorine	(Cl)	1774	Gadolinium	(Gd)	1886
Manganese	(Mn)	1774	Germanium	(Ge)	1886
Oxygen	(O)	1774	Argon	(Ar)	1894
Molybdenum	(Mo)	1782	Helium	(He)	1895
Tellurium	(Te)	1782	Krypton	(Kr)	1898
Tungsten	(W)	1783	Neon	(Ne)	1898
Uranium	(U)	1789	Polonium	(Po)	1898
Zirconium	(Zr)	1789	Radium	(Ra)	1898
Strontium	(Sr)	1790	Xenon	(Xe)	1898
Titanium	(Ti)	1791	Actinium	(Ac)	1899
Yttrium	(Y)	1794	Radon	(Rn)	1900
Chromium	(Cr)	1797	Europium	(Eu)	1901
Beryllium	(Be)	1798	Lutetium	(Lu)	1907
Niobium	(Nb)	1801	Protactinium	(Pa)	1917
Tantalum	(Ta)	1802	Hafnium	(Hf)	1923
Cerium	(Ce)	1803	Rhenium	(Re)	1925
Palladium	(Pd)	1803	Technetium	(Tc)	1937
Rhodium	(Rh)	1803	Francium	(Fr)	1939
Iridium	(Ir)	1804	Astatine	(At)	1940
Osmium	(Os)	1804	Neptunium	(Np)	1940
Potassium	(K)	1807	Plutonium	(Pu)	1940
Sodium	(Na)	1807	Americium	(Am)	1944
Barium	(Ba)	1808	Curium	(Cm)	1944
Boron	(B)	1808	Promethium	(Pm)	1945
Calcium	(Ca)	1808	Berkelium	(Bk)	1949
Magnesium	(Mg)	1808	Californium	(Cf)	1950
Iodine	(I)	1811	Einsteinium	(Es)	1952
Cadmium	(Cd)	1817	Fermium	(Fm)	1953
Lithium	(Li)	1817	Mendelevium	(Md)	1955
Selenium	(Se)	1817	Nobelium	(No)	1958
Silicon	(Si)	1823	Lawrencium	(Lw)	1961
Aluminium	(Al)	1825	Rutherfordium	(Rf)	1969
			Hahnium	(Ha)	1970

Elephant Largest living land animals. These thick-skinned mammals reach 3.5 metres in height and 6 tonnes in weight. The sensitive trunk (modified upper lip) is used for carrying food and water to the mouth, for spraying and for lifting. The African elephant is larger (especially the ears) and wilder than the Indian. The Indian elephant is often domesticated and trained to work.

Elgar, Edward (1857–1934) English composer who was knighted in 1904. His works include the *Enigma Variations*, a violin and a cello concerto, two symphonies, the five *Pomp and Circumstance* marches, and the oratorio *The Dream of Gerontius*.

Eliot, Thomas Stearns (1888–1965) American-born British poet, critic and dramatist who wrote *The Waste Land* and the verse drama *Murder in the Cathedral*.

Elizabeth I (1533–1603) Queen of England from 1558. She came to the throne at a time of political and religious unrest but her firmness of rule restored both stability and prosperity to England. She was ably served by men such as William Cecil and she encouraged overseas expansion. In 1588 the Spanish Armada was defeated, thereby confirming her new position as monarch of a great naval power.

Elizabeth II (*b* 1926) Queen of Great Britain and Head of the Commonwealth from 1952. She married Philip Mountbatten, Duke of Edinburgh, in 1947, and celebrated her jubilee in 1977. They have four children: Prince Charles, Princess Anne, Prince Andrew and Prince Edward.

Elk Largest of all the deer, standing nearly two metres high at the shoulder, elk live among the pine forests of Scandinavia and other sub-arctic regions. In North America it is called the moose. The male carries huge, flattened antlers.

Elm A family of large deciduous trees growing up to 30 metres tall. Elms were very common until in the 1960s and 1970s millions of them were killed by Dutch elm disease.

El Salvador Small republic in Central America on Pacific coast. The economy is based on agriculture, with coffee and sugar being the main cash crops and exports. El Salvador has been in a state of civil unrest since the early 1970s. Area: 21,400 km^2; Pop: 4,930,000; Cap: San Salvador.

Emu Australian bird, flightless but fleet of foot. It is related to the cassowary.

Energy Energy is the ability to do work. There are many different forms of energy, but there are two basic kinds – *potential energy* and *kinetic energy*. A wound-up spring or the water behind a dam both have stored up energy – potential energy. As the spring unwinds and the water flows through turbines the energy is changed to kinetic energy – energy of movement. Other forms of energy are electrical, chemical, heat, sound, radiant and nuclear. These different forms can be changed into each other.

Engineering The application of scientific principles to industry and transport. Engineering is basically to do with the construction and maintenance of engines, but now covers a much wider field.

Mechanical engineers deal with the operation of machinery. Civil engineers design roads, bridges, water supply systems, etc. There are also electrical engineers, mining engineers, chemical engineers, marine and aeronautical engineers, etc.

England Part of the United Kingdom of Great Britain and Northern Ireland. It is the most densely populated part of the kingdom, with the largest cities, including London. The landscape includes flat lands in the east; rolling downs in the south; moors and rocky coastlines in the west; lakes and fells in the north-west. Down the centre of the country run the Pennine Hills, dividing the industrial regions of the north-west and north-east. In the centre are the midland counties, once made rich by wool and later becoming the industrial heart of England. The south-east, around London, has crowded towns and suburbs.

Today, tourists visit England to see its historic towns and castles and admire its scenery. But its wealth comes mostly from its business activities, such as banking, insurance, trade and industry. Area: 130,000 km^2; Pop: 46,221,000; Cap: London.

English language Language spoken not only in Britain but widely throughout the world, including the United States. The English language developed through three periods: Old English (AD 700 to 1100), Middle English (1100 to 1500), and Modern English (1500 to the present).

English has absorbed words from many other European languages.

SCOTLAND
SOUTHERN UPLANDS
CHEVIOT HILLS
THE PENNINES
LAKE DISTRICT
NORTH YORK MOORS
IRISH SEA
NORTH SEA
WALES
CAMBRIAN MTS
ENGLAND
COTSWOLDS
CHILTERN HILLS
NORTH DOWNS
SOUTH DOWNS
EXMOOR
DARTMOOR
BODMIN MOOR
BRECON BEACONS
THE FENS
THE BROADS
ENGLISH CHANNEL
FRANCE
Channel Islands
Isle of Man
Isle of Wight
Anglesey
Holy Isle
North Channel
St. George's Channel
Cardigan Bay
Bristol Channel
Solway Firth
Strait of Dover
The Wash
Hadrian's Wall
London
Birmingham
Manchester
Liverpool
Leeds
Sheffield
Bristol
Cardiff
Newcastle upon Tyne
Belfast
Dublin
Plymouth
Kingston upon Hull
Nottingham
Leicester
Coventry
Stoke-on-Trent
Wolverhampton
Bradford
Sunderland
Middlesbrough and Teesside
Snowdon 1085m
Scafell Pike 978m
Snaefell 620m
Land's End
Lizard Point
Flamborough Head
Spurn Head
miles
0 20 40 60
0 20 40 60 80 100
kilometres

Wind erosion in Oklahoma, USA, stripped farms clear of soil overnight and created the famous Dust Bowl in the 1930s.

Enzymes Enzymes are chemicals that speed up chemical reactions in all animals and plants. The human body contains more than a thousand types of enzyme, all doing a specific job. Without these enzymes we could not digest our food, see or breathe. And enzymes have many other uses. Some detergents contain them to break down stains caused by protein matter. They are also used in the manufacture of beer, bread, cheese, antibiotics, and many other products.

Epilepsy A disorder of the nervous system causing periodic fits and loss of consciousness.

Equator An imaginary line around the Earth mid-way between the North and South Poles. The equator is 0° latitude.

Equatorial Guinea Republic in West Africa made up of a small forested mainland area between Gabon and Cameroon and a number of islands. The economy is based on agriculture, particularly cocoa and coffee. Area: 28,000 km^2; Pop: 275,000; Cap: Malabo (on Bioko I.).

Equinox Two points in the Earth's orbit where the tilt of its axis is sideways on to the Sun. All parts of the world then have 12 hours of light and 12 hours of darkness. The spring equinox occurs about March 21 and the autumn equinox about September 23.

Eros Greek god of love. He is represented as a winged boy with a bow and a quiver of arrows strapped to his back. (Roman equivalent Cupid.)

Erosion The wearing away of the land surface by water, wind and ice. Rivers carve valleys and carry rock debris to the sea. Ocean waves pound the shore and eat away at the coastline. Wind armed with sand grains sculptures desert rocks. And glaciers scrape the land clear of soil. But the material that is eroded is deposited elsewhere and builds up into new rocks.

Escape velocity This is the speed a spacecraft must reach before it can coast away from the pull of gravity. The required speed to escape Earth's gravity is 40,000 km/h (25,000 mph).

Eskimos Mongoloid people of the Arctic coasts of N America and Greenland. Traditionally nomadic hunters, they lived off seals, bears and walruses, eating the meat and using the skins for clothing, canoes and tents. Snow houses (igloos) were rare. Today Eskimo numbers are declining and more and more of them live in settlements.

Ethiopia Country in NE Africa, formerly called Abyssinia, with a northern coastline on the Red Sea. A land of hot deserts and high cooler plateaux. Many people live in remote highland villages, farming and raising livestock. The chief cash crop is coffee. Other products are animal hides and skins. Ethiopia has been an independent country for some 3000 years. It now faces a terrible onset of famine, caused by drought. Area: 1,222,000 km²; Pop: 31,998,000; Cap: Addis Ababa.

Eucalyptus Some 600 species of evergreen gum-trees of the myrtle family, native to Australia. Some grow 100 metres tall. They yield timber, gum and aromatic oil from the leathery leaves.

Euclid (*c* 300 BC) Greek mathematician who founded modern geometry. He is best known for his *Elements* in which he assembled all the mathematical knowledge of his time.

Euphrates River in south-west Asia, flowing from eastern Turkey through Syria and Iraq where it joins the Tigris and becomes the Shatt al Arab, flowing into the Arabian Gulf. Used for irrigation and HEP schemes. Length: 2860 km.

Europe A small, densely populated and highly developed continent. Much of the land is taken up by a large fertile plain reaching from Russia in the east to the Atlantic in the west. To the north are the forests and highlands of Scandinavia, to the south a series of mountain ranges - the Pyrenees, Alps and Caucasus - and the Mediterranean lands. Europe's farms are often small but highly efficient, and its industrial production ranks amongst the world's greatest. Area: 10,531,000 km²; Pop: 693,000,000. See map on pages 80 and 81.

European Economic Community (EEC) Group of 12 nations in western Europe, who trade freely and share a European parliament, court and civil service. The 12 members are France, West Germany, Italy, Belgium, Luxembourg, the Netherlands, Ireland, Denmark, the United Kingdom, Greece, Spain and Portugal. Though a powerful trading group, the Community has so far made little progress towards its original goal of becoming a United States of Europe.

Evaporation The conversion of a liquid to a gas at a temperature below boiling point of the liquid. The rate of evaporation increases with heat. The evaporation of water from the surface of the sea by the heat of the sun is responsible for the WATER CYCLE.

Everest, Mt Mountain in Himalayas, on the boundary between Tibet and Nepal. Highest mountain in the world. First climbed by Hillary and Tenzing in 1953. Height: 8848 metres.

Evergreen Plant that bears leaves throughout the year. Leaves are lost and replaced as part of a continual process. Most conifers are evergreen, as are a small number of broad-leaved trees, e.g. holly and holm oak.

Evolution The process by which organisms gradually change over successive generations, resulting in better adaptation to the environment and eventually producing new species. The theory of evolution was put forward by Charles Darwin in 1859.

Explosives Chemicals that produce explosions when they are struck or ignited. When an explosion takes place, the solids and liquids in the explosive substance change to gases and give out great amounts of heat. They also expand violently.

Eye The organ of sight. The human eye is a tough, fluid-filled ball with a lens suspended across the front. The lens can change shape to focus light onto a region at the back of the eye called the retina. This is lined with light-sensitive cells which send messages to the brain when light hits them. The brain decodes these messages to build up a picture.

Some creatures, such as insects, have simpler eyes called compound eyes. These are made up of many tiny units, or facets, each of which creates a tiny image. So the insect sees everything as a mosaic of hundreds of tiny pictures.

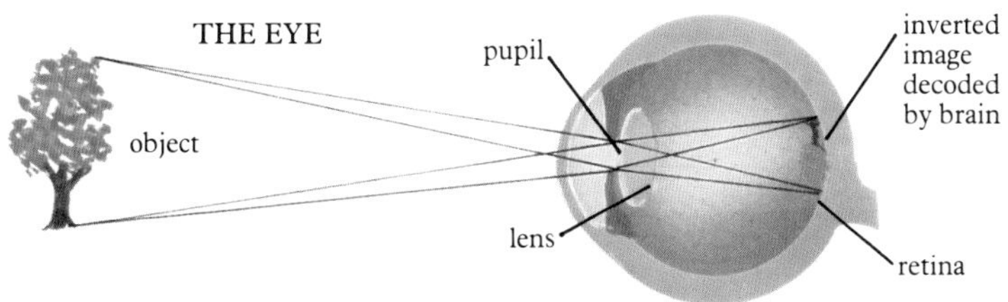

Europe (Map)

65°
A
B
D
E
ICELAND
Reykjavik
Arctic Circle
30°
miles
0
200
400
0
200
400
600
kilometres
NORWEGIAN SEA
Faroe Is.
NORWAY
Shetland Is.
55°
ATLANTIC
OCEAN
Bergen
Orkney Is.
Oslo
Stockholm
Lake Vänern
SWEDEN
Glasgow
Edinburgh
Göteborg
20°
Belfast
DENMARK
NORTH SEA
UNITED KINGDOM
Dublin
Copenhagen
IRELAND
Manchester
Liverpool
BALTIC
Birmingham
Hamburg
Gdańsk
Cardiff
Thames
NETH.
Amsterdam
WEST
Berlin
POLAND
Bristol
The Hague
Rotterdam
EAST
London
Antwerp
Essen
GERMANY
English Channel
BELGIUM
Cologne
Bonn
Brussels
Oder
Elbe
Seine
Rhine
Leipzig
Prague
Paris
LUX.
Frankfurt
45°
Stuttgart
CZECHOSLOVAKIA
Nantes
Loire
Munich
FRANCE
Zürich
Vienna
Bay of Biscay
Berne
LIECHTN.
Geneva
SWITZERLAND
AUSTRIA
Budapest
Bordeaux
HUNGARY
Lyon
ALPS
Milan
Po
Venice
Zagreb
Turin
Rhône
Oporto
Duoro
PYRENEES
Genoa
ITALY
Belgrade
PORTUGAL
ANDORRA
Marseille
MONACO
SAN MARINO
YUGOSLAVIA
SPAIN
Ebro
Madrid
Tagus
Barcelona
Corsica
Rome
ADRIATIC SEA
APENNINES
Lisbon
Minorca
Majorca
Valencia
Naples
Sardinia
ALBANIA
Seville
Ibiza
TYRRHENIAN SEA
MEDITERRANEAN SEA
Palermo
35°
Str. of Gibraltar
Gibraltar (U.K.)
Algiers
IONIAN SEA
Rabat
Tunis
Sicily
Casablanca
ALGERIA
MOROCCO
TUNISIA
MALTA
10°
0°
10°

G
H
J
K
Murmansk
White Sea
Arkhangel'sk
N Dvina
FINLAND
Lake Onega
Lake Ladoga
Helsinki
Leningrad
Gulf of Finland
Nizhniy Tagil
Sverdlovsk
Perm
U S S R
Gorki
Kazan
Riga
Moscow
W. Dvina
Kuybyshev
Tula
Penza
Ural
Minsk
Volga
Saratov
Voronezh
Kursk
Don
Kiev
Kharkov
Volgograd
Lvov
Dnieper
Donets
Dnestr
Donetsk
Dnepropetrovsk
Rostov
Krivoy Rog
Odessa
Sea of Azov
ROMANIA
Simferopol
Groznyy
CASPIAN SEA
Bucharest
Danube
BLACK SEA
CAUCASUS MTS
Tbilisi
Baku
Sofia
BULGARIA
Istanbul
Yerevan
Kizil
Ankara
AEGEAN SEA
Athens
TURKEY
IRAN
Tehran
IRAQ
Tigris
SYRIA
Euphrates
CYPRUS
Crete
2
3
4
5
70°
60°
30°
40°
50°

F

Fabre, Jean Henri (1823–1915) French entomologist whose *Souvenirs entomologiques* (1879–1907) provides a detailed study of insect behaviour.

Falcon Birds of prey, related to hawks but with longer pointed wings and tails. Examples are the handsome gyrfalcon and the small KESTREL.

Falkland Islands Group of islands in S Atlantic Ocean 770 km NE of Cape Horn. A British colony, the Falklands consist of two main islands, East and West Falkland. The land is mostly moorland, suitable only for sheep-rearing. The only settlement of any size is the port and capital of Stanley on East Falkland. The islands were invaded by Argentina in 1982 and recaptured by British forces. Area: 12,170 km^2; Pop: 1990.

Faraday, Michael (1791–1867) English physicist who founded the science of electromagnetism. In 1833 he succeeded Sir Humphry Davy as professor of chemistry at the Royal Institution. Among his discoveries and inventions were the electric motor and the first generator.

Faroe Islands Group of islands in the Atlantic Ocean, situated NW of the Shetland Islands. The islands belong to Denmark, though they are self-governed. The main town is Thorshavn on Strömö island. Pop: 42,000.

Fascism Extreme 'right-wing' political movement of the 1920s and 1930s, which gained power in Germany, Italy and Spain. The Italian Fascists were led by Mussolini, the Spanish by Franco, but the most evil were undoubtedly the German NAZIS, led by HITLER, who brought about World War II.

Fates In Greek mythology, three goddesses who controlled human destinies.

Fats One of the most important foods of all animals and plants. A large part of our body energy comes from eating fats. Hard fats include the fat of beef, mutton and other animals. Butter and margarine are soft fats. Vegetable oils come from the seeds of plants, mainly from soyabeans. When hard and soft fats are heated they turn into oils. Foods rich in fat provide energy for long storage but too much fat in the diet leads to obesity, digestive and other problems.

All these foods contain fat, though in some it is 'hidden'.

Fawkes, Guy (1570–1606) Catholic conspirator who tried to blow up the Houses of Parliament and King James I on November 5, 1605. He was discovered in time, tried for treason and executed.

Federal Bureau of Investigation (FBI) Name since 1935 of the chief investigative branch of the US Department of Justice. Its headquarters are in Washington. The FBI was founded in 1908, as the Bureau of Investigation. During the 1930s it waged war on gangsters. Today, as well as detecting criminals (drug traffickers, for example), the FBI is also involved in secret 'undercover' work and spy-catching. It is not a police force, however. It reports to the US Attorney-General, who decides what action to take.

Fermentation A chemical change that takes place in animal and vegetable matter brought about by yeasts, bacteria or enzymes. Examples of fermentation are the rising of bread dough, the souring of milk, and the digestion of food in our stomach. Alcoholic drinks such as beer, wine and spirits are also produced by fermentation.

Fermi, Enrico (1901–54) Italian-American nuclear physicist who in 1938 was awarded the Nobel Prize for his work on radioactive materials. His research aided the construction of the atomic bomb and he was responsible for the first nuclear reactor.

Fern A group of green flowerless plants that reproduce by spores. The spores develop in special capsules on the underside of the large leaves or fronds. Ferns are most abundant in warm damp regions, where species grow to 10 metres.

Fertilizer Plant foods, normally added to the soil to replace substances used up by crops or lost by other means. The chief soil nutrients are nitrogen, potassium, phosphorus, sulphur, calcium and magnesium. The traditional fertilizer is farmyard manure. Other natural fertilizers are bone-meal, which is rich in nitrogen and phosphorus, and guano (bird-droppings) which is rich in nitrogen and phosphates. Most fertilizers used today are chemicals such as superphosphate of lime, sulphate of ammonia, and sulphate of potash. Fertilizers may be applied to the soil before, during, or after planting.

Feudal system The principal structure of life in western Europe during the Middle Ages. It was based on land. The king granted estates to his chief nobles, in return for their loyalty and service in time of war. Lesser nobles in turn received smaller pieces of land from the chief nobles. At the bottom were freemen (who owned plots of land but had to work their lord's land as well) and peasants or serfs who owned no land, and in some countries, such as Russia, were virtually slaves. In return for their work, the freemen and peasants were protected by their lord.

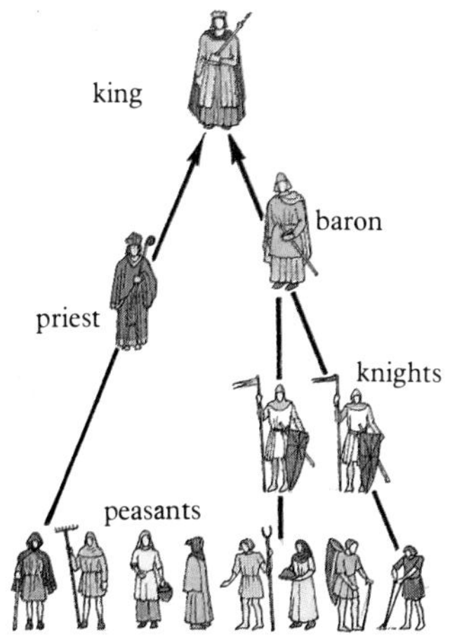

The Feudal System

Fibre optics The use of hair-thin strands of special glass to carry pulses of laser light. A laser beam sent along a glass fibre can carry much more information – telephone or television signals, for example – than an electric current in a copper cable. A single pair of hair-thin glass fibres can easily carry 200 telephone conversations, all going on at the same time.

Fibres Textile fibres come from several sources – from plants, animals or minerals. The main natural fibres are COTTON, WOOL, flax and SILK. Most natural fibres are fairly short and have to be spun to make a continuous strong yarn suitable for weaving.

Fiji Republic in the SW Pacific, consisting of over 800 islands of which approximately 100 are inhabited. Most of the larger islands are mountainous and volcanic. Area: 18,000 km^2; Pop: 686,000; Cap: Suva (on Viti Levu).

Film (photographic) Black and white film has a surface layer made of a compound of silver. When a camera's shutter is opened, light strikes the silver compound, partly changing it to silver. When the film is developed, the parts exposed to light are completely changed to silver. The silver forms a thin black layer, giving a negative image. A positive print is made from this negative.

In colour film there are three layers of light-sensitive silver compounds. Each layer is sensitive to different colours in the light.

Finch A large family of seed-eating birds that includes the redpoll, linnet and CROSSBILL, as well as the more common finches. They are most colourful birds with strong heavy beaks with which they can crack open the tough cases of seeds.

Fingerprints The pattern of ridges on a person's finger pads are unique and unchanging. The prints made by fingers are therefore a foolproof method of identifying people and are particularly helpful in criminal investigations.

Finland Republic in N Europe. Almost 70% of the country is forested, with numerous large lakes in the S and rugged highlands in the N. Poor soils and a cold northern climate combine to make less than one-tenth of the land suitable for growing crops. Timber is the mainstay of the economy and Finland is one of the world's leading pulp and paper producers. Shipbuilding, textiles, clothing and glass-

1
2
3
4
5
6
7
8
9
10

ware are other major industries. Area: 337,000 km^2; Pop:4,873,000; Cap: Helsinki.

Fir Group of 40 or so coniferous trees belonging to the pine family. Firs have flattened needles and woody cones that stand upright. The trees are widely grown for their timber. The Douglas fir is not a true fir and has cones that hang down.

Firefly Flying beetles which give out a bright light caused by a chemical reaction. The lights flash on and off intermittently and serve as a courtship signal. They are related to glow-worms.

Fireworks Most fireworks are made by putting gunpowder in paper tubes. Gunpowder, also called black powder, is a mixture of saltpetre, sulphur, and charcoal. Small amounts of other chemicals are added to create colours.

Fish An aquatic vertebrate, well adapted to a life in water with a streamlined body and a series of fins. Fishes take in oxygen from the water by means of gills. Most have scales on the skin and all are cold-blooded. There are three basic groups of fishes: the bony fishes, which include about 95 per cent of all species; the cartilaginous fishes, such as sharks and rays, which have cartilage (gristle) instead of bone; and the LAMPREYS and HAGFISHES, jawless fishes with cartilaginous skeletons.

Fission, nuclear The splitting of uranium atoms by bombarding them with atomic particles called neutrons. In the fission process, other neutrons are produced which can go on to split other uranium atoms. A chain reaction takes place, making a lot of heat. This chain reaction is controlled in nuclear reactors and the heat produced is used to make electricity. If the reaction is not controlled it can cause an explosion, as in the atomic bomb.

Flags Piece of cloth bearing a design, or emblem, used as a sign or signal. Flags were used in ancient Egypt, India and China, and brought to Europe by Arab invaders. In the Middle Ages, heraldic flags identified kings and knights in battle. Later came the idea of national (country) flags. Flags were also used for sending signal messages at sea, until largely replaced by radio. A selection of national flags appears on page 86.

Flatfish Member of a group of fishes that live at the bottom of the sea. The group includes PLAICE, flounders, TURBOT, SOLE, HALIBUT and several less familiar species. A flatfish that is only a few weeks old looks much like a herring of the same age. Then it changes: the body flattens and one eye migrates onto the other side of the head, so that the fish can lie on the sea floor with both eyes uppermost.

Flea The name given to a large group of small, wingless insects, all of which are blood-sucking parasites of mammals and birds.

Fleming, Alexander (1881–1955) Scottish bacteriologist who discovered penicillin in 1928. He shared the Nobel Prize for medicine in 1945, by which time his work had gained full recognition.

Flint A variety of quartz often found in chalk. Flint can be chipped to produce extremely sharp edges and was widely used by prehistoric people to make tools and weapon heads.

Floods Heavy rain or melting snow often causes rivers to overflow or burst their banks and flood the land. But worse floods are produced by the sea. Storms may drive high seas over low-lying land, especially in the tropics, and great waves called tsunamis can be generated by submarine earthquakes.

Florence Capital of Tuscany, in central Italy on R. Arno. Historic city of Roman origin and one of the world's major art centres. Ruled by the Medici family as an independent city state (1421–1737), it played a leading part in the Renaissance. Dante, Michelangelo, Leonardo da Vinci and Machiavelli are just a few of its famous citizens. Pop: 465,000.

Florida In the south-eastern USA, Florida is the home of many retired Americans and it receives about 40 million tourists a year. Miami Beach is one of several famous seaside resorts and other attractions include Disney World, near Orlando, the Everglades National Park and the Kennedy Space Center at Cape Canaveral. Area: 151,670 km^2; Pop: 9,746,000; Cap: Tallahassee.

Examples of different marine fish: garfish (1); herring (2); shark (3); John Dory (4); lamprey (5); cod (6); ray (7); lumpsucker (8); eel (9); plaice (10). Both the eel and the lamprey spend part of their lives in fresh water.

New Zealand

India

United Kingdom

Canada

China

United States

Australia

USSR

Zimbabwe

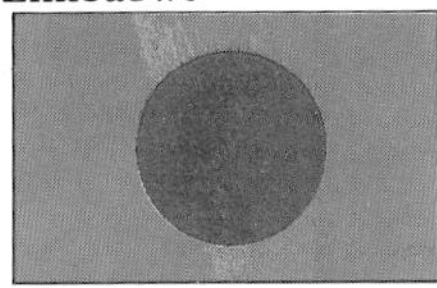
Bangladesh

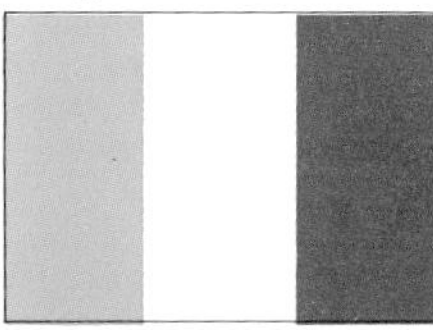
Italy

Brazil

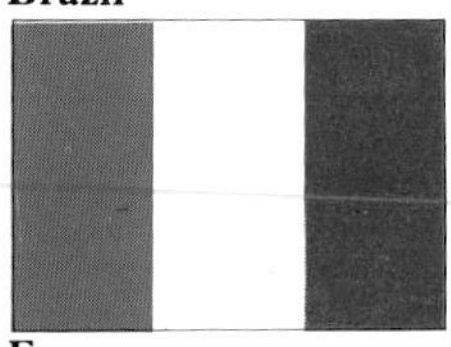
France

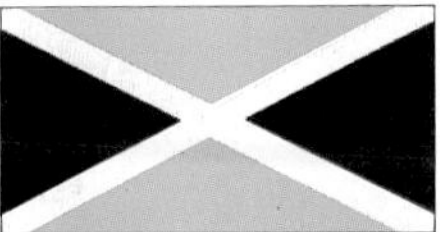
Jamaica

Denmark

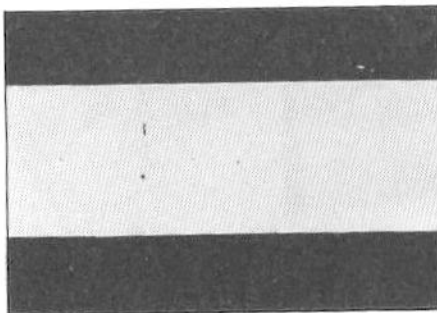
Spain

South Africa

Sweden

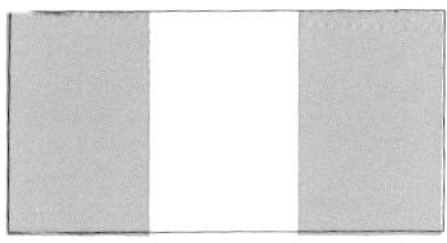
Nigeria

Israel

Japan

Trinidad

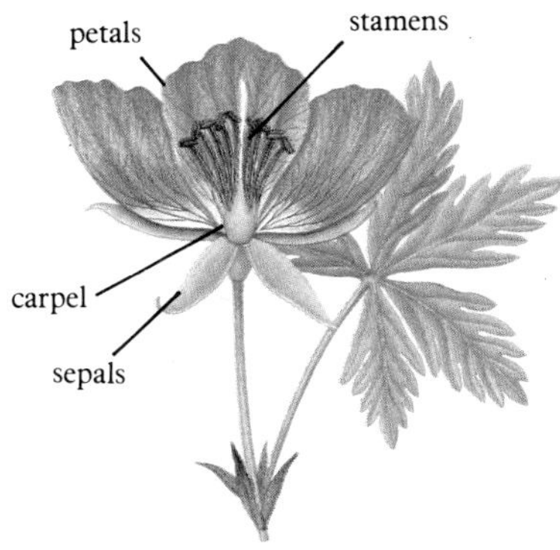

The parts of a flower.

Flower The reproductive part of seed-producing plants. A typical flower has a series of brightly coloured petals surrounded by a ring of leaf-like sepals. Inside the petals are the male, pollen-bearing stamens and, at the centre of the flower, the female carpel containing eggs.

Fluorine Pale yellow gas resembling chlorine. The most highly reactive of all gases, it is only found in nature in combination with other elements. Among these compounds (fluorides) is sodium fluoride which is added to drinking water to help prevent tooth decay. Chem. symbol F.

Fly A group of insects with only a single pair of wings. There are many species including fruit-flies, blue-bottles, house-flies and MOSQUITOES. Many feed and lay their eggs on dead animals or decaying plant matter and are liable to transmit diseases.

Flying fox Fruit-eating bats found in the tropics. They include the largest of all bats with a wingspan over one metre.

Flying phalanger Squirrel-like marsupials that can glide (but not fly) up to 30 metres from tree to tree. Found in Australia and New Guinea.

Flying squirrel Small squirrels able to glide (but not fly) from tree to tree. Found in the forests of western N America, India and Ceylon, and western Finland through northern Russia into Siberia.

Fog is caused by the condensation of water vapour in air that is chilled immediately above the ground. Fog is most frequent in autumn when on clear nights the land rapidly loses the heat it has gained during the day and chills the air lying above it. In coastal districts fog is often caused by warm, moist air from the sea passing over the colder land. The foggiest place in the world is Grand Banks off Newfoundland, where warm, moist air passing over the Gulf Stream meets the cold Labrador Current.

Food preservation Most food goes bad quickly unless we take steps to preserve it. The air is full of micro-organisms which settle on the food and begin to break it down. Chemical changes also take place inside the food, and it starts to go bad. Fortunately, there are ways of stopping or delaying this process. Preserving techniques include heat treatment, chilling, freezing, drying, curing, pickling, and the use of chemicals. Sterilization is a form of heat treatment in which the food is raised to a high temperature to kill any germs present. This is done in canning. Pasteurization is partial sterilization, using only a moderately high temperature to avoid spoiling the flavour of the food.

Football See **Association football, Rugby football**.

Force A force is something that acts to cause a change in motion. Force pushes and pulls. It starts, stops, or changes motion in some way. The force of gravity acts over vast distances to keep the planets in orbit around the Sun. Force is needed to keep a car or an aircraft moving at a constant speed because friction with the ground and the air act to slow them down. Force is measured in dynes.

Ford, Henry (1863–1947) American automobile manufacturer who used mass production to construct cheap cars. He founded the Ford Motor Company in 1903.

Forest More than 25 per cent of the world's land surface is forested. Coniferous forests reach across northern Asia, Europe and N America. To the south are the remnants of deciduous forests which have been largely cleared for farming or felled for timber. The other great forests are the tropical hardwoods of the Amazon basin, the Congo basin and SE Asia.

Fossil The remains or traces of plants and animals that lived long ago preserved in rocks. Fossilization can take place, for example, if an animal dies and is rapidly covered by mud. The soft parts decay but

Fossils can be dated from the rocks in which they are found. Trilobites crawled across the sea floor over 500 million years ago. Ammonites, molluscs with a coiled shell up to 2 metres across in some species, died out 65 million years ago. Protosuchus was a crocodile-like reptile living 225 million years ago. Fossilized bones enable scientists to reconstruct the original animal.

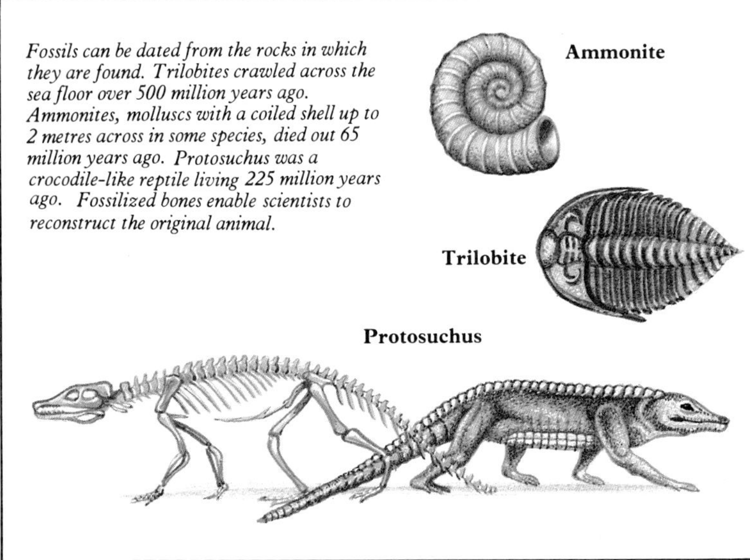

the bones are gradually replaced by minerals (they are petrified, or turned to stone) while the mud hardens to solid rock. From fossils, scientists have been able to build up a picture of the evolution of life on Earth.

Fox A long-legged, bushy-tailed carnivore belonging to the dog family found in many parts of the world. The red fox of Europe and N America is renowned for its cunning and some have adapted to life in cities. Others include the large-eared fennec fox of N Africa and the small-eared Arctic fox. The female is called a vixen.

Foxglove Several species of tall woodland plant with pinkish-purple tubular blooms arranged in long spikes. Foxgloves are poisonous plants but yield the valuable heart drug digitalis.

France A western European republic which held a world empire until the 1960s. The French Republic grew out of the French Revolution (1789), which ended thirteen hundred years of monarchy.

The country is an important EEC producer of cereals, root crops, dairy foods, wine and other goods, with more than half the population engaged in agriculture. Over one-quarter of the land is forested. Natural resources are used in the manufacture of, for example, cars.

France is mainly flat with a maritime climate in the north and west, and has higher regions and a Mediterranean climate in the south and east. Area: 547,000 km^2; Pop: 55,000,000; Cap: Paris.

Francis of Assissi, St (*c* 1182–1226) Born into a wealthy family he decided to lead a life of poverty, following the example of Jesus Christ. He founded the Franciscan Order of Friars and is supposed to have preached to animals.

Franklin, Benjamin (1706–90) American scientist and statesman. He conducted research into electricity and invented the lightning conductor. As one of the 'founding fathers' he took a leading role in the formation of the American constitution. He was also a successful diplomat, popular in both England and France.

Frederick II (The Great 1712–86) King of Prussia from 1740. A brilliant general, he seized Silesia from Maria Theresa of Austria and established Prussia as a great military power. With the first partition of Poland in 1772 he greatly increased the size of his own kingdom. He enjoyed music and poetry and promoted religious tolerance.

French Guiana (Guyane) Overseas dept. of France on NE coast of South America. Sugar-cane is the chief cash crop, gold and bauxite the chief minerals. Area: 91,000 km^2; Pop: 78,000; Cap: Cayenne.

French Revolution A political upheaval in France which began in 1789 with the storming of the Bastille (state prison) in Paris by a mob. The old regime in France was no longer able to govern the country properly, and the king was forced to consult representatives of the people. A new National Assembly was formed, which forced through drastic changes in French life and abolished the monarchy. King Louis XVI was accused of treason and executed in 1793. There followed the 'Reign of Terror' during which many aristocrats and counter-revolutionaries were sent to the guillotine. The motto of the Revolution was 'liberty, equality, fraternity'. After ten years of fierce revolutionary struggle and political experiment, Napoleon took charge of France, later becoming emperor.

Frequency The number of complete cycles of a wave motion that take place in a second. The alternating current (AC) in our homes has a frequency of 50 cycles per second or 50 hertz (50 Hz). The hertz is a unit equal to one cycle per second. Radio waves have a much higher frequency, and light waves much higher still. The higher the frequency, the shorter the length of each wave.

Freud, Sigmund (1856–1939) Austrian psychiatrist who founded psychoanalysis. He promoted the idea of each person having both a conscious and a subconscious mind. He believed that emotional problems could be traced back to events in infancy. His ideas were bitterly opposed at the time but have had a tremendous influence on modern thought.

Friction always happens when two things rub together. Smooth objects cause less friction than rough objects. Rolling objects cause less friction than sliding objects. If two things rub together they cause heat, as when we rub our hands together. When we want to slow something down, we apply more friction, as in the brakes on bicycles and cars.

Frog Tailless amphibian with long hind legs used for jumping and swimming. Frogs belong to the same group as toads, the main difference between them being that frogs have smooth skins and toads have rough ones. Some frogs and toads live almost permanently in water. But the majority live mostly on land, returning to the water to lay their eggs. These hatch into tadpoles: tiny legless larvae with tails, and gills with which they can breathe. Gradually the tadpoles develop legs and lungs, lose their tails and gills and leave the water.

Front In meteorology, the boundary between air masses of different characteristics. A warm front is the boundary between cold air and a following warm air mass. It can bring drizzle and steady rain. A cold front is the reverse and it can bring showers and blustery weather. Fronts are associated with DEPRESSIONS.

Frost Frozen moisture that forms on solid objects when the temperature falls to 0°C or below. The term is also used for air temperature at or below freezing point (degrees of frost).

Fruit The seed-containing body of flowering plants, formed by the ovary. There are many different types of fruit. Some are dry, such as nuts, the winged fruit of sycamores, or the ripe pods of peas. Others are fleshy, like plums and berries.

Fry, Elizabeth (1780–1845) Prison reformer who devoted her life to campaigning against the horrors of prison life at that time. She was even invited to tour the prisons of many European countries and later most of her suggestions for improvement were carried out.

Fuel cell A device that turns chemical energy into electrical energy. For many years scientists have been trying to improve the fuel cell so that it can replace the heavy electric battery for powering motor cars and other applications. High efficiencies are possible, but so far the ideal fuel cell has not been produced. However, it was the fuel cell that provided the on-board power for the American Apollo space programme.

Most fuel cells consist of two metal plates surrounded by fuel which may be solid, liquid, or gas. The fuel, which can be hydrogen or hydrocarbon, is fed in and ignited. A complex chemical reaction takes place between the molecules of the plates and the fuel, giving an electric voltage between the plates.

Fulmar A sea bird related to the shearwater. The fulmar is a grey and white bird which nests in colonies on rocky sea cliffs. It is a superb flier.

Fungus Member of a large group of flowerless plants that contains the MUSHROOMS, MOULDS and YEASTS among many others. Fungi have no leaves and are unable to make their own food. Instead, a mass of fine threads, called hyphae, spread over material such as dead plant matter and absorb nourishment from it. The mushrooms and toadstools that we actually see are the reproductive parts of the fungi – the fruiting bodies, usually produced only at certain times of the year.

Funnel-web spider Tropical spiders, known also as grass spiders, that spin sheet webs in long grass. At the back of the web is a funnel. The spider sits at the bottom and when a victim lands on the nest, it is quickly pulled down to its death. The Australian funnel-web spider can give humans a dangerous, but not deadly, bite.

Fuse A safety device in an electric circuit. If there is a fault in an electric circuit the current can rise and wires can become red hot, perhaps causing a fire. All circuits should have fuses to prevent this happening. A fuse is usually a piece of wire that melts easily. If the current rises too high, the fuse melts and breaks the circuit.

Fusion, nuclear A process in which different kinds of hydrogen atoms are forced to join together, or fuse. When this happens, huge amounts of energy are released, as in the hydrogen bomb. Scientists have not yet been able to harness nuclear fusion as a means of producing vast amounts of useful energy. Nuclear fusion is the process that gives the Sun its light and heat.

In the core of the Sun four atoms of hydrogen fuse to form one atom of helium, releasing enormous amounts of energy in the process.

G

Gabon Republic in West Africa on the Atlantic coast. Over 75% of the country is covered by equatorial rain forest. Agriculture employs the majority of the population and forestry is the main industry. Area: 268,000 km^2; Pop: 958,000; Cap: Libreville.

Gagarin, Yuri (1934–68) Soviet cosmonaut who in *Vostok I* was the first man to make an orbital flight of the Earth (April 12, 1961). He was killed in a plane crash.

Gainsborough, Thomas (1727–1788) British landscape and portrait painter who worked in oils. His portraits are famed for their grace and refinement. Among his best-known paintings are the portraits *The Blue Boy* and *Mrs Siddons* and the landscape *The Harvest Wagon*.

Galapagos Islands Group of islands in the Pacific Ocean. The islands belong to Ecuador and have a unique collection of plants and animals, made famous by Darwin. The most spectacular of these is the giant tortoise.

Galaxy A collection of stars held together by gravity. The Sun and its family of planets belong to the Milky Way galaxy, together with about 100,000 million other stars. Some galaxies are elliptical in shape; others, including the Milky Way, have spiral arms. Galaxies are separated by millions of light years of empty space.

Galileo (1564–1642) Italian astronomer and physicist who investigated natural laws by conducting practical experiments. He built the first astronomical telescope and his discoveries confirmed the theory of Copernicus that the Earth and other planets circle the Sun. His views were opposed by the Church and he spent the last eight years of his life under house arrest.

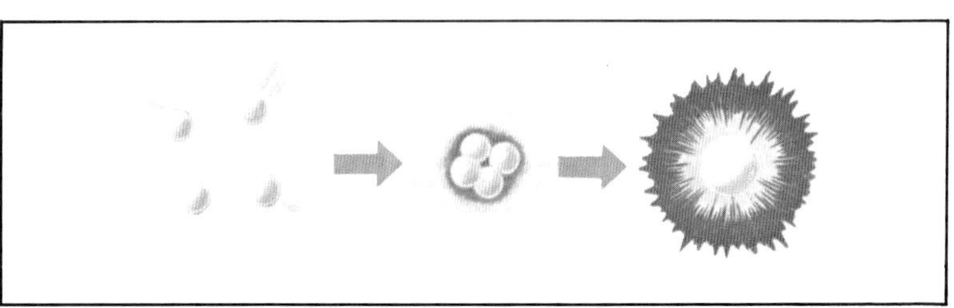

1 

2 

3 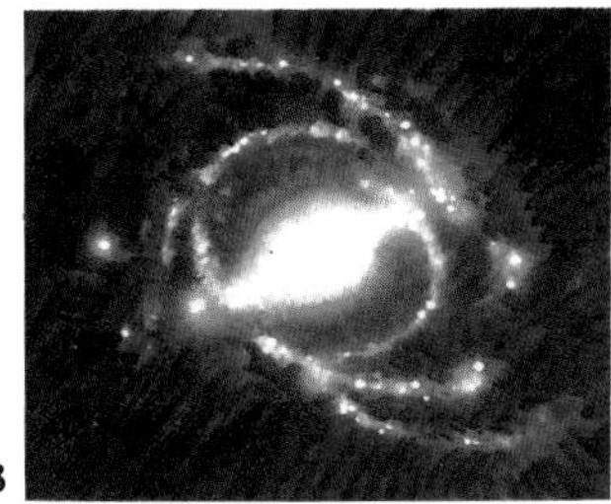

Galaxies take different shapes including elliptical (1), spiral (2) or barred spiral (3) forms.

Gall Abnormal growth of a plant caused by certain insects, mites or fungi. The oak-apple is a common example: it is caused by a gall wasp.

Galvani, Luigi (1737–98) Italian physiologist who conducted early experiments in electricity. He used frogs to demonstrate the theory of 'animal electricity'.

Gambia, The Republic in West Africa on the Atlantic coast, consisting of a strip of land on either side of the Gambia R. The economy is based on agriculture, with groundnuts and rice being the main crops. Area: 11,000 km^2; Pop: 725,000; Cap: Banjul.

Gandhi, Mohandas (1869–1948) Indian leader and moral teacher who was known as the Mahatma or 'great soul'. He worked vigorously for Indian independence from Britain. He advocated peaceful disobedience and was himself imprisoned several times. After independence he encouraged the peaceful integration of all Indians but was assassinated by a Hindu fanatic.

Ganges River in Asia, flowing from the Himalayas through India and Bangladesh into the Bay of Bengal which it enters through a massive delta. The Ganges is sacred to the Hindus. Length: 2400 km.

Gannet Sea bird which fishes spectacularly by diving into the water from the air. The gannet is a large bird, almost completely white save for dark wing tips and a yellowish patch on the head. Colonies of gannets nest on rocky cliffs.

Garibaldi, Giuseppe (1807–82) Italian patriot who created a unified Italy. He was forced to flee Italy on several occasions after unsuccessful plots, but in 1860 he conquered both Sicily and Naples with only 1000 men. Victor Emmanuel was proclaimed the first king of Italy in 1860.

Gas Gas is one of the three states of matter. The other two are LIQUID and SOLID. If some gas is placed in a container, it spreads out to entirely fill the container. If the temperature of a gas is lowered beyond a certain point it will become a liquid. If the temperature is lowered still further, the liquid becomes a solid.

Gas, natural See **Natural gas**.

Gas turbine An efficient kind of engine, usually called a 'jet engine'. A shaft carries two groups of fans – compressor fans and turbine fans. Air is sucked in by the compressor and its pressure increased. Then the air is mixed with fuel and ignited. This produces expanding hot gases which escape at high speed from the engine's exhaust, creating thrust. Before the gases escape they spin the blades of the turbine which drive the compressor.

Turbojet

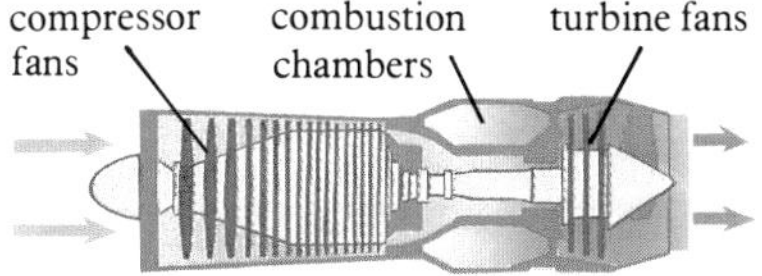

Gastropods Group of molluscs that includes slugs, snails, limpets and whelks. Many live in the sea, though there are freshwater and land forms; and most possess a single, often coiled shell.

Gauguin, Paul (1848–1903) French painter who spent the latter years of his life in Tahiti. He is remembered for his brightly coloured canvases.

Gazelle Dainty little antelope with lyre-shaped horns, found in Africa and Asia. The females have only short spikes or no horns at all. Grant's and Thomson's gazelles are the best known.

Gecko Lizards famed for their ability to climb and cling to smooth vertical surfaces thanks to small hooks on the toes. They vary from 2.5 to 35 cm in length.

Geiger counter An instrument for detecting and measuring RADIOACTIVITY. It contains a tube of gas with a wire inside it. As the radioactive particles pass through the gas they knock electrons from the gas atoms. These electrons travel to the wire and give a signal that is recorded on a meter or heard as a series of clicks from a loudspeaker.

Generator A machine that turns mechanical energy into electricity. The mechanical energy comes from some kind of engine or turbine, usually powered by coal, oil or falling water. A generator produces electricity because an electric current is generated in a loop of wire when it is rotated in a magnetic field. Large generators have many loops of wire which rotate on a shaft between powerful electromagnets. A motor is the opposite of a generator. It turns electricity into mechanical energy.

Genetics The study of the genes and the role they play in protein production and heredity (the inheritance of characteristics from parents by young). See DNA.

Geneva Capital of Geneva canton, Switzerland, situated on L. Geneva at exit point of R. Rhône. Major centre of jewellery and watch industries and popular tourist resort. Pop: 150,000.

Genghis Khan (*c* 1162–1227) Great Mongol leader whose vast empire included most of central Asia and part of SE Europe. He was a ruthless conqueror and his armies left a trail of destruction wherever they went.

Geography The study of the Earth's surface. It includes landforms, climates, plants and animals, mineral resources, and the way people live in different parts of the world.

Geology The study of the structure of the Earth, its rocks and surface features.

Geometry The branch of mathematics which deals with lines, angles, points, shapes, and surfaces.

George III (1738–1820) King of Great Britain from 1760. Though well-intentioned, he was politically inept. His choice of Lord North as Prime Minister (1770–82) contributed to the loss of the American colonies. His reign was marked by the Industrial and Agrarian revolutions, as well as by prolonged wars with France. By 1811 he had become virtually insane and a regency under the future George IV was established.

German Democratic Republic Country in NW Europe. A Communist state, it is usually called East Germany to distinguish it from its neighbour, the German Federal Republic (West Germany). East Germany is mostly flat country, broken by ranges of hills. Chief crops are cereals, potatoes and root crops. Metal-working, chemicals, iron and steel are the main industries.

The eastern part of Germany was conquered by the Russians during World War II and has remained in the Communist bloc since 1945. Half of the capital Berlin belongs to West Germany even though it is in the East. Area: 108,207 km^2; Pop: 16,718,000; Cap: East Berlin.

German Federal Republic Country in NW Europe often known as West Germany. To the east is the German Democratic Republic (East Germany). Northern Germany is a flat plain; the south has forests and mountains. To the west are the industrial regions of the Ruhr and the Saar. Among the crops grown are cereals, sugar beet and vines, while minerals include coal and iron ore. West Germany is a prosperous industrial country, with chemicals, electronics, engineering, machine tools and vehicles among its industrial products.

The Federal Republic came into being in 1949, four years after the defeat of Nazi Germany in World War II. It was a founder member of the EEC and is one of the most successful countries of post-war Europe. Area: 248,642 km^2; Pop: 61,387,000; Cap: Bonn.

Germination The early growth of a seed

that results in a new plant. The process requires moisture and warmth. First the seed swells up with water until the seed-coat bursts open. Then a root, or radicle, emerges and grows downwards into the soil. Finally the young shoot, or plumule, begins to grow upwards towards the light.

Geyser A spout of steam and hot water from the ground. Geysers and hot springs occur in volcanic regions where water is heated in subterranean rock chambers and periodically escapes through a surface vent. Geysers are found in New Zealand, Yellowstone Park, USA, and Iceland. The name derives from the Icelandic Geysir.

Ghana Country in W Africa, formerly called the Gold Coast. Ghana's farmers grow cocoa, the chief export, coffee, bananas, rubber and fruit. In the north livestock are reared. Area: 238,598 km²; Pop: 13,804,000; Cap: Accra.

Giant panda See **Panda**.

Gibbon The smallest and most agile of the apes. About one metre high, they have very long arms on which they swing rapidly through the trees. They live in the forests of SE Asia and feed mainly on fruit.

Gibraltar The Rock of Gibraltar is a peninsula jutting out from Spain commanding the entrance to the Mediterranean. Captured by Britain in 1704, it has remained a British possession since that date. Area: 6 km²; Pop: 26,500.

Gila monster Large poisonous lizard of SW United States. Its vibrant black and orange colouring gives fair warning of its venom.

Gill Structure by which many aquatic animals are able to breathe in water. Fishes have internal plates of gills at the side of the head. The gills are well supplied with blood and, as water passes over them, oxygen passes easily from the water into the blood. Other animals, including various young insects and young tadpoles, have feathery external gills.

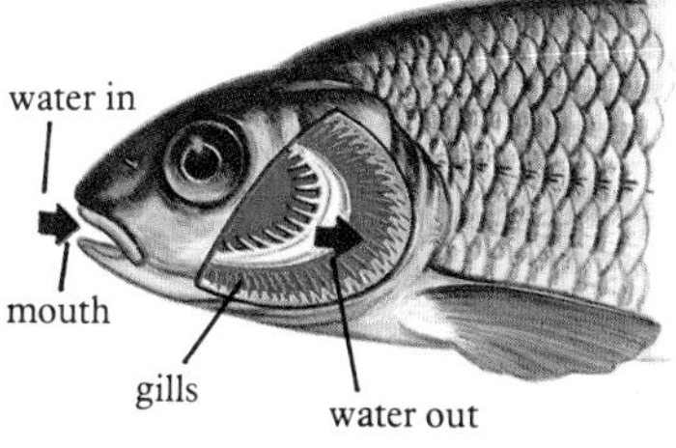

Ginkgo A deciduous tree native to China also called the maidenhair tree, and the only living representative of a group of trees that flourished millions of years ago. The leaves are heart-shaped and male and female flowers are borne on separate trees.

Giotto di Bondone (1266–1337) Florentine artist and sculptor who started a more realistic approach to painting by the study of nature.

Giraffe Hoofed African mammal and tallest animal in the world, able to browse on the savanna tree tops that no other animal can reach. Males may reach 5.5 metres in height.

Glacier A 'river' of ice that flows down a valley from a snowcap or mountain snowfield. Rock debris frozen in the ice enables a glacier to deepen and smooth its valley into a U-shape. There are many U-shaped valleys in Europe and North America created by glaciers which have long since melted.

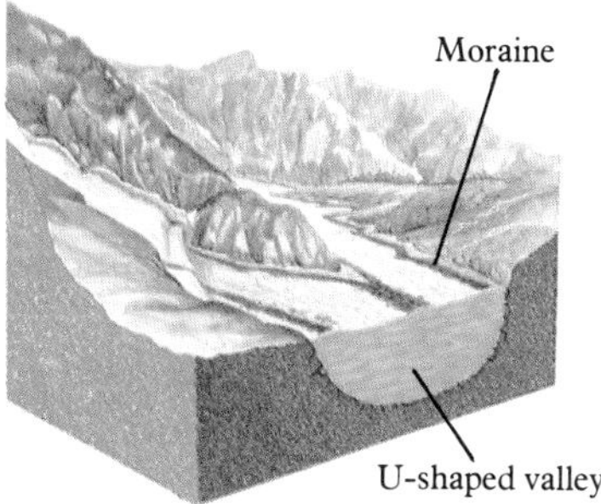

Valley glaciers in mountainous regions transport loose rock called moraine.

Gladstone, William Ewart (1809–98) British Liberal statesman who became prime minister four times. He supported Free Trade and Home Rule for Ireland.

Gland An organ which produces certain substances and passes them out into the body. Some glands, such as sweat glands in the skin and digestive glands in the gut, have ducts through which the substances pass. These glands are called exocrine glands and their products are known as secretions. Other glands, called endocrine glands, have no ducts but pass their products directly into the blood. Their products act like chemical messengers, and are called HORMONES.

Glasgow Capital city of Strathclyde region of Scotland. Situated on R. Clyde, it is a thriving port and was formerly a major shipbuilding centre. Important for manufacture of metal goods, textiles, printing and more recently micro-electronics. Its notorious slums have largely disappeared. Pop: 763,000.

Glass Sand, lime and soda are the basic ingredients of glass. These three simple materials are mixed in the right proportions and heated in a furnace until they become a thick, sticky liquid. This molten glass can then be made into almost any shape before it cools to become the hard, brittle material we see in windows, bottles, mirrors and glasses. Special strong glass can be made by adding other materials such as borax. Lead and potash are added to make LENSES.

Glow-worm Beetle related to the fireflies of southern Europe. The male has wings, but the wingless female spends her life on the ground. It is she who is the 'glow-worm', for she can give out a light to attract passing males.

Gluck, Christoph Willibald (1714–87) German operatic composer. Among his best known works are *Orfeo ed Euridice*, *Alceste* and *Iphigénie en Tauride*.

Glue A substance for sticking things together, often made from bones, skin, and other parts of animals. Heating these waste parts in water breaks down a protein called collagen and turns it into a clear solution. When this cools it is either glue or gelatin, depending on its purity. Other adhesives, often called glues, are gums, cements and epoxies.

Gnu Large, ungainly antelope of eastern and southern Africa, also known as wildebeest.

Gnu

Goat Horned ruminants related to sheep. Wild goats range from S Europe and NW Africa to Asia. All are expert climbers and feed on almost any vegetable matter from grass to the bark and leaves of trees. Male, or billy, goats have beards.

Gobi Vast desert region of Mongolia and China. Mainly scrubland with stony and sandy deserts and few oases. Inhabited by Mongol nomads. Area: 1,300,000 km^2.

Goethe, Johann Wolfgang von (1749–1832) One of Germany's greatest poets and dramatists. He won early recognition with his drama *Götz von Berlichingen* and his novel *The Sorrows of Young Werther*. *Egmont* is one of his best known plays, and *Wilhelm Meister's Apprenticeship* one of his most famous novels. In 1808, the first part of Goethe's great dramatic poem and life-work, *Faust*, was published. It was completed just before his death in 1832.

Gogh, Vincent van (1853–90) Dutch painter whose artistic career lasted only 10 years (1880–90). He led a life of poverty and suffered from periods of insanity before committing suicide. His work was as intense as his own character. He produced over 700 drawings and 800 oil paintings, but only one was sold during his lifetime.

Gold One of the precious metals, gold resists corrosion by most chemicals and has been highly prized throughout history. Normally alloyed with silver or copper for extra strength, it has been used since earliest times in jewellery and coinage. Today gold has many industrial uses. It is particularly important in the electronics industry because it is a superb conductor of electricity. Chem. symbol Au (from Latin *Aurum*).

Goldfish Ornamental fish of carp family derived from a plain Chinese ancestor. Bred in an immense array of varieties. In captivity they can live up to 25 years.

Goldsmith, Oliver (1728–74) Irish poet, novelist and dramatist best known for his play *She Stoops to Conquer* and the novel *The Vicar of Wakefield*.

Golf Game played by hitting a small ball with a stick called a club. The object of the game is to hit the ball around a course of up to 18 holes. At each hole, the golfer must try to hit his ball from the start point or 'tee' along the open fairway. His score for the round is the total number of shots needed for all 18 holes.

Goose Large birds related to ducks and swans. They have webbed feet and swim well, though they rarely dive. Geese often live in large flocks and make long migratory flights, flying in V-formations called skeins.

Gorilla The most massive of the apes, gorillas weigh about 200 kg and may stand nearly two metres high. Family groups lead a peaceful nomadic life in the rain forests of central Africa, feeding on fruit and leaves. See picture on page 149.

Gorki, Maxim (1868–1936) Russian writer with revolutionary views who spent long periods in exile. He wrote short stories and novels such as *Foma Gordeyev* and *Mother*. His most famous play is *The Lower Depths*. When he returned to Russia in 1928 he was hailed a national hero.

Gounod, Charles (1818–93) French composer whose opera *Faust* was for many years one of the most successful ever. Others include *Romeo and Juliet* and *Mireille*. He also composed widely for the Church and in other forms of music.

Government System for running a country. In a democracy, the people govern themselves by electing representatives to a PARLIAMENT or congress. In a dictatorship, a single strong leader rules, usually harshly. In countries with more than one POLITICAL PARTY, the party winning most votes in an election forms the government. In Communist states, however, only one party (the Communist) is allowed. Monarchy was the most common form of government in the past, but most countries today are republics, with a president as head of state.

Goya, Francisco José de (1746–1828) Famous Spanish artist, court painter and engraver whose works include a portrait of the Duchess of Alba, satirical etchings and caricatures.

Grammar In its simplest form, the rules of language, describing how LANGUAGE is organized for writing and speaking. Grammar describes such things as sentence structure, parts of speech (noun, verb, adjective, adverb and so on), and correct usage. The oldest known grammar describes the language called Sanskrit, and is 2500 years old.

Grand Canyon One of the world's natural wonders in NW Arizona, USA. Cut by Colorado R., the gorge is over 1.5 km deep and varies in width from 6 to 30 km. Spectacular colour-changes, as the sunlight strikes the multicoloured banded rock layers, make it a major tourist attraction.

Granite A hard igneous rock with large crystals formed by the slow cooling of magma beneath the surface of the Earth.

Grape Smooth-skinned, juicy fruit borne in bunches in woody vines. Since ancient times grapes have been eaten fresh and dried (sultanas, raisins, currants), and fermented to produce wine.

Graph Graphs are a way of showing how numbers and amounts compare. There are different kinds of graph. *Pie charts* are circle graphs cut into segments like slices of a pie. Various sized slices represent different fractions of the whole. *Bar graphs* show different numbers or amounts as long or short bars. *Line graphs* are the commonest kind. They show changes by a line that rises and falls as whatever is being measured rises and falls.

Grass The grasses form one of the largest families of the flowering plants. They have long thin leaves and tiny green flowers without petals that grow in spikes. Grasses grow almost everywhere. They include cereals such as wheat, barley, oats and rice.

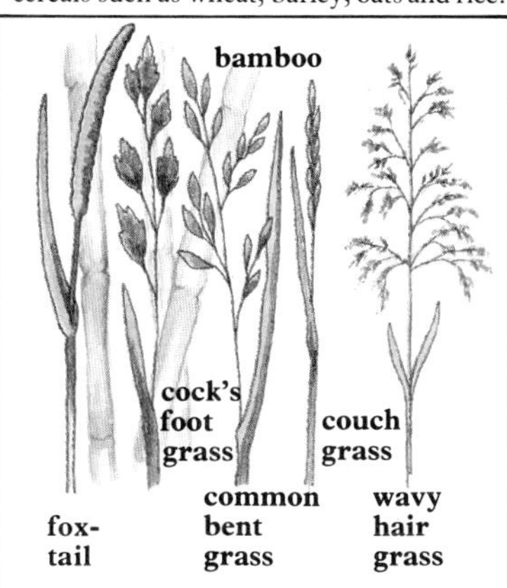

Grasshopper A group of jumping insects related to crickets and locusts, with long, powerful hind legs. Some of them can fly. Grasshoppers are active on warm, sunny days and are noted for their 'song' (called stridulation) which they produce by rubbing their hind legs against their wings.

Grass snake A snake found in damp places over most of Europe except the extreme north and Ireland. It is about 1 metre long and usually has distinct yellow and black markings on the neck. It is not poisonous but hisses and pretends to strike if cornered.

Gravitation The force that attracts any two bodies towards each other. Newton's law of gravitation says that any two objects are pulled towards each other with a force that is directly proportional to the product of their masses and inversely proportional to the distance between them. In other words, the more massive they are and the closer they are, the more strongly they are pulled together.

Great Barrier Reef Largest coral reef in the world extending some 2000 km along the NE coast of Australia, its distance from the shore varying between 8 km in the north and 240 km in the south.

Great Dividing Range Mountain range in eastern Australia running almost the entire length of the continent, from Queensland to Victoria. Highest point is Mt Koskiusko (2230 metres) in the Snowy Mts.

Great Lakes A group of five lakes in North America: Superior, Michigan, Ontario, Huron and Erie. The lakes are interconnected and linked to the Atlantic via the St Lawrence Seaway. They are badly polluted, and frozen throughout the winter.

Grebe Water bird similar to diver or loon. Grebes have boldly marked heads with ear tufts and crests. In the the mating season they perform a spectacular courtship dance, rushing to and fro across the surface of the water in an almost upright position.

Greco, El (*c.* 1541–1614) Spanish-Cretan painter whose original and brightly coloured works aroused much criticism among the Spanish religious authorities.

Greece Country on the Mediterranean coast of SE Europe, consisting of many islands and the southern part of the Balkan Peninsula. Most of the land is mountainous. Greece has a warm sunny climate and is visited by millions of tourists each year. Most of the Greek people live by farming, growing fruit, vines, olives, tobacco and wheat.

Greece has a long and splendid history, with great civilizations in Crete and on the mainland, where much of Western culture was born. Area: 131,979 km²; Pop: 9,984,000; Cap: Athens.

Greece, Ancient An early civilization of the Mediterranean region, at its height during the 'Classical' period in the fifth and fourth centuries BC. The ancient Greeks were the founders of European civilization, which was greatly influenced by Greek ideas on human life, law and government, art and architecture. Ancient Greece was divided into city-states, which sometimes had democratic governments (but also slavery). The leadership of Athens in the fight against Persian invaders made her the dominant state in the Classical period. Some of the finest works of Classical Athens – the Parthenon and other temples – can still be seen. After the conquests of Alexander the Great (356–323 BC), Greek culture was spread throughout a large empire, and was later taken all over Europe by the Romans.

Greenland Large island NE of North America. It is a self-governing part of the Danish Kingdom, inhabited mainly by Eskimos in coastal settlements. Most of the island lies within the Arctic Circle and is permanently ice-bound. Area; 2,175,600 km²; Pop; 50,000; Cap: Godthaab.

Grieg, Edvard (1843–1907) Norwegian composer who used folk songs of his native country as a basis for many of his works. Among his compositions are the Piano concerto in A Minor, the *Peer Gynt* suites and the *Lyric Pieces* for piano.

Grimm, the brothers **Jakob Ludwig** (1785–1863) and **Wilhelm Karl** (1786–1859) Famed for their *Fairy Tales* they were also able philologists. Jakob was responsible for the philological dictionary *German Grammar* and together they began a German dictionary in 1854 which was only completed in 1961.

Grouse Game birds, often reared on moors specifically for shooting. Grouse are stout birds which spend most of their time on the ground, only taking wing when alarmed. The red grouse and black grouse are common moorland species.

Guatemala Republic in Central America with coasts on both the Pacific and the Caribbean. The landscape varies from

Ancient Greece, especially Athens, saw a great flowering of art, architecture, literature and, above all, philosophy.

coastal plains to the mountainous areas of the interior which contain a number of active volcanoes. The economy is based on agriculture; coffee is an important cash crop and accounts for half of the country's exports. Area: 109,000 km^2; Pop: 8,077,000; Cap: Guatemala City.

Guillemot A seabird belonging to the auk family. The guillemot is a true ocean-dweller, seldom coming ashore except to breed. It is a dark-brown bird with a white breast, has webbed feet, and swims and dives with ease to catch fishes.

Guinea Republic in West Africa on the Atlantic coast. Coffee, bananas and pineapples are the main agricultural exports. Area: 246,000 km^2; Pop: 5,579,000; Cap: Conakry.

Guinea-Bissau Republic on Atlantic coast of W Africa. The economy is based on agriculture with rice grown in the wet coastlands, and groundnuts and some cattle farming in the interior. Area: 36,000 km^2; Pop: 843,000; Cap: Bissau.

Guinea pig Domesticated rodent related to S American cavy. Kept as pets and for scientific experiments.

Guitar Stringed instrument, played by plucking the strings with the fingers. The classical Spanish guitar has six strings. The folk guitar has 12 strings. The guitar's tone comes from its hollow wooden body. The electric guitar, however, has a solid body. The vibrations of its steel strings are amplified (increased) electronically and put out through a LOUDSPEAKER. Guitars were first made in the 13th century.

Gulf Stream A warm ocean current issuing from the Gulf of Mexico and flowing NE through the Atlantic. As the North Atlantic Drift it reaches the shores of Europe and brings mild winters to coastal lands.

Gull A group of medium to large seabirds with black, grey and white plumages. They are familiar birds of the seashore, uttering raucous cries as they squabble for scraps of food. Gulls are scavengers and are commonly found near human habitation in search of easy pickings.

Gun The word 'gun' is usually applied to all kinds of firearms from small pistols to giant artillery. Small-arms all work in more or less the same way. They have a barrel with a closed 'breech' at one end. A cartridge is placed in the breech and fired by pressing a trigger. The trigger releases a

Nine positions which the gymnast must attain to develop the required mobility and strength in: back and shoulders (1), back and stomach (2,3), hips and legs (4,5,6), shoulders and legs (7,8) and for elevation (9).

firing pin, which strikes the base of the cartridge and explodes a percussion cap. This fires the explosive in the cartridge, producing a large amount of expanding gas. The gas propels a bullet or lead pellets at high speed. Most guns have a rifled barrel which makes the bullet spin and keep on a straight course when it leaves the barrel.

Gunpowder An explosive made from saltpetre, sulphur, and carbon. Invented by the ancient Chinese, gunpowder was unknown in the western world until the 13th century.

Gunpowder Plot An attempt by GUY FAWKES and a group of English Roman Catholics to blow up the Houses of Parliament, in 1605.

Gutenberg, Johann (1397–1468) German printer who is believed to be the first European to print with movable type. The first book to be printed in his shop at Mainz was the *Mazarin Bible* (1456).

Guyana Republic in N South America. The landscape varies from the low-lying, humid coastal region, in which the population is concentrated, to the densely forested highlands of the interior. There are considerable deposits of bauxite which, together with sugar, make up the main exports. Area: 215,000 km^2; Pop: 794,000; Cap: Georgetown.

Gymnastics Sport in which competitors perform acrobatic movements using the floor and various pieces of apparatus (such as bars, rings, and vaulting horses). Points are awarded according to skill and the difficulty of the movement attempted. Gymnastics developed from the rather boring 'keep fit' drill movements taught in the 19th century, and is now an Olympic Games event. The various pieces of apparatus call for agility, strength and grace from the gymnast.

Gypsy Gypsies are nomadic (travelling) people, originally from northern India and wrongly supposed to have come from Egypt. They speak a language called Romany.

Gyroscope A gyroscope consists of a wheel that spins inside a frame, rather like a bicycle wheel. Once the wheel is spinning, the axle of the wheel always stays pointing in the same direction. A gyroscope can therefore be used as a compass. Gyroscopes are used to steer aircraft, ships, rockets and torpedoes.

H

Haddock A marine fish belonging to the cod group and easily recognizable by the large black spot above the pectoral fin. It can grow up to one metre long, though it is generally somewhat shorter. Haddock live close to the sea bed up to depths of 200 metres.

Hades (Pluto) Greek god of the underworld. He abducted Persephone, the daughter of DEMETER, and made her his queen. The name Hades (now synonymous with the underworld) was too fearsome to be spoken so the god was called Pluto. (Roman equivalent Dis.)

Hadrian (AD 76–138) Roman emperor who proved to be an able general and administrator. He suppressed revolts in Palestine and visited Britain in *c* AD 121. He had a great wall built between Bowness-on-Solway and Wallsend-on-Tyne to keep out the N British tribes.

Hadrian

Hagfish A primitive fish with an eel-like body and a sucking mouth with no jaws. A series of barbels surround the mouth and nostrils. Hagfishes live close to the sea bed, up to 2000 metres deep. They are blind but have a good sense of smell.

Hague, The City and seat of government, Netherlands, situated 3 km from the North Sea. Site of International Court of Justice. Pop: 465,000.

Haiti Republic in West Indies occupying the western third of the island of Hispaniola. The economy is based largely on agriculture with coffee accounting for almost half the nation's exports. Area:

28,000 km²; Pop: 5,654,000; Cap: Port-au-Prince.

Hake A marine fish belonging to the cod group. It is a fierce hunter in coastal waters, living during the day near the sea bed and rising closer to the surface at night to hunt fishes such as herrings, mackerel and sprats. It grows up to one metre long.

Halibut The giant of the flatfishes, growing up to three metres long. It is less flattened than many of the flatfishes. It lives at depths of up to 400 metres and feeds on small fishes. Halibut live up to 50 years.

Halloween Festival celebrated on October 31, the eve of All Saints' Day. Once a pagan celebration before the beginning of winter, it is still associated with ghosts, witches and weird events.

Hals, Franz (1580–1666) Dutch painter who is best known for his vividly life-like portraits and in particular for *The Laughing Cavalier*.

Hamburg Largest seaport and industrial centre, and second largest city in West Germany. Historic trading centre and a founder member of the Hanseatic League. Badly damaged by Allied bombing in World War II. Pop: 1,645,000.

Hamster Short-tailed rodent, considered a pest in the wild but popular as a pet.

Handball Two forms of game. The first is a court game, in which the player hits a ball with the hand – a version being 'fives'. The other handball, usually called team handball, has rules similar to those of Association football, except that the ball is caught, thrown or punched (and not kicked). The goalkeeper is the only player allowed to kick the ball. Team handball is played on an outdoor soccer pitch in summer, but indoors on a smaller pitch in winter.

Handel, George Frederick (1685–1759) Prolific German-born composer who, in 1726, became a British subject and spent most of his working life in England. Handel wrote over 40 operas including *Atlanta* and *Serse* and 32 oratorios such as the *Messiah* and *Israel in Egypt*. He also composed organ and orchestral music, including the popular *Water Music*. Handel, blind for the last eight years of his life, is buried in Westminster Abbey.

Hannibal (247–182 BC) Carthaginian general who conquered southern Spain and then led his army and elephants of war across the Alps. He won a series of brilliant victories against the Romans including the battle of Cannae (216 BC). He lacked the support to take Rome and was recalled to defend Carthage. He was defeated at Zama (202 BC) and later took poison to avoid capture by the Romans.

Hanoi Port and capital city of Vietnam on the Red River. Former capital of French Indo-China. Pop: 2,000,000.

Hapsburg or **Habsburg** Formerly one of the most powerful ruling houses of Europe. The Hapsburgs ruled in Austria from 1282–1918 and were crowned Holy Roman Emperors almost continuously from 1273–1806. Their policy of acquiring territory through brilliant marriage alliances rather than through war proved extremely successful. Some of the most famous members include Maximilian I, Charles V and Marie Antoinette.

Hardy, Thomas (1840–1928) English novelist and poet who first trained to be an architect. His novels include *Far from the Madding Crowd*, *Tess of the D'Urbervilles*, *The Mayor of Casterbridge* and *Jude the Obscure*.

Hare A mammal closely related to the rabbit but easily distinguished by its long hind legs and ears. The brown hare lives in open grassy country, resting by day in a **form** – an area of flattened grass. Brown hares are solitary animals except in spring, when they rush around in groups or stand up and 'box' with one another.

Brown hare

Harold, King (1022–66) Son of Earl Godwin, he was named heir to the throne of England by Edward the Confessor. He defeated his brother Tostig and Harold III of Norway at Stamford Bridge but at the battle of Hastings (1066) he was himself defeated by William (the Conqueror), Duke of Normandy.

Harp Musical instrument known since ancient Greece and with many local forms throughout the world. The harp is played in a sitting position, the player using both hands to vibrate the strings. Harps with a single rank of strings are easier to play than the three-ranked kind. The harpist may also use foot pedals.

Harpies In Greek legend terrifying monsters whose bodies were half woman and half bird.

Harrier Birds of prey belonging to the hawk family, with long slender wings and a graceful flight. They can usually be seen flying low over open country in search of small animals.

Hartebeest Common S African antelope with short horns and bulky body.

Harvestman Eight-legged relative of the spiders with rounded body. Known as daddy-long-legs.

Harvest mouse A tiny mouse measuring six cm in length and weighing only six grams. It makes its home in long grass, building a nest around the stems. Harvest mice are found in most parts of the world.

Harvey, William (1578–1657) English physiologist who discovered the circulation of blood. He acted as physician to James I and Charles I, and in 1628 his thesis on circulation was published.

Hastings, Battle of (1066) The battle which brought William, duke of Normandy, the English crown. The Normans under his command invaded England and were met near Hastings by the English army under Harold, whom most Englishmen accepted as king. Harold was killed in the battle, and William the Conqueror went on to vanquish all England.

Hawaii A group of 132 volcanic islands in the central Pacific Ocean, Hawaii became the USA's 50th state in 1959. Tourism is a major activity. Processed foods are the chief manufactures. Area: 16,706 km^2; Pop: 965,000; Cap: Honolulu.

Hawk moth Stout, fast-flying moths, most of which fly at night. One of the largest and best-known species is the death's head, which has a skull-like mark on its thorax, just behind the head.

Haydn, Franz Joseph (1732–1809) Austrian composer who is known as the 'father of the symphony'. He wrote 104 symphonies, over 80 string quartets and 20 operas, mostly while employed as musical director by the princely Hungarian family of Esterhazy. His last full-scale works were the two great oratorios *The Creation* and *The Seasons*.

Hazel A deciduous tree related to the birch. Hazels can grow up to 12 metres tall, but are usually cut down to form bushes. The catkins appear before the broad, hairy leaves, and eventually produce nuts which are popular with mice and squirrels as well as people.

Heart A vital organ that pumps blood around the body. It is actually like two pumps working closely together. The right side receives blood from the body and pumps it into the lungs where it collects oxygen. The blood returns to the left side of the heart and is then pumped around the body. Vessels leaving the heart, carrying oxygen-rich blood, are called arteries, those leading back to the heart are called veins.

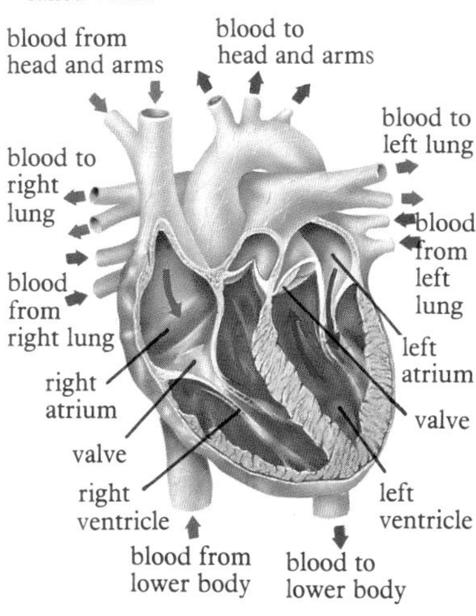

Heart

Heat A form of energy. An object becomes hot when the molecules that make it up start moving faster and bumping into each other. Most of the heat we use comes from burning fuels. But heat is also produced when electricity travels through a coil of wire, or by friction. Our main source of heat is the SUN.

Heat travels in three ways. It travels by *radiation*, when it moves through space, as it does from the sun or a fire. It travels by *conduction* through a solid, as it does when the handle of a pot gets hot. In *convection*, the hotter parts of liquids and gases rise above the cooler parts and cause currents.

Heath A large group of low-growing evergreen shrubs, commonly found on heaths and moors. They produce globular or bell-shaped flowers which are often purple, though some species have pink or white flowers. True heather, also called ling, has purple flowers and small triangular leaves.

Hebrides Group of islands off W coast of Scotland. The islands are separated into two groups, the Inner and the Outer Hebrides. The group includes the Isles of Skye, Mull, Arran, Lewis and Islay.

Hector In Greek legend the greatest of the Trojan heroes. He was eventually killed by Achilles.

Hedgehog An insectivorous mammal which measures about 25 cm in length. The hairs of its coat are very thick, with those on the back and sides forming stiff, sharp spines. When in danger, some hedgehogs can roll into a tight prickly ball that few animals are willing to attack. They are nocturnal creatures and hibernate during the winter.

Helen In Greek legend the beautiful wife of Menelaus, King of SPARTA. Her abduction by Paris to Troy sparked off the TROJAN WAR.

Helicopter An aircraft with horizontal rotor or rotors which act as both wings and propeller. There can be two rotors turning in opposite directions to prevent the helicopter body from spinning; otherwise a small rotor at the tail performs the same task. Helicopters can take off and land vertically, and move forward or backward as the rotor is tilted.

Helium The second lightest element after hydrogen, helium is one of the inert gases. It is non-inflammable and can safely be used for filling balloons and airships. Chem. symbol He.

Helsinki Seaport and capital of Finland. An important industrial and commercial centre, the city was founded to the north of its present position in 1550, was moved in 1640, and became capital in 1812. Pop: 490,000.

Henry VIII (1491–1547) King of England from 1509. His first wife, Catherine of Aragon, failed to produce a male heir, so he rejected papal authority in order to marry Anne Boleyn. Despite his subsequent marriages to Jane Seymour, Anne of Cleves, Catherine Howard and Catherine Parr, he remained immensely popular. His reign was marked by the dissolution of the monasteries and a move towards Protestantism.

Hephaestus Greek god of fire and blacksmith to the gods. (Roman equivalent Vulcan.)

Hera In Greek religion the Queen of Olympus and mother of many of the gods. The jealous wife of Zeus, she was also the protector of all women. (Roman equivalent Juno.)

Heracles (Roman Hercules) In Greek legend a hero who was famed for his courage and great physical strength. Having murdered his wife and children in a bout of madness, brought on by Hera who hated him, he successfully performed 12 labours as a form of penitence.

SH-60B Sea Hawk

Arms of England

Arms of Scotland

Arms of Wales

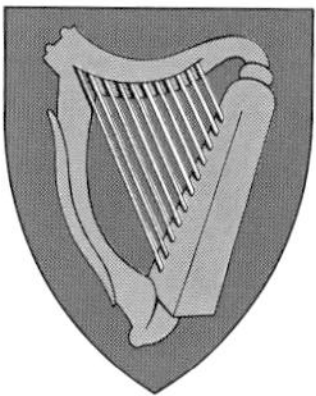

Arms of Eire

Heraldry In the Middle Ages knights bore 'arms', devices on their shields or banners with their own personal markings. From these badges arose the custom of heraldry. To this day each noble family has a coat of arms, and a complicated set of rules determines which marks, colours and emblems are used. Today businesses as well as individuals may display arms. In England the Heralds' College or College of Arms keeps the heraldic records and advises those seeking to obtain arms.

Herb A flowering plant that has no woody stem and which dies down after flowering. The term is also applied to plants used for flavouring food and for medicinal purposes.

Hercules See **Heracles**.

Heredity The process by which characteristics are passed on from parents to their young. The information transmitted from one generation to another is carried in the genes on the chromosomes.

Hereward the Wake An Anglo-Saxon folk hero who led the last resistance against William the Conqueror. His base on the island of Ely was taken in 1071 but he escaped and lived as an outlaw.

Hermes In Greek legend the messenger of the gods (Roman Mercury). He was also the god of thieves, merchants and physicians.

Hermit crab Unlike most crabs, hermit crabs have no protective shell. They hide their soft bodies in the old shells of other animals such as whelks. When the crab grows too big for its chosen home, it has to find a new one.

Herod the Great (73–3 BC) King of Judaea from 31 BC. He suffered from periods of insanity in his old age and executed a number of his sons. Ruling at the time when Jesus was born, he ordered the massacre of all small children at Bethlehem.

Herodotus (*c* 484–*c* 424 BC) Greek historian who was called 'The Father of History' by Cicero. He travelled extensively and kept records of all that he saw. His narrative deals in particular with the Persian Wars but also describes the customs and traditions of the peoples that he met.

Heron Very large water birds with long legs and necks. They stand patiently in shallow water waiting to seize fishes with their long, stabbing bills, sometimes shading the surface with their wings spread. The common or grey heron is found by rivers, lakes and estuaries.

Herring One of the most abundant marine fishes of the North Atlantic and neighbouring seas. Herring form huge shoals near the surface of the sea, feeding on plankton at night and migrating from one area to another. A fully-grown herring is about 40 cm long.

Hibernation The period of dormancy undergone by certain animals during the winter to avoid harsh weather conditions and lack of food. During hibernation an animal's body processes slow down, and the temperature of warm-blooded creatures drops to that of the environment. Animals that hibernate include land snails, queen wasps, frogs, toads, snakes, lizards and a few mammals such as dormice and hedgehogs.

Hieroglyphic Kind of picture writing used by Ancient Egyptians. The symbols (pictograms) stood for words, ideas and sounds.

Himalayas Massive mountain system in central Asia, running from N Pakistan, through N India, Bhutan and Nepal to China. Contains the world's highest mountain, Everest (8848 metres), and is the source of numerous great rivers, including particularly the Indus, Ganges and Brahmaputra.

The Hindu goddess Siva, whose dancing symbolises energy flowing through the world.

Hinduism The main religion of India which evolved some 4000 years ago and has absorbed many beliefs. It influences every aspect of its followers' lives: their conduct, society, laws, philosophy and even poetry. Brahma is the supreme deity. The Vedas, Brahmanas and Upanishads are sacred texts. Most Hindus believe in reincarnation and in the *caste* system of hereditary social classes.

Hippocrates (460–*c* 370 BC) Greek physician who is called the 'father of medicine'. He is supposed to have written many books but they were probably written by his followers. Many modern doctors take the Hippocratic Oath which obliges them to follow a strict ethical code.

Hippopotamus Bulky African mammal that spends most of its time wallowing in rivers and lakes. It may be four metres long and four tonnes in weight. The smaller pygmy hippopotamus is a native of West Africa.

History A systematic study of the past, involving the recording and interpretation of events. The following chart is a chronological record of significant events in world history from the earliest civilizations to the present day.

BC

5000 Continuous civilized communities develop along the banks of the Nile in Egypt, the Tigris and Euphrates in Mesopotamia and the Yellow River in China.

3500–3100 Sumerians build cities in the valleys of the Tigris and Euphrates. They used the wheel, bronze and cuneiform writing.

3400 Nile settlements united in two kingdoms, Upper and Lower Egypt. Hieroglyphic writing in use.

3100–2900 Menes unites Lower and Upper kingdoms into one nation and founds his capital at Memphis.

3000–1500 Civilization develops in Indus valley with well-planned cities such as Mohenjo-Daro and Harappa.

2870 First settlement at Troy.

2700–2500 Pyramids built as tombs for Egyptian kings including the Great Pyramid at Gizeh for King Cheops.

2500 Minoan civilization emerges on Crete with the city of Knossos and the earliest form of written Greek.

2400 Decline of Memphis; Thebes becomes new Egyptian capital.

2100–1800 Building and rebuilding of Stonehenge monument in England.

2000 Mycenaeans settle in Greece and develop flourishing civilization.

1815 The Assyrian Empire founded.

1800 Abraham, Patriach of the Jews, believed to have started the journey from Ur that led his people to Canaan.

1780 Lower Egypt overrun by the Hyksos (wandering raiders from the Syrian plateau).

1750 Hammurabi rules Babylonia and issues code of laws.

1600 Phoenetic alphabet in use in Phoenicia.

1580 Hyksos kings driven out by the Egyptians.

1523 Chinese civilization develops under Shang dynasty.

1450 Palace at Knossos destroyed and Minoan civilization declines.

1400 Mycenaeans become main power in Mediterranean.

1360 Tutankhamun, Pharaoh of Egypt.

1300 Sidon, Phoenician city-state, attains the height of its maritime power.

1292 Rameses II, Pharaoh of Egypt; great military figure and builder.

1250 Moses leads the Hebrews out of Egypt.

1230 The Hebrews under Joshua enter their 'Promised Land'.

1193 The Greeks of Mycenae at war with the Trojans.

1180 Traditional date of the fall of Troy.

1025 Saul anointed by Samuel as King of Hebrews.

960 Solomon builds a temple to Jehovah at Jerusalem.

933 Death of Solomon; kingdom of Hebrews divided into Judah and Israel.

814 Founding of Carthage by Phoenicians.
776 The first Olympiad. The beginning of the Greek calendar.
753 Traditional date of the founding of Rome.
722 Sargon II, King of the Assyrians, destroys the kingdom of Israel.
663 Assyria conquers Egypt.
612 Nineveh captured by Cyaxares, King of the Medes, who destroys forever the power of the Assyrians.
586 Nebuchadnezzar of Babylon captures Jerusalem, destroys the temple of Solomon, and leads the people of Judah into captivity.
558 Cyrus founds the Persian Empire.
538 Babylon falls to Cyrus, who allows Jews to return to Palestine.
536 The Jews commence rebuilding of the Temple.
525 Both Buddha and Confucius lived about this time.
510 Republic established in Rome.
508 Athenian democracy established.
490 Greeks defeat Persians under Darius at the Battle of Marathon.
485 Darius succeeded by Xerxes, who continues the war against the Greeks.
480 Xerxes invades Greece and defeats Greeks at Battle of Thermopylae. Later, Persian fleet defeated at Battle of Salamis.
478 Delian league is formed under the leadership of Athens.
447 Athenians begin building the Parthenon.
431 The Peloponnesian War between Athens and Sparta begins.
404 Athens captured by Spartans.
400 Athenians defeated by Persians. Retreat of the ten thousand under Xenophon.
372 Athenians and Spartans make peace.
367 Aristotle joins Plato in Athens.
338 Philip of Macedonia conquers Greece.
336 Macedonian troops enter Asia. Murder of Philip. Accession of Alexander the Great.
334 Battle of Granicus: Alexander defeats Darius III of Persia.
333 Battle of Issus: Alexander defeats Darius III again.
332 Egypt annexed by Alexander. Founding of Alexandria.
331 Final defeat of Darius III. Alexander captures Babylon.
330 Murder of Darius III and end of Persian Empire.
326 Alexander explores Indus valley, but retreats when his soldiers refuse to go any further east.
323 Alexander dies of typhus at Babylon: his generals share the vast empire amongst themselves. Ptolemy, one of the generals, becomes governor of Egypt.
320 Ptolemy captures Jerusalem.
312 Building of Appian Way, the first of the great Roman roads.
305 Ptolemy takes the title of Pharaoh. Alexandria becomes centre of Greek learning.
264–242 The first Punic War between Rome and Carthage begins.
221–210 Great Wall of China is built.
219 Second Punic War begins.
218 Hannibal, Carthaginian general, crosses Alps with elephants and enters Italy.
217 Hannibal wipes out a Roman army.
216 Battle of Cannae: another great Carthaginian victory.
215 First Macedonian War. Philip V of Macedonia attacks Rome. Ends in 205.
202 Hannibal defeated at Zama.
200–197 Second Macedonian War. Philip is defeated and forced to surrender Greece to Rome.
183 Death of Hannibal.
165 Jews revolt under Judas Maccabaeus and found independent kingdom of Judea.
149–146 Third Punic War. Scipio destroys Carthage and Roman province of Africa is founded.
146 Rome conquers Macedonia.
89 All Italians become citizens of Rome.
88–82 Civil war in Rome: Sulla emerges as victor and becomes dictator.
78 Death of Sulla.
73–71 Revolt of slaves in Sicily under Spartacus the gladiator.
55–54 Britain invaded by Julius Caesar.
44 Julius Caesar murdered. Mark Antony seizes Rome.
37 Herod the Great of Palestine recognized as King of Judea by Romans.
31 Battle of Actium: Julius Caesar's heir Octavian defeats fleet of Mark Antony and Queen Cleopatra of Egypt.
27 Augustus restores republic of Rome.
5 Probable date of birth of Jesus of Nazareth at Bethlehem.

AD Christian Era Begins
30 Crucifixion of Jesus.
37 Caligula Emperor of Rome.
41 On assassination of Caligula, Claudius elected Emperor by Praetorian Guard. Traditional date of founding of Christian Church by St. Peter.
43 Claudius begins Roman conquest of Britain.
46–47 Romans overrun kingdom of Caractacus.
50 Caractacus captured in Shropshire and taken to Rome. Britain becomes part of Roman Empire.
51–57 Missionary voyages of St. Paul.
54 Claudius poisoned; Nero becomes Emperor.
61 Boadicea, Queen of Iceni, leads a revolt against the Roman garrison in Britain.
64 Fire destroys Rome. First persecutions of the Christians.
66 Revolt of the Jews against Romans.
70 Roman legions under Titus take and destroy Jerusalem. Survivors are dispersed.
79 Vesuvius erupts and destroys the cities of Pompeii and Herculaneum.

117 Roman Empire reaches greatest extent under the Emperor Hadrian.
122 Hadrian's Wall built in Britain.
212 Roman citizenship bestowed on all freemen in the Empire.
247 Goths cross over the Danube and raid central Europe.
261 Romans defeat Scythian and Goth invaders.
300 Christianity becomes the recognized religion in Britain.
303 Persecution of Christians under Diocletian.
305 St. Alban martyred.
313–323 Roman Empire shared by Constantine in the west and Licinius in the east.
314 Constantine and Licinius at war. Edict of Milan: Christianity is tolerated in the Roman Empire.
324 Constantine reunites the Roman Empire.
330 Constantinople founded on site of Byzantium.
337 Constantine receives baptism on his death-bed.
350 Huns invade Europe.
360–367 Pict, Irish and Saxon invasion of Britain.
375 Huns invade Rome.
395 Death of Theodosius, last Roman ruler of a united Empire. Honorius and Arcadius, joint Emperors, redivide the Empire, this time permanently.
407 Romans withdraw from Britain.
410 The Goths under King Alaric take Rome.
425 Angles invade Britain. Barbarians overrun Roman Empire.
432 St. Patrick preaches in Ireland.
451 Attila, king of Huns, raids Gaul but is repelled by Romans.
455 Vandals from Africa sack Rome.
476 End of Roman Empire in the west.
477 Saxons invade Britain.
517 King Arthur of England may have lived at about this time.
553 St. Columba lands on Iona.
569 Birth of Mohammed at Mecca.
590 Pope Gregory the Great declares Rome to be the supreme centre of Christianity.
597 Death of St. Columba. St. Augustine lands in Britain and reintroduces Christianity.
602 Archbishopric of Canterbury founded.
611 Islam is proclaimed by Mohammed.
622 The Hegira: Flight of Mohammed from Mecca to Medina. Founding of Mohammedan religion.
629 Mohammed returns to Mecca.
632 Death of Mohammed.
638 Moslems capture Jerusalem.
664 Synod of Whitby: the Celtic Christian Church in England accepts the teachings of the Roman Church.
670–707 Moslems conquer North Africa.
673–678 Moslems besiege Constantinople without success.
711 Moslems invade Spain.
717–718 Constantinople again withstands Moslem attacks.
732 French defeat Moslems at Tours and halt their advance in western Europe.
735 Death of Venerable Bede.
757–796 Offa, King of Mercia.
772 Charlemagne becomes sole King of Franks.
779 Offa's dyke marks boundary between England and Wales.
786 Haroun-al-Raschid Caliph of Baghdad. Arab Empire at its greatest.
793 Sack of Lindisfarne: Viking attacks on Britain begin.
800 Pope Leo crowns Charlemagne Emperor of West at Rome.
802 Vikings dominate Ireland.
814 Death of Charlemagne.
827 Egbert becomes first King of all England.
836 Danes sack London.
844 MacAlpine unites Picts and Scots.
860 Danes sack Winchester.
871 Alfred the Great defeats Danes at Ashdown.
874 Iceland settled by Norsemen.
878 Danes defeated by Alfred at Ethandune.
885 Alfred takes London.
886 Alfred signs treaty with Danes establishing them in the Danelaw (northern England).
900 Death of Alfred.
940 Edmund, King of Wessex.
943 Malcolm I, King of Scotland.
958 Edgar, King of England.
975 Edward the Martyr, King of England.
979 Edward murdered; succeeded by Ethelred the Unready.
982 Norsemen discover Greenland.
991 Battle of Maldon: Ethelred buys off Vikings.
1000 Leif Ericsson discovers Nova Scotia.
1005 Malcolm II, King of Scotland.
1009 Danes attack London.
1016 Death of Ethelred. Canute is King of England, Denmark and Norway.
1035 Death of Canute.
1040 Duncan, King of Scotland, killed by Macbeth, who takes title.
1042 Restoration of English accession with crowning of Edward the Confessor.
1052 Edward founds Westminster Abbey.
1066 Death of Edward. Harold elected King. Battle of Hastings: death of Harold. William, Duke of Normandy crowned King of England.
1086 The Domesday Book completed.
1095–1099 Pope Urban II summons the First Crusade.
1096 The People's Crusade, led by Peter the Hermit, is massacred in Asia Minor.
1099 The Crusaders take Jerusalem.
1100 William II (Rufus) killed in the New Forest. Henry I, King of England.
1118 Founding of Order of Knights Templar.
1135 Stephen elected King. Henry II heir to throne. Period of civil war.
1147 The Second Crusade. Founding of kingdom of Portugal.
1154 Peace restored when Henry II ascends throne.

1169 Saladin, Sultan of Egypt.
1170 Murder of Thomas à Becket in Canterbury Cathedral.
1171 Norman conquest of Ireland.
1189 Jerusalem falls to Saladin. The Third Crusade.
1190 Richard I of England joins the Third Crusade.
1191 Siege and fall of Acre.
1192 Richard I held prisoner by Leopold of Austria.
1194 Richard returns to England.
1199 John, King of England.
1200–1450 Hanseatic League of German cities promotes trade.
1202 The Fourth Crusade.
1204 The Crusaders take Constantinople.
1206 Genghis Khan founds the Mogul Empire.
1212 The 'Children's Crusade': thousands of French and German children march towards the Holy Land. Many die or are sold into slavery. Possible origin of the 'Pied Piper' legend.
1215 John is forced to sign the Magna Carta, a statement of the barons' rights.
1216 Henry III, King of England. The first English Parliament.
1217 The Fifth Crusade.
1227 Death of Genghis Khan whose empire stretched from the Caspian to the Pacific.
1228–29 The Sixth Crusade secures Jerusalem by negotiations.
1244 Sultan of Egypt retakes Jerusalem.
1248–54 The Seventh Crusade: Louis IX leading attack on Egypt is captured and ransomed.
1260 Kublai Khan becomes the Great Khan.
1264 Battle of Lewes: Henry defeated by Simon de Montfort.
1265 De Montfort's Parliament: Commons meet for the first time. Battle of Evesham: de Montfort killed.
1271 Marco Polo begins his travels.
1282 Edward I subdues Wales.
1295 The Model Parliament – the first truly representative English Parliament.
1296 Annexation of Scotland by Edward I.
1297 William Wallace uprising. Battle of Stirling: Scots victorious.
1298 Battle of Falkirk: Wallace defeated by Edward I.
1306 Pope Clement V. Papal court moves to Avignon. Wallace executed at Smithfield. Robert Bruce rebellion.
1307 Edward II, King of England.
1314 Battle of Bannockburn: Scotland wins her independence.
1327 Edward II deposed and murdered; Edward III, King of England.
1337 Edward claims French crown: start of Hundred Years War.
1346 Edward III defeats French at Battle of Crécy.
1348 The Black Death ravages Europe.
1356 English under Edward the Black Prince defeat French at Poitiers.
1367 Tamerlane takes title of Great Khan.
1369 War with France renewed.
1375 Sole remaining English possessions in France include Calais, Bordeaux, Bayonne and Brest. Truce agreed.
1376 Death of Black Prince.
1378 The Great Schism: rival popes elected.
1381 Peasant revolt in England: Wat Tyler murdered before Richard II.
1399 Richard II deposed. Henry of Lancaster (Bolingbroke) becomes Henry IV.
1400 Owen Glendower leads a revolt in Wales.
1407 The Great Schism ends.
1415 Henry V renews war with France: English victory at Battle of Agincourt.
1429 Joan of Arc raises the siege of Orleans.
1430 Joan taken prisoner by Burgundians and sold to English.
1431 Joan of Arc martyred.
1453 Turks take Constantinople: end of Eastern Empire. All English possessions in France lost except Calais.
1454 Invention of printing from moveable type by Gutenberg.
1455 Battle of St. Albans: start of the Wars of the Roses.
1461 Lancastrian cause suffers defeat at Battle of Towton Field: Edward IV proclaimed King.
1470 Earl of Warwick ('the Kingmaker') deposes Edward IV.
1471 Battles of Barnet and Tewkesbury: Earl of Warwick dies at Barnet. Return of Edward IV.
1476 Caxton sets up his press at Westminster.
1478 Spain introduces the Inquisition.
1483 Edward V murdered after only two months' reign. Henry Tudor proclaimed Henry VII.
1485 Richard III, killed at Bosworth. Henry VII, King of England.
1486 Diaz sails round the Cape of Good Hope.
1492 Columbus discovers the New World. Ferdinand drives Moors from Spain.
1497 Vasco da Gama reaches India by the sea route.
1513 James IV of Scotland defeated and killed at Battle of Flodden.
1514 Wolsey becomes Archbishop of York.
1517 Martin Luther, founder of Protestantism, nails his 'Ninety-five Theses' condemning many Church practices to the door of Wittenberg church. This marks the beginning of the Reformation.
1519 Cortez takes Mexico. Magellan sails round the world.
1528 Peru subdued by Pizarro.
1529 Fall of Wolsey. He fails to arrange annulment of Henry VIII's marriage to Catherine of Aragon.
1530 Henry's quarrel with the papacy begins.
1533 Henry marries Anne Boleyn.
1534 Act of Supremacy. End of papal power in England.

1535 Loyola founds Jesuits. The first English printed Bible (Coverdale's).
1536 Dissolution of monasteries. Death of Catherine of Aragon. Anne Boleyn executed. Henry marries his third wife.
1537 Death of Jane Seymour.
1538 Henry excommunicated.
1540 In January Henry marries Anne of Cleves, whom he divorces. In July Henry marries Catherine Howard.
1542 James V of Scotland defeated at Solway Moss. Execution of Catherine Howard. Henry marries Catherine Parr.
1547 Edward VI. Somerset, Lord Protector.
1549 Act of Uniformity authorizing First Prayer Book.
1552 Second Prayer Book.
1553 Death of Edward. Mary proclaimed Queen. Catholic Church restored. Lady Jane Grey makes unsuccessful bid for the throne.
1554 Mary marries Philip of Spain. Execution of Lady Jane Grey.
1558 Loss of Calais. Elizabeth, Queen of England. Protestantism restored. Marriage of Mary Queen of Scots to French Dauphin.
1561 Mary Queen of Scots returns to Scotland.
1562 Huguenot wars.
1567 Revolt in Netherlands against Spain.
1568 Mary Queen of Scots flees to England; imprisoned by Elizabeth.
1587 Execution of Mary Queen of Scots.
1588 Defeat of the Spanish Armada.
1600 East India Company granted charter by Elizabeth.
1601 Poor Law established.
1603 James VI of Scotland becomes James I of England, uniting the two crowns.
1605 Gunpowder Plot.
1607 Colony of Virginia founded.
1611 Authorized Version of the Bible.
1618 Thirty Years War begins in Europe with revolt by Protestants in Prague.
1620 Pilgrim Fathers sail to America in the *Mayflower* to avoid religious persecution.
1629 Charles I reigns without Parliament until 1640.
1640 Charles in need of money summons the Long Parliament.
1641 Massacre of the English in Ireland.
1642 New Zealand and Tasmania discovered. Charles tries to arrest five Members of Parliament. Civil war begins.
1643 Louis XIV of France (He rules for seventy years).
1647 Charles surrenders to Parliament.
1648 The Treaty of Westphalia brings Thirty Years War to a close.
1649 Trial and execution of Charles. England becomes a republic under Cromwell.
1651 Charles II defeated at Battle of Worcester; flees to France.
1652 First Dutch War.
1653 Cromwell becomes Protector.
1658 Death of Cromwell; his son Richard becomes Protector.
1659 Resignation of Richard Cromwell.
1660 General Monk brings back Charles II.
1664 Second Dutch War. New Amsterdam (New York) captured.
1665 Great Plague of London.
1666 The Great Fire of London.
1667 Dutch fleet sails up the Medway and destroys British squadron.
1672–74 Third Dutch War.
1677 Princess Mary of England (daughter of Duke of York, later James II) marries William of Orange.
1685 Death of Charles II. James II, King of England. The Monmouth rebellion.
1688 Flight of James II. William of Orange and Mary offered throne. Protestant succession restored.
1689 William and Mary accept Bill of Rights limiting royal power.
1690 William defeats James II at Battle of the Boyne.
1692 The Massacre at Glencoe.
1694 Bank of England founded. Death of Queen Mary.
1701 Frederick I of Prussia.
1701–1713 War of Spanish Succession.
1702 Queen Anne. England joins war of Spanish Succession.
1704 British capture Gibraltar. Battle of Blenheim: Marlborough defeats French and Bavarians.
1714 George I of Britain.
1715 Jacobite rising in Scotland fails.
1727 George II of Britain.
1745 Charles Edward (Bonnie Prince Charlie) lands in Scotland. Battle of Prestonpans: Jacobite victory. They reach Derby but return again to Scotland.
1746 Battle of Culloden: Jacobites routed.
1752 Reformed Gregorian calendar adopted.
1756 Seven Year War begins with France and Austria. The 'Black Hole' of Calcutta.
1759 Wolfe captures Quebec.
1760 George III of Britain. Conquest of Canada completed.
1763 Peace of Paris ends Seven Years War. Britain keeps Canada.
1764 The Industrial Revolution. Hargreaves invents the spinning jenny.
1770 Captain Cook discovers New South Wales.
1773 Boston tea riots.
1774 American War of Independence begins.
1776 American Declaration of Independence.
1781 Surrender of General Cornwallis and British forces at Yorktown.
1782 Britain acknowledges the independence of the American States.
1788 First Congress of USA at New York. Colonization of Australia begins.
1789 George Washington becomes first president of the USA. Fall of the Bastille and outbreak of French Revolution.

1792 France becomes a republic – royalty abolished. France declares war on Austria.
1793 Louis XVI beheaded. Reign of Terror begins. Britain at war with France.
1795 Napoleon invades Italy as Commander-in-Chief.
1798 Napoleon in Egypt. Battle of the Nile. Nelson victorious.
1799 Napoleon made First Consul. Pitt introduces income tax.
1800 Legislative Union of Ireland and England. Austrians defeated by Napoleon at Battle of Marengo.
1801 Treaty between France, England and Austria signed.
1803 France sells Louisiana to USA. War with France renewed.
1804 Napoleon crowns himself Emperor.
1805 Nelson defeats French navy at Battle of Trafalgar. Napoleon victorious at Battles of Ulm and Austerlitz.
1806 Napoleon overthrows Prussia at Battle of Jena.
1807 Slave trade abolished throughout British Empire.
1808 Napoleon's brother, Joseph Bonaparte, King of Spain. Peninsular War begins in Spain.
1809 Napoleon divorces the Empress Josephine.
1810 Marriage of Bonaparte to Marie-Louise of Austria.
1811 The Prince of Wales becomes Regent owing to permanent insanity of George III. Luddite riots against mechanization of industry.
1812 USA declares war on Great Britain. France at war with Russia. Napoleon burns Moscow but is forced to retreat, losing most of his army.
1813 Wellington invades France. Napoleon defeated at Battle of Leipzig.
1814 Abdication of Napoleon and banishment to island of Elba. Peace between Great Britain and USA.
1815 Napoleon escapes from Elba. Battle of Waterloo: Napoleon finally overthrown; surrenders to British; exiled to St. Helena.
1819 Spain cedes Florida to USA.
1820 George IV of Britain.
1822 Declaration of Greek independence.
1824 Bolivar dictator of Peru.
1830 William IV of Britain. Louis Philippe proclaimed King of France.
1833 Slavery abolished in British Empire.
1836 Great Trek of Boers from British South African territory.
1837 Queen Victoria of Britain.
1840 Marriage of Queen Victoria and Prince Albert. Penny post introduced. Famine in Ireland results in massive loss of life and large-scale emigration.
1846 Repeal of the Corn Laws. Free trade established.
1848 Louis Philippe abdicates. French Republic proclaimed.
1851 The Great Exhibition in Hyde Park.
1852 Louis Napoleon Emperor in France.
1854 Outbreak of Crimean War.
1857 The Indian Mutiny.
1860 Garibaldi takes Naples and proclaims Victor Emmanuel first King of Italy.
1861 Abraham Lincoln, President of the USA. American Civil War.
1862 Bismarck chief minister in Germany.
1863 Lincoln abolishes slavery in the USA.
1864 Red Cross organization formed.
1865 End of American Civil War. Lincoln murdered.
1867 Dominion of Canada established.
1869 Opening of Suez Canal.
1870 France declares war against Prussia and is rapidly defeated. Fall of Napoleon III leads to Third French Republic.
1872 Election balloting system introduced in England.
1877 Queen Victoria proclaimed Empress of India.
1878 Afghan War. Paris Exhibition.
1879 Zulu Wars.
1880 First Boer War.
1881 Transvaal becomes a republic. Peace with Boers.
1891 Education Act, granting free education.
1899 Second Boer War.
1900 Attack on Ladysmith. Relief of Ladysmith and Mafeking.
1901 Death of Queen Victoria. Founding of Commonwealth of Australia.
1902 End of Boer War.
1904 Entente Cordiale between France and Great Britain.
1904–1905 Russo-Japanese War.
1906 San Francisco earthquake and fire.
1909 Blériot flies the English Channel. Union of South Africa established. Peary reaches N Pole.
1910 King George V of Britain.
1911 Amundsen reaches South Pole.
1912 China declared a republic. *Titanic* disaster.
1914 Irish Home Rule Bill passed. Panama Canal opened to traffic. Outbreak of World War I.
1917 Revolution in Russia. America declares war against Germany.
1918 Kaiser abdicates. Armistice signed.
1919 First aeroplane crossing of the Atlantic.
1920 First meeting of League of Nations.
1922 Tutankhamun's tomb discovered in Egypt. Founding of Irish Free State.
1924 Death of Lenin. Wembley Exhibition. First Labour Government.
1926 General Strike in Great Britain.
1933 Adolf Hitler becomes Chancellor of Germany.
1935 Saar returned to Germany. Italy at war with Abyssinia.
1936 Death of George V. Franco revolt in Spain. Edward VIII abdicates; George VI succeeds to throne.
1938 Germany annexes Austria.
1939 Outbreak of World War II.
1941 Germany invades Russia. Japan attacks the USA. USA at war with Germany.
1943 Allied invasion of Italy.

1944 Allied invasion of Normandy.
1945 Germany unconditionally surrenders. First atomic bomb dropped at Hiroshima: war with Japan ends.
1948 British railways nationalized. State of Israel created.
1950 North Korea invades South Korea: UN forces sent to the aid of the latter.
1953 Coronation of Elizabeth II. Summit of Mount Everest reached by British expedition. Cessation of hostilities in Korea.
1956 Suez Crisis: Anglo-French force invades Egypt to secure Suez Canal but is ordered to withdraw by the UN. Revolt of students and workers in Hungary crushed by Soviet troops.
1958 Soviet Union launches first space satellite.
1961 Soviet Major Yuri Gagarin makes first manned space flight. Berlin Wall is built.
1963 Assassination of President Kennedy.
1965 Death of Sir Winston Churchill. Rhodesia proclaims its independence.
1966 American involvement in Vietnam war increases.
1967 Six-day War: Israelis rout forces of Egypt, Syria and Jordan.
1968 Russians invade Czechoslovakia to destroy 'liberal' government.
1969 American troops begin withdrawal from Vietnam. American astronaut Neil Armstrong becomes first man to walk on Moon.
1973 Britain, Eire and Denmark become full members of the EEC. Cease-fire signed in Vietnam war. Yom Kippur war between Egypt, Syria and Israel ended by Soviet–US involvement.
1975 South Vietnam falls to communist forces. Oil begins to flow from Britain's North Sea fields.
1976 Supersonic airliner Concorde enters service.
1979 Ayatollah Khomeini establishes Islamic republic in Iran. Margaret Thatcher becomes Britain's first woman prime minister. End of illegal white rule in Rhodesia Zimbabwe. Russian troops invade Afghanistan.
1980 Iran and Iraq begin Gulf War.
1981 Polish government announces martial law and represses the workers' Solidarity movement.
1982 Argentinian forces invade the Falklands which are recaptured by a British task force. Israel invades Lebanon.
1983 Antinuclear protests throughout Europe against siting of US missiles. South Korean Jumbo airliner with 269 people aboard shot down after straying into Soviet airspace.
1984 Indian prime minister Indira Gandhi assassinated by Sikh extremists.
1985 The largest charitable event in history: Live Aid concert organized by Bob Geldof raises £50 million for Ethiopian famine victims. Earthquake in Mexico City kills 20–30,000 people. Eruption of Colombian volcano claims 23,000 lives.
1986 US Space Shuttle explodes in flight with the death of the seven people aboard.

Adolf Hitler

Hitler, Adolf (1889–1945) Austrian politician who from 1920 led the National Socialist (Nazi) Party in Germany. He became Chancellor in 1933 and Führer in 1934. He turned Germany into a powerful war machine, persecuting minority groups such as the Jews and Communists. He ordered the invasion of Poland in 1939 which began the Second World War. Faced with defeat, he committed suicide in Berlin on April 30, 1945.

Ho Chi-Minh (1892–1969) Revolutionary leader of Indo-China who won independence from France for North Vietnam after a long and bitter struggle. As president of North Vietnam from 1954 he led the guerilla war against US-backed South Vietnam; success came only after his death. Saigon, former capital of South Vietnam, was renamed Ho Chi-Minh City in honour of him.

Ho Chi-Minh City Port and largest city in Vietnam. Formerly Saigon before communist take-over, during which many of the inhabitants either fled or were driven out of the city.

Hockey Team game played with curved sticks, with which players hit the ball into a net to score goals. The positions of the players and rules are similar to those of soccer.

Hogarth, William (1697–1794) English painter, caricaturist and engraver who satirized the excesses of his time. His most famous engravings include *The Rake's Progress*, *Marriage à la Mode* and *Idleness and Industry*.

Holbein, Hans (the Younger) (1497–1543) German portrait painter and woodcut artist who settled in England and became court painter to Henry VIII. The *Last Supper* and *The Ambassadors* are among his best-known works.

Holly An evergreen shrub or small tree with leathery, glossy green leaves. Those leaves growing on the lower branches are spiny, while those higher up have wavy or even smooth edges. The male and female flowers grow on separate trees which explains why only some trees bear the characteristic scarlet berries.

Hollywood Now part of the US city of Los Angeles, California, but famous as the 'movie capital of the world' from the 1920s when the cinema industry became established there. Hollywood became the home of the large film studios, and of many famous film stars. Today, most of the studios produce television programmes.

Holography A way of producing 3-dimensional images. To make this happen, an object is lit by light from a LASER. The laser beam is split in two. One half strikes the object and reflects from it to a photographic plate. The other half is made to strike the plate directly. The two beams interact, and when the photographic plate is developed it is a hologram. When a laser beam is passed through the hologram a 3-dimensional image of the object is seen on the other side of the plate. The object appears solid.

Homer Greek poet of the 8th century BC, and presumed author of the *Iliad* and the *Odyssey*, narrative poems which were the models for all later epics.

Honduras Republic in Central America on Caribbean Sea with a small Pacific coast in the SE. The landscape is mainly mountainous and forested with fertile volcanic highlands in the south. The economy is based on agriculture, particularly bananas. Area: 112,000 km^2; Pop: 4,249,000; Cap: Tegucigalpa.

Hong Kong British dependency at mouth of Canton R. in China, consisting of Hong Kong Island and the mainland areas of Kowloon and the New Territories. One of the busiest ports in the world and a major financial and commercial centre with a large textile industry. The economy is booming despite an agreement for the colony's return to China in 1997. Area: 1000 km^2; Pop: 5,355,000.

Honolulu Capital and chief port of Hawaii, USA on Oahu I., with important international airport. Pop: 763,000.

Hoopoe One of the most exotic-looking birds found in Europe, Asia and Africa. It has a prominent black-tipped crest, black and white barred wings and pinkish-brown head and breast.

Horace (65–8 BC) Roman lyric poet who wrote *Epodes*, *Epistles*, *Satires* and *Odes*. He became poet laureate to Augustus.

Hormone A chemical 'messenger' produced by certain glands in the body and carried by the blood. Each hormone is responsible for regulating a specific activity inside the body. For example, the hormone insulin controls the amount of sugar in the blood. If the sugar level is too high, insulin is produced to help convert the sugar into glycogen (a sugar store) in the liver.

Hornet A large wasp, with a browner body then the familiar black-and-yellow wasp. Like other social wasps, hornets make large communal nests, generally in hollow trees. Unless disturbed, they are not usually aggressive.

Horse Hoofed mammal widely distributed over Europe and Asia in prehistoric times. The sole surviving wild example is Przhewalski's horse of central Asia. Horses were domesticated some 4000 years ago and there are now more than 60 breeds. For centuries horses were working animals; today they are mostly ridden for sport and pleasure.

Horse chestnut A deciduous tree, native to eastern Europe but widely planted elsewhere for ornament and shade. It has long conical clusters of showy white flowers and large, fan-shaped, compound leaves. Its seeds or conkers are borne inside spiny cases.

Horse-fly A group of true flies that make a loud humming noise in flight. The females feed by sucking blood from animals, particularly horses and cattle, and will also bite humans.

Horse racing Sport known since early times (certainly since the first Olympic Games in ancient Greece). Many of today's classic horse races began in the

18th century, including the English Derby, first run in 1780. The Derby is a flat race (the horses do not have to jump any obstacles). The most famous steeple-chase (race with jumps) is the Grand National, first run in 1839.

Horsetail A group of green flowerless plants which live mainly in damp places. Horsetails are related to ferns. They have tall ridged stems that snap easily at intervals, wherever there is a 'joint'. The joints are surrounded by a collar of tiny scale leaves: there are no proper leaves. The plants reproduce by means of spores.

House-fly A true fly which lives in and around houses, feeding on rubbish and human waste. It feeds by spitting on the food to make a paste which it can then suck up. House-flies spread diseases, since they move constantly from decaying matter to fresh food.

Hovercraft A vehicle that skims over the surface of water or land on a cushion of air. The air is forced under the craft, lifting it clear of the surface. There is therefore little friction or drag. The craft can travel easily at speed, usually propelled by propellers which can also be used to steer the hovercraft.

BN-7 Hovercraft

Hover-fly A large family of true flies which can hover in mid air. They feed on pollen and nectar. Many hover-flies look like bees and wasps but, being true flies, have only one pair of wings.

Hudson, Henry (d. 1611) English explorer and navigator who discovered the Hudson River and Hudson Bay while seeking a Northwest Passage to China. During his last expedition his crew mutinied and cast him adrift to die.

Hugo, Victor Marie (1802–85) French poet, novelist and dramatist. His works include the novels *The Hunchback of Notre Dame*, *Les Misérables* and *Toilers of the Sea*, and plays such as *Ruy Blas* as well as many poems.

Hummingbird Tiny birds that feed mostly on nectar. Named for the noise their wings make as they hover in front of flowers and dip their beaks in for the nectar. Found throughout the New World, the largest hummingbird is only 20 cm long, the smallest the size of a bumble bee.

Hundred Years War A series of wars between England and France. They lasted, off and on, from 1337 to 1453. The main cause was the claim of the English king to the throne of France. The English won many battles under Edward III and later under King Henry V. A peasant girl, Joan of Arc, who was inspired by nationalism and religion, raised French resistance in 1429–30, and by 1453 the English had lost nearly all their French possessions.

Hungary Landlocked republic in E Europe. Large fertile plains drained by the Danube and its tributaries cover the eastern half of Hungary, with rolling uplands and hills in the N and W. It is a mainly agricultural country with an emphasis on cereal crops. In 1949 a one-party communist state was proclaimed. This led to an anti-communist uprising in 1956 which was suppressed by Soviet troops. Area: 93,000 km^2; Pop: 10,681,000; Cap: Budapest.

Huns Fierce Mongoloid tribe that invaded the Roman Empire during the AD 400s. Under their leader Attila, they defeated the Barbarians and the Goths and invaded Gaul. Only after Attila's death did the subject nations oust the Huns.

Hurdling Race in which the competitors have to jump over obstacles or hurdles. In athletics, hurdle races are run over 100 and 400 metres. The hurdle is a light barrier, easily knocked over if the runner fails to clear it. The barriers used in the 3000-metre steeplechase race are much more solid.

Hurricane See **Tropical cyclone**.

Hwang Ho Also called the Yellow River from the colour of the silt it carries, the Hwang Ho is the second longest river in China. The Hwang Ho has been responsible for many devastating floods and has earned the name 'China's Sorrow'. Length: 4700 km.

Hybrid The offspring of two different species or varieties of organisms. In the animal kingdom a hybrid is usually infertile. An ass, for example, is the infertile offspring of a horse and a donkey. Many hybrid plants on the other hand are fertile.

Hydra A tiny freshwater animal with a tubular body (polyp) that moves around by gliding or by turning somersaults. Hydras catch their prey (worms and insect larvae) by means of stinging tentacles.

Hydraulics The branch of science that studies the behaviour of liquids. Hydraulic engineers build dams, canals, irrigation and water supply systems. Hydraulic machines can be divided into two main classes: TURBINES and PUMPS. Turbines are machines that work by the force of flowing water. Pumps are machines that do work on the water, such as raising it to a higher location.

Hydrocarbons Substances called organic compounds because they come from things that once were alive. They contain only hydrogen and carbon. Hydrocarbons are obtained from oil and natural gas. They are used to make plastics and synthetic fibres.

Hydrofoil A craft which rises clear of the water when it reaches a certain speed; it is then supported on wing-like foils fitted under the hull. As only the foils touch the water, friction is greatly reduced and the craft can reach high speeds with the use of little power.

Hydrogen The lightest of the elements, hydrogen is a highly inflammable gas. With carbon it forms a vast number of organic compounds – the HYDROCARBONS. Chem. symbol H.

Hyena Carnivorous dog-like mammals of Africa and Asia. They have large powerful jaws and hunt in packs. There are three species, brown, striped and spotted (laughing).

Hypnosis The induction of a state of trance in a person which makes him or her highly responsive to suggestion.

Hyrax Only 45 cm long itself, the nearest relative this little mammal can claim is the elephant. It lives in south-western Asia and Africa and looks like a guinea pig. It is also called a cony.

I

Alpine ibex

Ibex Wild mountain goat found in Europe and Asia. The Alpine ibex (male) is about a metre high at the shoulder and has backward sweeping horns some 75 cm long. The female's horns are shorter.

Ibis Wading birds related to herons and flamingoes. There are various species with long legs and necks and long curved beaks. Some like the scarlet ibis of tropical America are brightly coloured, others like the sacred ibis of Egypt are black and white. They nest in trees.

Ibsen, Henrik Johan (1828–1906) Norwegian dramatist whose works dealt with psychological and social problems. His plays include *Hedda Gabler*, *The Wild Duck*, *Ghosts*, *A Doll's House* and the dramatic poems *Brand* and *Peer Gynt*.

Ice The solid form of water. Pure water forms ice at 0°C (32°F). At this temperature the movement of the water molecules becomes so slow that the liquid crystallizes into ice. When water freezes it increases its volume by one-eleventh. Ice is therefore lighter than water, so it floats. Ice starts to melt when the temperature goes above 0°C, but until all the ice is melted the temperature of both water and the still-unmelted ice remains at 0°C.

Ice Age Several times during the Earth's history the climates of the world have grown cold and ice has covered large areas of land. The most recent occasion was the

Great Ice Age when ice sheets repeatedly spread out from Scandinavia and Canada, scraping the soil from the land and dumping it farther south. It is possible that the Great Ice Age has not ended.

Icebergs Large floating lumps of ice that 'calve' from glaciers and ice-shelves in polar regions. Icebergs may rise 100 metres above the sea, but beneath the surface there will be about nine times as much ice again. Icebergs drifting south in the Atlantic are a shipping hazard.

Ice hockey World's fastest team game, played on an ice rink. Each team has six players on the ice, wearing skates and carrying hockey sticks. The 'ball' is a flat leather object called a puck. The object is to score goals by hitting the puck into your opponents' net.

Iceland Island republic in N Atlantic. The landscape consists largely of barren plains and mountains, with large ice fields particularly in the south-west. The island has active volcanoes and is known for its thermal springs and geysers. With less than 1% of the land suitable for growing crops, the nation's economy is based on fishing, and fish products account for 80% of the exports. Area: 103,000 km²; Pop: 227,000; Cap: Reykjavik.

Iguana Large, long-tailed, rather grotesque lizards of tropical America and the Galapagos. Some are 1.5 metres long.

Immunity Resistance of the body to infection by harmful bacteria or viruses. Immunity relies on the ability of certain white blood cells to 'recognize' foreign substances and release ANTIBODIES to fight the infection. Artificial immunity can be induced by INOCULATION.

Impala Graceful African antelope with long (75 cm), lyre-shaped horns and famed for leaping ability. The female is hornless.

Incas Civilization of S American Indians based in Cuzco, Peru, which reached its height at the end of the 14th century. The Inca civilization was conquered by the Spanish under Pizarro in 1533.

India Country in Asia, with the second largest population in the world. It is a land of many landscapes: the high Himalayas in the north, the broad river plain of the

Magnificently clad elephants are a feature of Indian ceremonial processions.

Indus, Ganges and Brahmaputra Rivers, and a southern tableland, the Deccan. The wet tropical monsoon climate is good for rice-growing, and cereals are also grown. Other crops are cotton, sugar-cane, jute and tea. Cattle are seen in large numbers, but the Hindus (over 80% of the people) are forbidden by their religion to eat beef. India has coal and other minerals, and industry is developing rapidly, both in manufacturing and engineering. There are nine cities with over a million people, but many Indians still live in small villages. Poverty combined with a fast-growing population is a major problem. Area: 3,281,334 km²; Pop: 746,388,000; Cap: Delhi.

Indonesia Republic in SE Asia comprising numerous islands, including Sumatra, Java, a large part of Borneo, Sulawesi and the western part of New Guinea. Most of the islands are mountainous and there are many active volcanoes. The majority are densely forested and under-developed. Java, an exception, is the centre of a rapidly developing oil industry. The rich volcanic soils of this island, combined with continuous high temperatures and heavy rainfall, enable crops to be grown all year round. Rice is by far the most important crop, often grown in spectacular hillside terraces. Area: 1,904,000 km²; Pop: approx 150,000,000; Cap: Jakarta (on Java).

Indus River in Asia, flowing from Tibet through Kashmir and Pakistan into the Arabian Sea. Used extensively for irrigation and HEP schemes. Length: 2700 km.

Industrial Revolution The transformation of first Britain (from about 1760) and then other Western countries, in the eighteenth and nineteenth centuries, from nations of craftsmen and peasants into nations of factories and industrial workers. This was the result of many factors: a large and growing population; healthy trade; plenty of money to invest in business; a large stock of raw materials such as coal and iron; and most of all, new forms of power such as the steam engine, and more efficient methods of production made possible by new machinery.

Symbol of the Industrial Revolution, Stephenson's Rocket was built to haul passenger trains between the great industrial towns of Liverpool and Manchester.

Inert gases Group of gases including argon, helium, krypton, neon, radon and xenon which are notable for their lack of reaction with other elements. They are also called the rare gases because they occur naturally only in very small quantities, accounting for about one per cent by volume of air.

Inertia The tendency for anything to resist any change in its motion. Inertia has to be overcome to start an object moving. Once the object is moving, inertia has to be overcome again to stop it. The more massive an object is, the greater its inertia – it is easier to start pushing a bicycle than a motor car.

Infra-red radiation Infra-red rays carry heat. They are waves of ELECTROMAGNETIC RADIATION, like radio waves, X-rays and light waves. Infra-red radiation passes easily through many substances that will not let ordinary light through. Photographs can be taken in the dark or fog using infra-red rays. Many aerial photographs are taken by this means.

Inoculation A medical technique to safeguard a person against infection by a disease. It involves injecting the person with a preparation, usually a mild dose of the disease itself, that makes the body resistant to any future attack by the disease.

Inquisition Notorious system of tribunals set up by Roman Catholic Church to eradicate heresy in the 13th century and continuing for centuries thereafter. Suspected heretics were tortured and put to death. The separate Spanish Inquisition controlled by the secular authorities was particularly ruthless.

Insect The largest group of animals containing about one million known species. An insect's body is divided into three distinct sections - head, thorax and abdomen - and bears three pairs of legs and a pair of feelers or antennae. Most insects also have two pairs of wings. All adult insects breathe air and have holes (spiracles) along their sides leading to fine tubes (tracheae) which carry air through the body. Examples include DRAGONFLIES, GRASSHOPPERS, EARWIGS, BEES, BUTTERFLIES and BEETLES The largest insect is the African Goliath beetle with a body about 10 cm long and 5 cm thick.

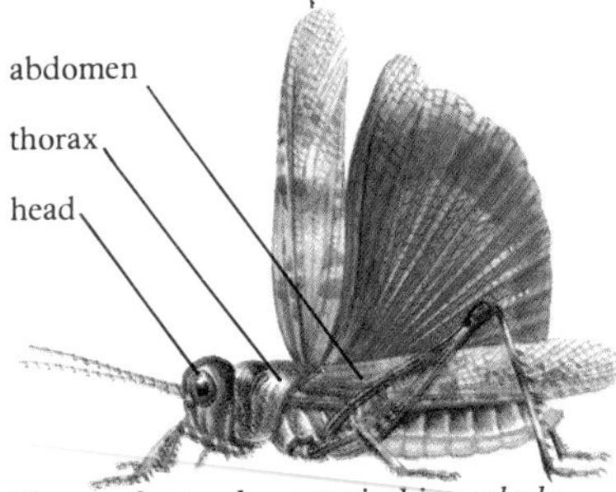

The grasshopper has a typical insect body with three clear sections, as well as two pairs of wings and six legs.

Insectivore Member of a group of insect-eating mammals with long snouts and sharp teeth. The group includes HEDGEHOGS, MOLES and SHREWS.

Instinct Animal behaviour that is hereditary rather than learnt. Examples of instinctive behaviour are shown in animal courtships, care of young and MIGRATION.

Intelligence The ability to assemble facts learnt from past experiences and use them to overcome new problems. A person's or animal's quickness to understand a situation is a measure of its intelligence.

Internal combustion engine An engine in which fuel is burned inside a chamber. The gases formed by this burning produce power in various ways. The best-known internal combustion engines are petrol, diesel and jet engines. In petrol and diesel engines, fuel is burned in cylinders. The hot gases produced drive pistons up and down, this up-and-down motion turning a crankshaft. In jet (GAS TURBINE) engines, fuel is burned in a combustion chamber to produce hot gases. As the gases escape from the engine they produce a forward thrust. The ROCKET is a special kind of internal combustion engine. As it carries its own supply of oxygen, it can operate outside the Earth's atmosphere.

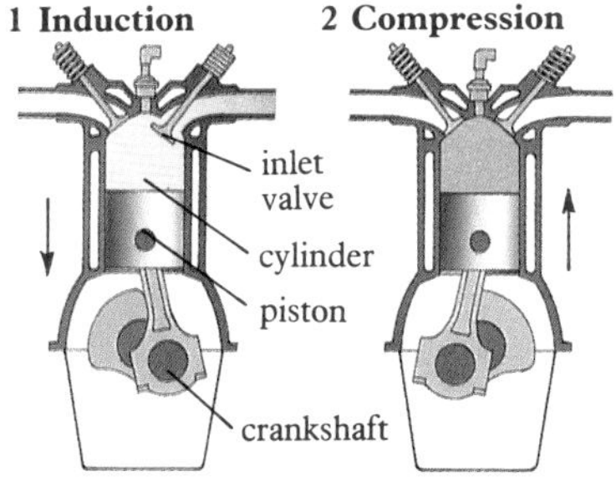

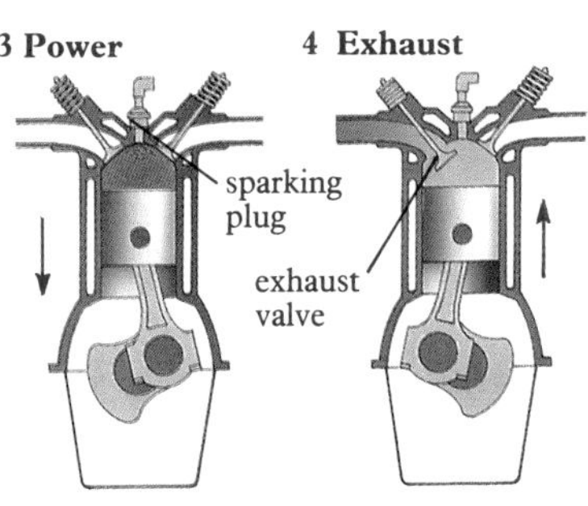

The stages of the four-stroke cycle

International Date Line Imaginary line roughly corresponding to the 180° line of longitude. Because time is measured east and west of Greenwich (0°) at the rate of one hour per 15 degrees, there is a difference of 24 hours at the 180° line of longitude. Travellers from west to east gain a day as they cross the line, those going east-west lose one.

International Monetary Fund (IMF) Organization set up in 1946 as an emergency fund into which member-states paid money (as currency or gold) and from which they borrowed when they needed to. The IMF does not lend money like an ordinary bank; it buys and sells gold and currencies. Its job is to help member-states get out of temporary financial difficulties. Making loans to poor nations is the responsibility of the International Bank for Reconstruction and Development (usually called the World Bank).

INTERPOL (International Criminal Police Organization) Based in Paris, France, Interpol helps police forces in countries throughout the world (though it has no members in communist countries). It began in 1923, and its main job is to store and give out information about criminals and crimes. It cannot, however, interfere in a country's affairs and Interpol detectives do not arrest criminals elsewhere.

Invertebrate Any animal without an internal skeleton of bones. Protozoans, crabs, worms and insects are all invertebrates.

Iodine Bluish-black, non-metallic element formerly obtained only from ribbon-wrack seaweeds. Iodine is used in photography, and dissolved in alcohol it forms the antiseptic 'tincture of iodine'. Chem. symbol I.

Iran Islamic republic in SW Asia. It is a country of mountains, plateaux and large deserts. Agriculture is restricted mainly to the limited lowland regions with some goat and sheep farming in higher areas. The economy is based on the massive oil deposits in the SW, and most industries with the exception of textiles are oil-related. Iran was a kingdom until 1979 when the Shah was exiled and the republic proclaimed. Area: 1,627,000 km^2; Pop: 34,000,000; Cap: Tehran.

Iraq Republic in SW Asia. The landscape is dominated by the rivers Euphrates and Tigris with large areas of desert. Agriculture is concentrated in the fertile river valleys. The economy is based on large oilfields in the north. Iraq is the centre of the ancient civilizations of Mesopotamia. Area: 435,000 km^2; Pop: 12,171,000; Cap: Baghdad.

Ireland Island in the Atlantic Ocean, separated from Great Britain by the Irish Sea, St George's Channel and North Channel. It is politically divided into NORTHERN IRELAND in the north-east (part of the United Kingdom) and the Republic of IRELAND. Area: 84,000 km^2; Pop: 4,888,000.

Ireland, Republic of Independent republic in W Europe occupying over 80% of the island of Ireland, and divided historically into the provinces of Leinster, Connacht, Munster and Ulster. There is a large central lowland surrounded by hills and rolling uplands. The mild, damp climate has contributed to the largely agricultural economy, in which livestock breeding and dairy farming are of major importance. Manufacturing industries are increasing and tourism is also important.

Ireland gained its independence from Britain in 1922 after centuries of strife and left the Commonwealth in 1948. Its constitution lays claim to Northern Ireland. Area: 70,000 km^2; Pop: 3,440,000; Cap: Dublin. See map on page 118.

Iron The most important metallic element and the second most abundant metal in the Earth's crust after aluminium. Iron is extracted from its ores by a process known as smelting in a blast furnace. By itself, iron is fairly weak and very prone to corrosion, but the addition of small amounts of other materials, particularly carbon, produces our most important alloy – steel. There are many different steels for different purposes. Extra strength, toughness, springiness and resistance to corrosion are some of the qualities which are produced in different alloys. Chem. symbol Fe (Latin *Ferrum*).

Iron Age The period following the Bronze Age, when people learned how to make tools of iron. In Mesopotamia (modern Iraq), men were working iron by 1500 BC, but the knowledge did not reach western Europe until nearly 1000 years later.

Irrawaddy Major river of Burma, flowing southwards the length of the country into the Bay of Bengal. Important for irrigation in a large rice-growing region. Length: 2000 km.

Irrigation Artificial watering of land in order to grow crops. It is generally employed where rainfall is less than 500 mm per year but may be vital in wetter lands for water-loving crops such as rice. Irrigation has been practised since ancient times; in the Nile valley, for instance, it has always been the only source of water.

Isis Ancient Egyptian nature goddess; a sister and wife of Osiris.

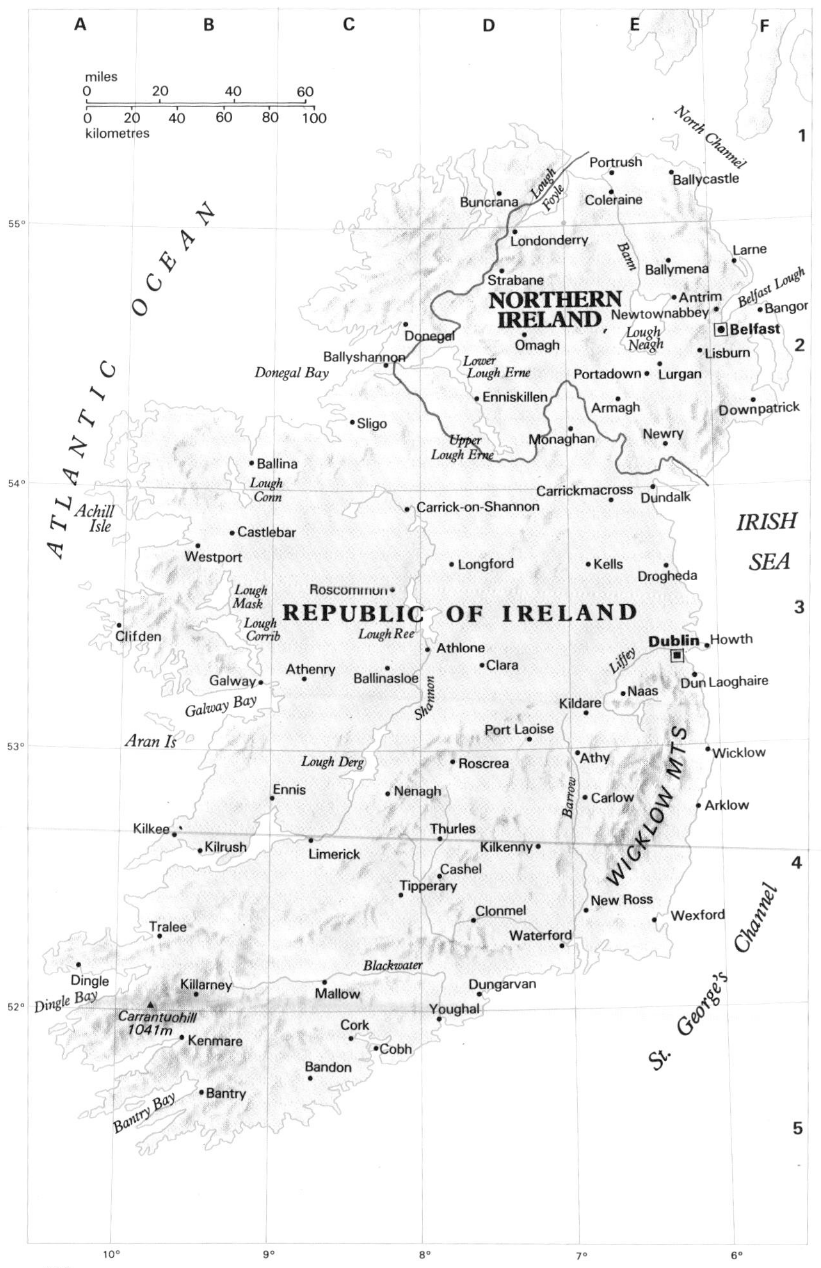
A
B
C
D
E
F
miles
0 20 40 60
0 20 40 60 80 100
kilometres
1
2
3
4
5
55°
54°
53°
52°
10°
9°
8°
7°
6°
ATLANTIC OCEAN
North Channel
IRISH SEA
St. George's Channel
NORTHERN IRELAND
REPUBLIC OF IRELAND
Portrush
Ballycastle
Coleraine
Buncrana
Lough Foyle
Londonderry
Bann
Larne
Ballymena
Strabane
Antrim
Belfast Lough
Bangor
Newtownabbey
Belfast
Donegal
Omagh
Lough Neagh
Lisburn
Ballyshannon
Lower Lough Erne
Donegal Bay
Portadown
Lurgan
Enniskillen
Armagh
Downpatrick
Sligo
Monaghan
Newry
Upper Lough Erne
Ballina
Lough Conn
Carrickmacross
Dundalk
Achill Isle
Carrick-on-Shannon
Castlebar
Westport
Longford
Kells
Drogheda
Lough Mask
Roscommon
Lough Corrib
Clifden
Lough Ree
Athlone
Dublin
Howth
Liffey
Athenry
Clara
Galway
Ballinasloe
Dun Laoghaire
Naas
Galway Bay
Shannon
Kildare
Port Laoise
Aran Is
Wicklow
Lough Derg
Athy
Roscrea
WICKLOW MTS
Ennis
Nenagh
Carlow
Barrow
Arklow
Kilkee
Thurles
Kilrush
Limerick
Kilkenny
Cashel
Tipperary
New Ross
Clonmel
Wexford
Tralee
Waterford
Blackwater
Dingle
Killarney
Mallow
Dungarvan
Dingle Bay
Carrantuohill 1041m
Youghal
Kenmare
Cork
Cobh
Bandon
Bantry
Bantry Bay

Muslims at prayer in a mosque. The walls are not decorated with pictures and statues but with abstract patterns.

Islam Mainly Eastern religion of followers of the prophet Mohammed, with almost 500 million adherents. Moslems, or Mohammedans, believe in the mercy and justice of the one god Allah and observe five pillars of faith: profession of faith, prayer (five times a day facing in the direction of the holy city of Mecca), almsgiving, fasting, and a once-in-a-lifetime pilgrimage to Mecca.

Islamabad Capital of Pakistan. A modern purpose-built city with a nuclear power station. Pop: 77,000.

Isle of Man Island in the Irish Sea belonging to the British crown but with its own parliament ('Tynwald'). Tourism is a major industry.

Isotope An isotope is an element that has had neutrons added to or taken away from the nucleus of its atoms. Some isotopes are radioactive. Radioactive isotopes are very useful because, while they retain the normal chemical properties of the element, their radioactivity allows their presence to be detected in various industrial processes. Isotopes are also used in medicine to track down and destroy diseased cells.

Israel Republic in SW Asia on the E Mediterranean coast. Its varied landscape includes the large Negev Desert in the S, the highland regions of Galilee and Judea, and the fertile coastal plains. The Mediterranean climate, often aided by irrigation, is ideal for the cultivation of citrus fruits and vegetables which are the leading cash crops and the chief exports. Mineral resources are limited, but manufacturing industries ranging from textiles to aircraft construction have been established with massive American aid.

Israel became an independent Jewish state in 1948 but has been in almost continuous conflict with its Arab neighbours and has fought four major wars. Area: 21,300 km^2; Pop: 4,021,000; Cap: Jerusalem.

Istanbul Seaport and largest city of Turkey situated on both sides of the Bosporus. Formerly known as Constantinople, the old city on the N shore was the centre of the Byzantine and Muslim empires. Pop: 2,535,000.

Italy Republic in S Europe consisting of a peninsula in the Mediterranean and the two principal islands of Sicily and

Sardinia. The mainland is dominated by the Apennine Mts which run almost the full length of the country. The Po valley in the north and the coastal plains are the main agricultural regions. Industry is also concentrated in the north using cheap hydroelectricity. Italy has a long cultural history as the centre of the ancient Roman Empire and the European Renaissance. This, combined with its Mediterranean climate, stimulates a large tourist industry. Area: 301,000 km^2; Pop: 56,651,000; Cap: Rome.

Ivan the Terrible (1530–84) First tsar of all Russia from 1547. A tyrannical and cruel ruler, he expanded the boundaries of Russia eastwards. His reign saw the opening of trade relations with Queen Elizabeth I of England and unsuccessful wars with Poland and Sweden.

Ivory Coast Republic on the Gulf of Guinea, West Africa. Much of the south is covered in dense tropical rain forest, though further north there are large plains and savannas. The economy is based largely on coffee and cocoa exports. Area: 320,000 km^2; Pop: 8,000,000; Cap: Abidjan.

Ivy An evergreen woody plant with glossy leaves that clambers over trees, rocks and walls. Ivy climbs by means of roots that grow from the stem and take hold in the tiniest crevices.

J

Jackal Ragged, yellowy-coloured members of the dog family found in Africa and southern Asia. They hunt small antelopes and other small mammals in packs, but also follow the large carnivores to pick up their leftovers.

Jackdaw A member of the crow family, the jackdaw is an inquisitive bird, well-known for its habit of stealing bright objects. It resembles the carrion crow but is slightly smaller with blue-black plumage, a grey nape and blue-grey eyes.

Jaguar Largest cat of S and C America. It weighs up to 150 kg and has a yellow coat with rosettes of black spots.

Jakarta Port in Java and capital of Indonesia. Pop: 4,546,000.

Jamaica Mountainous island country in the Caribbean Sea, west of Haiti. Jamaica has a warm, moist climate, cooler in the mountains. The people grow sugar-cane, bananas, coffee, fruit, coconuts, ginger and tobacco. Maize and rice are staple foods, and cattle are raised. Tourism is important, and industry has grown in recent years. Minerals include bauxite (aluminium ore), gypsum and petroleum. Area: 10,964 km^2; Pop: 2,388,000; Cap: Kingston.

James I (1566–1625) He reigned as James VI of Scotland from 1567 and as James I of England, Scotland and Ireland from 1603. Described as 'the wisest fool in Christendom', his uncertain religious views angered both Protestants and Catholics, as shown by the Gunpowder Plot in 1605 and the Puritan-inspired publication of the Authorized Version of the Bible in 1611. His reliance on favourites and his long years of personal rule without parliament furthered discontent.

James II (1633–1701) King of England and Scotland (as James VII) 1685–88. His marriage to the Catholic Mary of Modena in 1673 was unpopular. He quelled the Monmouth rebellion (1685) but the brutal sentences handed out to the prisoners at the Bloody Assizes by the ruthless Judge Jeffreys only increased his unpopularity. He tried to obtain religious toleration for Catholics but with the Glorious Revolution in 1688 he fled to France.

Japan Country in eastern Asia, made up of four large islands and 3000 smaller ones. It is a cool, mountainous land, much of it forested. Small farms produce rice, barley, wheat and soyabeans. Fishing is important, for the Japanese do not eat much meat. Coal and copper are mined, but most minerals have to be imported to supply Japan's many industries. It is the third largest industrial nation in the world, and Japanese exports include ships, cars, televisions and electrical goods.

Industrialization has transformed Japan, which was a little-known empire until the 1800s, when it opened its ports to outsiders and began to adopt new ways. In World War II Japanese troops overran much of Asia until defeated in 1945. Since then, Japan has made an astonishing recovery. Area: 372,409 km^2; Pop: 120,000,000; Cap: Tokyo.

Jason In Greek legend the leader of the Argonauts who sought the Golden Fleece. This belonged to Aeëtes, King of Colchis, and Jason was forced to perform a series of difficult tasks before he could take it.

Jay

Jay The most brightly coloured member of the crow family. It has a pinkish-brown plumage with black on the wings and tail, blue patches on the wings, and a conspicuous white rump. Jays imitate the calls of other birds. In spring they rob eggs from the nests of smaller birds.

Jazz Style of music with its origins in folk tunes and the African rhythms of the 19th century slave immigrants to the United States. Jazz was first played around 1900 by black musicians in the southern states of the USA, particularly in New Orleans. Much jazz is improvised, the players making up their own version of a tune as they go along.

Jefferson, Thomas (1743–1826) American lawyer, scientist and statesman who was responsible for the drafting of the Declaration of Independence. Founder of the Republican Party (forerunners of the present Democratic Party), he became president in 1801 and served two terms. His administration saw the purchase of Louisiana from France in 1803.

Jellyfish Sea creatures with transparent umbrella-shaped bodies ringed by long, hanging tentacles. Some species grow up to two metres across. Jellyfishes paralyse small fishes and other prey by releasing poison darts from stinging cells in their tentacles.

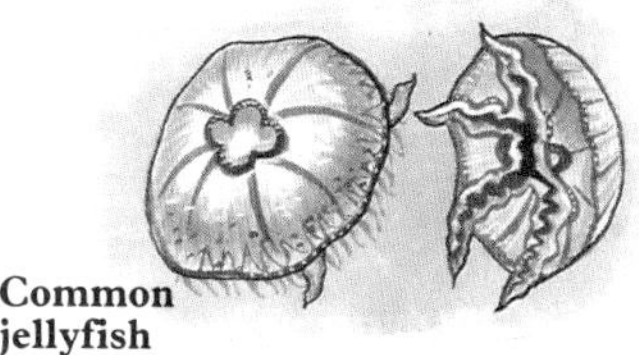
Common jellyfish

Jenner, Edward (1749–1823) English physician known as the 'father of immunology' who discovered a smallpox vaccine.

Jerusalem Historic city in central Palestine and capital of Israel. Sacred to three faiths – Judaism, Christianity and Islam – it was captured by the Crusaders in 1099 and regained by Muslims under the leadership of Saladin. Pop: 387,000.

Jesus Christ (*c* 4 BC–AD30) Founder of CHRISTIANITY. His followers believed him to be the son of God and the performer of many miracles; the Pharisees saw him as a revolutionary and persuaded Pontius Pilate, the Roman governor, to have him crucified. The teaching of Jesus Christ survived his death to become the foundation of Western civilization.

Jet engine See **Gas turbine**.

Jews See **Judaism**.

Joan of Arc, St (1412–31) French heroine known as the Maid of Orleans. She is supposed to have heard angels telling her to go to the aid of the Dauphin. She later led the French in a series of victories against the English in the Hundred Years War. Captured by the Burgundians, she was sold to the English who burnt her as a heretic.

Johannesburg City in Transvaal, South Africa. Centre of the Witwatersrand gold-mining region. Founded in 1886 after the discovery of gold, it has grown to be the largest city. Pop: 1,726,000 (met area).

John, King (1167–1216) The youngest son of Henry II, he reigned as King of England from 1199. During his reign Normandy was lost and in 1215 he was forced by the barons to sign the MAGNA CARTA.

Johnson, Samuel (1709–84) English lexicographer and writer whose *Dictionary* was published in 1755. He also wrote *Lives of the Poets* and was an outstanding literary figure of his day. His famous biography was written by James Boswell.

John the Baptist, St (d. *c* AD 29) Regarded as the forerunner of Jesus, he was a great prophet. He encouraged people to repent and heralded the coming of the Messiah. He was beheaded by Herod Antipas, the son of Herod the Great, king of Judaea.

Jordan Kingdom in the Middle East. The fertile highland plateau has a cool climate, with hot summers, but elsewhere it is hot most of the year and there are large areas of desert. During the Arab-Israeli war of 1967, Jordan lost its land on the West Bank of the R. Jordan. Today, one of its problems is the many Palestinian refugees who have made their home in the country. Area: 97,764 km²; Pop: 2,689,000; Cap: Amman.

Judaism Ancient religion of the Jews, based on the teachings and laws of the Old Testament, and from which both Christianity and Islam are derived.

Judo see **Martial Arts**.

Julius Caesar (*c* 101–44 BC) Great Roman general, statesman and writer. He conquered Gaul (58–49 BC) and in 55 BC invaded Britain. He defied the Senate's order to disband his army and defeated their general Pompey. He ruled as a dictator but introduced social reforms and was popular with the people. He was murdered in 44 BC.

Jupiter The largest planet in the Solar system (diameter 134,000 km) orbiting the Sun at a distance of 778 million miles. It is composed largely of hydrogen but may have a rocky core. The surface is hidden by swirling clouds containing a strange red spot. Jupiter has 16 moons.

Jute The name of an important natural fibre (and the plant from which it is derived). The fibre is soft but can be spun into tough, strong threads suitable for rope, sacking and matting. Jute is grown in warm, wet areas of India and Bangladesh.

K

Kabul Capital of Afghanistan, on R. Kabul. The city lies in a mountain valley, commanding routes to the Khyber pass. Pop: 377,000.

Kalahari Desert Semi-desert region in southern Africa. Lies mainly in Botswana, over 1000 metres above sea level. Inhabited by Bushmen. Area: 52,000 km².

Kampuchea (Cambodia) Communist state of SE Asia. The central part of the country is a low-lying plain crossed by the Mekong River. This is where the majority of the people live, growing rice in the fertile soil. In 1973 communist forces (Khmer Rouge) captured the capital and established a brutal regime that resulted in the death of one-third of the population. In 1978 Vietnamese forces invaded the country and set up a new government. Area: 181,000 km²; Pop: 6,118,000; Cap: Phnom Penh.

Kangaroo Australian marsupials with powerful hindlimbs and tails and short forelimbs. The great grey kangaroo of eastern Australia is a forest browser. It may stand almost two metres in height, can hop eight metres in a single bound and travel at 40 km/h. The plain-dwelling red

A Jewish scribe copies the Law (Torah) in Hebrew script.

kangaroo is smaller but more widespread. Kangaroo babies (joeys) remain in the mothers' pouch for six months.

Karachi City and seaport in Pakistan. Important for oil and gas industries and shipbuilding. Former capital of Pakistan. Pop: 3,469,000.

Karate See **Martial Arts**.

Kashmir Mountainous region in NW India and NE Pakistan which has been the subject of dispute between the two countries since 1947.

Keats, John (1795-1821) Great English romantic poet. His poems include *Endymion*, *The Eve of St Agnes*, *Hyperion* (unfinished), *La Belle Dame Sans Merci*, *Ode to a Nightingale* and *Ode on a Grecian Urn*.

Kennedy, John Fitzgerald (1917-63) The youngest candidate and first ever Roman Catholic to become president of the USA (35th). Elected to office in 1961, he was immensely popular. He was opposed to racial discrimination and ably dealt with the Cuban missile crisis (1962). He was assassinated by Lee Harvey Oswald in Dallas on November 22, 1963.

Kenya Country in E Africa bordering the Indian Ocean. Northern Kenya is hot and dry, with savanna and thorn scrub. The central highlands are cooler and wetter, and this is where the majority of the people live, farming the rich volcanic soil. The chief exports are agricultural: coffee, tea, sugar, cereals, maize and dairy products. Area: 582,800 km^2; Pop: 19,372,000; Cap: Nairobi.

Kepler, Johannes (1571-1630) German astronomer who worked out the law governing the motion of the planets. He based his calculations on the detailed observations of the Danish astronomer Tycho Brahe.

Kestrel A small falcon with a brownish plumage and a grey head and tail. The kestrel feeds mainly on mice and voles, and can frequently be seen hovering above roadside verges in search of prey.

Khartoum Capital city of Sudan, at junction of Blue and White Niles. Site of famous siege in 1884-85 by the Mahdists who killed General Gordon. Pop: 299,000.

Kidney The organ responsible for cleansing the blood of waste products which result from various chemical processes within the body. Kidneys contain many thousands of tiny units that filter the waste materials from the blood. Dissolved in water, the wastes then pass from the kidneys into the bladder. From here they are emptied out of the body as urine.

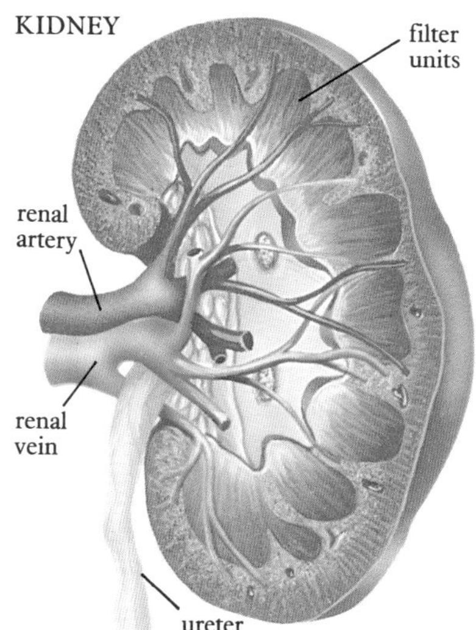

Kingfisher A small, brightly coloured bird, with a glossy blue-green back and orange underparts. Kingfishers are shy birds that live by streams and ponds. They dive into the water to catch fish.

Kipling, Rudyard (1865-1936) British writer whose work describes life in India under British rule, particularly *The Light that Failed* and *Kim*. He also wrote stories for children including *Jungle Book*, *Stalky and Co* and *Puck of Pook's Hill*.

Kiribati Country in the Pacific Ocean, consisting of a string of islands including the former Gilbert Islands. The soil is poor, though the climate is good. The chief crops are coconuts and pandanus fruit; the main food is fish. Area: 712 km^2; Pop: 60,000; Cap: Bairiki.

Kite A bird of prey, about the same size as the buzzard. It is recognized by its forked tail and soaring flight.

Kiwi Chicken-sized, flightless bird and emblem of New Zealand. It has hair-like feathers and a long sensitive beak with which it probes the forest litter for worms and insects. A shy creature, it hides by day and forages by night when the peculiar call for which it is named can be heard.

Knox, John (1505–72) Religious reformer who established Protestantism in Scotland.

Koala Although it was the model for the very first 'teddy bear', the koala is not a bear. It is an Australian marsupial of the phalanger family. By day it sleeps high in the blue gum-tree, by night it eats the leaves and buds. The mother carries her baby in her pouch for several months until it is ready to climb on to her back and pick food for itself.

Koran The sacred book of Islam. Moslems regard it as a series of revelations by God to Mohammed. The Koran is written in classical Arabic and memorized by Moslems.

Korea, Democratic People's Republic of Also known as North Korea, the country occupies the northern part of the Korean Peninsula in E Asia. It is mountainous and fringed by many coastal islands. Northern Korea has a harsh climate, with cold winters. Its people work on collective farms and in state-owned factories. Minerals include coal, iron ore, tungsten and gold. Area: 120,570 km^2; Pop: 19,630,000; Cap: Pyongyang.

Korea, Republic of Also known as South Korea, this republic occupies the southern part of the Korean Peninsula. It is mountainous, with hot, wet summers. Winters in South Korea are milder than in North Korea. Rice is the main crop, followed by barley, cotton and wheat. Silk is also produced. South Korea has advanced industries, including textiles, iron and steel, vehicles and electronics. Since the end of the Korean War in 1953, South Korea has progressed faster than the North. It now rivals Japan as an Asian industrial power. Area: 98,510 km^2; Pop: 41,999,000; Cap: Seoul.

Kublai Khan (1216–94) Grandson of Genghis Khan and one of the greatest Mongol emperors. He extended the boundaries of his empire and founded the Yuan dynasty in China (1260).

Kung fu See **Martial Arts**.

Kuwait Country in Arabia, at the head of the Arabian Gulf. A hot desert land, with scarcely any fertile pasture, Kuwait has become rich through oil. Oil drilling began in 1936, and today Kuwait enjoys free schools, hospitals and other modern services thanks to its oil revenues. Area: 17,824 km^2; Pop: 1,758,000; Cap: Kuwait.

L

7-spot ladybird

14-spot ladybird

Ladybird Family of beetles which feed on aphids and so are welcomed by gardeners. Common ladybirds are red with black spots – the number of spots varies with the species. Others are black with red spots, and some are yellow and black. The bright colours warn birds that ladybirds have an unpleasant taste.

Lagos Port and capital of Nigeria, W Africa, on Gulf of Guinea. The city was founded on Lagos Island as a slave trading post, later spreading to the mainland. Owing to overcrowding, the seat of government is being transferred to Abuja. Pop: 1,100,000.

Lamprey Primitive fish with a sucking mouth and no jaws. The sea lamprey is a long eel-like fish, up to 75 cm in length. It has circular rows of horny teeth and feeds by clenching the sides of fishes and sucking their blood. The river lamprey is similar but smaller.

Language A collection of 'sound signs' or words, used for communication. We use language when we speak and write. There are at least 2800 different languages in the world, and many more dialects (local variations). The language spoken by the greatest number of people is Chinese, followed by English. The ENGLISH LANGUAGE belongs to the Indo-European language family. It is very like Dutch and German. Also in the same language family are Romance languages, such as French and Italian. Although LATIN is still studied, no-one now speaks it.

Laos Country in SE Asia, that has a long eastern border with Vietnam. Very mountainous, the country's chief natural features are the Annam Mountains and the Mekong River, which forms part of the western border with Thailand. Much of the country is forested. Timber products are valuable, and rice, coffee and maize are grown. Tin is the chief mineral export.

The ancient kingdom of Laos has often been taken over by more powerful neighbours. From 1893 until 1949 it was part of French Indo-China. In 1975, after years of civil war, it came under partial Vietnamese control. Area: 236,862 km^2; Pop: 3,723,000; Cap: Vientiane.

La Paz Capital of Bolivia, S America, situated in the Andes at a height of 3675 metres – the highest capital in the world. Pop: 655,000.

Lapwing A bird also known as the peewit (from its whistling call). It has a feathered crest on its head, a metallic blue-green sheen across its back and wings, and a white breast. Lapwings flock in large numbers over ploughed fields and coastal mudflats. They feed on insects, slugs and worms.

Larch Group of coniferous trees belonging to the pine family. The leaves are borne in whorls and are shed in winter. The small upright cones have thin, almost papery scales.

Lark Birds noted for their sweet song and hovering flight. Larks have a small crest on their head. They have dull brown plumage which makes them difficult to spot on the ground where they make their nests.

Larva Stage in the development of many invertebrates, and certain vertebrates such as amphibians, which is markedly different in form from the adult. Caterpillars and tadpoles are both forms of larvae.

Laser A laser is an instrument that produces an intense beam of light so thin it can drill holes in steel plates and even in diamonds. A laser beam is powerful because, unlike ordinary light, all the light waves in it are in step. They reinforce each other to produce light of great energy. This light is said to be coherent.

Latent heat Changes of state – freezing, melting, and boiling – take place at certain fixed temperatures because of latent heat. For instance, latent heat has to be removed from a liquid to make it freeze. The temperature of the liquid drops until it begins to freeze, and then the temperature remains steady as freezing takes place. This is why it takes so long to make ice.

Latin Language once spoken by the Romans and spread by conquest throughout the ROMAN EMPIRE. Latin became the language of learning and science in Europe, and also the language of the Christian Church. Latin has given many words to other languages including English. So, although Latin is now a 'dead' language, it is still of interest to people studying history and the way language works.

Latitude and longitude Imaginary grid system over the Earth. Lines of latitude run parallel with the equator. Lines of longitude (meridians) run north-south. The latitude of any place is the angle it makes with the equator at the centre of the Earth. The longitude of any place is the angle it makes with the prime (0°) meridian at the centre of the Earth.

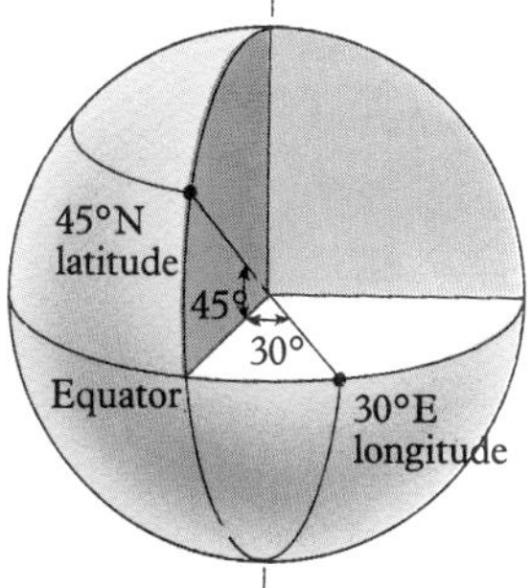

Laurel The name laurel is given to many kinds of ornamental bushes but the true European laurel is the sweet bay. It is a broad-leaved evergreen that can grow as high as 20 metres but is usually much shorter.

Law Rules of society, ultimately enforced by the POLICE and the courts. In Britain laws are made by parliament, and judges (assisted by juries) and magistrates administer it. Criminal law covers offences that are punishable by the state. Civil law covers cases concerning private rights. Countries with shared histories may have similar laws: Roman, British and Napoleonic law, for example, have influenced the laws of many countries.

Lawrence, D(avid) H(erbert) (1885–1930) English novelist whose works deal with the natural instincts and passions of people. Novels include *Sons and Lovers*, *The Rainbow*, *Women in Love* and *Lady Chatterley's Lover*.

Lead Soft, bluish-grey metal which is easy to cut and shape. For thousands of years it has been used for waterpipes. Today large amounts are used in car batteries. Pewter is an alloy of lead and tin, as are many solders used for joining metals. Chem. symbol Pb (Latin *plumbum*).

Leaf The main food-making part of a plant. The green colour is due to chlorophyll, which absorbs the energy of sunlight and uses it to power the food-making process called photosynthesis. Leaves vary tremendously in shape: some are smooth, some are toothed, and some are completely divided into separate leaflets.

Lebanon Country at the eastern end of the Mediterranean Sea, with Syria to the north and Israel to the south. Lebanon has a 'backbone' of high mountains, once forested, and a fertile valley, the Bekaa. Lebanon has few minerals or industries, but for centuries has been a centre for Middle East trade. Its recent history is one of invasion and civil war. Area: 10,400 km²; Pop: 2,601,000; Cap: Beirut.

Leech Blood-sucking worms, found mainly in fresh water. Leeches have sucking discs at each end of their bodies which enable them to cling to fishes and other animals and suck their blood. Doctors once used leeches to 'bleed' their patients in the mistaken belief that it would help them to heal more quickly.

Lemming A vole-like rodent of cold northern grasslands that lives in underground colonies. It does not hibernate during the winter but continues to live under the snow. About every four years the lemming population rises sharply and there is not enough food to go around. When this happens the lemmings emigrate in hordes. Many perish trying to cross rivers and lakes, but a few survive to set up new colonies.

Wood lemming

Lemur Tree-living primates found in Madagascar (Malagasy). They have large eyes and long bushy tails. The ring-tailed lemur holds its tail upright when it is running.

Lenin, Vladimir Ilyich (1870–1924) Russian revolutionary leader who founded the Communist party. He spent long periods in exile but returned in 1917 and after the 'November revolution' assumed power. His party won the civil war of 1918–20 and he ruled as virtual dictator. His mausoleum in Red Square in Moscow has become a communist shrine.

Leningrad Major port and second largest city of USSR, on R. Neva. Originally called St Petersburg, it was renamed Petrograd in 1905 and then Leningrad in 1924. Centre of Russian Revolution (1917) and besieged in 1944 by the Germans (at which time one million citizens died). Site of Winter Palace and Hermitage museum. Pop: 4,588,000.

Lens A device that changes light passing through it by bringing together the light rays or spreading them apart. A magnifying glass is a lens. It can bend light rays from all points on an object towards each other. This creates an enlarged image of the object. A magnifying glass is a *convex* lens – it is thickest in the middle. A *concave* lens is thinnest in the middle. It spreads light rays out and makes objects look smaller.

Lent The period of 40 days before Easter when Christians used to fast, remember their sins, and resolve to do better. People

Vladimir Ilyich Lenin

do not often fast in Lent now, but they often give up some small luxury or comfort.

Leonardo da Vinci (1452–1519) Italian artist, scientist and engineer. A RENAISSANCE genius who is best remembered for his *Mona Lisa* and *The Last Supper*. He was also an able anatomist and inventor who conducted advanced research into the principles of hydraulics, the circulation of the blood and the principles of flight.

Leopard Large cat (up to 2.5 metres long) found in Africa and Asia. The fur is yellow with black spots. The black leopard (panther) is a common variety. Leopards prey on antelopes and other mammals and are fierce hunters.

Lesotho Mountainous country in southern Africa, entirely surrounded by South Africa. The farmland is poor, there are few industries, and many people work in South Africa. Formerly the British colony of Basutoland, Lesotho became independent in 1966. Area: 30,362 km^2; Pop: 1,474,000; Cap: Maseru.

Liberia Country on the coast of W Africa. Inland, the dense forests are thinly populated. People live in small villages, growing rice and other crops. Near the coast the land is more suitable for farming, and rubber, coffee and bananas are grown for export. Liberia was founded in 1821 as a settlement for freed slaves from the USA. Area: 111,398 km^2; Pop: 2,160,000; Cap: Monrovia.

Library Collection of books, or the building in which books, records, documents and data of various kinds are stored. There was a library at Nineveh, in ancient Assyria, as early as 650 BC, and famous libraries in Ancient Greece, Egypt and Rome, and also in the Arab world and China. During the Middle Ages, libraries helped to preserve scientific knowledge. Public libraries began in the 19th century.

Libya Country in N Africa, with a Mediterranean coast. Most people live on the coastland, grazing livestock and growing crops of dates, olives, grapes and vegetables. Barley and wheat are grown too. Further south the country becomes part of the sandy Sahara Desert. Oil wealth has been used to irrigate the desert and to start new industries. In ancient times Libya was Rome's 'granary', growing wheat for the Roman Empire. The country is now run by a system of elected people's congresses. Area: 1,759,997 km²; Pop: 3,749,000; Caps: Tripoli and Benghazi.

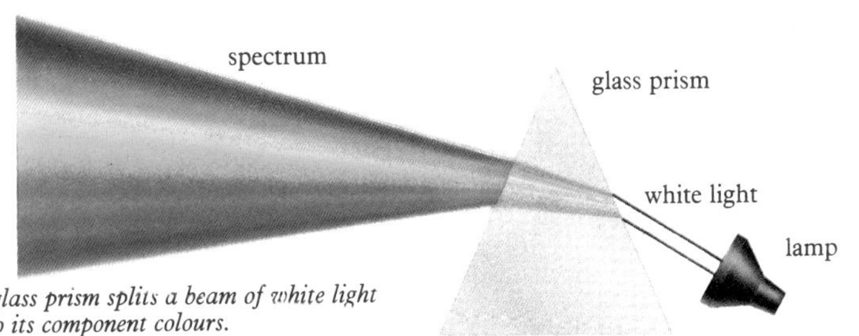

A glass prism splits a beam of white light into its component colours.

Lichens Unusual plants consisting of an intricate mixture of a fungus and an alga. The fungi in these partnerships cannot grow without their food-providing algal partners. Most lichens are extremely hardy and many grow on bare rocks in very hot or very cold places. Growth is slow and the plants are long-lived.

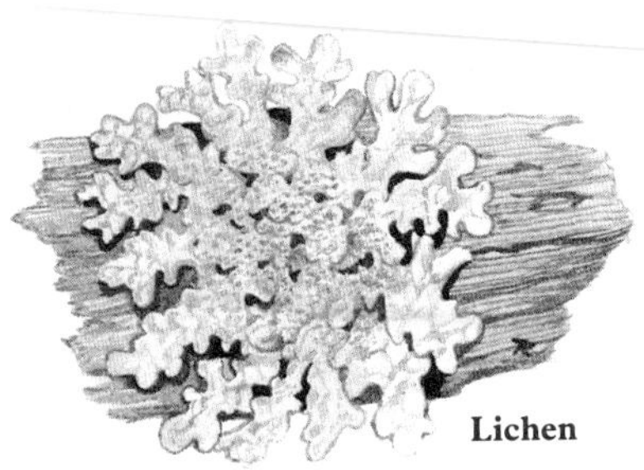

Lichen

Liechtenstein Small European principality between Switzerland and Austria. The western third of the land is taken up by the Rhine Valley, the remainder by the Alps. The economy depends heavily upon tourism and finance. There are close ties with Switzerland. Area: 158 km²; Pop; 27,000; Cap: Vaduz.

Light A kind of ELECTROMAGNETIC RADIATION, like radio, heat, X-rays, etc. It travels as waves at a speed of 300,000 kilometres (186,000 miles) per second. Its waves are very small – only a few millionths of a centimetre long. The length of the waves also determines the colour of light. Red light, for example, has a slightly longer wavelength than blue light. When white light from the sun is passed through a glass prism, the beam of light is split up into its various components – the colours of the rainbow. Light, like all other kinds of radiation, travels as tiny particles of energy called *quanta*. A quantum of light is called a *photon*.

Lighthouse The lights in early lighthouses were merely fires burning in metal baskets. Today's lighthouses, many of which are completely automatic, have powerful electric lamps that can be seen as far as 50 km away. The lens, usually large and barrel-shaped, is made to rotate around the lamp. This produces the flashing sequence by which navigators can recognize the lighthouse.

Lightning Gigantic spark of electricity which travels between a cloud and the ground during a thunderstorm. The tremendous electrical 'pressure' or voltage needed to make this happen is believed to be built up in the cloud through friction between ice crystals and water droplets in the turbulent air currents. Thunder is the noise of air violently expanding as it is heated by the lightning.

Light-year The distance travelled by a beam of light in one year. This is equivalent to 9.5 million million km. Light-years are used in astronomy to measure the vast distances of the stars. The nearest star to the Sun is Proxima Centauri, 4.3 light-years away.

Lima Capital of Peru, founded by Francisco PIZARRO in 1535. Twice devastated by earthquakes (1687 and 1746), and twice subsequently rebuilt. Pop: 3,158,000.

Limestone Rock consisting mainly of calcium carbonate, the purest form of chalk. Limestone is easily dissolved by rainwater containing carbon dioxide which makes it a weak acid. Limestone scenery is associated with caves and underground streams.

Limestone caves often contain spectacular formations of stalactites and stalagmites.

Limpet The name of various snails with conical shells. They cling tightly to rocks on the seashore, even in stormy seas, and each limpet shell grows to fit its own piece of rock. The animals move about to graze on algae on the rocks, but always return to their own 'home base'.

Lincoln, Abraham (1809–65) American lawyer who became a member of Congress in 1846. He bitterly opposed slavery and in 1861 became the 16th president of the United States. He led the Union through the Civil War, though there was constant friction between him and his generals. He was re-elected in 1864 but was assassinated by John Wilkes Booth in 1865.

Lindbergh, Charles (1902–74) American aviator who became a national hero when he made the first solo transatlantic flight in 1927. In 1932 his son was kidnapped and murdered.

Linen Woven fabric made from the fibre of the flax plant. Introduced to N Europe by the Romans, it became the main textile in the Middle Ages, with Flanders the most famous centre. Today Ireland is the chief producer.

Linnaeus, Carolus (Karl von Linné, 1707–78) Swedish botanist who founded a system of classification for plants and animals. He defined organisms by referring firstly to their *genus* and then to their *species*.

Lion Large cat found in Africa south of the Sahara. The fur is brownish-yellow. The male has a majestic mane and is the centre of the family group or pride. The lionesses hunt zebra and antelopes.

Lippi, Filippo (1406–69) Florentine artist whose beautiful frescoes can be seen in Prato Cathedral in Tuscany.

Liquid One of the three states of matter, the others being SOLID and GAS. In a liquid the molecules that make it up are not firmly fixed to each other, so that a liquid fills any container into which it is poured. If liquids are heated beyond a certain temperature they turn into gases. If they are cooled below a certain point they become solids. Different liquids have different freezing and boiling points. About 70 per cent of the Earth's surface is liquid.

Lisbon Port and capital of Portugal, with fine natural harbour at mouth of R. Tagus. Important cultural and commercial centre, with increasing industrialization. An earthquake in 1755 destroyed almost the entire city. Pop: 769,000.

Lister, Joseph (1827–1912) English surgeon who founded antiseptic surgery. He used carbolic acid and sterilized instruments to prevent infection, thereby reducing the mortality rate in hospitals.

Liszt, Franz (1811–86) Hungarian pianist and composer. His works include tone poems, symphonies, piano concertos and the *Hungarian Rhapsodies*.

LIVER

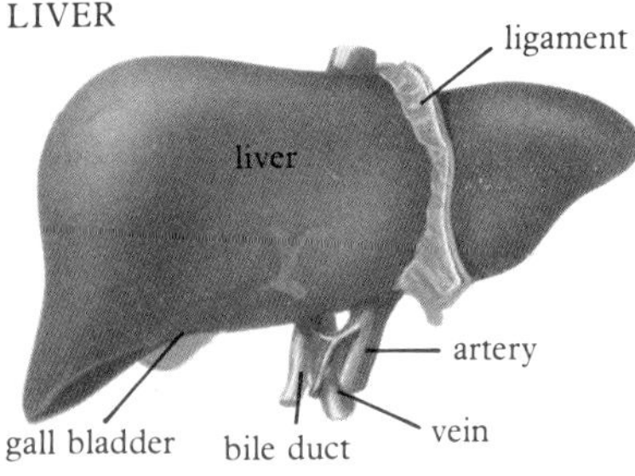

The liver is the largest gland in the body and is irreplaceable.

Liver A large gland with several important functions. It produces bile, a substance that helps break down fatty foods in the gut. It also produces several blood proteins. It stores sugars in the form of glycogen, as well as certain vital vitamins. The liver also breaks down old red blood cells and stores the iron they contain. Finally, as a result of all its chemical activity, the liver provides heat for the body.

Liverpool Port and admin centre of Merseyside, England, with some of the world's largest docks. Its commercial importance began in the 18th century with cotton and the slave trade. In 1830 the first entirely steam-hauled railway linked Liverpool with Manchester. Today, industry, especially food processing, is important. Pop: 540,000; Greater Liverpool 1,368,000.

Liverwort Green flowerless plants closely related to the mosses. There are two types: leafy liverworts that look very similar to mosses and flat liverworts that look more like green seaweed. Like mosses, liverworts can reproduce by spores.

Livingstone, David (1813–73) One of the greatest explorer-missionaries of Africa in the 19th century. He discovered the Zambezi River in 1851 and the Victoria Falls in 1855. He was found by Stanley in 1871 after he had been feared lost, but he later died while searching for the source of the River Nile.

Lizard Group of generally long-tailed reptiles related to snakes. Some species, such as the SLOW WORM, have no legs and look more like snakes. Most lizards feed on insects and other small creatures. They are widely distributed throughout the world, particularly in the warmer regions, and range in size from a few centimetres to the 3-metre komodo dragon of SE Asia.

Llama S American hoofed mammal of the camel family. Like its wild relative the guanaco, the llama has no hump. It is used as a beast of burden in the Andes and valued also for its meat and wool.

Lobster Large crustacean which lives on the sea bed. Lobsters have long antennae, eyes on stalks and five pairs of legs. The first pair form large pincers, or claws. Their colour varies from blue to dark green – lobsters only turn red when they are cooked.

Locomotive There are three main types of locomotive – steam, electric and diesel. Steam locomotives have, however, been largely replaced in western countries by other types. The most powerful diesel locomotives are diesel-electric. They have diesel engines that supply the power to turn electric generators. The generators make electric current that turns electric motors. These turn the driving wheels. Most of the world's electric locomotives take their power from overhead wires via a

The first steam locomotive was built by Richard Trevithick in 1804.

sprung arm called a *pantograph*. Other locomotives pick up current from a third rail.

Locust Insects related to grasshoppers. There are many species of locusts, some of which cause terrible damage to crops in Africa. They may swarm in vast numbers darkening the sky and can rapidly strip fields and trees bare of green vegetation.

London Capital city of the United Kingdom, situated on R. Thames. Seat of government and international financial, commercial and cultural centre. Imports of food and raw materials arrive at the busy Port of London, exports from the City of London depart 'invisibly'. With many historic buildings – St Paul's Cathedral, Westminster Abbey, the Tower of London – and attractive parks and streets, tourism has become a major industry. *Londinium* was founded by the Romans in 43 AD. In the Great Fire of 1666 much of the city, including over 100 churches, was destroyed. Again during the Blitz of World War II London suffered extensive damage, but little trace of the bombing survives and the town has greatly expanded. Pop: (Inner London) 2,497,000, (Greater London) 6,696,000.

Longfellow, Henry Wadsworth (1807–82) American poet whose poems include *The Village Blacksmith* and the long poem *The Song of Hiawatha*.

Longitude See **Latitude**.

Long March An episode during the struggle between the Nationalists and Communists in China. In 1934, the Communist forces in Kiangsi were forced out by Chiang Kai-shek's Nationalists. Led by Mao Tse-tung, they travelled about 13,000 km to Yenan, where they joined other Communist groups. Thousands died on the march.

Los Angeles Port and city in California, USA, situated in an important oil producing region. Home of Hollywood, the film centre of the USA. The city suffers from serious air pollution. Pop: 2,967,000 (met area 7,478,000).

Loudspeaker An instrument that turns small varying electric currents into sounds. Loudspeakers are usually of the moving coil type. This coil is attached to a stiff paper cone. Varying electric currents from the final amplifier of the radio, TV set or record player travel around the wire of the coil. The varying current makes the coil, which is inside a permanent magnet, vibrate. The loudspeaker's paper cone vibrates with the coil and the vibrating cone causes sound waves in the air. These sound waves travel to our ears and we hear the speaker's voice or the music just as it sounded in the studio.

Louis XIV (1638–1715) King of France from 1643. Known as the Sun King, he built the magnificent palace of Versailles and extended the boundaries of France through an aggressive foreign policy. He was responsible for the persecution of the Huguenots (over 400,000 fled the country), and he quarrelled with the Papacy. His last years were marked by costly and unsuccessful foreign wars.

Louis XVI (1754–93) King of France from 1774. A well-intentioned man who was unable to deal with the social unrest and economic problems of his time. Following the revolution of 1789, he and his family made an unsuccessful attempt to flee in 1791 and were imprisoned in 1792 for treason. Louis was guillotined in January 1793, and his unpopular and extravagant queen, Marie Antoinette, was executed in the October of the same year.

Human louse

Louse Wingless insects that are parasites of birds and mammals, including humans. Lice are flat and hairy, with strong claws for clinging to the fur or feathers of their host. Sucking lice feed on the blood of mammals; biting lice live mainly on birds, chewing the skin and feathers. Lice cause itching of the skin and carry disease.

Lung One of a pair of large organs used for breathing. Air is drawn into the lungs through the nose and down the windpipe. The windpipe then branches into each of the two lungs and continues to branch into a tree of tiny tubes, each ending in a tiny air sac called an alveolus. The alveoli are surrounded by blood vessels through which oxygen passes from the lungs into the blood to be transported through the body. The waste gas carbon dioxide passes back out in the opposite direction.

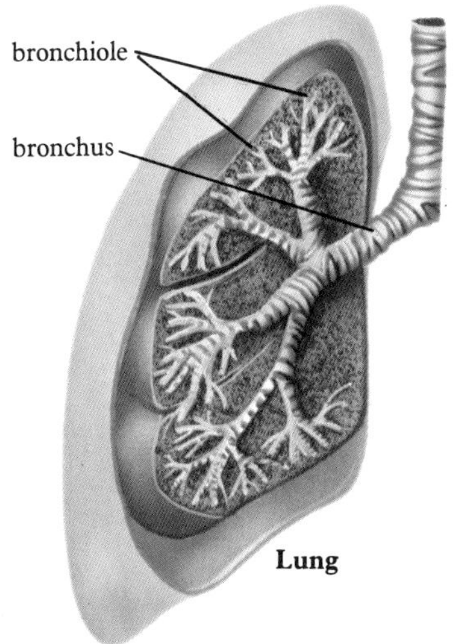

Lung

Lungfish Freshwater fishes found in S America, Africa and Australia. Unlike other fishes they have air-breathing lungs as well as gills and they can live in shallow or stagnant water. Some burrow in the mud when their rivers dry up.

Luther, Martin (1483–1546) German religious leader who attacked the corrupt practices of the Church of his day. His nailing of the '95 theses' to the door of Wittenberg church in 1517 is regarded as the start of the Protestant Reformation.

Martin Luther

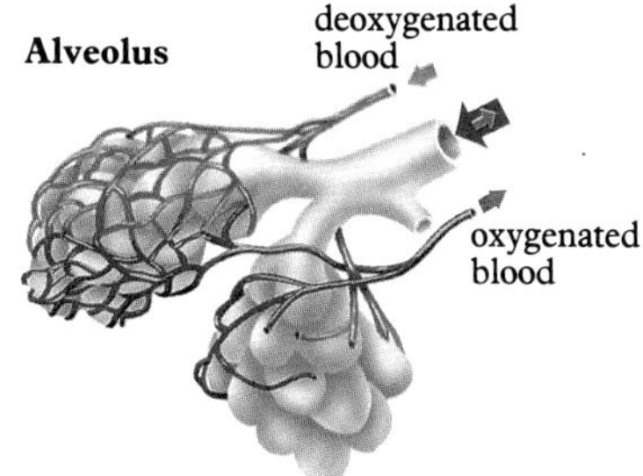

Alveolus

Luxembourg Small country in western Europe. Northern Luxembourg is forested, and hilly; the south is milder in climate with rolling plains and river valleys, good for farming. Luxembourg's wealth comes from industry, particularly iron and steel.

A duchy (dukedom) since the Middle Ages, Luxembourg's history has been closely linked with that of the Netherlands and Belgium. It became an independent country in 1839 and was a founder member of the EEC. Area: 2585 km^2; Pop: 366,000; Cap: Luxembourg.

Lynx Smallish spotted wild cat with short tail and tufted ears. The European lynx lives in the forests of northern Europe and Asia but is rare. The Canadian lynx is larger and less rare. The bobcat is a small N American lynx.

Lyre-bird Spectacular Australian bird with lyre-shaped feathers displayed to great effect during courtship.

M

Macao Small Portuguese colony in SE China on the estuary of Canton R. Port and gambling centre. Area: 15 km^2; Pop: 277,000.

Macaw Large, colourful, long-tailed parrots of tropical America. They feed on fruit and seeds, and nuts cracked open by their strong beaks.

Machiavelli, Niccolo (1469–1527) Italian statesman and author of *The Prince*. He believed that political power once achieved should be retained for the welfare of the state at whatever cost.

Machine gun An automatic weapon that can fire hundreds of rounds of ammunition in a minute. These weapons are of many types and are used on land and in the air. Their barrels range in size from .22 calibre to 30 mm. Ammunition is fed in from a magazine or a belt.

Mackerel A shoaling fish that spends winter in deep water close to the sea bottom. It spends the spring and summer in coastal waters feeding on a variety of fishes. It is usually about 40 cm long, with wavy blue stripes running down its back and a series of small fins in front of its tail.

Madagascar Island state off the E coast of Africa. On the coast, the climate is hot and damp. Inland, there are cooler highlands. Dense tropical forests cover much of the land. Rice, millet, manioc, coffee, tobacco, vanilla, cloves and bananas are the chief crops. The people of Madagascar are a

Lynx

mixture of Africans and Indonesians. Area: 587,194 km²; Pop: 9,665,000; Cap: Antananarivo.

Madras Port in S India. A textile and manufacturing centre. Pop: 2,469,000.

Madrid Capital of Spain. Situated on a plateau 655 metres high, it is Europe's highest capital. During the Spanish Civil War the city withstood a siege for 29 months. Pop: 3,146,000.

Magellan, Ferdinand (1480–1521) Portuguese navigator who in 1520 found a route round the south of S America to the Pacific through what is now called the Magellan Strait. He was killed by natives in the Philippines but one of his five ships completed the first voyage around the world.

Maggot The grub of certain types of flies. It has no legs and its head is minute. Maggots feed on the flesh on which the eggs are laid causing it to 'go bad'.

Magna Carta Royal charter issued unwillingly by King JOHN OF England in 1215 under pressure from the barons. Its main aim was to protect the rights of the barons themselves, but it also provided some protection for the less powerful. In later times it was seen as the foundation of English liberties.

Magnesium Light, silvery-white metal which burns in air with a brilliant white flame. Magnesium is extensively used in lightweight alloys for the aerospace industry. Chem. symbol Mg.

Magnetism Magnetism is a force that acts between certain objects. Magnets are used every day in compasses, telephones, TV and radio, and in producing electricity. A compass works because the Earth itself is a huge magnet that attracts the ends of the compass needle, pulling it in a north-south direction. If two magnets are brought near to each other, 'unlike' poles (north and south) attract each other, 'like' poles (north and north, or south and south) push each other apart. Iron is an easily magnetised substance, as are nickel and cobalt.

If a wire is wound round a piece of iron and an electric current is passed through the wire, the iron becomes magnetised. A device of this kind is called an ELECTROMAGNET.

Magnolia A tree or shrub widely cultivated for its beautiful, sweet-smelling flowers. There are several species, some of which are evergreen.

Magpie A black and white member of the crow family – though close up a great deal of the black plumage shows a green or dark blue sheen. Magpies are usually seen in pairs, hunting for food together. The birds eat eggs and young chicks. Like jackdaws, they like to collect bright objects.

Mahler, Gustav (1860–1911) Austrian romantic composer and conductor who wrote nine symphonies and many beautiful songs. His unfinished tenth symphony was completed to high critical acclaim by the Mahler scholar, D. Cooke, in the 1960s.

Mahogany Group of tall, tropical American trees with dark wood that is heavy but not too hard to be sawn and carved. African trees with similar timber are often called mahogany.

Maidenhair tree See **Ginkgo**

Maize Cereal crop whose grain grows in large cobs. Called corn in North America, it is cultivated as a food for animals and humans, and for its oil. See picture on page 45.

Malaria Tropical disease caused by a protozoan parasite and transmitted by mosquitoes. The female mosquito passes the parasite into the bloodstream when she bites. The fever comes and goes in waves as the microbes multiply rapidly and are then killed off by the body. Treatment is with quinine.

Malawi Country in E Africa, on the shores of L. Malawi. Much of the land is a high, cool plateau. Most people are farmers, growing their own food, but some work on plantations where crops such as coffee, tea and sugar are grown for export. Area: 118,515 km²; Pop: 6,829,000; Cap: Lilongwe.

Malaysia Country in SE Asia, a federation of 13 states. Most states are on the mainland (Malaya), but Sabah and Sarawak are on the island of Borneo. Both parts of the country have a tropical climate. Crops include rice, tea, pepper and pineapples. From the forests come teak and other hardwoods, palm oil, copra and rubber. Malaysia is the world's largest producer of natural rubber and tin. Area: 329,834 km²; Pop: 15,330,000; Cap: Kuala Lumpur.

Mali Country in W Africa. The northern part fringes the Sahara Desert; Timbuktu, a town in central Mali, is the last town

Woolly mammoth

before the travellers enter the desert. Further south, around the R. Niger, the land is greener. Chief crops are cotton, groundnuts, and cereals. The people are mostly farmers and wandering herdsmen. Area: 1,240,000 km^2; Pop: 7,562,000; Cap: Bamako.

Mallard A wild duck, common on marshes, coastal mud-flats and lakes. Mallards are often seen on ornamental ponds. The female bird is speckled brown; the male has grey and reddish-brown feathers, with a handsome dark green head.

Malta Mediterranean republic, made up of a cluster of islands, including Malta, Gozo and Comino. Malta, the largest island, is high and rocky, with a flat central plain. It is dry and hot, poor farmland, and has no minerals. The Maltese people fish and work in the dockyards and tourist hotels.

Malta is a key naval stronghold, controlling Mediterranean sea routes, and for this reason it has had many rulers in its long history. From 1813 it was British. In 1964 it became independent, and declared a republic in 1974. It now has close trade links with Libya. Area: 316 km^2; Pop: 356,000; Cap: Valletta.

Mammal Any of the large class of back-boned animals in which the female feeds her young with milk from her own body. All mammals have warm blood, and with a few exceptions they are clothed with hair. Apart from egg-laying MONOTREMES such as the PLATYPUS, they all give birth to active young. Badgers, cats, mice, whales and humans are all mammals.

Mammoth A large, woolly elephant which roamed the northern plains during the Great Ice Age. Mammoths were finally hunted to extinction about 10,000 years ago but whole animals have been found perfectly preserved in the icy subsoils of Siberia and Alaska.

Man, Isle of See **Isle of Man**

Manatee Bulky seal-like mammals up to 4.5 metres long that live around tropical coasts. Also called sea cows, they are thought to be the mermaids that sailors once claimed to see basking on the rocks.

Manchester Fourth largest city in England, on R. Irwell. Important commercial, industrial and cultural centre with major textile and engineering industries. The Manchester Ship Canal opened in 1894 allowing seagoing ships right into the city, but traffic later declined. Pop: 543,000; Greater Manchester 2,594,000.

Mandrill Forest-living baboon with face and rear-end decorated with naked patches of blue and pink skin. The fur is brown.

Manet, Edouard (1832–83) French impressionist whose paintings include *Olympia* and *Un Bar aux Folies-Bergères*.

Manganese Brittle, greyish metal which is widely used in steelmaking. Manganese removes impurities from the steel and strengthens it. Manganese steels are very tough. They are used for making machine parts. Chem. symbol Mn.

Mangrove Tall tropical trees of coastal swamps, with stilt-like roots, that thrive only in salty water.

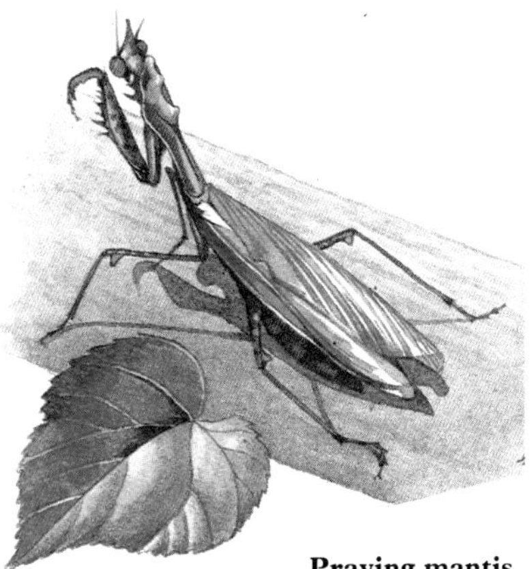

Praying mantis

Mantis Tropical insects related to cockroaches. They are also known as praying mantises because they maintain a prayerful attitude while waiting for their prey. When the prey approaches they seize it rapidly in their long, spiny front legs.

Maoris Aboriginal inhabitants of New Zealand who comprise 10 per cent of the population. Traditionally hunters, fishers and gatherers, they fought the white settlers and rival tribes with equal vigour. They are now integrated with the white population though many signs of their culture, especially their intricate wood carvings, are evident.

Mao Tse-tung (1893–1976) Founder of the Chinese Communist party and creator of the Red Army. After a long and bitter campaign against the Chinese Nationalists under Chiang Kai-shek, he became Chairman of the People's Republic of China in 1949. His *Thoughts of Mao Tse-tung* had great influence in China.

Map A representation of part or all of the Earth's curved surface drawn to scale. Physical maps concentrate on natural features such as rivers and mountains; political maps feature roads, cities, frontiers, etc; general maps combine these features. Maps are made from information supplied by surveyors and aerial photographs.

Maple A family of 150 species of deciduous trees. The leaves are broad and usually deeply lobed. The sap is rich in sugar (the original maple syrup) and the timber is hard. The leaf is the emblem of Canada.

Marathon Long distance race which commemorates the run of a soldier from Marathon to Athens to bring the news of the defeat of the Persians (490 BC). As an Olympic event, the distance is fixed at 42.18 km.

Marble Crystallized form of limestone changed by great heat and pressure. Marble can take a high polish and is widely used in building and sculpture.

Marconi, Guglielmo (1874–1937) Italian physicist and engineer who shared the Nobel Physics Prize in 1909. He contributed to the development of wireless telegraphy and in 1901 transmitted the first transatlantic radio signals.

Marco Polo (*c* 1254–1324) Venetian merchant who travelled all over Asia and was one of the first Europeans to enter China. He visited the court of KUBLAI KHAN and acted as envoy for the great Mongol emperor for many years. He returned to Venice a very wealthy man in 1295.

Margarine Butter-like spread prepared from vegetable oils (formerly animal fats including whale blubber were used), skimmed milk, salt, water and sometimes colouring and added vitamins. Both margarine and butter manufacturers claim their product to be better for people's health but many doctors think neither is particularly good.

Marjoram A fragrant, flowering plant related to the dead-nettle. Marjoram is widely cultivated as its leaves are used for flavouring food.

Marlowe, Christopher (1564–1593) English dramatist and poet whose plays include *Doctor Faustus*, *Tamburlaine* and *The Jew of Malta*.

Marmot, Alpine The only European ground squirrel, living mainly in the Alps and Pyrenees but introduced to some other mountain areas.

Mars The fourth planet in line from the Sun, about half the size of Earth. Known as the Red planet because of the colour of its surface rocks, Mars was the best prospect for the discovery of life in the Solar system. In 1976 two Viking spacecraft landed on the stony surface. They carried out tests but failed to find any signs of life. Diameter: 6800 km; distance from Sun: 228 million km; satellites: 2 (Phobos and Deimos).

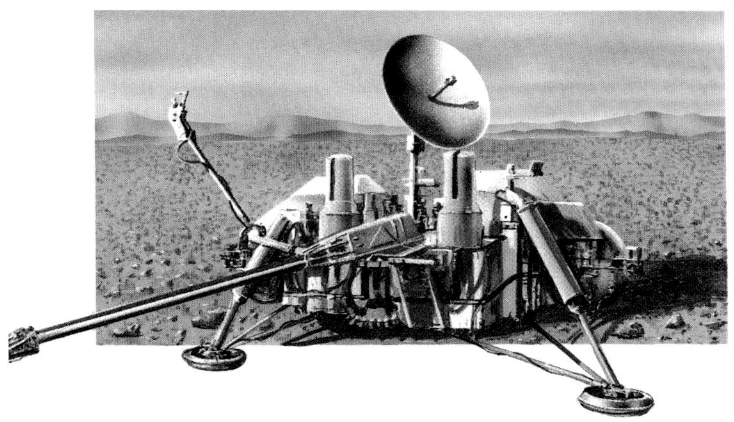

The Viking craft that landed on Mars in 1976 was even able to analyse the planet's red soil but it found no trace of life.

Marseille Leading commercial port and second largest city in France, on the Mediterranean coast. Rose to prominence when the Suez Canal opened up sea traffic between the Mediterranean and the East (1869). Pop: 912,000.

Marsupial One of the three kinds of mammal; the other two are placental mammals which give birth to live young and monotremes which lay eggs. All three types feed their offspring on milk. Marsupials differ from the others by caring for their newborn babies in a pouch. The babies may be less than two centimetres long when born. They climb up into the mother's pouch and are suckled by teats inside it. Marsupials include KANGAROOS, KOALAS and WOMBATS from Australia and the OPOSSUM of America.

Marten A carnivore, similar in shape to its cousin the stoat, only larger – about the size of a cat. There are two very similar species, both mainly nocturnal. The pine marten lives in forests and climbs trees. The beech marten hunts mostly on the ground.

Martial arts Combat sports based on Eastern philosophies. They were first used for self-defence in China some 4000 years ago, and later practised in India, Korea and Japan. The martial arts expert trains his mind as well as his body, to achieve complete self-control – for some martial arts techniques are dangerous. Judo, karate and kung fu are all forms of unarmed combat. Judo was the first Eastern martial art to become well known in the rest of the world, and is now one of the events in the OLYMPIC GAMES.

Martin Migratory birds similar to swallows but with far shorter forked tails. They fly north for the summer from southern Africa and can usually be seen high in the sky catching insects on the wing. The two most common European species are the house and the sand martin.

Marx, Karl Heinrich (1818–83) German philosopher and founder of modern Communism. Together with his friend Engels he wrote the *Communist Manifesto*, published in 1848. The following year he moved to London where he wrote *Das Kapital* (1867). His revolutionary doctrines have profoundly influenced the political thinking and events of the 20th century.

Mary I (1516–58) A Roman Catholic who reigned as Queen of England from 1553. Her marriage to Philip II of Spain in 1554 was very unpopular. She re-established papal authority and burnt nearly 300 protestants including the bishops Cranmer, Latimer and Ridley. Despite her intention to govern fairly and kindness to the poor, she earned her name of 'Bloody Mary'.

Mary, Queen of Scots (1542–87) She became Queen of Scotland when only one week old and as a descendant of Henry VII held a strong claim to the throne of

England. Briefly married to Francis II of France, she returned to Scotland (1561) after his death. In 1565 Mary married her cousin, Lord Darnley, and only 13 weeks after his murder, she married the earl of Bothwell, the man suspected of the killing. Forced to abdicate in 1568, Mary fled to England. The focus of numerous Catholic plots, she was executed for treason.

Mass The mass of an object is the amount of material in it. The mass of something does not vary, unlike weight, which is the force by which a body is pulled towards the centre of the earth. In space, a body is weightless, but its mass is the same as it would be on earth.

Mathematics The science of numbers and shapes. The branch of mathematics that deals with numbers is called ARITHMETIC. ALGEBRA uses symbols such as *x* and *y* instead of numbers. GEOMETRY deals with lines, angles, and shapes such as triangles and squares.

Matisse, Henri (1869–1954) French painter who is famed for his use of violent colours to express shape and form.

Maugham, William Somerset (1874–1965) English writer who was a master of the short story. His novels include *Of Human Bondage*, *Cakes and Ale*, *The Moon and Sixpence* and *The Razor's Edge*.

Mauritania Country in W Africa. It is mostly hot, dry desert. Only a few wandering Arab and Berber herdsmen live here, driving sheep and goats from oasis to oasis. Further south there is enough rainfall for crops to be grown; these include groundnuts, dates, rice and millet. The most important resources are minerals, chiefly copper and iron ore. Area: 1,030,969 km²; Pop: 1,623,000; Cap: Nouakchott.

Mauritius A volcanic island in the Indian Ocean, E of Madagascar. Together with several smaller islands it forms the independent state of Mauritius. The island is an important producer of sugar-cane which accounts for 90% of the exports. It is also becoming a popular tourist resort. Area: 2000 km²; Pop: 960,000; Cap: Port-Louis.

Maya Civilization of the Yucatán peninsula in Central America which reached its zenith between the 4th and 9th centuries AD. Pyramidal temples, hieroglyphic inscriptions and stone calendars show a knowledge of astronomy and mathematics.

Mayfly Insects, related to the dragonflies, which live near water. Mayflies have long slender bodies, delicate wings and long trailing tails. The young, called nymphs, spend their lives in the water. The adults have very short lives, rarely more than a week and only a few hours in some species.

Mecca Sacred capital of Islam in Saudi Arabia. Birthplace of Mohammed and place of pilgrimage for all Muslims. Pop: 367,000.

Mechanics The branch of science that deals with the effects of forces on bodies. Engineers use mechanics to find out about stresses on dams, bridges, etc. Astronomers use the science to study the motions of the stars and planets. There are two branches of mechanics – *dynamics* and *statics*. Dynamics deals with bodies in motion, statics deals with stationary bodies.

Medals See **Decorations**

Medici Powerful Florentine family of merchants and bankers who acquired immense wealth and were great patrons of the arts. They included **Cosimo** the Elder (1389–1464), the first ruler of Florence, his grandson **Lorenzo** the Magnificent (1449–92) and **Catherine** de Médicis (1519–89) queen of France.

Medicine The art and science of the treatment and prevention of diseases. The ancient Greek physician Hippocrates is known as the 'father of medicine'. An important advance in medical knowledge was made with the discovery of blood circulation in 1628 by William HARVEY. The 19th century saw the introduction of microscopes and antiseptics, and further advances have been made with the use of antibiotics, vaccinations and blood transfusions.

Mediterranean Large sea bounded by S Europe, W Asia and N Africa. It is connected to the Atlantic by the Strait of Gibraltar, to the Red Sea by the Suez Canal and to the Black Sea by the Dardanelles. The Mediterranean has many islands including Cyprus, Crete, Sicily, Corsica, Sardinia, Malta and the Balearic Islands. The sandy Mediterranean coasts, especially those of Spain, France and Italy attract many tourists.

Medusa In Greek legend one of the three Gorgon sisters who had live snakes for hair. She was killed by Perseus.

Melanin A pigment responsible for the brown colours of many animals. Sun-tan is a result of extra melanin production during exposure to strong sunlight.

Melbourne Major port and capital of Victoria, Australia, situated at mouth of R. Yarra in rich agricultural region. Founded in 1835, the city experienced rapid expansion when gold was discovered nearby. In 1901 it became the temporary capital of Australia and was the site of the first assembly of the Federal Parliament. Pop: 2,804,000 (met area).

Melville, Herman (1819–91) American novelist. His works include *Moby Dick*, *Typee* and *Billy Budd*.

Mendel, Gregor Johann (1822–84) Austrian botanist and monk who studied the similarities between successive generations of pea plants. Using the results of his research he formulated the principles of heredity as Mendel's Law, which when published in 1866 was largely ignored. Full appreciation came in 1900.

Mendelssohn, Felix (1809–47) German composer and conductor who was born into a wealthy family. Among his best-loved works are the overtures *A Midsummer Night's Dream* and *The Hebrides*, the E Minor violin concerto, the Italian symphony and the oratorio *Elijah*.

Mercury (metal) The only metal that is liquid at room temperature. Often called quicksilver, mercury is used in thermometers, barometers and other scientific instruments. Chem. symbol Hg (Latin *Hydroargyrum*).

Mercury (planet) One of the smallest planets and the closest to the Sun, Mercury is an airless, waterless world scarred by craters like our own Moon. The side facing the Sun is roasted to a temperature of 350°C, while the night side freezes at –170°C. Diameter: 4880 km; distance from Sun: 58 million km.

Mermaid See **Manatee**.

Metals These are elements or ALLOYS that are usually good conductors of heat and electricity, have quite a high density, and can usually be worked by beating or drawing into wire. The most important metal is IRON because it is the basis of steel. ALUMINIUM and COPPER follow in importance. All metals are solid at normal temperature except MERCURY, which is a liquid. Most metals are found in the Earth as ores combined with other elements. They have to be processed to produce the pure metal. Gold, silver, platinum and copper can be found in their pure state.

Metamorphic rock Rock that has been changed by heat or pressure in the Earth's crust. MARBLE, for instance, is metamorphosed LIMESTONE, and SLATE is metamorphosed SHALE.

Metamorphosis A total change of form during the life of an animal. Good examples can be found among frogs and toads, which start life as legless tadpoles, and also among insects – the butterfly grows from a caterpillar, and the house-fly from a wriggling maggot.

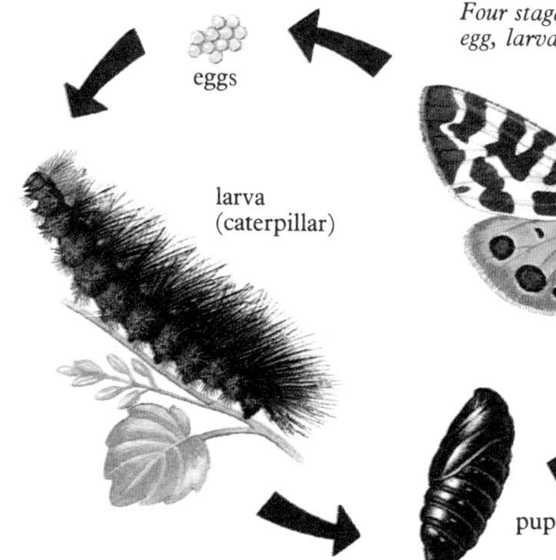

Four stages in the metamorphosis of a moth: egg, larva, pupa and adult.

The impact of an iron meteorite made this vast crater in Arizona about 20,000 years ago.

Meteor A fragment of rock, normally the size of a grain of sand, that plunges into the Earth's atmosphere from space. Friction with the air makes the fragment glow white-hot. Most meteors burn up in the atmosphere, but larger ones may reach the ground as meteorites. About 20,000 years ago a meteorite blasted a crater 1.2 km wide in Arizona, USA.

Meteorology The study of the Earth's atmosphere at all levels. The study of WEATHER is confined mainly to the levels near the ground.

Mexico Country in Central America. A land of mountains, volcanoes and high plateaux, with a wide flat peninsula, Yucatan, in the SE. At one point, at the country's 'waist', the Atlantic and Pacific Oceans are less than 250 km apart. The lowlands are hot and humid, the north dry, and the mountains much colder. The forests provide timber, while the farmland yields beans, coffee, cocoa, cotton, fruit and vegetables. Cattle and other livestock are raised. Industry is developing rapidly, aided by large oil reserves. Other minerals include gold, silver and copper. Area: 1,973,000 km^2; Pop: 77,659,000; Cap: Mexico City.

Mexico City Capital of Mexico, 3000 metres above sea level. Largest Latin American city and growing daily. An important industrial and commercial centre, it has fine business, cultural and admin buildings but is surrounded by shanty towns and subject to great pollution. Extensive damage was caused by an earthquake in 1985. Pop: 9,191,000 (14,750,000 including suburbs).

Michelangelo (Buonarroti, 1475–1564) Italian Renaissance painter, sculptor and poet. Among his greatest works are the statues of David in Florence and Moses in Rome, and his paintings on the ceiling of the Sistine Chapel in Rome of biblical scenes and on the wall behind the altars of the Last Judgement.

Microchip See **Silicon chip**.

Microfilm Film on which printed pages, documents, etc, are reduced to a miniature size convenient for storage. A microfiche is a piece of microfilm measuring 10 cm by 15 cm, on which several pages are normally recorded. The pages are read through a special projector.

Micro-organism Any microscopically small plant or animal, such as a bacterium or a protozoan.

Microphone A device for translating sound into electrical signals as in the mouthpiece of a TELEPHONE.

Microscope An instrument for looking at objects that are too small to be seen clearly by the naked eye. Microscopes contain a number of lenses and are used extensively in science to see details of plants, animals, and other objects. The highest magnification possible in ordinary microscopes is about × 1600. The electron microscope is much more powerful. It can magnify up to two million times, using beams of electrons instead of light rays.

Midas, King of Phrygia (*c* 8th century BC) In Greek legend everything he touched turned into gold.

Middle Ages Period in European history between the fall of the Roman Empire and the Renaissance, from about the 5th to the 15th century. The early Middle Ages are sometimes called the DARK AGES. The main features of society in the Middle Ages were the FEUDAL SYSTEM, in which land was held in exchange for certain duties, the dominance of the Roman Catholic Church, the use of Latin by those who could write, and the Gothic style in art and architecture.

Middle East Term with no precise meaning normally used to describe an area east of the Mediterranean including Syria, Lebanon, Jordan, Israel, Iraq, the Arabian peninsula and Egypt. It is an area of considerable unrest and tension, partly due to the long-standing Arab-Israeli dispute and partly because of its vast oil resources. See map on page 142.

Midge Small mosquito-like flies often seen in swarms on warm summer evenings. Biting midges feed by sucking blood, but the non-biting and gall midges are harmless to other animals.

Migration The regular movement of animals from one area to another and back again, usually on a seasonal basis. Birds are great migrants. Swallows, for example, spend the summer in Europe and then fly to Africa in the autumn.

Many northern birds, including lots of ducks and geese, come to Britain and southern Europe for the winter. They do this to avoid the snow and ice of the far north. Various butterflies, fishes and mammals also migrate.

Eels spawned in the Sargasso Sea travel 4000 km across the Atlantic. During the three-year journey they turn from larvae into elvers. They spend their adult lives in European rivers. Then they make the return trip and die.

A
B
C
D
E
BLACK SEA
CAUCASUS MTS
PONTINE MTS
TAURUS MTS
TURKEY
Istanbul
Edirne
Gallipoli
Sea of Marmara
Izmit
Adapazari
Bursa
Ankara
Eskisehir
Izmir
Afyon
Lake Tuz
Konya
Kizil
Sinop
Samsun
Sivas
Kayseri
Mt Erciyas 3916
Malatya
Maras
Adana
Gaziantep
Mersin
Antakya
Urfa
Batumi
Tbilisi
Kirovabad
Yerevan
Erzurum
Mt Ararat 5165
Lake Van
Diyarbakir
Siirt
Mardin
Rezaiyeh
Tabriz
Lake Urmia
Maragheh
Rhodes
CYPRUS
Nicosia
MEDITERRANEAN SEA
Latakia
Halab
Hama
SYRIA
Tripoli
Homs
Beirut
LEBANON
Damascus
Euphrates
Mosul
Erbil
Kirkuk
Tigris
Tharthar Basin
IRAQ
Baghdad
Karbala
Hilla
An Najaf
Hamadān
Qahremānshah
Khorramabad
Hor al Hammar
Ahvaz
Khorram
Basra
Abadan
KUWAIT
Kuwait
Haifa
Irbid
Syrian Desert
Zarqa
Amman
Tel-Aviv-Yafo
ISRAEL
Jerusalem
Dead Sea
JORDAN
Elat
Matruh
Alexandria
El Mahalla el Kubra
Port Said
El Mansura
Tanta
Suez Canal
El Gîza
Cairo
Suez
Beni Suef
Gulf of Suez
Gebel Katherina 2637
El Minya
Asyût
Nile
Al Jawf
Tabūk
An Nafud
Hafar
Hail
EGYPT
Luxor
HEJAZ
Al Kharj
Ramah
Aswân
Medina
Riyadh
Yanbu'al Bahr
RED SEA
Lake Nasser
SAUDI ARABIA
Wadi Halfa
Nubian Desert
Jiddah
Mecca
At Tā'if
ASIR
Dongola
Port Sudan
Suakin
Rub
SUDAN
Jizan
Khartoum North
Omdurman
Khartoum
Kassala
Massawa
Asmara
YEMEN
Sana
SOUTH YEMEN
Hodeida
Wad Medani
Sennar
ETHIOPIA
Taizz
Aden
40°
35°
30°
25°
20°
15°
45°

F
G
H
J
K
1
2
3
4
5
6
7
Tashkent
U. S. S. R.
Samarkand
Amu Darya
Dushanbe
Ashkhabad
KOPET RANGE
Faizabad
HINDU KUSH
Gilgit
Babol
Gorgan
BURZ MTS
Mashhad
Mazar-i-Sharif
Baghlan
Tirich Mir 7690
Demavend 5604
Tehran
Rey
Charikar
Jalalabad
Peshawar
Islamabad
Kabul
Khyber Pass
Shah Fuladi 5143
Dasht-e-Kavir
Herat
Wah
Rawalpindi
Ghazni
Gujrat
RAN
AFGHANISTAN
Gujranwala
Birjand
Sargodha
Lahore
Esfahan
Farah
Faisalabad
Helmand
Kandahar
Yazd
GROS MTS
Multan
Dasht-e-Lut
Quetta
Kermān
SULAIMAN RANGE
Bahawalpur
Kalat
Shiraz
Indus
Bikaner
PAKISTAN
Sukkur
INDIA
Bandar Abbas
Bandar-e-Lengeh
Jodhpur
Strait of Hormuz
Hyderabad
OMAN
Gwadar
Sharjah
Dubai
Doha
Chah Bahar
Karachi
Gulf of Oman
Abu Dhabi
Ahmadabad
Khaburah
Muscat
Tropic of Cancer
UNITED ARAB EMIRATES
Jamnagar
Rajkot
OMAN
ARABIAN SEA
miles
0 100 200 300
0 100 200 300 400 500
kilometres
Salala
Qishn
55°
60°
65°
70°
75°

Milan Capital of Lombardy, N Italy. Major industrial and commercial centre. Site of Gothic cathedral and renowned opera house (La Scala). Pop: 1,706,000.

Mildew A group of parasitic fungi that form on the leaves of plants. The term is also more widely used to describe any fungal growth that covers a surface with fine threads or hyphae.

Milk The most nutritious and natural food, milk contains proteins, fats, carbohydrates, minerals and vitamins. It is secreted by the mammary glands of all female mammals to nourish their young, and cows are bred to produce surplus milk for human consumption. Commercially produced milk is tested and pasteurized (see PASTEUR), and sometimes homogenized – the fat is distributed throughout the liquid instead of rising to the top. It must then be cartoned or bottled, stored under refrigeration and distributed. One of the largest industries in United States and Britain. Europe as a whole has a problem of over-production.

Milky Way A faint band of starlight crossing the night sky. When viewed through a telescope the Milky Way resolves into an enormous number of stars. It is in fact the plane of the galaxy to which the Sun belongs. The Milky Way galaxy is shaped like a vast lens with spiral arms. It contains some 100,000 million stars and measures 100,000 light-years across.

Millipede A group of many-legged arthropods that feed on decaying vegetation. Most species are long and slender with almost every segment of their bodies bearing two pairs of legs.

Milton, John (1608–74) English poet who was an ardent Puritan. He devoted much of his energies to the Parliamentary cause and was a firm believer in the freedom of the press. Milton became blind in 1652, and it was after being forced into retirement that he wrote, by dictation, his epic poems *Paradise Lost* and *Paradise Regained*. Other works include *Samson Agonistes*, *Comus* and *Lycidas*, as well as many sonnets.

Mime Form of acting in which the performer says not a word, expressing meaning only by movements of face, limbs and body. Mime was popular on the Greek stage, and also in ancient Rome. In Europe in the 16th century mime was performed in the Commedia dell'Arte.

Mimicry The resemblance of a harmless creature to a poisonous or otherwise unpleasant one. Some of the best examples of mimicry are found among insects. Many HOVER-FLIES, for example, are remarkably like various wasps and bees.

Mimosa An evergreen tree, native to Australia, but widely grown elsewhere as an ornament, especially for its yellow flower clusters. It belongs to the pea family and is also called the silver wattle. Its fern-like leaves are covered with fine silvery down. See also ACACIA.

Minerals Substances that make up rocks. Most are combinations of the ELEMENTS that occur in the Earth's crust. Quartz, for instance, is a chemical combination of the two most common elements, silicon and oxygen, and is the main ingredient of sandstone. Some minerals are valuable sources of metals and are called ores. Others are highly-prized gemstones.

Mining Extracting or mining minerals from the ground is one of the world's most important industries. In addition to coal and oil, dozens of different minerals are mined. Some can be obtained fairly easily by *open-cast* mining when the mineral is on or near the surface. But the majority of deposits can only be obtained by sending down miners. In modern mines, machinery is used on a large scale. Coal can be cut entirely by machines. Main tunnels are supported by permanent steel and concrete ribs, and a plentiful supply of air is pumped down to provide the miners with fresh air and to rid the mine of dust and dangerous gas.

Mink A nocturnal carnivore whose brown fur is highly prized. The European mink is about 38 cm long with a long body and tail and short legs. It is found mostly in France. The larger American mink has escaped from fur farms and is found in Scandinavia and the British Isles. Mink live near water and are excellent swimmers.

Minnow One of the smallest fishes of the carp family – a full-grown minnow is only 4 to 9 cm long.

Minoan civilization Forerunner of classical Greek civilization which existed in Crete from about 3000 to 1200 BC. Crete was the centre of a maritime empire and, by 1700 BC, a rich BRONZE AGE culture. Archaeologists have revealed splendid palaces at Knossos and Phaestos. Some

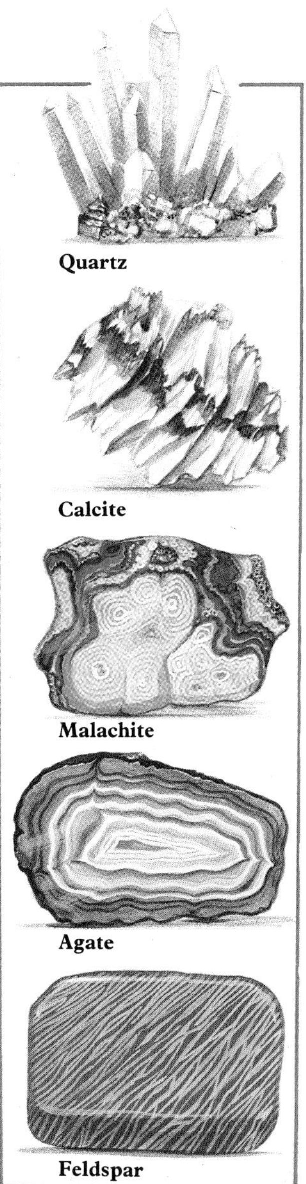
Quartz

Calcite

Malachite

Agate

Feldspar

disaster, such as an earthquake, ended the Minoan civilization about 1400 BC.

Minotaur In Greek legend, a creature half man – half bull which lived in the labyrinth (maze) built for Cretan King Minos. Each year it ate seven Athenian youths and seven maidens. The hero Theseus found his way through the maze with the help of Minos's daughter, slew the monster and won her hand.

Mint A number of sweet-smelling plants belonging to the same family as the dead-nettles. Mints have square stems and dense whorls or spikes of small purple flowers. The broad leaves are the most fragrant part of the plant and are used to flavour food.

Mirage An optical illusion caused by the refraction and reflection of light which occurs in very hot weather. The air near the ground is hotter than the air above it. Light rays are bent when they pass from cool to warm air, causing objects to be seen in places where they do not exist.

Mirrors Light rays come from everything we can see. When you stand in front of a mirror, some of the light rays that come from you strike the mirror. The mirror REFLECTS the rays back to your eyes. You see a *mirror-image* of yourself. Your right side appears to be on the right. But when real people face you, their right side is always on your left. This is because the mirror reflects light rays from your right side back to you on the right.

A mirror is made from a flat sheet of glass on the back of which is sprayed a thin layer of aluminium or silver. The back of the metal is then painted. Light is reflected from the metal through the glass.

Mississippi Major river of North America flowing from NW Minnesota to the Gulf of Mexico which it enters through a large delta. The river drains approximately 3,000,000 km^2, but causes considerable flood-control problems. Length 3750 km.

Missouri Longest river in the USA. The Missouri is the main tributary of the Mississippi, flowing through the states of Missouri, Nebraska, Iowa, North and South Dakota, and Montana. The Missouri is extensively used for irrigation and HEP stations. Length: 3960 km.

Mistletoe A semi-parasitic woody plant that grows on the branches of trees, especially those of the apple and poplars. The mistletoe produces sticky white

Moles

berries in winter, and is widely used as a Christmas decoration.

Mohammed (*c* 570–632) Arabian prophet and founder of ISLAM born in the now holy city of MECCA. He was inspired by a vision of the angel Gabriel who brought God's message: instead of worshipping idols, people were to submit to one god, Allah. The word Islam means submission. Mohammed wrote the words of Allah in *The Koran*. His words were not heeded at first in his own land but were taken up elsewhere and today his followers form one of the largest religious groups.

Mohammedanism See **Islam.**

Mole A small insectivore that spends most of its time underground. It is a tube-shaped creature about 14 cm long, with large spade-like front feet that are ideally suited to digging. The mole lives in a maze of underground tunnels and feeds mainly on earthworms and other small creatures. Its eyesight is very poor and it relies mainly on smell and hearing.

Molecule A molecule is the smallest amount of a chemical substance that can exist by itself. It is made up of one or more atoms. A water molecule has in it one oxygen atom and two hydrogen atoms. If any of these atoms is removed, what is left is no longer a water molecule. Some organic molecules contain millions of atoms.

Molière, Jean-Baptiste Poquelin (1622–73) Great French dramatist who was also an actor. His plays include *Le Bourgeois Gentilhomme*, *Tartuffe*, *Le Malade Imaginaire* and his greatest, *Le Misanthrope*.

Mollusc Any member of the large phylum of animals that includes the SLUGS and SNAILS, BIVALVES, and the SQUIDS and OCTOPUSES. The name simply means 'soft' and refers to the animals' soft bodies, although many are actually protected by a hard shell. The phylum is the second largest in the animal kingdom, with about 90,000 species. Only the arthropods have more than this.

Molluscs

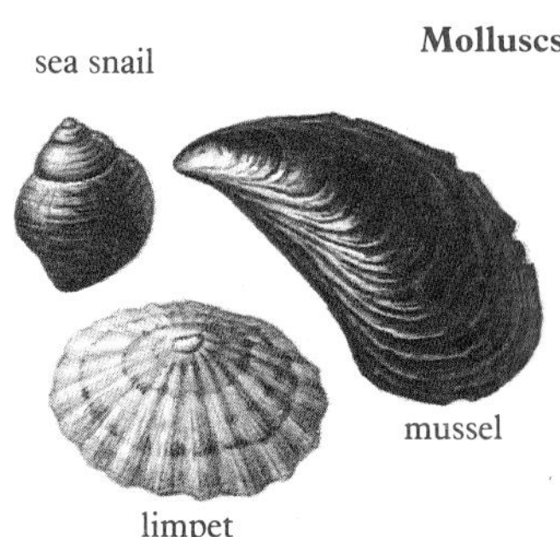

Molybdenum Hard, white metal whose chief use is in steelmaking. It enables the steel to retain its strength and hardness at high temperatures, a quality needed, for instance, by high-speed cutting tools. Chem. symbol Mo.

Momentum Momentum can be defined as the velocity of a moving body multiplied by its mass. A lorry driving at 60 km/h has a greater momentum than a car driving at the same speed because it has a greater mass. The impact of the lorry striking an object would be greater than the car's impact.

Monaco One of the world's smallest countries, on the SE coast of France. Its Mediterranean climate, hotels and casino attract many tourists. Its people are called Monégasques. Monaco is a self-governing state, protected by France. Area: 1.9 km^2; Pop: 27,100; Cap: Monaco.

Monarchs, British England did not really become one kingdom until the reign of ALFRED, greatest of the Saxon kings. Saxon rule was overthrown by the Normans, under WILLIAM I, in 1066. At first the English monarch had almost absolute power, but gradually the power of PARLIAMENT grew. The English kings ruled Wales from 1282, and from the reign of JAMES I (1603) both England and Scotland had the same king. James succeeded one of the greatest English sovereigns, Queen ELIZABETH I. During the CIVIL WAR (1642–49) the Parliament executed King CHARLES I, but the monarchy was restored in 1660 with CHARLES II. The longest reigning British monarch was Queen VICTORIA. By her time, power rested firmly with Parliament and the monarch's powers were mainly symbolic. Today, however, the sovereign is still head of state and head of the Church of England, and plays an important part in state affairs. See lists of English and Scottish monarchs right and overleaf.

Monastery The Greek word 'monos' means alone. To devote themselves to God and prayer many people wish to be alone, to withdraw from the world. Once people became hermits; later, Christian communities of monks and nuns grew up where people with religious vocations could live apart. Orders of monks and friars include the Benedictines, Dominicans, Franciscans, Carmelites and Trappists.

ENGLISH MONARCHS

Saxons	
Egbert	827–839
Ethelwulf	839–858
Ethelbald	858–860
Ethelbert	860–866
Ethelred I	866–871
Alfred the Great	871–899
Edward the Elder	899–924
Athelstan	924–939
Edmund	939–946
Edred	946–955
Edwy	955–959
Edgar	959–975
Edward the Martyr	975–978
Ethelred II the Unready	978–1016
Edmund Ironside	1016
Danes	
Canute	1016–1035
Harold I Harefoot	1035–1040
Hardicanute	1040–1042
Saxons	
Edward the Confessor	1042–1066
Harold II	1066
House of Normandy	
William I the Conqueror	1066–1087
William II	1087–1100
Henry I	1100–1135
Stephen, Count of Blois	1135–1154
House of Plantagenet	
Henry II	1154–1189
Richard I	1189–1199
John	1199–1216
Henry III	1216–1272
Edward I	1272–1307
Edward II*	1307–1327
Edward III	1327–1377
Richard II*	1377–1399
House of Lancaster	
Henry IV	1399–1413
Henry V	1413–1422
Henry VI*	1422–1461
House of York	
Edward IV	1461–1483
Edward V	1483
Richard III	1483–1485
House of Tudor	
Henry VII	1485–1509
Henry VIII	1509–1547
Edward VI	1547–1553
Mary I	1553–1558
Elizabeth I	1558–1603

continued overleaf

House of Stuart

James I	1603–1625
Charles I**	1625–1649

(Commonwealth 1649–1659)

Lord Protectors	
Oliver Cromwell	*1653–1658*
Richard Cromwell	*1658–1659*

House of Stuart *(restored)*

Charles II	1660–1685
James II*	1685–1688
William III } jointly	1689–1702
Mary II } jointly	1689–1694
Anne	1702–1714

House of Hanover

George I	1714–1727
George II	1727–1760
George III	1760–1820
George IV	1820–1830
William IV	1830–1837
Victoria	1837–1901

House of Saxe-Coburg

Edward VII	1901–1910

House of Windsor

George V	1910–1936
Edward VIII***	1936
George VI	1936–1952
Elizabeth II	1952–

* deposed. ** beheaded. *** abdicated.

Monet, Claude (1840–1926) French impressionist who specialized in atmospheric scenes. He used broken colour to produce special lighting effects and is perhaps best known for his depictions of water.

Money Form of exchange, or currency, used to buy and sell goods. In early times, people used to exchange or barter goods. Later, merchants carried gold and silver coins. By the Middle Ages commerce was becoming too complicated for this system to continue. So instead of carrying gold, merchants used paper money issued by banks. Modern coins and notes have no value of their own, being made of paper or cheap metal. The money is really only worth the goods it will buy, or the amount of another country's currency that it will buy. All currencies are valued against the US dollar and their exchange rates fluctuate according to the value put on them in international markets.

Mongolia Large country N of China and S of USSR. Mongolia is a high windy plateau, with mountains in the west and the GOBI DESERT in the south. Most people live in the north. Many are nomads, herding livestock over the vast plains, or steppes. They are expert horsemen. The country's chief products are hides, wool

SCOTTISH MONARCHS

Kenneth I	836–860
Donald I	890–863
Constantine I	863–877
Aedh	877–878
Eocha	878–889
Donald II	889–900
Constantine II	900–943
Malcolm I	943–954
Indulf	959–962
Duff	962–967
Colin	967–971
Kenneth II	971–995
Constantine III	995–997
Kenneth III	997–1005
Malcolm II	1005–1034
Duncan I	1034–1040
Macbeth (usurper)	1040–1057
Malcolm III Canmore	1057–1093
Donald Bane	1093–1094
Duncan II	1094
Donald Bane (restored)	1094–1097
Edgar	1097–1107
Alexander I	1107–1124
David I	1124–1153
Malcolm IV	1153–1165
William the Lion	1165–1214
Alexander II	1214–1249
Alexander III	1249–1286
Margaret of Norway	1286–1290
(*Interregnum* 1290–1292)	
John Balliol	1292–1296
(*Interregnum* 1296–1306)	
Robert I (Bruce)	1306–1329
David II	1329–1371
House of Stuart	
Robert II	1371–1390
Robert III	1390–1406
James I	1406–1437
James II	1437–1460
James III	1460–1488
James IV	1488–1513
James V	1513–1542
Mary	1542–1567
James VI*	1567–1625

* Became James I of Great Britain in 1603.

and livestock. Coal and oil reserves are being developed. Since 1924 Mongolia has been a communist republic, under Russian influence. Area: 1,565,406 km^2; Pop: 1,860,000; Cap: Ulan Bator.

Mongols Warlike nomadic tribes of Asia united in 1200's under GENGHIS KHAN who commanded an empire that stretched from China to eastern Europe. The empire broke up at the end of the 14th century.

Mongoose Fierce little carnivores of Africa and S Asia that are sometimes tamed and kept for killing snakes. They feed on birds' eggs, small mammals, toads, and reptiles. Because of their amazing speed, they can seize even a poisonous cobra.

Monkey Small mammals related to apes, although less intelligent. They live mostly in forests and are active by day, feeding on fruit and leaves and occasionally small animals.

The two groups of monkeys – Old World and New World – have one striking difference. All New World (American) monkeys have long, prehensile (gripping) tails which they use as an extra limb. They include the howler, spider, squirrel, woolly and capuchin monkeys and the kitten-sized marmoset, the smallest of all monkeys.

The long-nosed monkeys of the Old World do not have prehensile tails. They include the BABOONS, the colobus, proboscis and rhesus monkeys, and the barbary ape of Gibraltar.

Monkey puzzle An evergreen coniferous tree with a strange branching form. Also called the Chile pine, it gets its popular name of monkey puzzle because it looks too difficult for even a monkey to climb. The tree comes from S America, and is commonly grown as an ornament.

Monocotyledon The smaller of the two groups of flowering plants, whose seeds contain a single seed leaf, or cotyledon. Grasses and daffodils are both examples of monocotyledons. The other groups are the DICOTYLEDONS.

Monorail A train that runs on a single rail. The rail is normally supported above the ground and the train either hangs from wheels that run on the rail, or it runs directly on the rail which lies beneath the centre of the train. Monorails can be built above city streets and take up very little space.

Monotremes Egg-laying mammals of Australia and New Guinea. The ECHIDNA (spiny anteater) and the duck-billed PLATYPS are the only living species. They lay eggs like reptiles but feed their young on mother's milk like other mammals.

Monsoon A wind system in which the prevailing direction is reversed from summer to winter. Most marked in India where high pressure in winter leads to winds blowing off the land, while intense low pressure in summer leads to moisture-laden winds blowing in from the sea and the 'bursting' of the monsoon rains.

Mont Blanc Mountain in the Alps, on border between France and Italy. Highest Alpine peak. The road tunnel which runs beneath it is the second longest in the world. Height: 4807 metres.

Montfort, Simon de (1160–1218) English

statesman who led the barons in a successful revolt against Henry III and summoned the Great Parliament which included representatives from the towns as well as knights from the shires. He was later defeated and killed at Evesham.

Montreal Port and city of Quebec province, Canada, at confluence of St Lawrence and Ottawa Rs. Canada's principal port and largest city. Major manufacturing and commercial centre. The population is largely French-speaking. Pop: 1,080,000.

Moon Natural satellite of the Earth which orbits every 29½ days, always keeping the same face turned towards us. The Moon is waterless, airless and lifeless. It has huge lava plains (called maria), rugged mountains and a surface pitted with craters from meteorite impacts. Diameter: 3500 km; distance from Earth: 384,000 km.

Moore, Henry (1898–) Great English sculptor who works in bronze, stone and wood. He is renowned for his reclining figures which are generally female. His work can be seen in many parts of the world.

Moorhen A water bird similar to the coot, but slightly smaller and with a red patch at the base of its yellow bill. It swims with a head-jerking motion, and on land constantly jerks its tail. Moorhens feed on insects, worms and water plants and animals.

The Moon's phases: half the Moon is always lit by the Sun, but we see different amounts of the sunlit half as the Moon orbits the Earth. The phases go from 'new', to crescent, through half to full and back again.

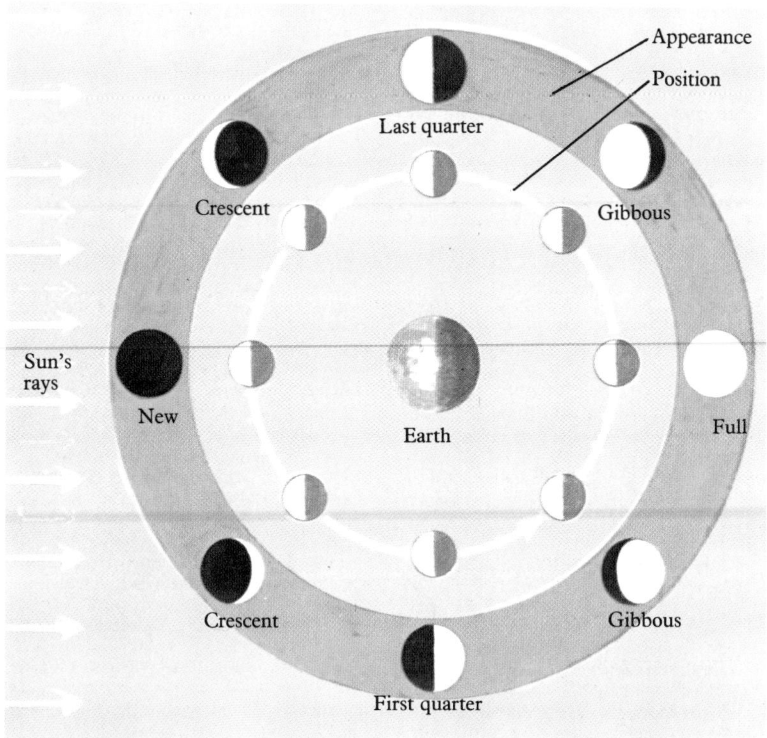

Moors Nomadic N African people who became Muslims in the 8th century and conquered Spain where their influence can still be seen, especially in city of Granada which was their stronghold. They were driven out by Christians in 1492.

Moose See **Elk**.

Morel Member of a group of edible mushrooms with distinctive, crinkled caps. The common morel is found in grasslands and light woodlands.

More, Sir Thomas (1478–1535) English scholar, statesman, writer and Roman Catholic saint. His refusal, as Chancellor, to accept Henry VIII's divorce from Catherine of Aragon led to his conviction and execution for treason. His book *Utopia* describes the ideal state.

Morocco Country in NW Africa, crossed by Atlas Mts. Much of the country is dry desert, but the northern hills are wooded and more fertile. The climate is good, especially on the coast, sheltered from hot Saharan winds. The people grow cereals, fruit, olives, vegetables, dates and figs. The chief mineral export is phosphates. Area: 446,666 km^2; Pop: 23,565,000; Cap: Rabat.

Morse code System of dots, dashes and spaces devised by Samuel Morse in 1840 for his telegraph machine. Used for more than a century, it has now been replaced in telegraphy by teleprinters and facsimile machines.

Moscow Capital city of USSR, on R. Moskva. The city, built mainly of wood, was largely burnt to the ground during Napoleon's occupation (1812). Among Moscow's famous landmarks are the Kremlin, Red Square and St Basil's Cathedral. The underground stations are noted for their splendour. Pop: 8,011,000.

Moses Jewish patriarch and biblical prophet who led the Jews out of captivity in Egypt and received the Ten Commandments on Mount Sinai.

Moslem See **Islam**.

Mosquito Blood-sucking flies notorious for their irritating bite. Not all mosquitoes bite people, but in some species the female sucks human blood and in so doing passes on malaria or yellow fever.

Moss A group of green flowerless plants. Mosses grow in damp places forming soft mats or cushions on the ground. They have short slender stems with thin leaves. There are no proper roots but short hairs anchor the plants to the ground. Mosses reproduce by SPORES.

Moth Along with BUTTERFLIES, moths form a large insect group, the *Lepidoptera*, which means 'scale wing'. Their wings are covered with tiny scales which give them their colour. Most moths fly at night and keep their wings flat when at rest, unlike butterflies which usually fly by day and rest with wings folded together above their bodies. A better way of telling the two apart is by the shape of their antennae. Butterflies have antennae with small knobs at the end. Moths have antennae of many shapes, often feathered, but never with knobbed ends.

Gypsy moth

Peppered moth

Motion When a body changes its position in space, it is in motion. Isaac Newton's first law of motion says that an object will remain at rest or will continue to move in a straight line unless it is acted upon by a force. This means that anything moving will go on moving in a straight line for ever unless something either stops it or changes its motion in some way, for example the force of gravity or friction.

Motor car See **Automobile**

Motor cycle The first motor cycle was built by Gottlieb Daimler and Wilhelm Maybach in 1885, using a Benz petrol engine in a hand-built wooden machine. European machines dominated the world markets until the end of the 1950s, when Japanese models swept the board in the space of a few years. Motor cycle racing

Kawasaki Z1 300

began in the early 1900s. One of the major events is the Isle of Man TT (Tourist Trophy) held since 1907.

Motor racing Competitive sport which began in France in 1895. Emile Levassor, winner of the race from Paris to Bordeaux and back, achieved an average speed of 15 mph. Today's racing cars average 100–120 mph. The first Grand Prix (big prize) race was held at Le Mans in 1906. The great names of racing – Alfa-Romeo, Bugatti, Duesenberg, Delages, Maserati and Mercedes, vied with each other to produce winning cars.

Mould The name given to many fungi that spread all over the materials on which they grow and cover them with fluffy or spongy coats. Penicillium is a bluish-green mould that grows on many stale foods, including cakes and bread. PIN MOULDS are fluffy white moulds, also found on our foods, that produce their spores in tiny black 'pin heads'.

Mountains The great mountain ranges are formed by the collision of TECTONIC PLATES beneath the ground. Rock layers are squeezed and buckled as if in a giant vice and rise up to form great 'fold' mountains such as the HIMALAYAS, ROCKIES, ANDES and ALPS. Other mountains are created by volcanoes or where 'blocks' of land are raised by pressures in the Earth's crust.

Mouse A small rodent closely related to rats. It looks like a vole but has a longer snout and tail, and larger ears. The tail is almost naked. Most species of mouse live in the wild but the house mouse lives in close association with humans.

Elis de Angelis and Colin Chapman's Essex-Lotus 81

Essex-Lotus 81

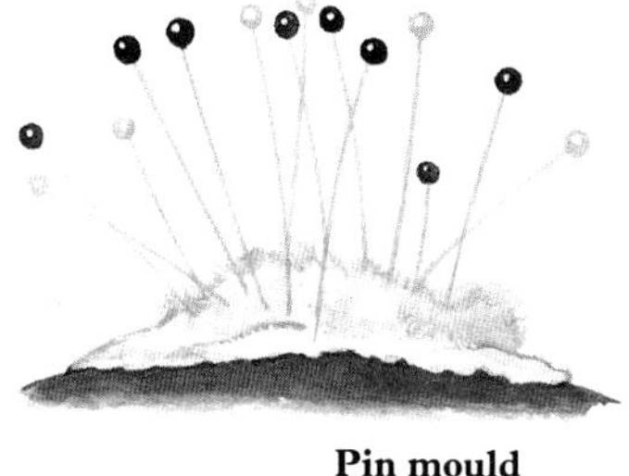

Pin mould

Penicillium mould

HIGHEST MOUNTAINS	
Asia	*Metres*
Everest (Nepal/Tibet)	8848
K2 (Godwin Austen, Kashmir)	8611
Kanchenjunga (India/Nepal)	8598
Makalu (Nepal/Tibet)	8481
Dhaulagiri (Nepal)	8172
Nanga Parbat (Kashmir)	8126
Annapurna (Nepal)	8078
North America	
McKinley (Alaska)	6194
Logan (Canada)	6050
Orizaba (Mexico)	5700
Popocatepetl (Mexico)	5452
South America	
Ancohuma (Bolivia)	7014
Aconcagua (Argentina)	6960
Ojos del Salado (Argentina/ Chile)	6880
Africa	
Kilimanjaro (Tanzania)	5895
Kenya (Kenya)	5199
Europe	
Elbrus (USSR)	5633
Mont Blanc (France)	4807
Monte Rosa (Switzerland)	4634
Oceania	
Wilhelm (Papua New Guinea)	4695
Cook (South Island, New Zealand)	3764
Kosciusko (Australia)	2228
Antarctica	
Vinson Massif	5140

Fold mountains are formed when two plates are pushed against each other. As one plate slides under the other, it melts. The melted rock may rise to the Earth's surface through volcanoes.

Mozambique Country in E Africa bordering the Indian Ocean. Most of its people live either on the coastal plain or in the valleys of the Limpopo and Zambezi Rs. The chief product is cashew nuts; tea, sugar and cotton are also grown, and there is timber in the forests. New factories use HEP from the Cabora Bassa scheme on the Zambezi. Area: 801,798 km^2; Pop: 13,402,000; Cap: Maputo.

Mozart, Wolfgang Amadeus (1756–91) Austrian composer and child prodigy. Much of his childhood was spent playing for the wealthy throughout Europe. Composing in all forms of music, he finally settled in Vienna in 1781. Despite his great musical genius, Mozart lacked sufficient financial support and died in poverty. His works include almost 50 symphonies, many great operas including *The Marriage of Figaro*, *The Magic Flute*, *Don Giovanni* and *Cosi Fan Tutti*, 25 piano concertos, much church music and many string quartets.

Munich Capital of Bavaria, W Germany, situated on R. Isar. Major brewing centre famed for its Oktoberfest. More than half the city was destroyed during World War II. Pop: 1,299,000.

Murray Principal river of Australia, rising in the Snowy Mountains and flowing westwards to enter the sea at Encounter Bay. For almost 2000 km the river forms the boundary between New South Wales and Victoria. The Murray is part of a major irrigation scheme and has several HEP stations. Length: 2600 km.

Muscle The contractile tissue inside the body that is responsible for movement. Muscle consists of large bundles of fibres attached to the bones across the joints. As a muscle contracts it pulls on one of the bones, causing it to move around the joint. Because muscles can only contract and pull, and cannot expand and push, they work in pairs, one muscle pulling a bone in one direction, another muscle pulling it back again.

Muses In Greek legend the nine goddesses of the arts and sciences: Clio, Erato, Euterpe, Thalia, Melpomene, Terpsichore, Polyhymnia, Urania and Calliope. Daughters of Zeus and Mnemosyne.

Mushroom A term used for a small group of edible toadstools, but also used in a wider sense for all the umbrella-shaped fungi. See picture on page 155.

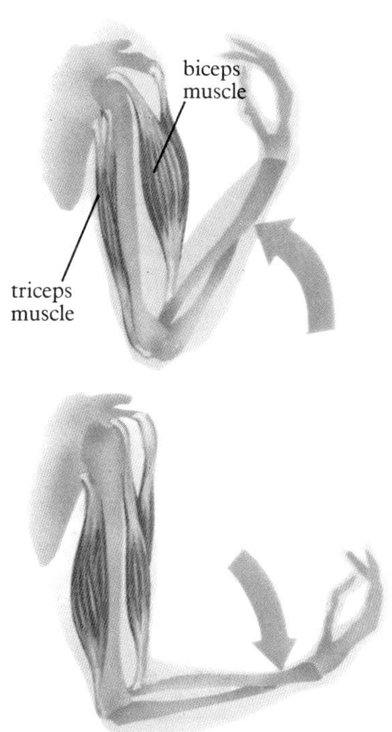

When you bend your arm, your biceps muscle contracts and your triceps muscle relaxes. The reverse happens when you straighten your arm.

Music Sounds arranged in patterns of rhythm and melody. The art of making music is a human activity, although some natural sounds, such as birdsong, may be called musical. Music is produced by the human voice and by instruments including PERCUSSION INSTRUMENTS, STRINGED INSTRUMENTS and WIND INSTRUMENTS. It can be played or sung by solo performers, by small 'chamber' groups or by large choirs and orchestras. Great music has been written by composers such as BACH, BEETHOVEN and MOZART, but it can also be performed without written music, as with early JAZZ, or be handed down from generation to generation, as with folk music.

Musk-ox Cattle of N American Arctic and Greenland. They have shaggy hair, curved horns and short legs. When threatened they form a circle round the calves to protect them.

Muskrat N American rodent which lives in a river-bank burrow and exudes an unpleasant musk-like odour. Muskrats are farmed for their fur (musquash).

Mussel A group of bivalve molluscs found in both fresh and salt water. Marine mussels are most often found on rocky shores. They cling to rocks by thin threads, known as the beard or byssus, and open their shells to feed. Freshwater mussels lie partly buried in the mud of lake and river beds but are not fixed by threads.

Mussolini, Benito (1883–1945) Founder of the Italian Fascist party, he became dictator in 1922. He conquered Ethiopia and as an ally of Hitler led Italy into World War II in 1940. He was overthrown in 1943 and later shot by resistance fighters while trying to escape to Switzerland.

Myths Traditional stories handed down from ancient times, often recounting deeds of gods and heroes. Local myths are found in every part of the world and are often closely linked to religious beliefs. The warriors of Scandinavia, for example, believed that death in battle would grant them a place in Valhalla, the hall of heroes, in the company of Odin, chief of the Norse gods.

N

Namibia Large, sparsely populated country in SW Africa. Much of the land is an arid plateau, with the Namib Desert in the west bordering the Atlantic and the Kalahari Desert in the east. The central grasslands support cattle and karakul sheep but the economy depends heavily upon diamonds, Namibia being a major world producer. The country is ruled by South Africa but is the scene of much unrest. Discussions are taking place between the UN and South Africa over independence. Area: 824,000 km²; Pop: 1,070,000; Cap: Windhoek.

Nansen, Fridtjof (1861–1930) Norwegian explorer, scientist and statesman, who was the first to cross Greenland in 1888. To prove that the ice of the Polar sea drifted from Siberia to Spitzbergen, he built the *Fram*, a ship shaped so as not to be crushed by the ice.

Naples Port and city in S Italy, at foot of Mt Vesuvius. Originally a Greek colony, it is an historic city with many fine churches. Great poverty still exists in the city but it attracts many tourists to its spectacular setting in the Bay of Naples. Pop: 1,255,000.

Napoleon I (1769–1821) Soldier and statesman of Corsican birth who became Emperor of France in 1804. A brilliant general, he conquered most of Europe and installed his brothers as Kings of Naples, Holland and Westphalia. He was later defeated in Spain by Wellington and his allies (the Peninsular War), and his invasion of Russia (1812) proved disastrous. Napoleon was eventually defeated at Leipzig in 1813 (The Battle of the Nations) and abdicated in 1814. He returned after 100 days' exile on the island of Elba in 1815 and rallied the French forces, but was narrowly defeated again at Waterloo by British forces led by the Duke of Wellington and Prussians under Blücher. He was exiled to St Helena where he died.

Napoleonic Wars Series of European wars from 1798 to 1815, in which France, under Napoleon, was ranged against shifting alliances of European states. France's citizen-armies and Napoleon's military genius secured many victories and, at the

Napoleon reviews his troops at the Tuileries in Paris in 1804.

peak of his conquests, Napoleon controlled practically all of mainland Europe. In 1812 he made the mistake of invading Russia, and his forces never recovered from the long, freezing retreat from Moscow. After defeat at Leipzig (1813), he abdicated, but returned for a final campaign which ended at WATERLOO.

Narcotics A group of drugs that suppress the nervous system and are used as sedatives, painkillers and sleeping pills. Many narcotics, such as heroin and morphine, are derived from opium, which comes from poppy seeds. Most narcotics are highly addictive and very dangerous if taken without proper medical supervision.

Narwhal Small whale of the Arctic Ocean. It is about five metres long with a straight spiralled tusk half as long again. The purpose of the tusk is unknown.

National Park An area set aside by law for the protection of wildlife and scenery. Many animals have been hunted to the brink of extinction and others have disappeared with the destruction of their habitats. In 1872 the first American national park covering 9000 km^2 was established at Yellowstone. Today national parks exist in many countries. One of the most famous is the Kruger National Park in South Africa (21,000 km^2).

NATO See **North Atlantic Treaty Organization.**

Natural gas This is a mixture of gases that have formed naturally from organic matter deep below the Earth's surface. Natural gas is nearly always found in association with oil and has to be drilled for in the same way. The gas is made up mainly of methane and has to be piped to a refinery, where it is purified. It is then piped to homes and factories.

Natural selection The driving force behind EVOLUTION. Any individual born with an advantage over other members of its species is more likely to live to produce young. If the characteristic is hereditary, the number of individuals possessing it will gradually increase while those individuals without it will eventually die out. This process of selection is often called 'survival of the fittest'.

Nautilus Cephalopod mollusc with coiled, pearly shell made of increasingly large gas-filled chambers. The animal lives in the largest, most recently made chamber.

Nazism National Socialism, the political theory of the party led by Adolf Hitler in Germany from the early 1920s. Nazism rejected the idea of justice in favour of power. To be strong was to be right. It was also racist, claiming that Germans were a superior breed and that others, especially Jews, were worthless. After the Nazis came to power in 1933, these beliefs led to Germany's attempt to conquer as much of the world as possible and to the slaughter of millions of people (including six million Jews) in special murder camps.

The Orion nebula glows from the light of new-born stars at its centre.

Nebula A mass of gas and dust in space believed to be the birthplace of stars. Some nebulae glow – the Orion nebula (a faint misty patch beneath the three stars that make up Orion's belt) appears through the telescope as a flaming blue, red and white cloud. Other nebulae are dark and obscure the stars behind them.

Nelson, Horatio (1758–1805) British naval hero who lost his right eye and right arm in battle against the French. In 1793, while on duty in Naples, Nelson first met Lady Hamilton. Later their love affair was to cause a public scandal. In 1798 Nelson defeated the French fleet in the Battle of the Nile. His greatest victory was the destruction of a combined Spanish and French fleet at the Battle of Trafalgar in 1805 in which he was fatally wounded.

Nematode Any of the huge group of animals commonly known as roundworms. Most are very small and live in the soil, feeding on decaying matter. Others are parasites on plants and animals.

Neon One of the INERT GASES present in air in small quantities. Widely used in discharge tubes for advertising signs where it produces a brilliant crimson glow. Chem. symbol Ne.

Nepal Mountainous kingdom in Asia, between China (Tibet) and India. Among many Himalayan peaks is Mt EVEREST. On the green valley slopes, the people cultivate terraced fields. Nepal exports rice, timber, cereals and cattle. Tourism is growing in importance. Area: 140,834 km^2; Pop: 16,578,000; Cap: Katmandu.

Neptune The eighth planet in line from the Sun, Neptune has an atmosphere containing large amounts of methane gas and appears greenish through the telescope. Diameter: 49,500 km; distance from Sun: 4500 million km; moons: two.

An artist's impression of Neptune seen from one of its moons.

Nero (AD 37–68) Dissolute Roman emperor and last of the Caesars. He murdered his chief rival, his mother and his wife and persecuted the Christians. A keen musician, he is said to have 'fiddled while Rome burned', though this accusation has no more basis in fact than his own accusation that the Christians started the great fire. Nero killed himself in the face of a successful revolt.

Nervous system The control system of the body that monitors and co-ordinates all activities, both conscious and unconscious. The brain is the main control centre, from which extends a long cord, the spinal cord, that passes down the middle of the backbone. The brain and spinal cord together form the central nervous system. Thirty-one pairs of nerves leave the spinal cord at regular intervals, branching out to form a network of nerves throughout the body. This is called the peripheral nervous system.

Netherlands Country in Europe also known as Holland. Flat and low-lying, the Netherlands includes areas reclaimed from the sea. Canals and rivers criss-cross the country. Windmills are a familiar sight, as are colourful fields of spring flowers. The chief rivers are the Rhine, Maas, Yssel and Scheldt. Farm products

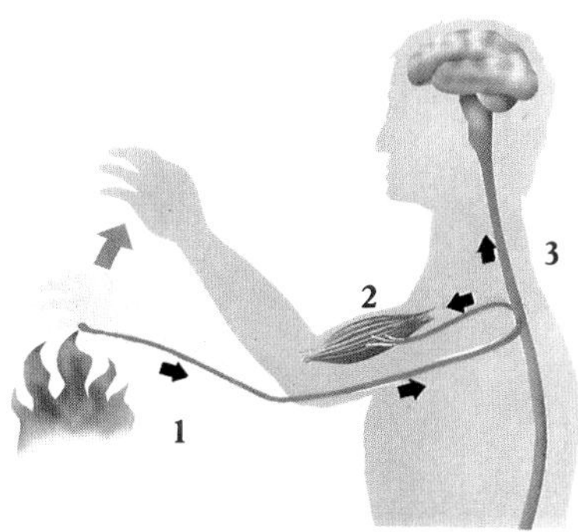

A reflex action happens before you know it. Your hand jerks away from fire (1) because nerves in the spinal cord pass a warning to the arm muscles (2) before the brain is informed (3).

include cereals, dairy products (especially butter and cheese), fruit and vegetables. Industries flourish, despite the lack of minerals; the country has shipyards, engineering and chemical works, and obtains energy from natural gas offshore. Area: 40,855 km^2; Pop: 14,437,000; Cap: Amsterdam (seat of government, The Hague).

Nettle Flowering plants noted for the stinging hairs on their stems and leaves. These hairs protect the nettle from hungry animals. The plants called dead-nettles have similar leaves but do not sting, and belong to a different plant group.

Newcomen, Thomas (1663–1729) Inventor of a steam engine used for pumping water out of Cornish tin mines.

New Guinea See **Papua New Guinea.**

New Orleans Port and city in Louisiana, USA, on Mississippi R. Centre of American cotton trade with oil and sugar refining. Home of Dixieland jazz. Pop: 558,000.

Newspaper Publication which presents news and comments on events of public interest. They are usually published daily or weekly. Newspapers began to appear regularly in the 17th century. The first daily paper in England was the *London Daily Courant* of 1702, followed in 1785 by the *Daily Universal Register*, which later became *The Times*. Today's news is collected and written by journalists and prepared for publication by sub-editors, under the leadership of the editor. Papers are printed on poor quality paper called *newsprint* and are either *broadsheets* or *tabloids*. Most 'popular' papers are tabloids.

Newt A small lizard-like amphibian closely related to salamanders. Unlike lizards, newts have no scales and are easily

Crested newt

distinguished by their flattened (rather than rounded) tails. They live either in or close to water and all species lay their eggs in water.

Newton, Sir Isaac (1642–1727) English scientific genius who made important advances and discoveries in physics, mathematics and astronomy. The first to state the laws of gravity (in his *Principia*), he invented integral and differential calculus, constructed a reflecting telescope and showed how light is made up of a spectrum of colours by passing it through a prism. He is buried in Westminster Abbey.

New York Port and city in SE New York state, USA, at mouth of Hudson R. The five boroughs of the city – Manhattan, the Bronx, Queens, Brooklyn and Richmond – are spread across the mainland, Long Island and Manhattan island. Largest city and principal port of USA. It was founded in 1610 as 'New Amsterdam' by the Dutch West Indian Company, who bought Manhattan for $24 worth of trinkets from the Indians. The city is famous for its skyscrapers including the World Trade Centre in the financial district, the Empire State Building (for long the tallest building in the world), the Statue of Liberty and the United Nations Building. Pop: 7,072,000 (9,120,000 met area).

New Zealand Country in SW Pacific, consisting of two main islands, North Island and South Island. North Island has a central volcanic area, with hot springs.

South Island has high mountains, the Southern Alps. The climate is temperate, with good rainfall. New Zealand's animal life includes species, such as the kiwi and the tuatara, not found elsewhere.

Most New Zealanders live in cities, but farming is an important activity. Sheep, meat, dairy products, wool, wheat and fruit are exported. Industries include timber, paper, and manufacturing. New Zealand became an independent parliamentary democracy within the Commonwealth in 1907. Area: 268,746 km²; Pop: 3,251,000; Cap: Wellington. See map on page 27.

Niagara Falls Two large waterfalls of the Niagara R. on the boundary between Canada and USA, and separated by Goat Island. Horseshoe Falls in Canada are 48 metres high, and American Falls in the USA are 51 metres high. The falls are a major tourist attraction and provide HEP.

Nicaragua Country in Central America, with long Atlantic and Pacific coastlines. Natural features include the swampy Mosquito Coast, the large L. Nicaragua, and several active volcanoes. The climate is hot and tropical. Earthquakes are common. Most Nicaraguans are farmers. The chief products are cotton, coffee, beef, gold, sugar, bananas and timber.

From 1936 the Somoza family held power as dictators, until overthrown by a socialist revolution in 1979. Area: 130,033 km²; Pop: 2,934,000; Cap: Managua.

Nickel Silvery-white metal with great resistance to corrosion. Widely used for plating other metal and in stainless steels. Cupronickel, an alloy of copper and nickel, is the basis of most 'silver' coinages. Chem. symbol Ni.

Niger Country in W Africa, north of Nigeria. It borders the Sahara Desert and is a hot, dry land with few trees. The people live by herding cattle, goats and camels. Millet, maize and dates are grown. Area: 1,267,329 km²; Pop: 6,284,000; Cap: Niamey.

Nigeria Large country in W Africa. The northern part is hot and dry; further south the country is wetter, with grassland and rain forest. The coasts are fringed with mangrove swamps. The people live by farming, forestry and fishing. Oil and natural gas provide most of the national income. The people of Nigeria include Ibos, Yoruba, Hausa and Fulani.

Once a haunt of European slavers, Nigeria was a British territory from 1861. It became independent in 1960. Area: 924,007 km²; Pop: 88,148,000; Cap: Lagos.

Nightingale A bird belonging to the thrush family. It is rather dull to look at, but is considered to be one of the finest singers of all birds. It gets its name from its habit of singing at night, but it also sings by day.

Nightingale, Florence (1820–1910) English nurse who did much to relieve the sufferings of the wounded soldiers in the Crimean War (1854–56). Though faced with much opposition she organized an efficient nursing service and came to be known as 'the lady with the lamp'.

Nightjar A bird, also called the goatsucker, which is rarely seen by day. At night it flies in search of insects, catching them in its gaping mouth. Its night cry is a continual 'chirring' sound.

Nightshade The name of a large family of plants including POTATO, TOBACCO and TOMATO. Some nightshades are poisonous, especially deadly nightshade which has purple flowers and deadly-poisonous black berries.

Black nightshade

Nile River in NE Africa and one of the longest in the world. Its two main branches are the White Nile whose source is L. Victoria in Uganda and the Blue Nile whose source is L. Tana in Ethiopia. These join to form the Nile proper in Sudan. Interrupted by a series of cataracts (rapids) the Nile flows northwards through Egypt and enters the Mediterranean via a large delta. The river has always been essential to the Egyptian economy, since it is virtually the only source of water for crops. As well as irrigation the river provides HEP for industries. The most important station is the Aswân Dam. Length: 6670 km.

Nitrogen Colourless gas without taste or smell which makes up nearly four-fifths of the atmosphere. Nitrogen compounds are essential to plants and animals and are extensively used in fertilizers. Chem. symbol N.

Nobel, Alfred Bernhard (1833–96) Swedish chemist and engineer who invented dynamite. From his discovery he amassed a great fortune and bequeathed a fund for five annual prizes, to be awarded in physics, chemistry, physiology or medicine, and literature. An additional award, in economic science, was set up by the Bank of Sweden and first given in 1969.

Nomads People who wander from place to place with their herds of camels, goats, sheep and horses in search of pasture. Nomads are found in the deserts of Africa and Asia. They generally live in easy-to-carry dwellings, such as tents, and take few belongings with them. Among the most famous are the Bedouins of Arabia.

North America The third largest continent occupying one-fifth of the Earth's land area. It consists of a vast central plain bordered by the Appalachian Mts in the east and the Rocky Mt system in the west which continues down through Mexico and Central America. North America is a rich continent, blessed with huge mineral resources and fertile farmlands. The inhabitants of the United States and Canada enjoy one of the highest standards of living in the world. Area: 24,346,000 km². See map on page 162.

North Atlantic Treaty Organization (NATO) A defensive military alliance formed in 1949. Its members are Britain, France, West Germany, Belgium, the Netherlands, Luxembourg, Denmark, Norway, Iceland, Italy, Portugal, Greece, Turkey, Canada and the USA. The armies, navies and air forces of the NATO countries train together. The Communist countries of Eastern Europe, led by the USSR, belong to a similar alliance known as the WARSAW PACT.

Northern Ireland Part of the United Kingdom, but geographically part of Ireland. It is made up of six of the nine counties of the Irish province of Ulster. The farmland is rich, the climate mild and moist. There is one great city, BELFAST. Industries include textiles, shipbuilding and engineering.

Northern Ireland was settled from the 1500s by English and Scots. When Ireland became self-governing in 1922, Northern Ireland chose to remain part of the United Kingdom. Division between the Catholic population (some of whom want Northern Ireland to unite with the rest of Ireland) and the Protestants (most of whom want to stay part of the United Kingdom) has caused much bitterness. Area: 14,000 km²; Pop: 1,488,000; Cap: Belfast.

North Sea Part of the Atlantic Ocean, E of Britain, W of Norway, Sweden, Denmark, West Germany, the Netherlands and Belgium, and N of France. The North Sea supports an important fishing industry and has major oil and gas deposits.

Norway A long, narrow country, Norway has a coast remarkable for long sea inlets or fjords. Inland are high mountains, while offshore are 15,000 small islands. Glaciers and fast-flowing rivers are plentiful. The climate is cold in winter, but the warm Gulf Stream keeps Norway's ports free of ice. Farmers grow cereals, potatoes and vegetables. Fishing is important, and Norway has a large merchant fleet. Energy is provided by North Sea oil and gas, and HEP. Area: 324,303 km²; Pop: 4,145,000; Cap: Oslo.

Novel A story, usually long, written in prose. Novel means new and the form we know today dates only from the 18th century, when it was 'new'. It grew from traditional tales of the East, from stories by Greek and Roman writers, and from such medieval romances as the stories of King Arthur. Early novel-like books were *Don Quixote* by the Spanish writer Miguel CERVANTES and *Robinson Crusoe* by the English writer Daniel DEFOE. The 19th century produced many great novels by writers such as Jane AUSTEN, Charles DICKENS, Victor HUGO and Leo TOLSTOY. By the 20th century the novel had become the most widely read form of literature.

Nuclear energy When the nucleus of an atom is broken apart, a large amount of energy is released. This is nuclear energy. The atoms of some substances – the radioactive elements – split apart by themselves. One of these elements is uranium. Uranium-235 is an ISOTOPE of uranium. When a neutron shoots away from the nucleus of a uranium-235 atom it crashes into another U-235 atom and knocks loose another neutron. This is

GREENLAND
(Denmark)
Godthaab
Davis Strait
Baffin Bay
Baffin Island
Ellesmere I.
ARCTIC OCEAN
Victoria Island
Banks I.
BEAUFORT SEA
Arctic Circle
NORTHWEST TERRITORIES
Great Slave Lake
Mackenzie
Hudson Bay
NEWFOUNDLAND
Newfoundland
St. John's
QUEBEC
St. Lawrence
ONTARIO
MANITOBA
CANADA
Lake Winnipeg
Winnipeg
MINNESOTA
NORTH DAKOTA
SASKATCHEWAN
Saskatoon
ALBERTA
Edmonton
Calgary
Missouri
MONTANA
ROCKY MOUNTAINS
BRITISH COLUMBIA
Vancouver
Seattle
WASHINGTON
Portland
OREGON
IDAHO
Snake
Vancouver I.
Queen Charlottes Is.
YUKON
Mt. Logan 6050
BROOKS RANGE
ALASKA
(U.S.A.)
Yukon
Mt. McKinley 6194
Anchorage
A
B
C
D
E
F
G
H
1
2
40
60
160

OF AMERICA
IOWA
Omaha
Denver
COLORADO
Colorado
Arkansas
KANSAS
Kansas city
Wichita
Chicago
Detroit
Hamilton
Lake Ontario
Lake Erie
Buffalo
N.Y.
MASS.
CONN.
R.I.
N.H.
Boston
Toledo
Cleveland
Newark
New York
N.J.
Philadelphia
PENNSYLVANIA
Pittsburgh
ILLINOIS
INDIANA
OHIO
Indianapolis
Columbus
Cincinnati
Baltimore
MARYLAND
DEL.
Washington D.C.
St. Louis
MISSOURI
Ohio
Louisville
WEST VIRGINIA
VIRGINIA
KENTUCKY
Norfolk
Los Angeles
CALIFORNIA
Long Beach
San Diego
Tijuana
Mexicali
ARIZONA
Phoenix
Tucson
Albuquerque
NEW MEXICO
Oklahoma City
OKLAHOMA
Tulsa
ARKANSAS
Memphis
Nashville
TENNESSEE
NORTH CAROLINA
PACIFIC OCEAN
Ciudad Juárez
El Paso
Fort Worth
Dallas
Red
TEXAS
Birmingham
Mississippi
MISSISSIPPI
ALABAMA
Atlanta
GEORGIA
SOUTH CAROLINA
ATLANTIC OCEAN
3
BERMUDA
Hermosillo
Gulf of California
SIERRA MADRE OCCIDENTAL
Chihuahua
Rio Grande
Austin
San Antonio
Houston
LOUISIANA
New Orleans
Jacksonville
Culiacán
Torreón
Monterrey
MEXICO
FLORIDA
Tampa
Lake Okeechobee
Gulf of Mexico
Miami
BAHAMAS
Nassau
Tropic of Cancer
San Luis Potosi
León
Guadalajara
Havana
Mexico City
Popocatepetl 5452
Puebla
Veracruz
Acapulco
Campeche Bay
Yucatán Peninsula
CUBA
Santiago de Cuba
Gulf of Honduras
HAITI
Port-au-Prince
DOMINICAN REPUBLIC
Santo Domingo
San Juan
PUERTO RICO
ANTIGUA
GUADELOUPE (Fr.)
DOMINICA
MARTINIQUE (Fr.)
St. LUCIA
St. VINCENT
GRENADA
4
Belmopan
BELIZE
JAMAICA
Kingston
GUATEMALA
Guatemala City
San Pedro Sula
HONDURAS
San Salvador
EL SALVADOR
Tegucigalpa
CARIBBEAN SEA
NICARAGUA
Managua
Lake Nicaragua
San José
COSTA RICA
Panama Canal
Panama City
PANAMA
Barranquilla
Cartagena
COLOMBIA
Maracaibo
Maracay
Caracas
Valencia
VENEZUELA
miles
0 200 400 600
0 200 400 600 800 1000
kilometres
20
80
100

The AGM-86B ALCM (air launched cruise missile) is carried by some B-52 bombers. Its range is 2500 km and it carries a thermonuclear warhead.

repeated throughout the piece of uranium in a flash and is called a *chain reaction*. If the piece of uranium is large enough and this reaction is not controlled, there is an atomic explosion. In nuclear power stations the chain reaction is slowed up by various means and the heat produced is used to drive electric generators. (See also FISSION, NUCLEAR.)

Nuclear weapons The first nuclear weapon was exploded on 16 July 1945. It was a test carried out by the United States. Two atomic bombs were dropped with devastating effect on Hiroshima and Nagasaki in August 1945 to end World War II. There are now more than enough nuclear weapons to kill all the people in the world. Atomic bombs can be of the *fission* or *fusion* type. FISSION bombs get their power from the splitting apart of uranium or plutonium atoms. FUSION or hydrogen bombs are much more powerful. The enormous power comes from the nuclear fusion of atoms of deuterium and tritium.

O

Oak A group of 250 or so species of large broad-leaved trees, all of which produce acorns as fruit and have long, lobed leaves. Some oaks are deciduous, others evergreen. They grow slowly and live for centuries.

Oasis An area in a desert where there is water. Many oases are springs, but the term also covers river valleys: the valley of the Nile, running through the Sahara desert, is the largest oasis of all.

Observatory A place from which astronomers study the sky. The first observatories are believed to have been circles of stones aligned on particular rising and setting points of the Sun and Moon. Modern observatories house optical instruments, usually in a dome. A slit in the dome opens to afford the telescope a view of the sky, and the dome rotates to allow the telescope to point wherever it is required. Unmanned orbiting observatory satellites have been launched in space to study the stars without the interference of the Earth's atmosphere.

Ocean The oceans cover 71 per cent of the Earth's surface. They can be divided into three zones: the continental shelves, the continental slopes and the abyss. The abyss contains plains, mountain ranges, volcanoes and deep trenches. The average depth of the oceans is 3550 metres, but a record depth of 11,033 metres has been measured in the Marianas Trench in the W Pacific. The tallest submarine mountain is the volcano Mauna Kea in Hawaii. It rises 10,023 metres from the ocean floor, though only 4204 metres are above sea level.

Two views of the watery earth: the top shows the vast Pacific Ocean, the lower the land masses.

Ocean currents Great 'rivers' of water moving through the oceans. Surface currents are generated by the prevailing winds. They take the form of circular movements of water – clockwise in the N hemisphere, anticlockwise in the S

The ocean bed has the same kind of dramatic scenery as the land, caused by movements of the crustal plates.

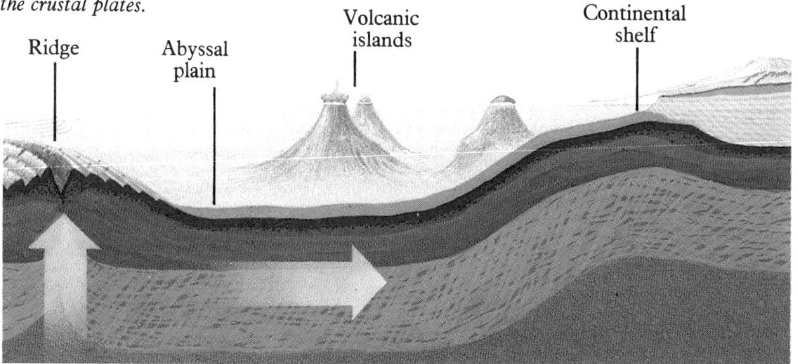

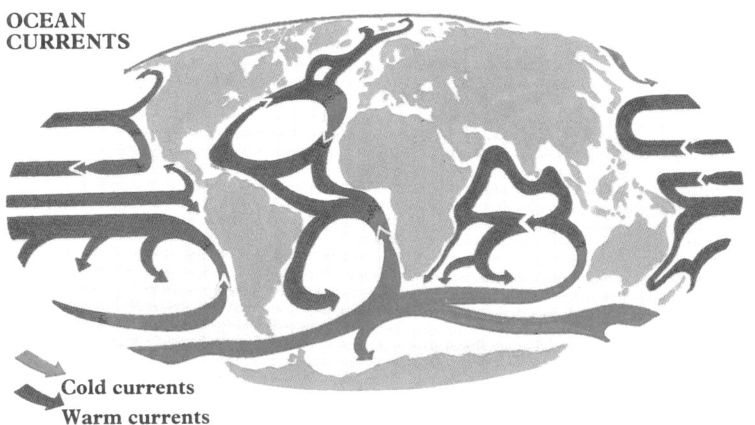

hemisphere. Notable currents include the Gulf Stream that warms W Europe in the winter and the Labrador current that chills the E coast of N America.

Ocelot Wild S American spotted cat, less than half a metre long.

Octopus Marine molluscs related to squids and cuttlefish. An octopus has eight suckered 'arms' which it uses to seize prey such as crabs. It has a bag-like body, large eyes, and a beaked mouth. It moves rapidly by shooting out a jet of water. Octopuses are found in many parts of the world and range in size from a few centimetres across the tentacles to as much as ten metres.

Odysseus In Greek legend one of the leaders of the Greek armies during the Trojan War. He invented the famous wooden horse that led to the final downfall of Troy. His later wanderings and the eventual recapture of his kingdom are told in Homer's *Odyssey*. (Roman equivalent Ulysses.)

Oedipus In Greek legend the son of Laius, King of Thebes, and Jocasta. It was prophesied that he would kill his father and marry his mother. Left on a mountain to die he was rescued and brought up by the King of Corinth. He later met Laius and killed him in a quarrel, then unwittingly married his mother.

Oil See **Petroleum**

Okapi Almost as distinctive as its relative the giraffe, but much smaller, the okapi stands just under two metres tall. It lives in the central African rainforest. The white bands on its legs stand out against its reddish hide.

Olive Mediterranean tree cultivated for its fruit. The trees are long-lived and many have stood for centuries. Their leaves are grey-green and the bark is gnarled. Olives, the fruit of the tree, are an important crop, both for eating and for making into oil. Italy is the world's leading olive oil producer.

Olympic games Sports festival held every four years, based on the games of ancient Greece. The ancient games involved running races, wrestling, poetry and other events. The modern games began in 1896 at the suggestion of Baron Pierre de Coubertin. The first modern Olympics were held in Athens and only 13 countries took part. Today thousands of competitors from many countries assemble for the games.

Oman Country on the SE coast of the Arabian peninsula. This mainly desert land has grown wealthy from oil. Formerly called Muscat and Oman, the country was a British protectorate until 1970. Area: 212,441 km²; Pop: 1,181,000; Cap: Muscat.

Omar Khayyam (*c* 1050 - 1123) Persian poet and mathematician. He is best known for his long poem the *Rubáiyát* which was translated into English by Edward Fitzgerald in 1859.

Omnivore Any animal that regularly eats both plant and animal material. Humans and badgers are both examples of omnivores.

OPEC See **Organization of Petroleum Exporting Countries**.

Opera A DRAMA told in musical form so that the words are sung rather than spoken. Opera was first performed in Italy around 1600. At first the words were mainly recited, but soon separate songs called arias were added. Many great composers, especially MOZART, have included operas among their works. Others, such as WAGNER, VERDI and PUCCINI, are known chiefly for their operas.

Opossum American marsupials with long prehensile tails. In some species the young are first carried in the mother's pouch and then on her back. The expression 'playing possum' comes from this animal's habit of feigning death in order to escape predators.

Pythia

Oracle In Ancient Greece the answer given to questions by gods and goddesses through priests and priestesses. The most famous oracle was that of Apollo at Delphi. The Pythia (above) sat on a special tripod to deliver oracles. She may have taken drugs to induce visions.

Orange Citrus tree with round orange fruit, abundant in ascorbic acid (vitamin C). Originally from China, the common sweet orange is widely cultivated in Europe and North America for eating and for its juice. The bitter Seville orange is grown for making marmalade.

Orang-utan Somewhat rare tree-dwelling ape from Sumatra and Borneo. Its name means 'man of the woods'. It has sparse reddish hair and stands upright at about 1.3 metres. Its armspread is considerably greater than its height. It swings through the branches on long, strong arms delicately picking and eating fruit. See picture on page 16.

Orb-web spiders Name for those spiders, such as the garden spider, which spin orb-shaped webs to catch their prey.

Orchestra Group of instrumental players. In the theatres of ancient Greece the orchestra was the space in front of the stage where the chorus danced. In modern theatres the orchestra still sits in front of the stage, in the 'pit'. An orchestra can be any group of musical instruments but usually describes that which developed after 1600 with the growth of opera in Italy and ballet in France. By the 18th century the basic symphony orchestra was established. It had four sections: woodwind and brass (WIND INSTRUMENTS), PERCUSSION INSTRUMENTS and STRINGED INSTRUMENTS. Modern orchestras have about 100 players sitting in a semicircle and following the commands of a conductor.

Orchid A large family of over 20,000 species of flowering plants, most of which grow in the tropics, living on other plants as *epiphytes*. The flowers vary greatly in shape, and are much prized by growers.

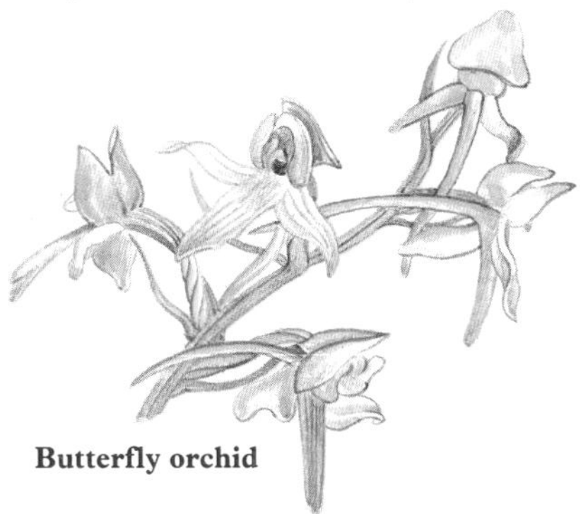

Butterfly orchid

Organization of Petroleum Exporting Countries (OPEC) Countries belonging to OPEC are mostly in the Middle East, but include Venezuela and Nigeria. OPEC meets to fix the price of oil, the most important fuel needed by the industrialized countries. In the 1970s the price of oil rose steeply, bringing about the 'energy crisis' and a worldwide slump in manufacturing and trade. Some OPEC members, such as Saudi Arabia, have grown immensely wealthy from the sale of oil and have used this wealth to modernize their countries.

Oriole Forest songbirds of Asia and Europe. The golden oriole has striking black and yellow plumage. The orioles of America are of a different family.

Orkney Islands Group of islands in North Sea, off NE Scotland. Chief town is Kirkwall on the largest island, Mainland (Pomona). Main industries are North Sea oil, dairy farming and fishing. Pop: 19,000.

Orpheus In Greek legend a skilled musician who went to Hades in search of his dead wife Eurydice. She was allowed to leave with him on condition that he did not look at her until they had returned to Earth. Forgetting his promise, he turned and she vanished for ever.

Oryx Three desert-dwelling species of antelope with long, slender horns and beautiful white or fawn coats. They are the gemsbok, the scimitar oryx and the almost extinct Arabian oryx.

Oscilloscope An electronic instrument in which an electric current, or anything that can be turned into an electric current, is shown as a moving graph on a cathode-ray screen.

Osiris Ancient Egyptian god of the Underworld, husband and brother of Isis.

Oslo Capital city and largest port of Norway, at the head of Oslo Fjord. Chief commercial and industrial centre with many wood-based manufactures. Pop: 452,000.

Osmosis A process which occurs when two solutions of different concentrations are separated by a semi-permeable membrane. It involves the movement of the solvent from the region of low concentration to that of high concentration. Osmosis is the method by which plant roots draw water out of the soil, made possible by the highly concentrated sap inside the root.

Osprey A bird of prey which hunts fish and is also known as the fish hawk. It is mostly brown, with white mottled underparts. The osprey dives into the water to catch its prey, seizing the fish in its talons. It is found in Europe, Asia and North America.

Ostrich The largest living bird, the flightless ostrich (male) stands up to 2.5 metres high. It has a long neck and long legs on which to run from danger.

Ottawa Capital city of Canada, in Ontario province. Founded in 1827, it began as a small lumbering settlement. It became the seat of government in 1858 and the capital in 1865. Pop: 304,000.

Otter A carnivore belonging to the weasel family. It is 75 cm long with a long body and tail and short legs. The feet are webbed and the fur is shiny and dark brown. Otters live on the banks of rivers and lakes, and also by the sea. They hunt in the water at night, feeding on fish and other water animals.

Otter

Ottoman empire Turkish state from the 14th to the early 20th century, named after its founder. From a small region of Anatolia (modern Turkey), the Ottoman sultans created an empire which, at its height in the 16th and 17th centuries, stretched from eastern Europe to Iraq and North Africa. The Ottoman empire shrank steadily after that, but it continued to exist until 1922, when the modern republic of Turkey was created.

Ovid (43 BC-AD 18) Roman poet who was originally a lawyer. Among his works are *Metamorphoses* and *The Art of Love*.

Owl A nocturnal bird of prey found in most parts of the world. The plumage consists of fluffy feathers which make its flight noiseless. Owls have flattened disc-shaped faces with sharply hooked bills and large forward-facing eyes. Species include the barn owl, horned owl, screech owl, long- and short-eared owls, tawny owl and smallest of all the elf owl.

Ox Family of hoofed ruminants that includes domestic CATTLE, BISON, BUFFALO, MUSK-OXEN and many others. Domesticated oxen are valuable beasts of burden in poorer countries.

Oxidation A chemical process in which a substance is combined with oxygen. This may be slow like the rusting of iron in damp air, or rapid and accompanied by a flame producing heat and light (combustion). The term oxidation is also used for similar reactions involving other substances, such as sulfur.

Oxygen Gas vital to plant and animal life which makes up about one-fifth of the atmosphere. It is the most abundant element in the Earth's crust, where in various compounds it accounts for 46% of the total. And combined with hydrogen in the form of water, it makes up over 85% of the oceans by weight. Chem. symbol O.

Little owl

Oyster A group of edible bivalve molluscs found in shallow, muddy coastal waters. If grit enters the shell the oyster protects its soft body by encasing the grit in a PEARL.

Oyster catcher A bird of the seashore, related to the plovers. It has handsome black and white plumage and a long, bright orange bill. Its diet includes shellfish (not often oysters), shrimps and worms.

Ozone A form of oxygen in which each molecule has three atoms instead of two. It is formed by electrical sparks in normal oxygen, and can be used as a bleach or a sterilizer. A layer of ozone in the upper atmosphere absorbs harmful ultraviolet radiation from the Sun.

Oxen pulling the plough in Ancient Rome.

P

Pacific Ocean Largest and deepest ocean in the world, extending from the Americas to Asia and Australia and from the Arctic Circle to Antarctica. It contains numerous islands, many volcanic. Area: 166,000,000 km^2; Greatest depth: 10,914 metres.

Paine, Thomas (1737–1809) English writer and agitator who wrote the pamphlet *Common Sense* in support of the American colonies in their struggle for independence. He also supported the French Revolution and his *Rights of Man* appeared in 1792.

Painting Work of art created in paint, chalk, ink or similar material. The oldest paintings known are those made on cave walls in prehistoric times, mostly of hunting scenes. Painting is common to East and West and is often religious in subject. Most European works of the Middle Ages were made for the church. A great change came with the RENAISSANCE, when painters began using perspective to create depth and distance in their pictures and brought more realism to the subjects. These and later artists worked for rich patrons who often demanded portraits. Others wanted landscape paintings of rural scenes. Among modern developments in art have been Impressionism, which tries to capture the mood of a scene, and abstract painting, which emphasises shape and form.

Pakistan Islamic republic in S Asia. The Himalayas rise in N Pakistan and great plains descend from the foothills to the R. Indus. Apart from the mountainous north and the river valley, Pakistan is mostly arid. Crops of cereals, rice, cotton and sugar need irrigation. Farmers also raise livestock. About a quarter of the people live in towns, the biggest of which are Lahore and Karachi. Chief industries are textiles, cement, sugar, paper, fertilizers and engineering products. Area: 803,882 km^2; Pop: 96,628,000; Cap: Islamabad.

Palaeontology The study of prehistoric life forms through FOSSILS – traces of plants and animals found in rocks.

Palestine See **Israel**.

Palm Group of some 2500 species of tropical trees and shrubs. A typical palm has a tall unbranched trunk crowned by a large fan of evergreen leaves. In poor countries the leaves and trunks are used in construction, and the trees are grown for their fruit and oil. Economically important palms include the DATE and COCONUT.

Pampas See **Prairie**.

Pan Greek god of fertility, huntsmen and shepherds. The lower half of his body was that of a goat and horns grew out of his head. He loved music and usually carried his pipes, made of reeds of different lengths and fastened in a row. (Roman equivalent Faunus.)

Panama Country lying on the narrow strip of land between North and South America. Running across the country is the Panama Canal which links the Caribbean and the Pacific. The country gains most of its wealth from trade passing through the Canal. The land is mountainous, with fertile plains and valleys. Rice is the main crop and staple food. Bananas are exported, together with sugar-cane. Area: 75,643 km^2; Pop: 2,000,000; Cap: Panama City.

Pancreas Gland inside the body with two major functions: it produces digestive enzymes which help to break down foods and two important hormones, insulin and glucagon, which control the amount of sugar in the blood.

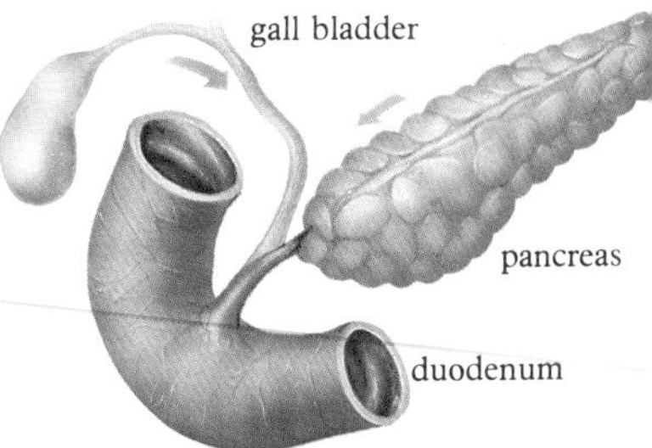

Digestive juice from the pancreas and bile from the gall bladder flow into a tube called the duodenum below the stomach.

Panda The giant panda is a black and white bear-like creature that lives in the bamboo forests of Tibet and China. Now carefully protected, its numbers were decreasing because of the destruction of its habitat. A few specimens can be seen in zoos outside China where they are fed almost exclusively on bamboo shoots. The lesser panda is red and looks rather like a racoon.

Pandora In Greek legend the first woman on Earth. The gods gave her a box which unbeknown to her contained all human ills. Curious, she opened it and released evil and misery to spread all over the world.

Pangolin Forest-dwelling mammals of Africa and Asia. Sometimes called scaly anteaters, the animals feed on ants and termites. Their long slender bodies are covered by overlapping scales, and some species can roll up to defend themselves.

Pansy Flowering plants similar to their close relatives, the violets, but with larger, flatter flowers.

Paper The first paper was made by the ancient Chinese about AD 100. They mashed tree bark into a wet pulp, squeezed out the water, pressed the pulp into flat sheets, and left the sheets to dry in the sun. Today, paper is made by large machines, but the process is still very much the same. The cheaper paper is made from wood pulp. Fine paper comes from rags. Different kinds of paper and different surfaces can be produced by varying the kinds of rollers the paper passes through.

Papua New Guinea Country in the Pacific Ocean, north of Australia. It includes the eastern part of New Guinea, islands of the Bismarck Archipelago, and the Solomon Islands. The climate is tropical and the central highlands are densely forested. Until recently the island was largely unexplored and its people little known. Area: 461,655 km^2; Pop: 3,266,000; Cap: Port Moresby.

Papyrus Grass-like water plant of Africa and Asia. The ancient Egyptians used its tough stems to make boats, cloth and a writing material called papyrus, the first 'paper'.

Paraguay Landlocked republic in central South America. The chief occupation is farming. Nearly 6 million cattle graze the rich pasturelands, and meat products are among the chief exports. Crops include cotton, rice, maize, soya beans, wheat and tobacco. Area: 406,720 km^2; Pop: 3,623,000; Cap: Asunción.

Parakeet Small brightly coloured members of the parrot family, mostly living in Australia and Tasmania. Some species, including budgerigars, are kept as pets. The Carolina parakeet is an extinct American bird.

Parasite A plant or animal that lives on or in another species and takes food from it without giving anything in return. Tapeworms and nematodes living in an animal's food canal are internal parasites, while fleas living in an animal's fur and sucking blood are external parasites. Dodder is a parasitic plant with no leaves or chlorophyll. It steals all its food from other plants by pushing suckers into them from its own thread-like pink stems.

Paris In Greek legend a Trojan prince who took Helen away from her husband, Menelaus, and thereby caused the Trojan War.

Paris Port and capital of France on R. Seine. Major commercial, cultural and fashion centre. The beautifully-designed city is divided into two almost equal parts: the northern or Right bank with its wide boulevards and the Left bank containing the famous Latin quarter. Many famous buildings including Notre Dame, the Arc de Triomphe and the Eiffel Tower attract tourists. Pop: 2,291,000.

Parliament Literally a 'talking place', where elected representatives meet to discuss and pass laws. The British parliament has two houses: the Commons and Lords. The real power lies in the Commons, whose members are elected representatives of the people. The House of Lords has a mainly advisory role, and its members are either hereditary peers (nobles), law lords or life peers (people given titles for service to the country). Bishops also sit in the House of Lords. Other countries have similar parliaments, though in many there is only one house and only one political party.

Parrot Brilliantly coloured birds with large generally hooked bills, and a powerful squawk. They are popular as caged birds and are excellent mimics. In the wild, parrots live in the warmer parts of America, Africa, Asia and Australia. Among them are the macaws (up to a metre long), cockatoos, true parrots, parakeets and lories.

Parthenon Ancient Greek temple which stands on the Acropolis in Athens. It was built in the 5th century BC and dedicated to the goddess Athena. Besides the deceptively simple beauty of the building itself, it was decorated with some of the most beautiful sculpture of classical Greece.

Partridge A game bird that looks rather like a plump, short-legged pigeon.

Passover (Pesach) The most important Jewish festival which occurs in March or April. At this time Jews remember how God delivered them from Egypt and spared the firstborn Jewish children when he killed those of the Egyptians.

Pasteur, Louis (1822–1895) French scientist who made major advances in chemistry, medicine and the food industry. He showed that bacteria are present though unseen almost everywhere. He invented the process of heating milk to kill bacteria (pasteurization) and of vaccinating animals and humans to make them immune to various diseases. He also made discoveries of great use in brewing and wine-making.

Paul, St (AD ? – *c* 64) Originally named Saul, he was a persecutor of the Christians. On his way to Damascus he 'saw the light' and became a disciple of Jesus. He made three missionary journeys to Asia Minor and Europe before being arrested and imprisoned in Rome. There he wrote some of the Epistles and was eventually executed.

Pea A group of flowering plants which includes the edible garden pea and blackeyed pea or cowpea, as well as the sweet pea (cultivated only for its flowers).

Peacock Peafowl are spectacular birds about the size of a turkey. The male has a magnificent train of feathers which it raises into a fan. The greeny-blue feathers are marked with bold 'eye' spots. The peahen is smaller and plainer with no train. The peacock is the emblem of India.

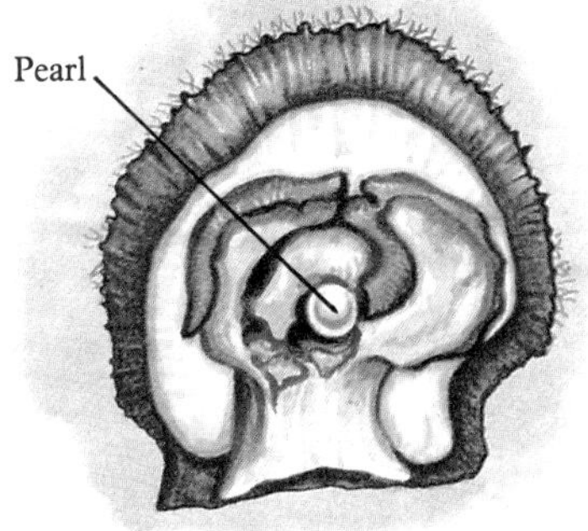

Pearl Valuable gem formed inside oysters and other molluscs. The oyster's shell is lined with a substance called nacre (mother-of-pearl). When a piece of grit gets inside the shell, it irritates the oyster and the animal coats it with smooth nacre, eventually forming a pearl. Pearl divers collect naturally formed pearls from the sea bed but pearls are also cultured, the impurities being injected into farmed oysters.

Pegasus In Greek legend an immortal winged horse which sprang from the head of the Gorgon Medusa, slain by Perseus.

Peking Capital of China and for centuries the seat of Chinese rulers, including Mongol, Ming and Manchu dynasties. The inner city contains the old imperial palace, formerly the 'Forbidden City', now a museum and tourist attraction. Pop: 7,750,000.

Pelican The world's largest web-footed birds, pelicans have a large pouch under the beak into which they scoop fish. They live in Australasia and North America. The American white pelican is the largest with a wingspan of over three metres.

Pendulum A simple pendulum is a weight on the end of a piece of string. If pulled to one side and released, the weight swings backward and forward in a fixed, even time called its *period*. This time is the same whether the swing is large or small and whatever the size of the weight. It depends only on the length of the string. This unvarying swing time is used to control the movement of clocks and was discovered by the great Italian scientist Galileo.

Penguin Flightless black and white birds that live on Antarctic and sub-antarctic coasts and feed on fish. They raise their young on land, standing on the ice in large rookeries. For two months the emperor penguin incubates the solitary egg laid by his mate, while she goes back to the sea. He holds the egg on his feet where it is kept warm by his belly feathers.

Penicillium A green, mat-forming mould that grows on bread, overripe fruit and many other foods. The mould produces penicillin, the antibiotic that is used in medicine to fight germs.

Pepys, Samuel (1633–1703) English diarist and naval official who became secretary to the Admiralty. He is best known for his diary (1660–69), written in cipher, which vividly portrays contemporary life in England. It was not until 1825 that it was published.

Perch Family of freshwater fishes that includes, along with the common perch, the zander and ruffe. Members have two dorsal fins, the front one of which is very spiny.

Perching birds The largest order of birds, the *Passeriformes*, whose toes are adapted for gripping branches. They include most familiar garden birds but also some exotic ones.

Percussion instruments Musical instruments which produce a sound when beaten or shaken. There are two groups. One includes instruments of fixed pitch, such as cymbals, bells, gong, tambourine and castanets. The other includes instruments of variable pitch, such as the drum, which sounds when a taut material, stretched across a hollow cavity, is struck. Some percussion instruments, such as gongs or cymbals, are used only for rhythm. Others, including the bells and xylophone, can be made to play a tune.

Perfume Fragrant substances used since ancient times to make the body and home smell pleasant. Perfumes are made largely from plant and animal oils distributed in alcohol, though many cheap varieties use synthetic substances instead. Musk, which is secreted by many mammals to attract their mates, is the base of many scents.

Periodic table An organized arrangement of the chemical elements in order of increasing atomic number. The atomic number of an element is the number of protons in the nucleus of each atom (also the number of electrons). In the table, elements with similar chemical properties fall in vertical columns called *groups*.

Periscope A device for seeing objects out of the line of vision by means of an arrangement of mirrors and lenses. Simple periscopes are used to see over the heads of crowds. Complex periscopes are employed in submarines.

Perseus In Greek legend the son of Zeus and Danaë. He killed the snake-haired Gorgon Medusa, and married Andromeda after saving her from a sea monster.

Perth Capital of Western Australia on Swan River. Founded in 1829, it experienced rapid growth during the 1890s, the population expanding fourfold. Pop: 918,000 (met area).

Peru Republic and third largest country in South America. The Andes Mountains run through the centre and the R. Amazon rises in the rainforests to the east. In the mountains there are remains of Inca cities destroyed by the Spanish conquerors in 1533.

About half of Peru's people are farmers, growing cotton, coffee and sugar and raising sheep, llamas and alpacas. Most wealth comes from minerals such as copper, iron, silver, lead, zinc and oil. Area: 1,285,116 km^2; Pop: 19,000,000; Cap: Lima.

Peter, St (? – *c* AD 64) A fisherman called Simon who became the leading disciple of Christ and preached the first Christian sermon after his death. He was named Peter by Jesus. He is credited with founding the Church in Rome and was later crucified there.

Petroleum Petroleum or crude oil is a greenish-black fossil fuel that is pumped from the earth, refined and turned into petrol, kerosene, diesel oil, fuel oil, lubricating oil, and many plastic products.

Petroleum and natural gas are found together in underground pools trapped between layers of impervious rock.

Pewter A grey alloy made mainly from tin. In the Middle Ages the best pewter was made by mixing tin with copper or brass to harden the metal. Lead was used for pewter of inferior quality. Today, antimony and copper are most often used. Pewter has been made since Roman times. It is still used to make plates, candlesticks, drinking cups and similar objects.

Pharaoh Ruler of ancient Egypt. The pharaohs were believed to be gods as well as kings. They ruled through their officials, who were often members of their family, and presided over big religious festivals. When they died they were buried with great ceremony in a PYRAMID or rock tomb. The Egyptians believed they went to join the other gods, and would continue to protect them.

Pheasant Large birds with colourful plumages and long tails. Pheasants came originally from Asia, but are now found world-wide. The game pheasant is reared for shooting and the table; the male bird is much more colourful than the female.

Philadelphia Port and city in Pennsylvania, USA, on Delaware R. In the late 18th and early 19th century it was the most important city in America, and briefly the capital (1790–1800). Declaration of Independence was signed here in 1776. Pop: 1,688,000 (4,717,000 met area).

Philippines Republic in SE Asia, separated from the continent by the South China Sea. The country is made up of over 7000 islands, some mountainous and volcanic, others small coral atolls. The land is fertile and most people farm. Chief crops include rice, maize, coconuts, sugar, tobacco, hemp, fruit and timber. A rich variety of minerals includes copper, oil, iron and

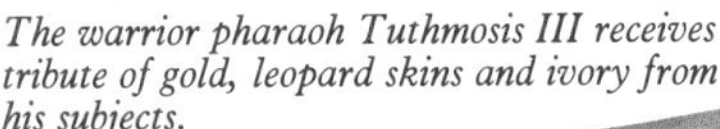

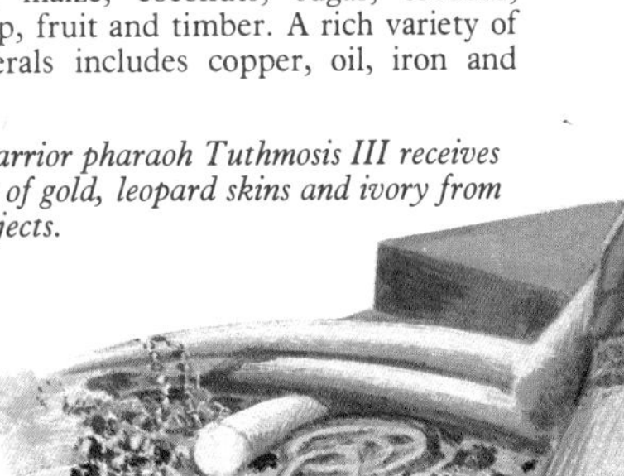

The warrior pharaoh Tuthmosis III receives tribute of gold, leopard skins and ivory from his subjects.

gold. Area: 299,976 km²; Pop: 55,528,000; Cap: Manila.

Philosophy The study of learning itself. The word philosophy comes from two Greek words meaning love of wisdom. Philosophers seek wisdom by thinking about the material and abstract worlds and about thinking itself.

Phoenicians Ancient people who were living on the coast of Syria soon after 2000 BC. They were great sailors and merchants, and from the 12th to the 6th century BC they controlled trade in the Mediterranean. They founded cities in N Africa, including Carthage which became their chief centre, and in southern Spain. In writing, the Phoenicians used an alphabet which is the ancestor of the modern alphabet.

Phoenix In Egyptian myth a bird which lived in the Arabian Desert. Every 500 years it consumed itself in fire and rose anew from the ashes.

Phosphorus Non-metallic element which glows in the dark and bursts into flame on contact with air. It forms many compounds and is an essential element of plants and of the bones and teeth of animals. Chem. symbol P.

Photography When a photograph is taken, rays of light from the object photographed pass through a LENS and enter the CAMERA. The light rays form an image on the light-sensitive FILM at the back of the camera. This image shows up when the film is developed in special chemicals. The film has become a *negative*. From the negative, positive final photographs are printed.

Photon A photon is a tiny packet of energy (a quantum) of ELECTROMAGNETIC RADIATION such as light. When light strikes something, it behaves as though it is made up of particles of energy instead of continuous waves. These particles are photons.

Photosynthesis The food-making process of green plants. It can take place only in sunlight. The green substance chlorophyll absorbs light and uses its energy to make glucose sugar from water and carbon dioxide gas. Oxygen is given off in the process.

Phylum The largest category used in the classification of plants and animals. All members of a phylum have basically the same structure, although they may differ greatly in size and appearance.

Physiology Study of the ways in which plants and animals function and of the various processes involved.

Piano (short for pianoforte) Musical instrument in which wires are struck by hammers moved when keys are pressed on a keyboard. The modern piano was invented in Italy in 1709 and followed earlier keyboard instruments such as the harpsichord. The piano gave performers greater control over tone and phrasing and quickly became popular. CHOPIN and LISZT composed many works for the piano.

Picasso, Pablo (1881–1973) Spanish painter and sculptor who had a profound influence on 20th century art. He worked in many different styles throughout his life and was the pioneer of Cubism. Perhaps his most famous work is the mural *Guernica* (1937), a response to the carnage of the Spanish civil war.

Pig Stout domestic animals developed from the wild boar. Extensively farmed for their meat (pork and bacon), fat (lard) and leather (pigskin). The United States (where they are called hogs) and China are the leading producers.

Pigeon The name given to a group of plump seed-eating birds. Some are called doves though that is simply an alternative name. All pigeons have deep cooing or booming voices, and a repetitive song.

Wood pigeon

Pigment A coloured substance that is used to colour other substances such as paper or cloth. Most pigments occur in plant or animal tissue but some are made artificially. When powdered pigments are mixed with a liquid to form paint they do not dissolve in the liquid. They remain

suspended, unlike DYES which are soluble.

Pike A voracious freshwater fish known to reach 1.5 metres in length with a flattened head and large jaws bristling with teeth. Pike are notorious predators and can take fish up to half their own weight.

Pilchard A marine fish, up to 25 cm long, related to the herring. It is found in large shoals in the Atlantic and the Mediterranean.

Pilgrim Fathers First English colonists in New England. They wanted freedom to practise their own form of religious worship outside the Church of England. Sailing in the *Mayflower*, they founded Plymouth Colony, Massachusetts, in 1620. With the help of friendly Indians, the little colony survived alone until more colonists began to arrive in 1628.

Pine A group of cone-bearing trees with needle-shaped leaves, found mainly in the cooler northern parts of the world. The trees are evergreen and are commonly planted for their timber or for ornament. The Scots pine is a common species, growing up to 35 metres high.

Pineapple S American plant with sharp sword-shaped leaves and a cone-shaped flower spike which develops into the large juicy fruit. Pineapples are produced commercially in Hawaii.

Pin mould There are several similar kinds of pin mould, so named because their spore capsules, raised on slender stalks, resemble tiny pins. The fluffy mycelium grows on dung, as well as on bread and many other foods. See page 153.

Piranha Carnivorous fish of S American rivers. They range in size from 10 to 40 cms, but all have viciously sharp teeth. They travel in shoals of up to a thousand individuals and together can devour the flesh of a large animal in a few minutes.

Pirates Robbers who commit their crimes at sea. In the 16th and 17th centuries there were many pirates. Some, called privateers, had official authorization to attack foreign ships. Most famous were the Caribbean buccaneers, such as Henry Morgan and William Kidd. Most feared perhaps was Edward Teach (Blackbeard) who terrorized the SE coast of N America until he was killed in a battle with a British man-of-war. Recently the term has been extended to include the sale of illegally copied books and video recordings.

Pitt, William, the Younger (1759–1806) British statesman who was prime minister from 1783–1801 and again from 1804–06. During his term the union of the Irish and British parliaments was accomplished and income tax was introduced (1799).

Pizarro, Francisco (*c* 1474–1541) Spanish conquistador who discovered and conquered Peru with only 180 men, thereby overthrowing the great Inca Empire. In 1541 he was assassinated by one of his own men.

Plague An infectious disease. Although it is uncommon today, plague caused terrible epidemics in Asia and Europe in earlier times. The last serious outbreak in England was in 1685. Plague causes swellings and other nasty symptoms, and the worst form, which affects the lungs, is nearly always fatal. See also BLACK DEATH.

Plaice The commonest flatfish in European waters. It lives on the sea bed and grows to a length of 55 cm. Its upper side is commonly grey-brown with red spots, though the fish can change colour to some extent to match its background.

Plane Family of tall deciduous trees frequently seen in cities because they can tolerate polluted air. The grey bark flakes to reveal yellow patches.

Planet A heavenly body which orbits the Sun and shines by reflected sunlight. There are at least nine planets in our SOLAR SYSTEM.

Plankton Free-floating plant and animal life in the surface waters of seas and lakes. The plant life, consisting of millions of tiny plants, is called phytoplankton. This forms the 'pastures' of the sea. A host of tiny animals, the zooplankton, feeds on the phytoplankton. Plankton is the food source of many sea creatures.

Plant Organism belonging to one of the two basic divisions of living things – the plant kingdom. Most plants are able to make their own food in a process known as photosynthesis, using the energy of sunlight. These plants are the basis of life on Earth, both on land and in the sea. Plants range from microscopic marine ALGAE to the giant REDWOOD.

Plasma In physics, plasma is an extremely hot gas whose atoms have been stripped of their electrons. The atmospheres of the stars are plasmas because of the enormous heat. Plasma can be deflected by magnetic and electric fields.

Plastics There are many different kinds of plastics, each with different uses and properties. They are all made up of long-chain molecules called *polymers* and can be easily shaped when soft. Most polymers are made from oil or coal. The two main types of plastic are *thermoplastics* and *thermosetting plastics*. Thermoplastics soften and melt when heated, and harden again when cooled. Thermosetting plastics remain hard when heated. Most plastic products are made by moulding.

Plate tectonics See **Tectonic plates**.

Platinum Scarce precious metal which has a high resistance to corrosion. It can be rolled into wafer-thin sheets or the finest wire. Platinum's chief use is in jewellery and as a CATALYST in the chemical industry. Chem. symbol Pt.

Plato (*c* 427–*c* 347 BC) Greek philosopher who was the pupil of Socrates and, in the Academy he founded, the teacher of Aristotle. His works in the form of dialogues include *The Laws*, *Apologia*, *Phaedo* and *The Republic*. In the latter he describes the ideal state and the wise men who would govern it. He believed in a world of ideas superior to the material world. His theories had a profound effect on Western philosophy.

Platypus The duck-billed platypus is an egg-laying mammal (monotreme) with a bill like a duck, a furry body and webbed feet. It lives in Australia, in a river-bank burrow where the female nurses her newly hatched young.

Pluto In Greek mythology, ruler of the underworld. His real name, HADES (now synonymous with the underworld), was too fearsome to be spoken.

Pluto Smallest and most distant of the planets in the Solar system, Pluto and its moon Charon are believed to be snowballs of frozen gas and dust. Pluto has an eccentric orbit that sometimes takes it nearer the Sun than Neptune. Diameter: 3000 km; average distance from Sun: 5900 million km.

Po River, the longest in Italy, flowing from the Alpes Maritimes to the Adriatic Sea. It drains a wide plain that is Italy's foremost agricultural region. Length: 650 km.

Poetry Work of literature, mostly using rhythmical forms and sometimes rhyme. Early stories, recited to a strict rhythm, often told of heroic deeds and became known as epic poems. Among them were the *Iliad* and *Odyssey* of HOMER. There are many more forms of poetry, including the 14-line sonnet and the story-telling ballad. Rhyme is a feature of much formal poetry, but it is not used in the blank verse of SHAKESPEARE or the free verse of modern poets, which has no strict rhythm either.

Poisons Substances that kill or sicken living things. Many plants are poisonous, including the deadly death-cap toadstool. Poisons such as heroin, opium, belladonna and strychnine come from plants. Many animals from spiders to snakes produce poisonous venom, but few are deadly. Other poisons, such as arsenic, lead and mercury are metallic. There are also poisonous acids, gases and bacteria. Poisons are not always harmful: given in the right doses, some save lives.

Poland Republic in eastern Europe bordered by the Baltic Sea. The land is mainly flat apart from a plateau in the south which is the main area for farming, mines and industry. Textiles, iron and steel are major industries, as well as engineering. Minerals include lead, coal, zinc and sulphur.

Constantly fought over and divided, Poland became independent only in 1918. During World War II, sandwiched between Germany and Russia, it suffered dreadfully. A communist government was set up in 1947 but there is considerable opposition to it. Area: 312,654 km^2; Pop: 36,887,000; Cap: Warsaw.

Polar bear Large, white carnivorous mammal, weighing as much as 700 kg, that lives on the shores of the Arctic Ocean and on the ice itself. During the cold, dark winter the female hibernates in a den in the snow and gives birth to two or three cubs. The cubs remain with their mother for up to three years. The males roam the ice all year hunting seals.

Polaris A star less than 1° from the Celestial North Pole – a point in the sky immediately above the axis of the spinning Earth. Also called the Pole Star and North Star, it is important in navigation.

Polecat A nocturnal carnivore closely related to the stoat and found over much of Europe and Asia. It can produce a strong unpleasant smell from musk glands at the base of the tail when frightened. The ferret is a domesticated form of the polecat.

Poles The geographic N and S poles are imaginary points on the Earth's surface at the axis of the spinning Earth. The magnetic poles as indicated by a compass do not correspond exactly with the geographic poles and their position changes over the years.

Police Civilian law-enforcement organization. Until the 1800s law and order were maintained by village constables, sheriffs and other local officials. The police force came into being in the 1800s, as towns and cities grew too large to police in the old way. Many countries today have national police forces. But in Britain and the United States police forces are locally run. Police usually wear uniforms and (except in Britain) carry guns.

Political parties Organizations of people with similar political views who are concerned with obtaining power to run a country. In PARLIAMENT representatives of the same party work together, either in government or in opposition. Because it does not have proportional representation

Polar bear

Britain has a two party system, with either the Conservative or Labour party winning a majority in parliament. Other parties including the Liberal and Social Democratic parties have little chance of power until the system is changed. In America the two great parties are the Republicans and Democrats.

Pollination The transfer of pollen from the stamens to the stigmas of a flower - either the same flower or a different flower of the same kind - which results in fertilization and the formation of seeds.

The wind and insects are the main agents carrying pollen from flower to flower. Wind-pollinated flowers are generally dull in colour and have no scent or nectar. But they produce lots of pollen to blow away on the breeze. The hazel is a familiar example, scattering pollen from its catkins as early as January. Insect-pollinated flowers generally have brightly coloured petals and sweet scents which attract bees and other insects. Most also have sweet nectar.

Pony A horse less than 14 hands (140 cm) high. Few European ponies are truly wild; they are mostly domestic varieties that are left to roam wild, such as the New Forest and Exmoor ponies of Britain. The Shetland pony is the smallest of all. It stands only 100 cm high at the shoulder and is very hardy.

Pope Leader of Roman Catholic Church. The word pope means father and Catholics believe that Jesus made St Peter (Simon) father of the Church when he said 'Thou art Peter [meaning rock] and upon this rock I will build my Church'. They also believe that the authority vested in St Peter is passed on to all subsequent popes in 'apostolic succession'. Of recent popes, John XXIII was most renowned.

Poplar A group of deciduous trees belonging to the willow family. Poplars are fast-growing and can withstand strong gales, for which reason they are frequently grown as windbreaks along roadsides. Most have triangular leaves.

Poppy A family of plants whose bright red

or yellow flowers add a vivid splash of colour to corn fields and wasteland. The common poppy has bright red petals and black stamens.

Porcelain Form of CERAMIC, which is whitish in colour and glass-like, in that it allows some light to shine through it. Porcelain was first made in China in the 7th century. It is made by mixing kaolin (china clay) and a form of feldspar, and heating them to over 1300°C. The result is porcelain, so hard that a steel blade will not cut it. The secret of making porcelain reached Europe in the 18th century.

Porcupine Hairy rodent with sharp quills on its back. Once stuck into an enemy's flesh they are difficult to remove and very painful. There are two porcupine families, the Old World and the New World, the latter being smaller.

Porpoise Small whales less than two metres long. They are distinguished from the 'beaked' DOLPHINS by their blunt snouts.

Portugal Republic of W Europe, bounded by Spain and the Atlantic Ocean. It includes the islands of Madeira and the Azores. Less well developed than most of W Europe, it relies largely on farming and fishing. Cereals, vegetables, fruit, olives and figs are grown. Fine grapes and wines are produced. Portugal is the world's chief producer of cork. Portugal was accepted for membership of the EEC from 1986. Area: 92,075 km^2; Pop: 10,045,000; Cap: Lisbon.

Poseidon Greek god of the sea and of horses. He is usually shown carrying a trident and surrounded by nymphs and tritons. (Roman equivalent Neptune.)

Post Office Organization which delivers mail. The first 'posts' were inns, which acted as staging-posts for horse riders carrying urgent messages. Later stage-coaches were used to carry mail. Today, the post offices of the world handle many millions of letters, increasingly sorted automatically by machine.

Postage stamp In 1840, at the instigation of W. Rowland Hill, the Post Office issued small gummed labels which people could buy at a penny each to stick on their mail. These 'Penny Blacks' were the world's first postage stamps. 'Twopenny Blues' were also issued for overweight letters. Other countries soon adopted the idea of postage stamps and people began to collect them. The Penny Black is not a rare stamp – over 60 million were printed – but a good

Poseidon, the Greek god of the sea, and Boreas, god of the north wind, create a storm.

The Penny Black (shown at more than twice its actual size).

postmarked example costs the collector £50 to £100. The most sought-after stamp in the world is probably the British Guiana one cent of 1856, only one of which is known to exist. In 1980 this scrap of paper was sold at an auction for £420,000.

Potassium Soft, white metal which reacts violently with water. It is an essential element for plant growth and is widely used in fertilizers. Potassium nitrate, or saltpetre, is an important ingredient of gunpowder. Chem. symbol K (German *Kalium*).

Potato Widely grown vegetable of nightshade family introduced to Europe from S America in 16th century. The potato is a tuber, an underground stem rich in starch. The USSR is the world's largest producer, though the United States is the largest consumer of potato crisps. The plant is vulnerable to blight and to infestation by the COLORADO BEETLE.

Pottery Kinds of CERAMIC ware, including earthenware and stoneware. Pottery is one of the most ancient crafts. At first wet clay was simply shaped and dried in the sun to make cooking pots and drinking cups. Later, some 5000 years ago, people discovered how to shape pots on a wheel. They learned also how to fire pots slowly in a kiln, and how to glaze them with a coating of copper or lead to make them stronger and more attractive. Today the pottery industry uses machines and electric kilns, but some jobs (such as fine painting) are still done by hand. PORCELAIN, which is fired to a greater heat so that it becomes almost glassy, is more expensive than earthenware pottery.

Poultry The name given to chickens, turkeys, ducks, geese and other birds farmed for their meat or eggs.

Power station Most of the world's power stations burn coal, oil or natural gas in furnaces to heat water in boilers and raise steam. This steam drives turbines, which in turn drive the electricity generators. Some power stations use gas turbines.

In nuclear power stations, the heat from controlled nuclear reactions is used to drive the turbines.

Prague Capital city of Czechoslovakia, on R. Vltava. Grew to considerable importance in 14th century as capital of Bohemia. Pop: 1,193,000.

Prairie An area of extensive, undulating grassland. The word 'prairie' is French in origin and was used by French explorers to describe the wide grasslands of the Canadian plains and the Mississippi valley. In former times great herds of bison roamed the N American prairies. Then European settlers used them as cattle ranches and later as wheat fields. Similar grasslands exist in Argentina (pampas) and SW Russia (steppes).

Prairie dog Rabbit-sized N American ground squirrels with dog-like bark. They live in extended family groups in deep burrows. Considered pests by farmers.

Prawn A group of crustaceans related to the shrimps but usually bigger. Like shrimps, prawns have hunched backs, long antennae and small claws.

Precious stones Minerals which when cut and polished are used as gemstones in jewellery. Diamond, a pure form of carbon and the hardest mineral known, is the most highly prized. Others include the green emerald (a form of beryl), the red ruby and the blue sapphire (both forms of corundum). Semi-precious stones include many varieties of quartz, such as amethyst, agate and citrine.

Prehistoric life We know about prehistoric animals and plants from fossils found in the rocks. The chart on page 182 shows the geological periods during which animals evolved from soft-bodied creatures to fishes, amphibians, reptiles (including DINOSAURS), the first birds, mammals and eventually man.

Jellyfish
PRE-CAMBRIAN TIMES
Trilobite
Millions of years ago
570
Cambrian period
500
Ordovician period
PALAEOZOIC ERA
435
Silurian period
395
Devonian period
345
Carboniferous period
Permian period
Trilobite
Nautilus
Early land plants
MESOZOIC ERA
Triassic period
Jurassic period
Cretaceous period
Early reptile
Dinosaur
CENOZOIC ERA
Early birds
Sabre-toothed tiger

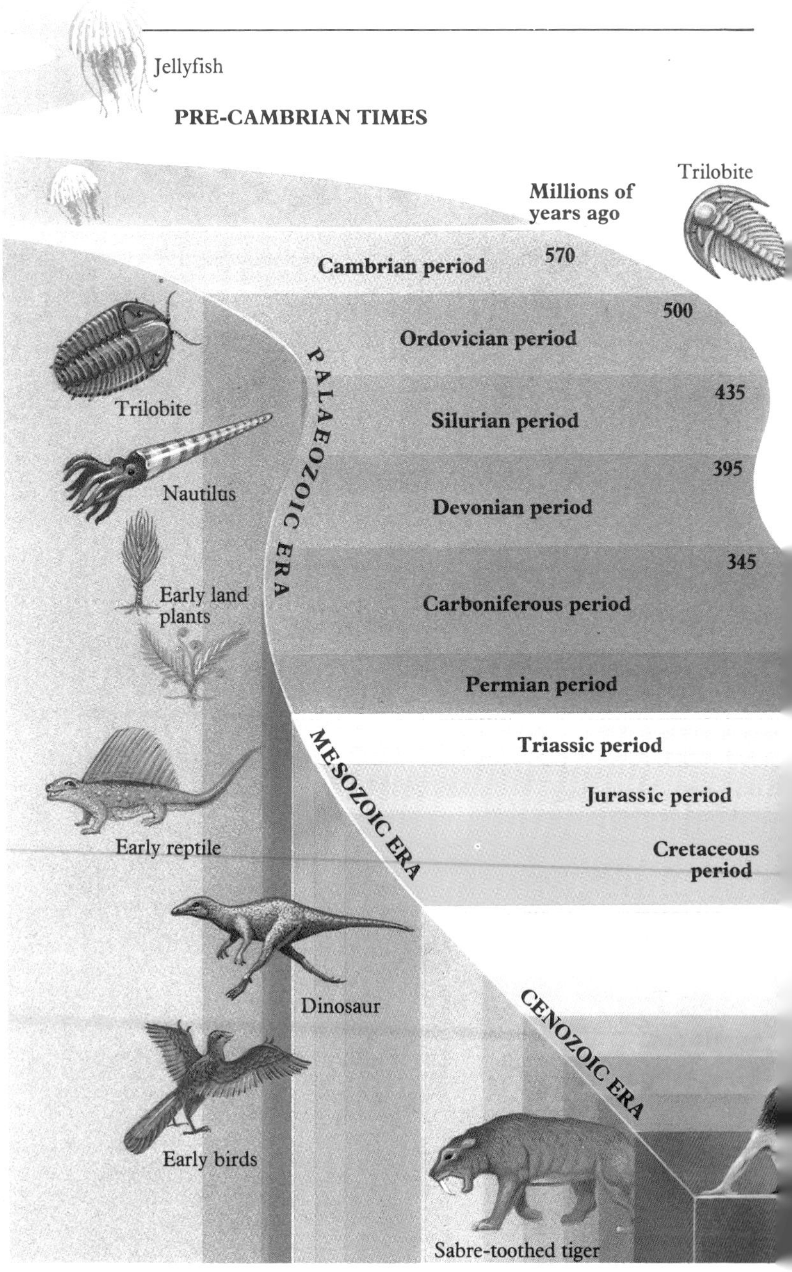

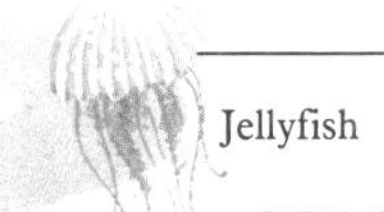

Presidents of USA In the USA the president is both head of state and leader of the government. He is also commander-in-chief of the armed forces. The first US president was George Washington, in 1789. Since then there have been 40 presidents, the 40th and current president being Ronald Reagan. Under the US constitution, the president is elected for a four-year term and can be voted back for a second term of office. The official home of the president is the White House, in Washington DC. See list on page 184.

Pressure The pressing or pushing of one body on another because of its weight or other force. It is measured in force per unit area – newtons per square metre or dynes per square centimetre.

Pretoria City in Transvaal and admin capital of South Africa. Founded in 1855 and named after Andries Pretorius, a prominent Boer leader. Pop: 739,000 (met area).

Primates Order of mammals that includes lemurs, monkeys, apes and humans.

Prime ministers of Britain The chief minister or premier, and head of the government. The first real prime minister of Britain was Sir Robert Walpole (1676–1745). It is the prime minister's duty to advise the Queen who is the head of state and a 'constitutional' monarch only. The prime minister's official London home is at 10 Downing Street, close to the Houses of Parliament. Nowadays, the prime minister is always a member of the House of Commons, and may be questioned during debates by other members. Among the most famous British prime ministers have been William Pitt, Benjamin Disraeli, William Ewart Gladstone, and Winston Churchill. The present prime minister, Margaret Thatcher, was the first woman to become British prime minister, in 1979. See list on page 184.

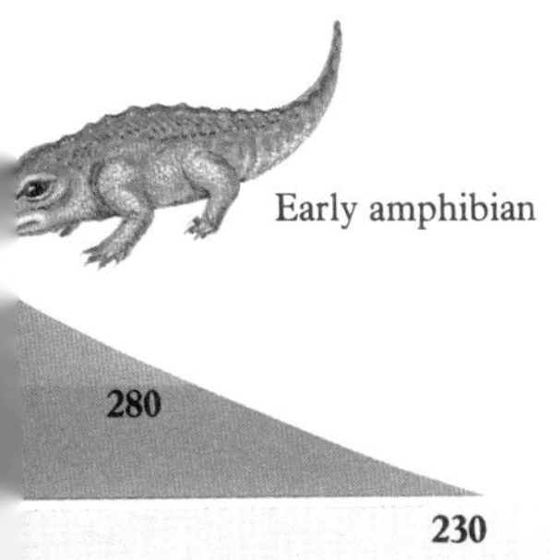

AMERICAN PRESIDENTS

	President (Party)	Term
1	George Washington (F)	1789–1797
2	John Adams (F)	1797–1801
3	Thomas Jefferson (R)	1801–1809
4	James Madison (R)	1809–1817
5	James Monroe (R)	1817–1825
6	John Quincy Adams (R)	1825–1829
7	Andrew Jackson (D)	1829–1837
8	Martin Van Buren (D)	1837–1841
9	William H. Harrison* (W)	1841
10	John Tyler (W)	1841–1845
11	James K. Polk (D)	1845–1849
12	Zachary Taylor* (W)	1849–1850
13	Millard Fillmore (W)	1850–1853
14	Franklin Pierce (D)	1853–1857
15	James Buchanan (D)	1857–1861
16	Abraham Lincoln † (R)	1861–1865
17	Andrew Johnson (R)	1865–1869
18	Ulysses S. Grant (R)	1869–1877
19	Rutherford B. Hayes (R)	1877–1881
20	James A. Garfield † (R)	1881
21	Chester A. Arthur (R)	1881–1885
22	Grover Cleveland (D)	1885–1889
23	Benjamin Harrison (R)	1889–1893
24	Grover Cleveland (D)	1893–1897
25	William McKinley † (R)	1897–1901
26	Theodore Roosevelt (R)	1901–1909
27	William H. Taft (R)	1909–1913
28	Woodrow Wilson (D)	1913 1921
29	Warren G. Harding* (R)	1921–1923
30	Calvin Coolidge (R)	1923–1929
31	Herbert C. Hoover (R)	1929–1933
32	Franklin D. Roosevelt* (D)	1933–1945
33	Harry S. Truman (D)	1945–1953
34	Dwight D. Eisenhower (R)	1953–1961
35	John F. Kennedy † (D)	1961–1963
36	Lyndon B. Johnson (D)	1963–1969
37	Richard M. Nixon (R)	1969–1974
38	Gerald R. Ford (R)	1974–1977
39	James E. Carter (D)	1977–1981
40	Ronald Reagan (R)	1981–

F = Federalist. R = Republican. W = Whig. D = Democrat. * Died in office. † Assassinated in office.

BRITISH PRIME MINISTERS

Prime Minister (Party)	Term
Sir Robert Walpole (W)	1721–1742
Earl of Wilmington (W)	1742–1743
Henry Pelham (W)	1743–1754
Duke of Newcastle (W)	1754–1756
Duke of Devonshire (W)	1756–1757
Duke of Newcastle (W)	1757–1762
Earl of Bute (T)	1762–1763
George Grenville (W)	1763–1765
Marquess of Rockingham (W)	1765–1766
Earl of Chatham (W)	1766–1767
Duke of Grafton (W)	1767–1770
Lord North (T)	1770–1782
Marquess of Rockingham (W)	1782
Earl of Shelburne (W)	1782–1783
Duke of Portland (Cln)	1783
William Pitt (T)	1783–1801
Henry Addington (T)	1801–1804
William Pitt (T)	1804–1806
Lord Grenville (W)	1806–1807
Duke of Portland (T)	1807–1809
Spencer Perceval (T)	1809–1812
Earl of Liverpool (T)	1812–1827
George Canning (T)	1827
Viscount Goderich (T)	1827–1828
Duke of Wellington (T)	1828–1830
Earl Grey (W)	1830–1834
Viscount Melbourne (W)	1834
Sir Robert Peel (T)	1834–1835
Viscount Melbourne (W)	1835–1841
Sir Robert Peel (T)	1841–1846
Lord John Russell (W)	1846–1852
Earl of Derby (T)	1852
Earl of Aberdeen (P)	1852–1855
Viscount Palmerston (L)	1855–1858
Earl of Derby (C)	1858–1859
Viscount Palmerston (L)	1859–1865
Earl Russell (L)	1865–1866
Earl of Derby (C)	1866–1868
Benjamin Disraeli (C)	1868
William Gladstone (L)	1868–1874
Benjamin Disraeli (C)	1874–1880
William Gladstone (L)	1880–1885
Marquess of Salisbury (C)	1885–1886
William Gladstone (L)	1886
Marquess of Salisbury (C)	1886–1892
William Gladstone (L)	1892–1894
Earl of Rosebery (L)	1894–1895
Marquess of Salisbury (C)	1895–1902
Arthur Balfour (C)	1902–1905
Sir Henry Campbell-Bannerman (L)	1905–1908
Herbert Asquith (L)	1908–1915
Herbert Asquith (Cln)	1915–1916
David Lloyd-George (Cln)	1916–1922
Andrew Bonar Law (C)	1922–1923
Stanley Baldwin (C)	1923–1924
James Ramsay MacDonald (Lab)	1924
Stanley Baldwin (C)	1924–1929
James Ramsay MacDonald (Lab)	1929–1931
James Ramsay MacDonald (Cln)	1931–1935
Stanley Baldwin (Cln)	1935–1937
Neville Chamberlain (Cln)	1937–1940
Winston Churchill (Cln)	1940–1945
Winston Churchill (C)	1945
Clement Atlee (Lab)	1945–1951
Sir Winston Churchill (C)	1951–1955
Sir Anthony Eden (C)	1955–1957
Harold Macmillan (C)	1957–1963
Sir Alec Douglas-Home (C)	1963–1964
Harold Wilson (Lab)	1964–1970
Edward Heath (C)	1970–1974
Harold Wilson (Lab)	1974–1976
James Callaghan (Lab)	1976–1979
Margaret Thatcher (C)	1979–

W = Whig. T = Tory. Cln = Coalition. P = Peelite. L = Liberal. C = Conservative. Lab = Labour.

Primrose A common flowering plant that often forms thick patches in woods and on waysides. It has solitary yellow, five-petalled flowers borne on hairy stems, and the long oval leaves grow straight from the roots.

Printing Printing as we know it began 500 years ago when Johannes Gutenberg invented printing with pieces of metal for each letter of the alphabet. These metal pieces could be used over and over again. Printing today is done by one of three processes. In *letterpress*, the printing surface is raised; in *lithography*, the printing surface consists of ink-absorbent areas and other areas which are made ink-repellent; and in *gravure*, the printing surface is etched.

Prism A block of glass or other transparent material used to split up (refract) light or other rays. White light is made up of rays of slightly different wavelength. When white light is passed through a prism, the different wavelengths are refracted at different angles, producing a beam showing the colours of the rainbow.

Prison Place of confinement for people who have been found guilty of a crime. In the past prisons were grim dungeons, unhealthy and overcrowded. The most infamous of all prisons was the Bastille in Paris whose liberation was the major event of the French revolution. The most infamous in Britain were the Tower of London where people convicted of treason were confined and the Fleet prison where debtors were sent. In America the most famous prison is Alcatraz on an island off San Francisco. In the 1700s reformers, including Elizabeth Fry, worked to improve prison life. Today, rehabilitation and training of prisoners is considered more important than punishment.

Probability A measure of the likelihood that something will happen. If an event cannot happen, its probability is zero. If an event is certain to happen, its probability is one. All other degrees of probability are fractions. For example, if we toss a coin it has an equal chance of coming down head or tail. The probability of a head is $\frac{1}{2}$; the probability of a tail is also $\frac{1}{2}$.

Prokofiev, Sergei (1891–1953) Leading Russian composer. Among his works are symphonies, concertos, the operas *Love of Three Oranges* and *War and Peace*, and the ballets *Romeo and Juliet* and *Cinderella*. He also wrote film music and the orchestral fairy tale *Peter and the Wolf*.

Prometheus In Greek legend he stole fire from Heaven and gave it to mankind. As a punishment he was chained to a rock where vultures devoured his liver.

Propaganda Information propagated particularly by governments or other organizations to assist their cause. In Nazi Germany in the 1930s, Goebbels had special responsibility for broadcasting false information that would shed good light on his party. Not all propaganda, however, has an evil purpose. The Allies also used propaganda and so do many worthy charities and organizations today.

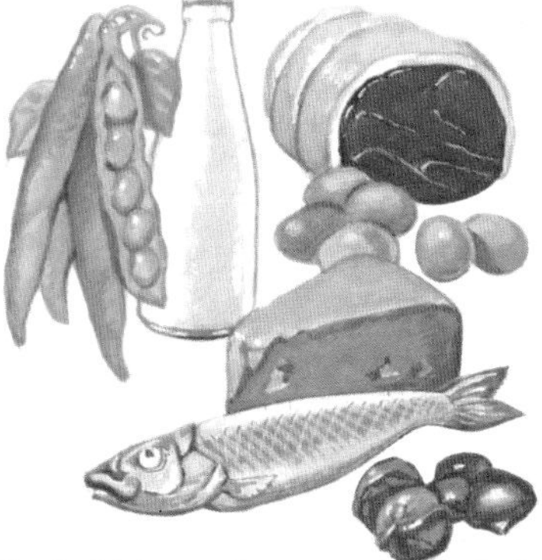

Foods rich in protein are necessary for body-building.

Proteins Proteins are chemicals that are a vital part of every animal and plant cell. We obtain proteins from foods such as milk, eggs, meat, fish, nuts and beans. Our digestive system breaks down these foods into *amino acids*, and the amino acids are then built up into other proteins.

Protestantism Christian Churches, with the exception of the Roman Catholic and Orthodox. Protestantism resulted from the Reformation when reformers protested against the authority of the Church. Today there are hundreds of denominations who basically believe in the authority of the Bible rather than dogma. Main branches are Anglican, Calvinist, Lutheran, Methodist, and Quaker.

Protozoan Any of the many very tiny animals whose bodies consist of just a single cell. Very few can be seen with the naked eye. Most live in watery surroundings and many move about by waving minute hairs.

Psychology Study of the mind and behaviour and the way people react with their environment. The best-known psychologist was Sigmund Freud, founder of psychoanalysis.

Ptarmigan A game bird related to the grouse. It lives on mountains and northern tundra, and in winter its sandy-grey plumage changes to almost completely white.

Pteridophyte Any member of a large group of flowerless plants that includes ferns, horsetails and clubmosses. These plants all reproduce by scattering dust-like SPORES.

Pterosaur Extinct flying reptile of the Mesozoic Era, with bat-like wings. *Pterodactylus* was the size of a sparrow but its relative *Quetzalcoatlus* had a 10-metre wingspan.

Dimorphodon must have been a clumsy creature with its heavy body and a wing span of only 1.5 metres.

Ptolemy Greek astronomer who lived about the middle of the 1st century AD. He claimed that the Earth was stationary and that the Universe revolved around it – a theory that remained unchallenged until the 16th century.

Puccini, Giacomo (1858–1924) Italian composer, regarded as the successor to VERDI. He wrote a number of famous operas including *La Bohème*, *Tosca*, *Madame Butterfly* and *Turandot*.

Puffball One of a group of almost spherical fungi containing a mass of dark spores, and attached to the ground by a slender thread. The skin of the ball generally splits to form a small hole when ripe and the spores are puffed out in clouds when the fungus is touched.

Puffin A bird of sea coasts and islands, related to the auks. A stout bird, with a black and white plumage and short legs, the puffin is distinguished by its gaudily coloured bill – grey, blue, scarlet and yellow.

Pulsar A rapidly rotating star that emits an immensely strong radio or optical pulse as it spins. Pulsars are believed to be only 10–30 km across and to consist of tightly packed neutrons with a density millions of times that of lead.

Puma Large cat, also known as the cougar or mountain lion. It stalks the mountains of western N and S America and has an ear-piercing wailing call.

Pump Pumps are machines for moving liquids or gases. Some pumps have a piston which moves to and fro in a cylinder to produce the required pressure. Valves allow the fluid to pass in one direction only. Other pumps work by fast-turning propeller blades, or with vanes that make the fluid move by centrifugal force.

Punctuation The use of marks in writing which make the meaning of a sentence clearer, and mark the natural pauses of speech. The marks include the question mark (?), the exclamation mark (!), quotation marks (“ ”), brackets (), the comma (,), semi-colon (;), colon (:) and full stop (.).

Purcell, Henry (1659–1695) Also known as the father of English music he was the organist at Westminster Abbey from 1679. He composed simple dignified music and among his beautiful church compositions are the *Te Deum* and the anthem *Thou knowest, Lord, the secret of our hearts*. He also wrote much ceremonial music for Royal and State occasions. His best known opera is *Dido and Aeneas*.

Pyramids Gigantic stone buildings built by the ancient Egyptians. A pyramid is square at the base, with four sloping sides rising to a point at the top. The Great Pyramid at Giza, the largest, is 146 metres high and 230 metres along each wall. The Egyptian pyramids were tombs for the pharaohs and other important people. Pyramids were also built in Mexico by the Maya and the Aztecs.

Pyrenees Mountain range forming natural boundary between France and Spain, running from the Bay of Biscay to the Mediterranean. Highest peak is Pico de Aneto (3404 metres).

Python Large constricting snakes, some over nine metres long, found throughout the Old World tropics. They eat small mammals and birds and are expert climbers and swimmers. The Asian reticulated python is the largest.

Q

Qatar A small country on a peninsula reaching into the Arabian Gulf, E of Bahrain. Qatar has grown rich from oil, but has also started other industries, including chemical production. Natural gas supplies power to make sea water drinkable in this desert country. Area: 11,000 km^2; Pop: 291,000; Cap: Doha.

Quail A small game bird related to the partridge. There are nearly 100 species living all over the world. Quail fly very little and normally keep within a metre or so of the ground.

Quantum In 1900, the German scientist Max Planck suggested that radiant energy such as light is sent out or absorbed in tiny

Ancient Egyptian peasants labour in the fields while behind them dead pharaohs lie entombed in treasure-filled pyramids – waiting to be robbed.

units called *quanta*. We now know that this theory was correct, and scientists talk about *quantum mechanics*, which is widely used in atomic research.

Quartz A common mineral found in many rocks, particularly sandstone. The hard, glassy crystals are a chemical combination of silicon and oxygen. Pure quartz is called rock crystal. Many semi-precious stones, such as amethyst, citrine, agate and jasper, are varieties of quartz with traces of impurities. Opal is an amorphous (non-crystalline) variety of quartz.

Quasars Quasi-stellar radio sources, or quasars, are brilliant bodies far off in space which produce the energy output of 100 bright galaxies from a space not much larger than our own Solar system. They were first detected in 1963.

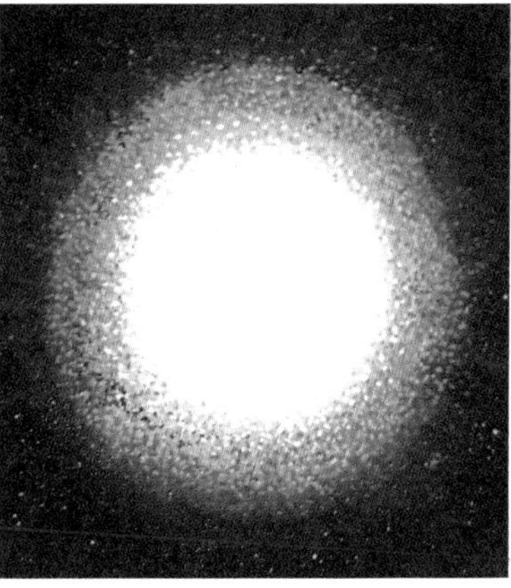

Quasars are believed to be galaxies at an early stage in their evolution.

Quebec Port and capital of Quebec province, Canada, on the St Lawrence River. It is built on two levels: Lower Town lying along the waterfront, and Upper Town on Cape Diamond Bluff, 100 metres above. The inhabitants are predominantly French-speaking. Pop: 177,000.

Quetzal Spectacular bird of S America with a long green train of feathers. The feathers were used as a symbol of authority by the Ancient Maya.

Quito Capital of Ecuador, situated on a plateau in the Andes, 2890 metres above sea level and about 25 km south of the equator. Pop: 557,000.

R

Ra Ancient Egyptian sun god. Early Egyptian kings claimed descent from him.

Rabbit A close relative of the hare with shorter ears and limbs. Rabbits live in extensive burrows or warrens. Their diet consists of grass and other green vegetation – including crops. When introduced into Australia and New Zealand rabbits did immense harm.

Rabies Viral disease that attacks mammals including humans. The word rabies means rage in Latin, and victims of the disease, animal or human, do foam at the mouth and act in a wild way. The disease is also called *hydrophobia* (fear of water) because all victims shun water. The disease is widespread in continental Europe but is unknown in Britain. Britain has rigorous quarantine laws to prevent infected animals entering the country. The disease can be treated, within 24 hours after exposure, by vaccination.

Racoon American carnivore related to pandas. About one metre long with dark bands on tail and head. They live in forests but occasionally venture into towns at night to scavenge amongst the garbage.

Rachmaninov, Sergei (1873–1943) Russian composer and pianist who emigrated to America after the Russian revolution. His best-known works include the *Second Symphony*, the *Second Piano Concerto* and the *Rhapsody on a Theme by Paganini*.

Radar Radar stands for Radio Detection And Ranging. It is a system by which distant objects can be located and their direction and distance plotted. Radio waves are sent out in short pulses which are reflected back from the distant object. The reflected signals can be displayed on a cathode-ray tube. Radar has extensive uses in the military and navigational fields.

Radio A radio transmitter is a device that makes electrons vibrate in an electric circuit. These vibrations travel outward at the speed of light as invisible radio waves. When the waves strike a receiving aerial they make electrons in the aerial vibrate at the same rate. A transmitter sends out a continuous *carrier wave*, on which are carried the electric current vibrations from a microphone or TV camera. Circuits in the receiving set select these varying currents, amplify them, and feed them to a loudspeaker. We then hear the original sounds that reached the microphone.

Radioactivity Some of the atoms in certain elements shoot out streams of particles or radiation. These atoms (ISOTOPES) are said to be radioactive. The best-known radioactive elements are radium and uranium. Three main kinds of radiation are shot out by these elements - alpha-particles, beta-particles, and gamma-rays. The radiation sent out by radioactive substances can be harmful to people. This applies especially to gamma-rays. But small amounts of radiation are used in some forms of medical treatment.

Robot manipulators allow radioactive materials to be 'handled' without danger to the operator who is safe behind leaded glass.

Radio astronomy The study of radio waves emitted naturally by objects in space. Radio astronomy has led to the discovery of objects such as QUASARS and PULSARS.

Radio telescope Device for collecting radio waves from space. Most radio telescopes are dish-shaped and work in a similar fashion to optical reflectors: they collect radio waves and focus them on to a detector. This is connected to amplifiers which make the signal stronger. Because radio waves are much longer than light waves, radio telescopes have to be bigger than optical telescopes. The largest fully steerable dish antenna is 100 metres in diameter, near Bonn, W Germany.

Radium Rare, naturally occurring, radioactive metal discovered by Marie and Pierre CURIE in 1898. Radiotherapy, the use of X-rays from radium, is employed in the treatment of cancer. Chem. symbol Ra.

Rail Birds with long legs and short tails, belonging to the same family as the coot and crakes. Rails are shy, secretive birds and seldom fly. The water rail usually hides among the reeds in marshes and lakesides. The land rail, also known as the corncrake, lives in grassy fields and meadows and its call is a loud 'crake'.

Railways The first public railway was the Stockton–Darlington which opened in 1825 with George Stephenson's *Locomotion* as its first engine. Neither idea was new: railways had been used in mines and Richard Trevithick had demonstrated a steam rail locomotive in 1804. The first railway to use steam locomotion exclusively was the Liverpool–Manchester (1830) with Stephenson's famous *Rocket*. Soon railways were opened up all over the world and rail transport was unchallenged until the arrival of the motor vehicle and the airliner. Modern developments include welded track for smoother running, trains that travel at over 200 km/h, and ever more reliable safety devices.

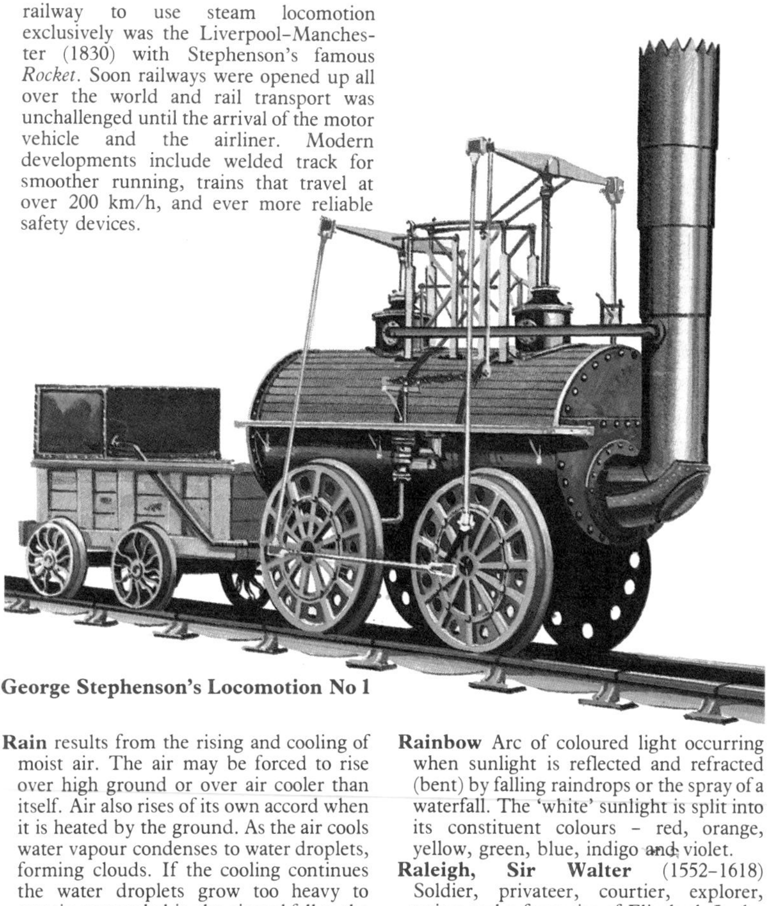

George Stephenson's Locomotion No 1

Rain results from the rising and cooling of moist air. The air may be forced to rise over high ground or over air cooler than itself. Air also rises of its own accord when it is heated by the ground. As the air cools water vapour condenses to water droplets, forming clouds. If the cooling continues the water droplets grow too heavy to remain suspended in the air and fall to the ground as rain. In very cold air the clouds are made of ice crystals. These may melt on their way to the ground or fall as snow.

Water droplets in a cloud increase in size until they fall as rain.

Rainbow Arc of coloured light occurring when sunlight is reflected and refracted (bent) by falling raindrops or the spray of a waterfall. The 'white' sunlight is split into its constituent colours – red, orange, yellow, green, blue, indigo and violet.

Raleigh, Sir Walter (1552–1618) Soldier, privateer, courtier, explorer, writer and a favourite of Elizabeth I who introduced tobacco and potatoes to Britain. He helped to quell an Irish rebellion in 1580, took part in expeditions against Spain and financed the unsuccessful settlement of 'Virginia' in 1585. He fell from favour under James I, was tried for treason and executed.

Ramadan The outstanding event in the Muslim year, this is a whole month of fasting, when people must not eat or drink between dawn and dusk. It ends with the feast of 'id al-fitr'. Since the Muslim calendar is based on months of the moon it does not tie in with the usual calendar and Ramadan may fall in any season.

Ranching Livestock farming in which the animals roam free to graze on the land. Ranching can be carried out on land that is unsuitable for crop farming, being either too dry or too infertile. But a lot of land is needed. An average cattle ranch in the W United States covers about 40 square kilometres. In Australia some ranches, or stations, cover several thousand square kilometres.

Rangoon Port and capital of Burma, in delta of R Irrawaddy. Major port and centre of an important rice-growing region. Pop: 3,660,000.

Raphael, Santi (1483–1520) One of the great Italian Masters whose varied works include frescoes, cartoons, portraits, pieces of sculpture and drawings.

Rasputin, Grigori Yefimovich (1871–1916) Russian monk who gained great power over Tsar Nicholas II and his family after supposedly curing the sickly tsarevich. He was eventually murdered by a group of nobles led by Prince Yussopov.

Rat A rodent with large naked ears and long, almost naked tail found world-wide. Rats do enormous damage to food and spread disease. Among many species are the black or ship rat, about 20 cm in length, and the slightly larger brown rat. The black rat was responsible for the spread of bubonic plague from Asia to Europe.

Ratel Nocturnal, omnivorous, black and grey badger-like animal related to the wolverine, and found in Africa and S Asia. A habit of raiding bees' nests for honey gives it its other name of honey badger.

Rattlesnake Poisonous N American snakes of pit viper family. The 'rattle' is the sound made by horny rings of cast-off skin.

Raven A large bird with black plumage belonging to the crow family. The raven feeds on carrion, small animals and fruit. Its call is a harsh 'croak'.

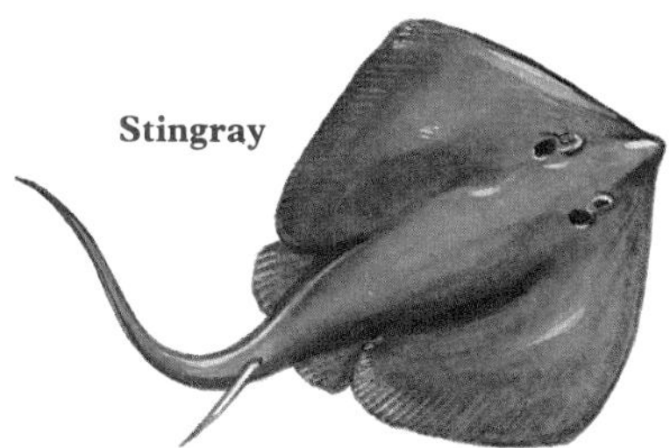
Stingray

Ray A group of cartilaginous fishes related to the sharks, and including skates. Rays have flattened bodies with huge pectoral fins which give them their distinctive diamond shape. They use these fins to propel themselves through the water instead of using their tails. Rays live mainly on the sea bed. Most species produce their eggs in horny cases, frequently called 'mermaids' purses'.

Rayon Synthetic fibre made from cellulose, usually obtained from wood pulp.

Razorbill A seabird similar in appearance to its close relative, the GUILLEMOT, but with a much broader bill. Razorbills spend most of their lives at sea and only come ashore to breed on high sea cliffs.

Record player Machine used for playing back pre-recorded sound from a flat vinyl disc, or record. The record is 'cut' using a special engraving tool, or cutting stylus, that vibrates in response to electrical signals from a microphone. The microphone transforms sound waves (vibrations) into electrical signals and a small device in the cartridge holding the stylus turns the signals back into vibrations. A record player reverses the procedure, using a playback stylus to pick up the vibrations which are then converted to electrical signals. Loudspeakers are used to reproduce the sound and amplifiers strengthen the signal.

Thomas Edison and Emil Berliner were pioneers of sound recording. Berliner manufactured his first 'gramophone' in 1894 in the USA. In those days, large horns were used to amplify the sound and there was no use of electrical signals.

Red Cross International society for relief of suffering in war or disaster. Founded through the efforts of Henri Dunant in 1863, its workers are guaranteed safe conduct by the Geneva convention. Called Red Crescent in Muslim countries.

Redstart

Redstart Small member of the thrush family with a red tail and, in the male, a russet breast. Found in woodlands and gardens.

Redwood A large coniferous tree of the western United States related to SEQUOIAS. Redwoods are the tallest trees in the world, growing to over 100 metres, and many live for thousands of years.

Reflection Light travels in a straight line, but it can be deflected from a straight course by reflection. It is reflected from shiny surfaces such as mirrors. When you look in a flat mirror you see what is called a *virtual* image: rays bouncing off a flat mirror appear to spread out from a point as far behind the mirror as the object is in front of the mirror. Curved mirrors produce images that are larger or smaller than the object looked at.

Reformation Great religious crisis in the Christian Church which resulted in the division between the Roman Catholic Church and various others which are together known as Protestant. It began in 1517 when Martin Luther made public some criticisms of the activities of priests. It developed into an attack on the authority of the Pope and on certain religious beliefs. Luther and others at first wanted to *reform* the Church. But no agreement was possible, and a complete split developed. In some countries, such as England, Protestantism became the state religion. Thus, the Reformation became a political matter as well as a religious quarrel.

Refraction Light is refracted when it passes from one medium to another. For example, when light passes from air into water, or from air into glass, it changes speed slightly. When the speed changes, the light rays bend. When a rod is half in, half out of a glass of water it appears to be broken at the surface. This is because the light slows down at the water's surface. It is because of refraction that LENSES make objects look larger or smaller, depending on the curve of the glass.

Refrigeration The process of reducing the temperature of substances. Refrigerators work because heat will only flow from a hot object to a colder object. Inside the refrigerator, a liquid called a refrigerant moves through a pipe. As it does so, it evaporates and cools. Heat flows from the inside of the refrigerator into the vapour in the pipe. The vapour then moves outside the refrigerator to a condenser, where it becomes liquid again and gives out its heat to the surrounding air. The liquid then moves back inside the refrigerator and the process is repeated. The inside of the refrigerator becomes cold because heat is constantly being taken from it.

Reindeer A semi-domesticated form of the CARIBOU found in northern Europe and Asia.

Relativity EINSTEIN'S *Special Theory of Relativity*, published in 1905, said that length, mass and time are all affected by motion. In fact, at the speed of light, a body would have no length and an infinite mass, and time for the body would stand still. Einstein deduced that mass and energy are related to one another. He formulated this in his famous equation $E=mc^2$, in which E is energy, m is mass, and c is the speed of light multiplied by itself. This means that a little mass is equal to a vast amount of energy, as was proved when nuclear power was released.

Religion An organized system of belief in a god or gods. Many different religions have been developed through the ages, with their own form of prayer and worship, their sacred writings or scriptures, and rules for everyday life. The main religions today include CHRISTIANITY with some 1000 million followers, ISLAM and HINDUISM (about 500 million each) and BUDDHISM (200 million). There are also about 15 million Jews (see JUDAISM).

Rembrandt (1606–69) Dutch painter whose vast output includes numerous self-portraits, group scenes and landscapes. A master of light and colour, his paintings have a vitality and simplicity of style that has placed him among the world's greatest artists. Among his most famous works are *The Anatomy Lesson* and *The Night Watch*.

Renaissance Period in European history which divides the Middle Ages from the Modern period. Its name means rebirth and refers to the revival of the ideas, art and learning of the classical period (ancient Greece and Rome). Equally important were the new ideas which developed partly as a result of this interest and are known by the general name, 'humanism'. The Renaissance began in Italy and was at its height between 1450 and 1550. The spread of Renaissance ideas was greatly assisted by the invention of printing.

Renoir, Pierre Auguste (1841–1919) French impressionist painter renowned for his pictures of ballet dancers. His best-known works include *Danseuse, Les Parapluies* and *La Première Sortie*.

Reproduction The production of young plants or animals by older ones. Sexual reproduction involves the joining of special male and female cells to produce the new generation, and this is the commonest form of reproduction in both plants and animals.

Non-sexual or asexual reproduction does not involve any joining of cells. Bacteria and many protozoans reproduce merely by splitting in two when they reach a certain size. Most fungi simply scatter spores which grow directly into new individuals.

Reptile Any member of a group of back-boned animals that includes SNAKES and LIZARDS, TORTOISES, and CROCODILES. They are all air-breathing animals, although many live in the water, and they are all covered with scales. All are cold-blooded and they are active only in warm weather.

Respiration A term used for two closely connected processes in animals and plants. It refers to the exchange of gases (breathing) that supplies an organism with oxygen and removes the waste gas carbon dioxide, and also to the chemical processes that take place inside the cells and result in the production of energy.

When you breathe in (left), your chest muscles raise your ribs and a flat muscle called the diaphragm moves downwards. This pulls air in to the lungs. When you breathe out (right) the diaphragm relaxes and rises, pushing air out.

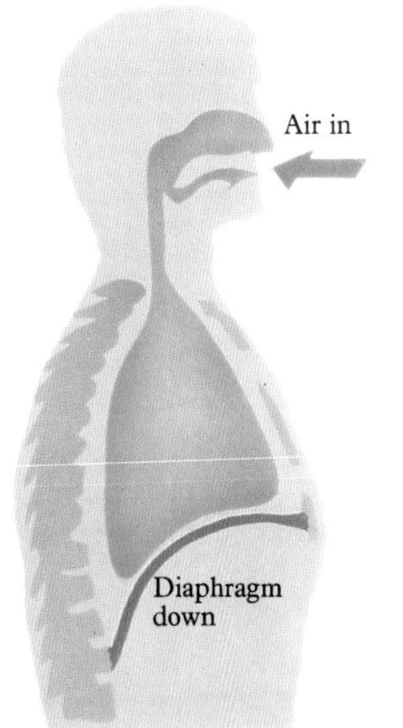

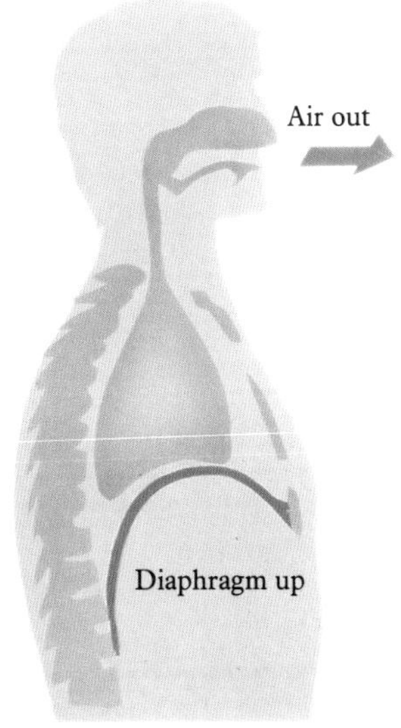

Reykjavik Port and capital of Iceland, with important fishing industry. Founded by Vikings in AD 874. Pop: 85,000.

Reynolds, Sir Joshua (1723–92) English portrait painter who became the first President of the Royal Academy in 1768. He painted about 2000 portraits; perhaps the best known is *Mrs Siddons as the Tragic Muse*.

Rhine River in Europe, flowing from Switzerland through W Germany and the Netherlands and entering the North Sea by two main arms – the Waal and the Lek. The Rhine is Europe's major commercial waterway with a heavy traffic of huge barges as far upstream as Basel on the Swiss border. The river is renowned also for its beauty, particularly the vineyards, towns and castles of the gorge section between Mainz and Bonn. Length: 1320 km.

Rhinoceros Huge lumbering mammals of Asia and Africa with exceptionally thick hide and one or two horns. The Indian rhino, weighing some 2.5 tonnes, is the largest of the five kinds. The others are the Javan, Sumatran, the black, and the white – the last two so named despite their identical grey colouring.

Rhodes, Cecil John (1853–1902) British statesman who was prime minister of the Cape Colony from 1890–96. He made a fortune from diamonds and directed the white settlement of Rhodesia (now Zimbabwe). He resigned in disgrace after the unfortunate raid into the Transvaal led by Sir Leander Jameson (1896).

Rhododendron Large evergreen shrub with showy bowl-shaped flowers that come in a range of colours from rich reds and purples to soft pinks and white. Rhododendrons are native to Asia where they grow at high altitudes.

Rhône River flowing from the Rhône glacier through Geneva in Switzerland, then through SE France into the Mediterranean. The river divides in the Camargue forming a large delta. Many vineyards and olive groves cover the fertile Rhône valley. The river is used extensively for irrigation. Length: 810 km.

Rice The staple diet of more than half the world's people, rice is mostly grown in the hot, wet regions of Asia. It is a cereal grass with nutritious, starchy grain. The young plants are transplanted into irrigated plots called paddies. Sometimes two crops can be grown in one year.

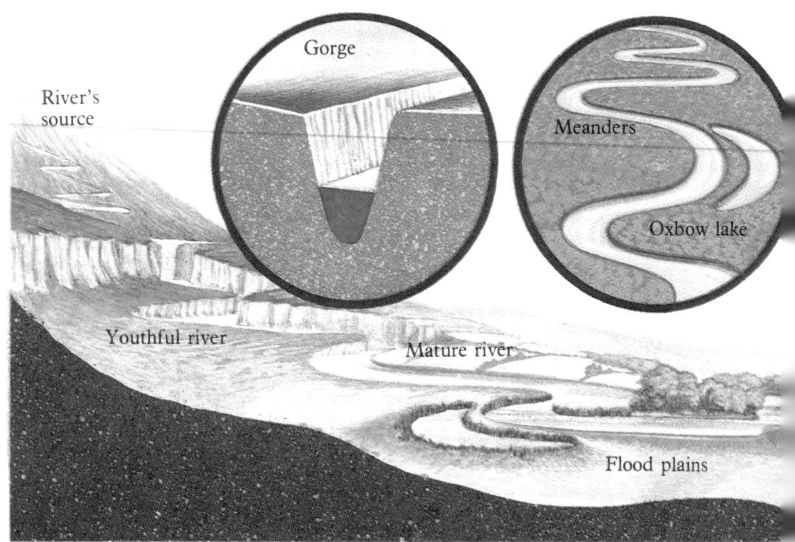

Richard I (1157–99) King of England from 1189, he was also known as Richard Lion-Heart. He led the Third Crusade against the Turks (1190) and captured Acre. He failed to retake Jerusalem and on his return journey was imprisoned first in Austria and later in Germany. An enormous ransom was paid for his release. He was fatally wounded in a skirmish while fighting in France.

Richelieu, Cardinal (1585–1642) French ecclesiastic who became cardinal in 1622 and chief minister to Louis XIII in 1624. Virtual ruler of France, he persecuted the Protestant Huguenots and kept the powerful nobles under control.

Rimsky-Korsakov, Nicolai (1844–1908) Russian composer and master of orchestration. He composed 17 operas based on Russian legendary themes, and three symphonies. His best-known works are the orchestral suite *Scheherazade* and *The Flight of the Bumble Bee*. He also rescored other composers' works, notably operas by Mussorgsky and Borodin.

Rio de Janeiro Seaport and former capital of Brazil, situated on large and beautiful natural harbour dominated by the imposing Sugar Loaf mountain. Pop: 5,094,000.

Rio Grande River in North America, flowing from Colorado state to the Gulf of Mexico, which forms much of the boundary between Mexico and the USA. Length: 3000 km.

River Streams and rivers drain water from the land and carry rock debris to the sea. The Mississippi alone dumps 700 million tonnes of sediment in the Gulf of Mexico each year. The area drained by a river and its tributaries is called the river basin. Largest is the basin of the Amazon in S America. Historically, river valleys were the cradles of civilization in China, Egypt and Mesopotamia.

LONGEST RIVERS

	km
Nile (Africa)	6670
Amazon (S America)	6437
Mississippi – Missouri – Red Rock (USA)	5971
Yangtze (China)	5470
Ob-Irtysh (USSR)	5410
Hwang Ho (China)	4672
Zaïre (Congo) (Africa)	4667
Amur (Asia)	4506
Lena (USSR)	4400
Mackenzie (Canada)	4241
Mekong (SE Asia)	4184
Niger (Africa)	4168
Paraná (S America)	4000
Murray-Darling (Australia)	3718
Volga (USSR)	3530

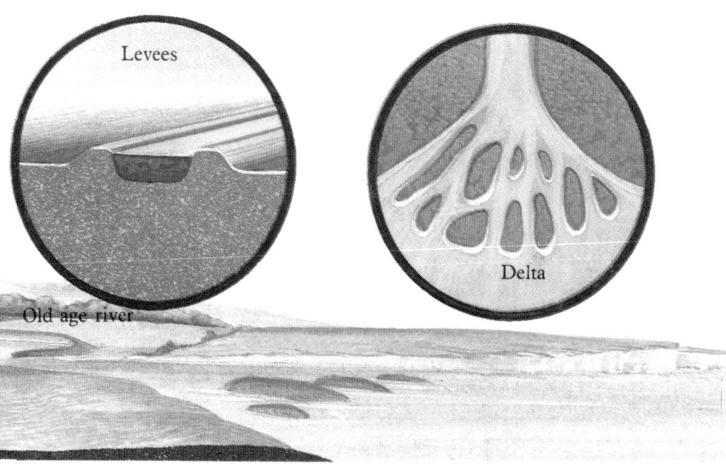

Roads The Romans were the first great road-builders. They laid a foundation of large stones, on which they spread rubble and mortar. Then they laid down broken bricks or tiles, and finally put down a surface of flat slabs. They cambered their roads to allow water to drain off.

Roads did not change much until the 1700s, when John McAdam started to tar the surface. Today's roads must have solid foundations to stand up to heavy traffic. Often materials such as cement and bitumen have to be added to strengthen the road bed. The surface layer may be concrete or asphalt.

Robotics Today's robots bear no resemblance to human beings. They are mechanical and electronic devices that imitate the actions of human arms, and are controlled by computers. Most of them work in factories, doing anything from delicate construction work to moving heavy loads. With the help of computer 'brains', robots may someday become as clever as people.

Robot miners, controlled from above ground, can work seams that are inaccessible or dangerous to humans.

Robespierre, Maximilien (1758–94) French lawyer who led the Jacobins after the Revolution of 1789 and was responsible for the 'Reign of Terror' in which many of his rivals (including Danton) were executed. He himself was arrested by his opponents and guillotined.

Robin The name applied to a number of familiar garden birds with a red breast in different parts of the world. The original robin redbreast is the European robin, a plump, aggressive little bird, with a reddish-orange forehead, throat and breast in both sexes.

Robin Hood (c 1200s) Legendary outlaw who robbed the rich to give to the poor. He and his band of followers supposedly lived in Sherwood Forest, Nottingham.

Rock The material of the Earth's crust. There are three major types of rock: igneous rocks are formed by the cooling of molten material from inside the Earth (e.g. granite and basalt); sedimentary rocks are composed of fragments of older rocks compressed and cemented together by minerals (e.g. sandstone) or of chemicals precipitated from water (e.g. limestone); metamorphic rocks have been changed by intense heat or pressure (e.g. marble).

The diagram shows how a 'liquid' rocket works.

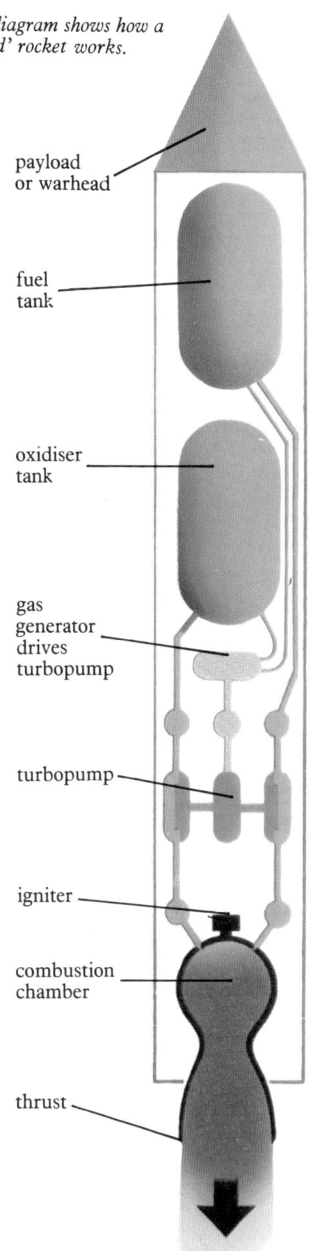

Rocket Rockets are the only known means of propelling vehicles in space. Jet engines need oxygen from the air to operate. Rockets carry oxygen in their propellant, so they can function in the airless conditions of space. The early rockets, like today's fireworks, were propelled by gunpowder. The Saturn rockets which launched Apollo astronauts to the Moon were 111 metres high and had as much thrust as 40 jumbo jets.

Rocky Mountain goat Sharp-horned ruminant that lives high in the mountains of the north-western United States. It resembles a goat but is more closely allied to the antelopes. Despite a clumsy appearance it is very sure-footed.

Rocky Mountains Mountain system in western North America, running from Alaska to Mexico. It consists of a number of parallel ranges with numerous peaks, the highest of which is Mt Logan (6050 metres).

Rodent Any of a group of mammals that includes rats and mice. These animals are all basically vegetarians and all have large chisel-like gnawing teeth at the front of the mouth. The teeth grow continuously to make up for wear at the tip. Rodents form the largest group of mammals and, as well as rats and mice, they include squirrels, beavers, porcupines and guinea pigs.

Rodeo Sport in which cowboys compete in such events as bronco riding, steer-roping and other tests of horsemanship and skill. Rodeos are popular in North America and developed from the contests staged by cowboys after rounding up the herds of cattle on the vast ranches. The riders would show off their skills and bet against one another. Today's rodeo stars are professionals, who travel from show to show.

Rolling Stones English pop group that rose to fame in the 1960s, led by Mick Jagger and Keith Richard.

Rolls, Charles Stewart (1877–1910) British pioneer motorist who together with the engineer Sir Henry Royce (1863–1933) founded Rolls-Royce Ltd, producing high-quality automobile and aero engines.

Roman Catholicism The main division of Christianity. It acknowledges the Pope as the spiritual leader of the Church, as the successor of St Peter, the apostle appointed by Jesus to be the head of His Church.

Roman Empire Dominant civilization in Europe and the Middle East from about the 1st century BC to the 5th century AD. Rome was a republic until 27 BC, when Octavian became the Emperor Augustus. It reached its greatest extent in the 2nd century AD, stretching from Scotland to Albania, Syria and Morocco, then declined until the last emperor was deposed in 476.

Roman civilization was based on the earlier civilization of Greece. While the Greeks were better thinkers and artists, the Romans were better builders, engineers and soldiers. They had a greater effect on the development of European culture than any other influence except, perhaps, the Christian Church.

Romania Republic in SE Europe. The Carpathian Mountains cover much of the country. In the west and south are fertile plains. Barley, maize, potatoes, grapes, sugar beet, sunflower seeds and tobacco are grown. The central mountains are forested and rich in minerals, among them oil, natural gas, coal and iron. Area: 237,482 km^2; Pop: 22,683,500; Cap: Bucharest.

It was the army which made Rome a great power. Victorious generals were allowed to hold a 'triumph'. They drove through the streets with their troops, their prisoners and their booty.

Rome Capital of Italy, situated on R. Tiber. Major religious, cultural and tourist centre. According to legend it was founded by Romulus and Remus in 753 BC. It was the capital of the Roman Empire and there are many famous relics of this period, including the Colosseum, Trajan's Column and the Forum. Pop: 2,848,000.

This 3rd-century coin shows Romulus and Remus, the wolf-reared twins said to have founded Rome in 735 BC.

Romney, George (1734–1802) English portrait painter who was a contemporary of GAINSBOROUGH and REYNOLDS. He is best known for his paintings of society figures such as Lady Hamilton.

Röntgen, Wilhelm Konrad (1845–1923) German physicist who discovered X-rays and was awarded the Nobel Prize in Physics in 1901.

Rook A bird belonging to the crow family, with a black plumage and a patch of greyish-white skin around the beak. The rook's bare face and its 'baggy trousers' help to distinguish it from its slightly larger cousin the carrion crow. Rooks live near farmland and eat grain and caterpillars.

Roosevelt, Franklin Delano (1882–1945) President of United States from 1933–45. He became governor of New York in 1929 despite a crippling illness. His economic reforms, or 'New Deal', helped to end the Great Depression and he ably led the United States through World War II.

Roosevelt, Theodore (1858–1919) President of the US from 1901 and champion of the rights of the 'little man'. He did much to regulate 'big business' through Anti-Trust legislation. He was awarded the Nobel Peace Prize in 1906 for bringing peace between Russia and Japan.

Root The part of a plant that anchors it in the ground and absorbs water and minerals from the soil.

Rose A large group of flowering shrubs, widely cultivated for their colourful, fragrant blooms. Roses have thorny stems and white, pink, or red, five-petalled flowers (though cultivated species come in a wider range of colours).

The dog rose (top) is simple and delicate compared to today's cultivated species.

Roses, Wars of the (1455–85) Contest for the English throne between the House of Lancaster and the House of York. The Lancastrian king, Henry VI, and the Yorkist claimant were both directly descended from Edward III. Both sides gained the upper hand at different times, and a Yorkist prince became Edward IV (1461–83). His brother, Richard III (1483–85), was overthrown by Henry VII (1485–1507), who ended the conflict by marrying a Yorkist princess.

Rossetti, Dante Gabriel (1828–82) British painter and poet who, with others, started the Pre-Raphaelite art movement.

The Tudor Rose (centre) is a combination of the red rose of Lancaster (left) and the white rose of York (right).

Rossini, Gioacchino Antonio (1792–1868) Successful Italian composer of 36 operas. All composed between 1810–29, the most popular is his comic opera *The Barber of Seville*. Many of his overtures are more widely known, like *The Thieving Magpie*, *William Tell* and *The Silken Ladder*.

Rotterdam Port and city in Netherlands, on the Nieuwe Maas. It is Europe's busiest port and an important industrial centre. Most of the city centre was destroyed during World War II. Pop: 590,000.

Rousseau, Henri (1844–1910) French customs official and self-taught primitive painter. He is best known for his colourful jungle scenes.

Rousseau, Jean Jacques (1712–78) French philosopher, political theorist and novelist. He abhorred the corruption of politics and in his *Contrat social* described the ideal democratic state in which individual freedom was subordinate to the general good. His ideas inspired the leaders of the French revolution.

Rowing Sport in which oarsmen race, usually on a lake or river, but also sometimes at sea. A rowing competition is called a regatta; one of the most famous is held at Henley-on-Thames. Rowing is an event in the Olympic Games: there are races for single rowers, pairs, fours and eights. The Boat Race between Oxford and Cambridge universities, held every year on the River Thames, is one of the most historic rowing races. The boats used in modern rowing are special lightweight craft, suitable only for calm water.

Rubber Elastic substance made from the latex of rubber trees, or nowadays produced synthetically from chemicals. It is air-tight, resistant to water, shock-absorbent and does not conduct electricity.

All these properties make it exceedingly useful, not least for the wheels of our cars.

Rubens, Sir Peter Paul (1557–1640) Regarded as the greatest of the Flemish painters, his most famous works include *Peace and War, The Rape of the Sabines* and *The Felt Hat*.

Rugby football Fifteen-a-side game played with oval ball which is handled and kicked. Originated at Rugby School. In professional Rugby League there are only 13 players in each side.

Ruminant Any mammal that chews the cud. Deer, sheep, goats and cows are ruminants. They are all grazing or browsing animals with multi-chambered stomachs. Food is initially gulped into the first chamber – the rumen – and later brought back into the mouth as cud to be chewed at leisure before it is finally digested.

Russia The largest of the soviet republics of the USSR and a name sometimes used to mean the USSR itself. Russia stretches from the Baltic Sea to the Pacific, and from the Arctic Ocean to the Caspian Sea. Area: 16,839,000 km^2.

Russian Revolution Political upheaval which ended with the creation of the Union of Soviet Socialist Republics (USSR). In 1917 Russia was suffering badly, mainly as a result of World War I. A reforming government was formed under Alexander Kerensky which forced the tsar to abdicate but continued with the war. In November, more extreme revolutionaries, known as Bolsheviks, under the leadership of Lenin and Trotsky, overthrew Kerensky and withdrew from the war. They set up a Communist government which, after two years of civil war, controlled the whole country.

Rutherford, Ernest (1871–1937) British physicist who was awarded the Nobel Chemistry prize in 1908 for his work on radioactivity. He was the first to split the atom (1919) and his study of the atom's structure contributed greatly to the advances made in nuclear physics in the 20th century.

Rwanda Small, thickly populated republic. in E central africa. The people are from two warring tribes – the Hutu and the Tutsi. At independence in 1962, power was held by the Hutu after a massacre of the Tutsi. Area: 26,336 km^2; Pop: 6,017,000; Cap; Kigali.

S

Sabre-toothed tiger Extinct prehistoric cat that lived in N America. Larger than a modern tiger, it had a pair of 25-cm teeth as sharp and curved as a sabre.

Sahara The largest desert in the world, situated in N Africa. It stretches from the Atlantic coast to the Red Sea and includes areas of sand dunes, stony wastes and mountains. Sparsely populated by nomadic tribesmen. Rich in oil and mineral deposits. Area: over 16 million km^2.

St Lawrence River in Canada, flowing NE from L. Ontario into the Gulf of St Lawrence on Atlantic coast. Length: 1250 km. The St Lawrence Seaway, a system of canals, locks and dams, has opened the way for ocean-going vessels to the Great Lakes.

Saints According to the Roman Catholic and other orthodox Churches, good people go to heaven when they die. Those who do are saints. Certain people whose lives on Earth have been exemplary are *canonized* (declared saints). Usually they are already revered by people who have prayed to them for miracles. Evidence of miracles is normally required. Among the most honoured saints are: Michael the Archangel, Andrew the apostle, Anthony of Padua, Thomas Aquinas, Augustine, Catherine, Dominic, Francis of Assisi, Ignatius Loyola, James and John the apostles, Joan of Arc, John the baptist, Mary, Matthew, Mark, Luke and John the evangelists, Thomas More, Paul of Tarsus, Simon Peter, Stephen the first martyr, Theresa of Lisieux and Francis Xavier.

Saladin (1138–93) Sultan of Egypt and Syria who defeated the Crusaders at the Battle of Hattin in 1187 and captured Jerusalem. Greatly outnumbered, he prevented Richard I of England from retaking the city in 1189, and the peace terms negotiated between the two leaders gave Saladin most of the disputed area, including Jerusalem. Revered by his fellow Muslims, he was also admired by his opponents.

Salamander A group of amphibians with tails, found in moist spots over much of the northern hemisphere. Most are under 15 cm in length but the giant salamander of Japan may reach 1.75 metres.

Salmon A highly prized game fish related to the trout found in the northern parts of Europe, Asia and N America. Adult salmon live in the sea but they return to breed in the same clear, upland stream where they hatched, leaping rapids and waterfalls on their journey upstream.

Salt In chemistry, a compound formed by the reaction of a BASE with an ACID. Common salt is a compound of two elements, sodium and chlorine, and is known chemically as *sodium chloride*. It is a part of sea water but is obtained mainly from salt flats and lakes, and from rock salt. Salt is an essential part of the human diet and is an important raw material in industry.

Salvation Army Religious organization run on military lines. As well as religion it brings food, warmth, shelter and counselling to the poor. Famous for its tambourine-ringing bands and rousing songs, its members raise money and preach the gospel at the same time. It was founded by William Booth, a Methodist preacher, in 1878. It publishes a magazine called the *War Cry*.

Sandstone One of the most common sedimentary rocks. As the name implies it consists of grains of sand, mostly QUARTZ, which have been compacted and cemented together by minerals. The colour depends upon the cementing mineral: often it is iron oxide, which stains the rock red.

San Francisco Port and city in California, USA, on San Francisco Bay which is spanned by the famous Golden Gate Bridge. The city is so hilly that public transport includes cable-cars. In 1906 it was largely destroyed by an earthquake. Pop: 679,000 (3,250,000 met area).

San Marino The smallest republic in the world. It grew from a 9th-century monastery in Italy and earns money largely from tourism and the sale of stamps. Area: 60 km^2; Pop: 20,000.

São Paulo The largest city in Brazil. It developed rapidly in late 19th century after a large immigration of Europeans, and has become a massive industrial and commercial centre. Pop: 8,491,000.

Sardine Small fish of herring family which live in vast shoals in Mediterranean and around the coasts of western Europe. Important for fishing and canning industry. A sardine is a young PILCHARD.

Sardinia Island in the Mediterranean, S of Corsica, and a self-governing region of Italy. A mountainous island with fertile lowlands. Pop: 1,582,000.

Satan Personification of evil and enemy of God, also called the devil. Features in Judaism, Christianity and Islam. Powerfully described in *Paradise Lost* by Milton.

Satellite A satellite is any object that moves around another of larger size. The Moon is a satellite of the Earth; the Earth and the other planets are satellites of the Sun. Man-made spacecraft that orbit the Earth are also satellites. Some carry scientific instruments for astronomical study, others send down information about the weather or the earth's surface.

Saturn Famous for its system of rings, Saturn is the second largest planet in the Solar system, sixth in line from the Sun. The rings, consisting of countless rocky fragments coated with ice, stretch 275,000 km from side to side, yet are only one km thick. Saturn has 15 moons; the largest, Titan, is bigger than the planet Mercury. Diameter: 120,000 km; distance from Sun: 1430 million km.

Satyrs In Greek legend a tribe of creatures that lived in the mountains and forests. They were usually represented as small hairy men with tails and goat-like ears.

Saudi Arabia Country occupying most of the Arabian Peninsula, with a long Red Sea coast and a shorter coast on the Arabian Gulf. This hot dry land, where Arab people lived by nomadic herding, was transformed by the discovery of oil in 1933. Money earned from oil has paid for roads, schools, hospitals and new industries in the desert. Sea water is turned into fresh water to irrigate market gardens. Area: 2,149,524 km^2; Pop: 10,794,000; Cap: Riyadh.

Schiller, Friedrich von (1759–1805) Leading German dramatist and poet whose works include *Don Carlos*, *Wallenstein*, *William Tell* and *The Maid of Orleans*.

Schubert, Franz (1797–1828) Austrian composer and the greatest songwriter of all time. He wrote over 600 'lieder' of great beauty. A lyrical genius, he died in poverty at the age of 31. Among his greatest compositions are the B Minor symphony (*The Unfinished*) and the C Major symphony (*The Great*), the incidental music for *Rosamunde*, *The Trout* quintet, and numerous piano sonatas.

Schumann, Robert Alexander (1810–56) German romantic composer noted for his piano music, songs, orchestral music, including four symphonies, and choral works. His piano concerto in A Minor was composed for his wife Clara, a great pianist. Suffering bouts of insanity, his last years were spent in an asylum.

Schweitzer, Albert (1875–1965) German missionary, musician and philosopher. He established a hospital at Lambaréné in French Equatorial Africa for people suffering from leprosy and sleeping sickness. He raised funds by giving organ recitals in Europe.

Scorpion Poisonous arachnid (spider family) found in most hot, dry parts of the world. The sting is carried in the tail which arches over the back. Some grow up to 20 cm but most are small. The sting is painful to humans but not deadly.

Scotland The northernmost part of the United Kingdom. Much of the country is heather-covered moors, with mountains, islands, and deep lochs (lakes) in the west. Further south the land is lower-lying. Towns and industries have grown up in river valleys, such as those of the Clyde and Forth, and North Sea oil has brought new industries to eastern coastal areas. About 9% of Britain's population lives in Scotland.

In 1603 James VI of Scotland succeeded to the English throne, as James I. In 1707 the Act of Union set up a single parliament for both England and Scotland. Area: 78,000 km^2; Pop: 5,116,000; Cap: Edinburgh. See map on page 204.

Scott, Robert Falcon (1868–1912) English naval officer and explorer who in 1911 led an expedition to the South Pole. He reached the Pole in January 1912 but found that Roald AMUNDSEN had beaten him to it by just over a month. He and his party died on the way back, some 11 miles from their base camp.

Scott, Sir Walter (1771–1832) Scottish poet and father of the historical novel. Gained recognition with his poem *The Lay of the Last Minstrel*. His novels include *Waverley*, *Guy Mannering* and *The Bride of Lammermoor*. His last years were marred by the bankruptcy of the publishing house in which he was closely involved.

Sculpture Technically complex skill and art form, that involves carving and modelling in a range of mediums from wood to stone. Typically the sculptor chips away at a block of marble to produce a perfect bust, figure or frieze. But sculptors model as well as carve, making representations of their subjects in wax or clay and then using the model to make a cast for a bronze or plaster statue. Some of the greatest sculpture was produced in ancient Greece and in Renaissance Italy, but modern times have seen the innovative work of Rodin, Giacometti and Henry MOORE.

Ancient Greek sculptures show the human body in perfect lifelike poses.

Sea anemone A group of marine animals with soft tubular bodies and a mouth fringed with tentacles. Stinging cells on the tentacles stun fishes and other animals on which the anemones feed. Anemones cling to rocks and are frequently found in rock pools. They pull in their tentacles and shrink to a blob of jelly if they are left uncovered by the tide.

Sea cow See **Dugong**; **Manatee**.

SCOTLAND

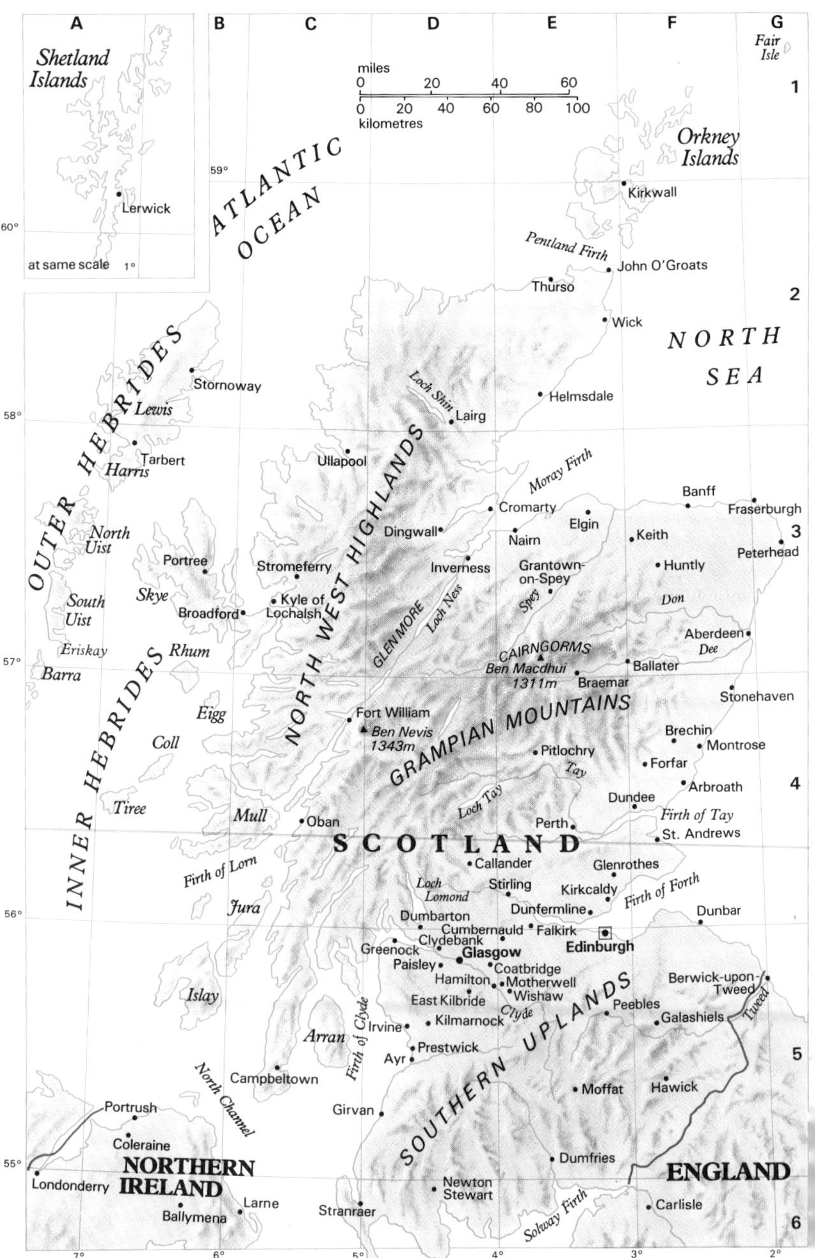
A
B
C
D
E
F
G
1
2
3
4
5
6
Shetland Islands
Lerwick
at same scale
1°
60°
59°
58°
57°
56°
55°
7°
6°
5°
4°
3°
2°
miles
0
20
40
60
0
20
40
60
80
100
kilometres
Fair Isle
Orkney Islands
Kirkwall
ATLANTIC OCEAN
Pentland Firth
John O'Groats
Thurso
Wick
NORTH SEA
OUTER HEBRIDES
Stornoway
Lewis
Loch Shin
Lairg
Helmsdale
Tarbert
Harris
Ullapool
NORTH WEST HIGHLANDS
Moray Firth
Banff
Fraserburgh
Cromarty
Elgin
North Uist
Dingwall
Nairn
Keith
Peterhead
Portree
Stromeferry
Inverness
Grantown-on-Spey
Huntly
South Uist
Skye
Kyle of Lochalsh
Broadford
Spey
Don
GLEN MORE
Loch Ness
Aberdeen
Dee
Eriskay
Rhum
CAIRNGORMS
Ben Macdhui 1311m
Ballater
Barra
Braemar
Stonehaven
INNER HEBRIDES
Fort William
Ben Nevis 1343m
GRAMPIAN MOUNTAINS
Eigg
Brechin
Montrose
Coll
Pitlochry
Forfar
Tay
Arbroath
Tiree
Mull
Loch Tay
Dundee
Firth of Tay
Oban
Perth
St. Andrews
SCOTLAND
Callander
Glenrothes
Firth of Lorn
Loch Lomond
Stirling
Kirkcaldy
Firth of Forth
Jura
Dunfermline
Dunbar
Dumbarton
Cumbernauld
Falkirk
Clydebank
Edinburgh
Greenock
Glasgow
Paisley
Coatbridge
Hamilton
Motherwell
Berwick-upon-Tweed
Islay
Wishaw
East Kilbride
Clyde
Peebles
Galashiels
Tweed
Irvine
Kilmarnock
SOUTHERN UPLANDS
Arran
Firth of Clyde
Prestwick
Ayr
North Channel
Campbeltown
Moffat
Hawick
Portrush
Girvan
Coleraine
NORTHERN IRELAND
Dumfries
ENGLAND
Londonderry
Newton Stewart
Larne
Ballymena
Stranraer
Solway Firth
Carlisle

Seahorse Small odd-shaped fish about 20 cm long with a long snout and a prehensile (gripping) tail. The male has a pouch in which eggs spawned by the female are hatched.

Seal A group of carnivores that are specialized for life in the sea, with tapering bodies and powerful flippers. Most find movement on land difficult, one exception being the sea lion.

Seasons The rhythm of the seasons is caused by the tilt of the Earth's axis (23½° from upright) as it circles the Sun. This tilt points first one hemisphere and then the other towards the Sun during the orbit, bringing summer and winter to the northern and southern hemispheres at opposite times of the year.

Sea urchin Small round animal with a spiny shell that lives along rocky coasts. The shell or test is made up of hundreds of chalky plates. Sea urchins move about on water-filled tube-feet which stick out through pores in the test. Some species have poisonous spines.

Seaweed A large group of marine algae found mostly around the shore. Seaweeds do not have leaves as such, though many are leaf-like. The main part of the plant is called the frond. Seaweeds are attached to surfaces by a sucker-like organ called a holdfast. There are three basic types of seaweed, green, brown and red.

Sedimentary rocks are those formed from sediments, such as rock fragments worn from the land (e.g. sandstone), the remains of once living things (e.g. coal and some limestones) or chemicals precipitated from water (e.g. chemical limestone). These sediments accumulate in layers which are compressed and slowly cemented together by minerals.

Seed The reproductive body of flowering plants and conifers. It consists of a miniature plant, known as the embryo, surrounded by a tough coat. The seed also contains a store of food which may be inside the embryo or packed around it. The embryo uses this stored food when it starts to grow.

Seismology The study of shock waves travelling through the rocks. The largest result from earthquakes and are measured according to their intensity on the open-ended Richter scale. Oil prospectors set off small explosions and record the passage of the shock waves as a seismogram. From the pattern of the waves they can establish the nature of the underground rock structures and assess the probability of finding petroleum.

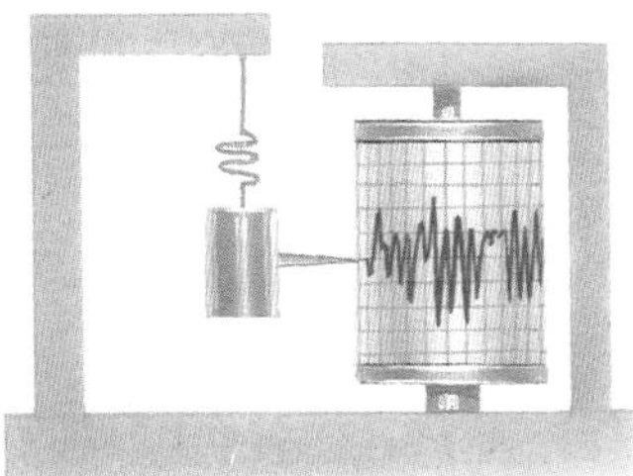

A seismograph: the heavy weight stays still while the support shakes. The tremors are recorded on a drum.

Semiconductor These materials are neither good conductors of electricity nor insulators. They have a low conductivity which increases with temperature. Silicon and germanium are the best known semiconductors and are often used for integrated circuits in electronics.

Senegal Republic in W Africa, mostly low-lying with savanna vegetation in the south and desert scrub in the north. Unreliable rainfall has led to droughts and famines in recent years. Peanuts are the chief export. Area: 196,177 km²; Pop: 6,541,000; Cap: Dakar.

Senses The various faculties of the body which provide the brain with information about the external world. They are sight, hearing, touch, taste and smell. The sensory organs, e.g. EYE and EAR, contain nerve endings called sensory receptors which respond to a stimulus, such as light or sound, by sending electrical impulses to the brain. The senses of taste and smell work closely together. Taste receptors (taste buds) are located on the tongue. They respond to only four different tastes, sweet, sour, bitter or salty. The smell receptors on the back of the nose are sensitive to a far wider range of scents and smells. What most people attribute to a sense of taste is actually attributable to smell.

Seoul Capital of S Korea on Han R. and historic capital of Korea from 14th century. Pop: 6,876,000.

Sequoia, giant A coniferous tree that grows wild in the mountains of California.

The world's biggest trees (but not the tallest), they are estimated to live for more than 3000 years. The bark of the mature tree is so soft that you can punch it without discomfort. The largest individual tree is known as the General Sherman. It weighs over 2000 tonnes.

Seven Wonders of the World At the time of Alexander the Great, Pliny the Elder compiled a list of what the sightseers of ancient times considered were the most remarkable of the many marvellous monuments built by man. They were: The Great Pyramid of Egypt; The Temple of Diana, at Ephesus in Asia Minor; The Tomb of Mausoleus, at Halicarnassus in Asia Minor; The Hanging Gardens of Babylon; The Pharos Lighthouse near Alexandria, Egypt; The Colossus of Rhodes and The Statue of Zeus at Olympia. Of the seven landmarks, the Great Pyramid of Egypt is the sole survivor today.

Severn Longest river in England, flowing in an arc from the Cambrian Mts to the Bristol Channel. Famous for its tidal bore. Length: 344 km.

Sextant An instrument used in navigation at sea. A movable mirror in the sextant is adjusted until the reflection of a star appears alongside the horizon when viewed through the eyepiece. A fixed scale on the sextant then indicates its angle of elevation. By noting the elevation of several stars along with their bearing and the exact time of observation, the navigator can calculate the position of his ship from special tables.

Seychelles A group of more than 80 islands in the Indian Ocean which form an independent republic. Tourism is Seychelles' main industry. Area: 445 km^2; Pop: 65,000; Cap: Victoria.

Shag A large bird of the seashore, like the CORMORANT in appearance, but smaller. Shags are superb in the water, diving and swimming to catch fish.

Shaftesbury, Earl of (1801–85) English humanitarian who did much to relieve the misery of the working classes. He introduced legislation that prohibited women and children from working in coal mines and reduced the working hours in factories to ten per day.

Shakespeare, William (1564–1616) English poet and dramatist whose works are performed the world over and whose expressions have passed into the language. He was born at Stratford-upon-Avon. As a young man he worked as an actor, becoming a partner in the Globe Theatre in 1599. His plays include: histories (outstanding among them, *Henry IV* [parts I and II], *Richard II*, *Richard III* and *Henry V*); comedies (including *As You Like It*, *A Midsummer Night's Dream*, *Twelfth Night* and *Much Ado About Nothing*); and tragedies (including his four great masterpieces *Othello*, *Macbeth*, *Hamlet* and *King Lear*. Had he written no plays at all, Shakespeare would still be remembered for his poems, long ones like *Venus and Adonis* and also numerous sonnets. He was married to Anne Hathaway whose home can still be seen in Stratford together with the poet's tombstone on which are carved these warning words:

'GOOD FREND FOR JESUS SAKE FORBEARE,
TO DIGG THE DUST ENCLOASED HEARE:
BLESE BE Y MAN Y SPARES THES STONES,
AND CURST BE HE Y MOVES MY BONES'.

Shale One of the most common sedimentary rocks formed from the consolidation of silt or clay. Shale splits easily into thin layers and has few uses, but some deposits contain petroleum.

Shanghai Major port and largest city in China, on the delta of Yangtze River. China's leading manufacturing centre with large textile, steel, shipbuilding, engineering and oil-refining industries. Pop: 11,320,000.

Shannon Longest river in Ireland, flowing into the Atlantic via a number of lakes and a large estuary. Length: 390 km.

Shark Most feared of all fish, sharks have torpedo-shaped bodies with large tails and a fin which sticks up from the water. They range in size from 50 cm to 15 metres, but their ferocity is not related to their size. The largest, the whale shark, is harmless to man. Man-eaters include the blue, white, leopard and tiger sharks. They live mostly in tropical waters. Many are fished for food, including the little dogfish which is sold as rock salmon. Like the skates and rays, sharks are cartilaginous fish.

Shaw, George Bernard (1856–1950) Irish-born dramatist, critic, essayist and active socialist who settled in England. His plays include *Man and Superman*, *Pygmalion*, *Caesar and Cleopatra*, *Saint Joan* and *The Apple Cart*.

Sheep Horned mountain animals reared since prehistoric times for their wool and meat. Wild sheep include the moufflon and the argali. Domestic sheep have been bred into many varieties. Australia and the USSR are the world's leading sheep-farming nations, followed by New Zealand (where there is one person for every 20 sheep).

Sheffield City in Yorkshire, England, once a major centre of iron and steel industry (based on local coal deposits), more recently known for its cutlery and silver plate. Pop: 537,000.

Shell A hard coat, such as that of snails and many other molluscs. It may be in one piece or, as in bivalves, made of two halves. These shells are made largely of lime secreted by the animal itself.

Shelley, Percy Bysshe (1792–1822) English romantic poet whose poems include *Adonais*, *Ode to the West Wind*, *Prometheus Unbound* and *To a Skylark*. A great friend of BYRON, he was drowned while out sailing.

Sheridan, Richard Brinsley (1751–1816) British politician and dramatist whose plays include *The Rivals* and *The School for Scandal*.

Shetland Islands Group of islands in the North Sea, situated about 100 km NE of Scotland. The main industries used to be fishing and textiles, but oil has become an important source of employment. The chief town is Lerwick situated on the largest island, Mainland. Pop: 27,000.

Ship Term for large, sea-going vessel. The Egyptians, Greeks and Phoenicians relied upon oars and a central, square sail to power their vessels, as did the Vikings centuries later. About AD 1000 the triangular *lateen* sail was developed which enabled ships to sail into the wind as well as with the wind. This led to the classic *fully-rigged* ship with square sails and a rear lateen sail. This arrangement lasted throughout the era of sail, including the very fast clippers of the late 19th century. But by the mid 1800s steam was replacing sail and iron was replacing wood. In 1894 the introduction of the steam turbine brought a breakthrough in engine propulsion, and in subsequent years oil and even nuclear power replaced coal as the means of raising steam for the turbines. Other modern developments include the introduction of the diesel engine, stabilizers, container ships, vast oil-tankers and, most recently, rigid sails.

Nelson's flagship Victory, shown cut away to reveal the gun decks and the hold.

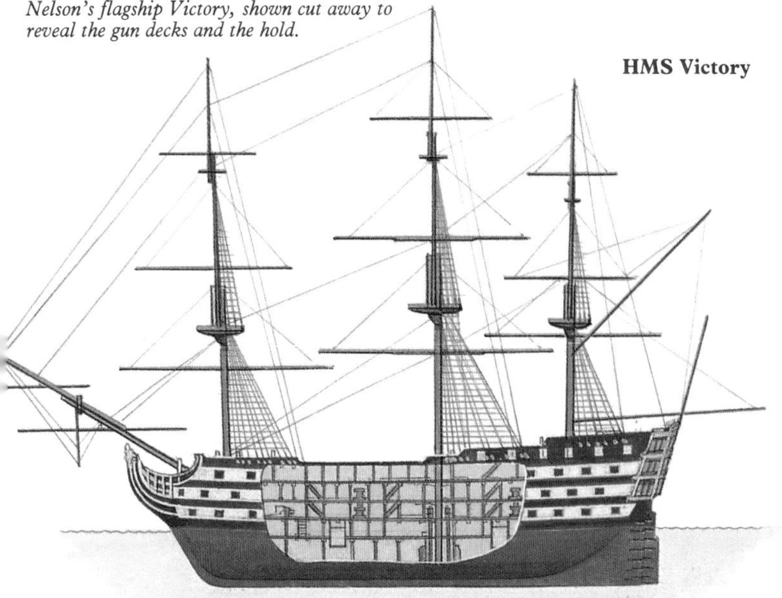

Shipbuilding Over the past few decades ship construction has changed considerably. To some degree, assembly line methods are used and a large part of the vessel under construction is prefabricated away from the shipyard itself. Whole sections of the ship's hull are welded together in an assembly shop, and the ship is built up section by section. In the past, hundreds of steel plates were riveted together, one by one, and the plates had to overlap. Now the plates are welded together with no overlap, saving metal and weight. During construction, the ship is supported by heavy wooden blocks under the keel. When the construction is complete, the vessel is ready for launching. A greased slipway is built to guide the vessel into the water. After launching, the ship goes to the outfitting dock where engines and other machines are installed, and decoration and furnishing are completed.

Shorthand Method of rapid handwriting. The most famous and popular shorthand was invented by Isaac Pitman in the 1830's. It employs a variety of symbols that represent the sounds of the language. It is extremely ingenious and is used by court and parliamentary shorthand writers who need to be able to take down dictation at 150–200 words a minute. Gregg shorthand (which also uses symbols), speedwriting (which abbreviates normal longhand) and stenograph machines (for shorthand typing) are also used to record speech, even though, nowadays, there are more than enough machines that can actually record the human voice.

Shrew The smallest of all mammals, shrews look like mice but have more pointed snouts. The common shrew is about 7 cm long with a long tail and has sharp, red-tipped teeth. Active day and night, it eats its own body weight in food every day. Its diet consists of insects and other small creatures.

Shrike Birds commonly called butcher-birds. They catch smaller birds, mice and insects, storing the bodies in a 'larder' by impaling them on thorns.

Shrimps Marine crustaceans rather like tiny lobsters, and closely related to prawns. Shrimps are an important food for many fishes.

Sibelius, Jean (1865–1957) Great Finnish composer and patriot who, at the age of 32, was given an annual grant by the state so that he could concentrate on composition. His works include a violin concerto, seven symphonies, several tone poems which include the popular *Finlandia*, and many songs.

Siberia Vast area of sparsely populated forests, mountains and plains occupying most of Asiatic USSR. For hundreds of years Siberia has been a place to send political exiles, a practice which continues today. Many of these people have been used to develop farms and industries. Area: 12,700,000 km^2.

Sicily Largest island in Mediterranean and a self-governing region of Italy, separated from the mainland by Straits of Messina. Mountainous landscape includes Mt Etna. Pop: 4,940,000.

Sierra Leone Country in W Africa, with a hot damp climate. Palm oil is the chief product, along with some coffee, ginger and rubber. Diamonds, iron and chrome are valuable minerals. Area: 71,735 km^2; Pop: 3,784,000; Cap: Freetown.

Sikhism Monotheistic religion founded in the hope of uniting Hindus and Moslems in India. Its followers live mostly in the Punjab. Their holiest shrine is the Golden Temple at Amritsar and their holy book is the *Granth*.

Silicon Non-metallic element abundant in the Earth's crust. Rock-forming silicon minerals include silica (*quartz*) and feldspar. With the addition of certain impurities, silicon becomes a SEMICONDUCTOR and the raw material for the manufacture of microchips. Chem. symbol Si.

Silicon chip Small wafer of silicon processed to produce an integrated circuit. Electronic calculators and computers all use silicon chips.

Silk A natural fibre produced by silkworms. The silkworm is a moth larva which spins a silk cocoon on mulberry leaves. A single cocoon gives a strand of silk over 600 metres long. Four strands are normally twisted together to make a usable thread. Half of the world's production of silk comes from Japan, but during this century the fibre has been largely replaced by synthetic materials.

Silver White precious metal which can be easily shaped and has a high resistance to corrosion. It is also the best metallic conductor of heat and electricity. Silver has long been used in jewellery and for coinage (though modern 'silver' coinage is

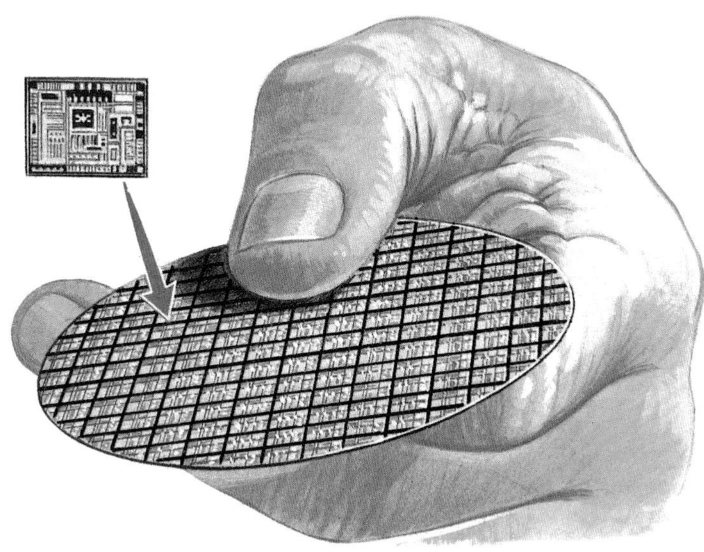

About 300 separate and identical chips are obtained from a single 'wafer' of silicon.

an alloy of copper and nickel). Some silver compounds are light-sensitive and are used in photography. Chem. symbol Ag (Latin *argentum*).

Silverfish A small wingless insect often seen running in baths and sinks. It belongs to a group of insects known as bristletails and has a three-pronged tail.

Singapore Island state in SE Asia, at tip of Malay Peninsula. Singapore is a busy, prosperous port and manufacturing centre. Banking and communications are also important. Area: 580 km^2; Pop: 2,532,000; Cap: Singapore.

Siphon If a bent tube full of liquid is taken from one glass of liquid to another glass of liquid at a lower level, liquid will flow from the upper to the lower glass. This is a siphon. A siphon depends on air pressure.

Sirens In Greek legend sea nymphs who by their singing lured sailors to their deaths on a rocky coast.

Skate See **Ray**.

Skating Movement over ice wearing skates (boots with a metal blade). For hundreds of years simply a winter pastime, today it is an event in the Olympic Games. There are speed skating events, competitions for figure skating and for dancing.

Skeleton The bones of an animal make up its skeleton. In vertebrates, animals with backbones, the skeleton acts as a framework for the body. Muscles attached to the bones enable movement at the joints. Some animals, such as snails and crabs, have skeletons outside their bodies which protect their soft bodies and prevent them from drying up.

Skiing Winter sport and Olympic event. Ski races are held in Europe and North America. The skiers race downhill, one at a time, the winner being the racer who sets the fastest time. In the slalom race, the skiers have to twist in and out of a series of 'gates'. Ski-jumping demands even more nerve. Here the skiers launch themselves from a mountainside ramp into mid air, landing far below. The longest jump wins.

Skin The outer covering of the body. It protects the internal organs from physical damage and infection by harmful bacteria and viruses. It helps to control body temperature in several ways; for example, if a person is hot, the blood flow through the skin is increased to cool the blood down. Sweat, produced by special glands in the skin, evaporates on the surface, also helping to reduce temperature. Sweat also contains waste materials, so sweating helps

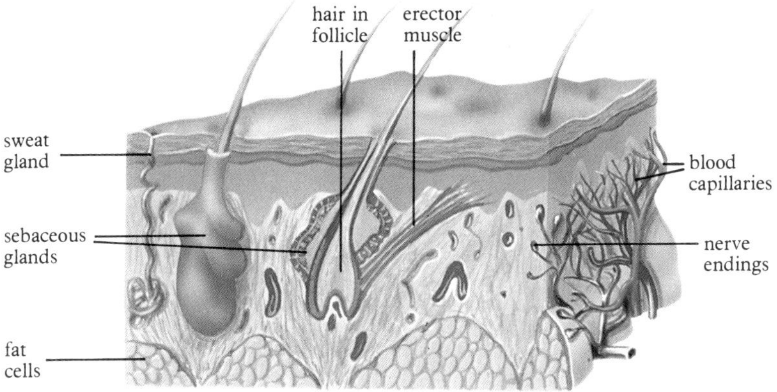

A section through the skin: the surface consists of dead cells which flake off.

to cleanse the system. The skin is also a major sense organ, containing different types of nerve endings that are sensitive to touch, pressure, heat, cold, pain, etc.

Skua Aggressive seabirds, renowned for their habit of chasing seagulls and other birds and forcing them to drop their prey which the skuas then swoop down and catch.

Skunk Black and white, omnivorous mammal of weasel family, notorious for its unpleasant odour. When frightened the animal turns on its enemy, raises its bushy tail and squirts a fine spray from glands on its rear as far as three metres. Skunks live in N and S America.

Sky diving Sport in which people wearing parachutes leap from aeroplanes. The sky diver can 'fly' for a brief time, as he or she falls towards the distant ground, before pulling the cord that opens the parachute. The aim then is to land as near as possible to a target on the ground, by guiding the parachute as it lowers the diver earthwards.

Skylark A bird noted for its beautiful song, heard as the bird hovers in flight. Skylarks live in open meadowland and nest on the ground. They run rather than hop, and feed on insects and seeds. The skylark is a brownish bird, with pale underparts and a small head crest.

Skyscraper Tall buildings built around a framework of concrete or steel. The walls of the building take no load at all, so they can be made of light materials. Given firm foundations, the frame of the building is created first. As each part of the frame is completed, other fitting stages can begin. Ready-made units are used to speed construction. Skyscrapers were only made possible by the development of the safe lift.

Slate A fine-grained metamorphic rock derived from shale. It splits into thin layers and is sometimes used for roofing.

Slavery Ownership of people as servants. The idea that each person has a right to his or her own freedom has been accepted by everyone only in recent times. Many early societies had slaves, and slavery was not always cruel.

The largest and worst form of slavery existed in the Americas from the 17th to the 19th century, when the slaves were mostly Africans brought by force to work for European masters. Slavery became illegal in Britain in 1833 and in the United States, where it helped to cause the Civil War, in 1863.

Sloth Slow-moving, coarse-haired mammal of S and C America that hangs upside down in the trees of the tropical rain forests, occasionally stretching out a long clawed hand to pick leaves and fruit. The two main species are the two-toed and the three-toed sloth.

Slow worm A legless, shiny brown lizard. It is about 50 cm long and usually lives in damp places. As its name suggests it moves slowly, but it speeds up when danger threatens. It feeds largely on earthworms and slugs.

Slug Gastropod mollusc, closely related to the snail but with only a tiny shell or no shell at all. Slugs are found in damp places, and usually come out to feed at night; most kinds eat plants, but some slugs are carnivorous. Slugs are disliked by gardeners for the damage they cause to vegetables.

Smallpox Once common, and often fatal, viral disease that at best left its victims with disfiguring scars. Today the disease has virtually disappeared, thanks to the use of vaccination programmes, though vaccine is still kept in laboratories.

Smell See **Senses**.

Smuggling Secret trade, usually in illegal goods, to avoid taxation or imprisonment. In the past smugglers traded in goods such as wine and tobacco, to evade the government taxes. Today, smuggling is often more serious, involving harmful drugs, such as heroin. Drugs are carried in secret from the countries of Asia and S America and smuggled into Europe and the United States. Countries work together, through INTERPOL and other organizations, to put an end to drug smuggling.

Smuts, Jan Christiaan (1870–1950) South African statesman and soldier. Though he had been a Boer general in the war of 1899–1902 he fought on Britain's side in World War I. He was prime minister of South Africa from 1919–24 and again from 1939–48.

Snail Gastropod mollusc found on land, in fresh water and in the sea. Some 50,000 species of snail are known. Most eat plants, but some eat other animals. The snail's shell protects it from enemies and also stops it from drying out.

Snake Legless reptiles related to the lizards. Snakes have long slim bodies and tails, and scaly skins. They cannot close their eyes. They move easily across rough ground either by looping their bodies sideways and pushing back against lumps in the surface, or by digging the broad scales on their bellies into the ground and pulling themselves forward. Snakes can eat prey far larger than themselves because the lower jaw is not connected to the skull. They swallow their prey whole. Some snakes kill their prey by squeezing (constricting) it to death; others have poisonous fangs. No snakes are found in Ireland.

Snipe Wading bird of moorland and marshes, mottled brown in plumage with dark stripes on the head. Snipe fly in a zigzag manner when alarmed, and during courtship, the male 'drums' with his tail and wings. Snipe nest on the ground and feed on insects and worms.

Snow Delicate ice crystals with an infinite variety of hexagonal (six-sided) shapes which form in air below freezing point and fall to the ground. The snow line is the level above which there is permanent snow cover. This varies from about 4800 metres in the tropics to sea level near the poles.

Snow crystals

Soap and detergents We need soap because water by itself simply rolls off greasy dirt without 'wetting' it. Soapy water penetrates the dirt and breaks it up into tiny particles. The soap surrounds the particles and floats them away. Soaps are made from alkalis such as caustic soda and caustic potash. Vegetable oils such as cottonseed are also widely used.

When we talk about 'detergents' we usually mean synthetic products which are more efficient 'wetters' than soaps. Detergents are made from oil by-products treated with sulphuric acid.

Soccer See **Association Football**

Social insect Any of those insects that live in an organized community – which is always a family unit – and co-operate with each other for the good of that community. All ANTS and TERMITES are social insects, and so are many BEES and WASPS.

Socialism Political idea based, like COMMUNISM, on the principle of sharing wealth. Socialists believe in equality; socialist ideas developed from the 1700s and grew stronger during the INDUSTRIAL REVOLUTION when workers in towns generally lived in poor and unhealthy conditions. Unlike Communists, socialists do not necessarily believe that revolution is the only way to achieve equality. In a democracy (such as France or Britain) socialist governments are peacefully elected to power. A simple form of socialism is the commune, in which all the people on a farm, for example, may share in the work and, after the harvest, share in the profits.

Socrates (*c* 469–399 BC) Greek philosopher whose ideas were written down by his pupil Plato. Socrates used a question-and-answer technique to find out what was good and what was bad, believing that evil sprang from ignorance and good from knowledge. His views caused so much offence in Athens that he was tried on a trumped-up charge of corruption and sentenced to death or exile. Preferring death, he took hemlock and died as nobly as he had lived.

Sodium Very soft, white metal which reacts violently with water. It occurs naturally in a wide range of compounds including sodium chloride (common salt) and sodium nitrate (Chile saltpetre). Chem. symbol Na (Latin *natrium*).

Sofia Capital of Bulgaria close to Yugoslavian border. Historic city, founded by Romans in 2nd century AD. Pop: 1,014,000.

Soil Topmost layer of the Earth's surface. It consists of broken-down rock, basically either sandy or clay, with varying degree of acidity. Organic material (humus) within the soil provides nutrition for the plants that grow in it.

Solar energy The energy given off by the Sun. It comes from atomic reactions that take place inside the Sun when hydrogen atoms are turned into helium atoms – a process called nuclear fusion. Only about one two-billionth of the Sun's energy ever reaches the Earth, but this tiny fraction still amounts to an immense amount of energy, some of which can be collected and put to use. It can be converted to electricity by photo-electric cells. This technique is used to power artificial satellites. Solar energy can also be used to supply power for homes, and efforts are being made to reduce the cost of this form of heating and lighting.

Solar system The system of nine planets, their moons, and countless smaller heavenly bodies such as asteroids, comets

and meteors, which circle the Sun. The radius of the Solar system – the distance from the Sun to the outermost known planet, Pluto – is over 5,600,000,000 km. Astronomers believe that there may be many such planetary systems in space.

Sole A flatfish found mostly on sandy or muddy sea beds around the coasts of Europe. Its range does not extend as far north as that of many other flatfishes. The fish is about 40 cm long. It buries itself in the sand by day and hunts at night.

Solid Solid is one of the three states of matter, the others being LIQUID and GAS. A solid has a fixed shape, unlike liquids and gases. The atoms or molecules of most solids are arranged in fixed patterns called CRYSTALS. When a solid is heated to a certain temperature it melts to become a liquid.

The planets of the solar system showing their relative distance from the Sun (from left to right): Pluto, Neptune, Uranus, Saturn, Jupiter, Mars, Earth, Venus and Mercury. The asteroid belt lies between Mars and Jupiter. On the far right is Earth as seen from space.

Solomon, King (?–*c* 932 BC) Son of David, he became King of the Jews *c* 972. He was very wealthy and was revered for his wisdom. He built the Temple at Jerusalem but his heavy taxes led to a revolt.

Solution A solution is a mixture of two or more substances which cannot be separated by being filtered or left to settle. When sugar is dissolved in a cup of tea it will never settle at the bottom of the cup, nor can it be filtered out. In solutions, the substance in which another substance dissolves is called the *solvent*. Usually the solvent is a liquid, but the substance dissolved can be a solid, another liquid, or a gas. The amount of a substance that can be dissolved in a certain quantity of solvent is a measure of its *solubility*. The solubility of most solids increases considerably if the solvent is heated. More than twice the quantity of sugar will dissolve in boiling water than in ice-cold water.

Somalia Arid country in NE Africa where sheep, camels and goats graze in large herds. Drought and famine are a serious problem. Area: 637,609 km^2; Pop: 6,393,000; Cap: Mogadishu.

Sonar A device that uses sound waves to find the depth of water under ships and locate submarines. Sound waves of frequencies between 5000 and 25,000 hertz (cycles per second) are sent out from under the ship's hull. These sound waves fan out, and when they meet an object they are reflected back. The distance to the object is found by automatic measurement of the time taken by the sound waves to return to the ship.

Sound Sounds are vibrations which travel through air or some other medium and can be detected by the ears. Sound waves cannot travel in a vacuum. When an object such as a violin string or a bell vibrates, waves of high and low pressure travel through the air to our ears. The vibration of our eardrums sends messages to the brain and we 'hear' the sound. Sound travels through air at 1222 km/h, with slight variations for atmospheric pressure and temperature. It travels faster through denser mediums such as water or steel.

We can tell one sound from another by its *pitch* (its highness or lowness) and its *loudness*. The higher the frequency of the sound waves, the higher the pitch. We can hear low notes from about 20 hertz (cycles per second) to high notes of about 20,000 hertz.

Sound recording In 1877 Thomas Alva Edison invented the first machine to record and play back sound. Electric recording did not appear until 1925. Plastic tape coated with magnetic iron oxide was first used to record sound in Germany in 1935. Long-playing discs were introduced in 1948, and it was not until 1958 that the stereo disc as we know it came on the market. Today, laser-produced compact discs offer practically perfect reproduction in durable form.

South Africa Country at the southern tip of Africa, consisting largely of a rolling grassy plateau – the High Veld – averaging over 1000 metres in height. In the south-east the Drakensberg Mts, rising to over 3300 metres, flank a narrow, fertile coastal plain. Much of the interior is dry and requires irrigation to grow crops. But the farms of South Africa produce more than enough food for the nation's needs. There are rich mineral resources. South Africa leads the world in gold production and has major deposits of coal, copper, uranium and diamonds.

The white people, mainly of Dutch and British ancestry, hold power, while the majority – the black Africans who make up 70% of the population – have no share in government. Area: 1,220,900 km²; Pop: 31,698,000; Caps: Pretoria (admin), Cape Town (legislative).

South America The fourth largest continent, occupying 15 per cent of the world's land area. S America is a developing continent. It has vast mineral reserves in the Andes, fertile farms on the plains and great reserves of timber in the Amazon basin. Yet more than half the people are peasant farmers who can barely produce enough food for their own needs. Industries are rapidly being expanded but the cost of this has put most of the continent deeply into debt. Area: 17,819,000 km².

Soviet Union See **Union of Soviet Socialist Republics**.

Soya A native plant of China, now cultivated in many parts of the world for its nutritious beans which are rich in protein and oil. Soya is used for making meal and flour, and, increasingly, for the production of meat substitute.

Space probes Both the USA and the USSR have sent space probes to the Moon and beyond. Possibly the most exciting were the American *Viking* probes which landed on Mars in 1976 to look for life, though in the event none was found. Equally ambitious are the *Voyager* probes to the more distant planets. In 1979 they took spectacular photographs of Jupiter and some of its moons. The following year *Voyager I* gave astronomers their first good look at Saturn and its rings. *Voyager II*, which reached Saturn in 1981 and Uranus in 1986, is scheduled to reach Neptune in 1989.

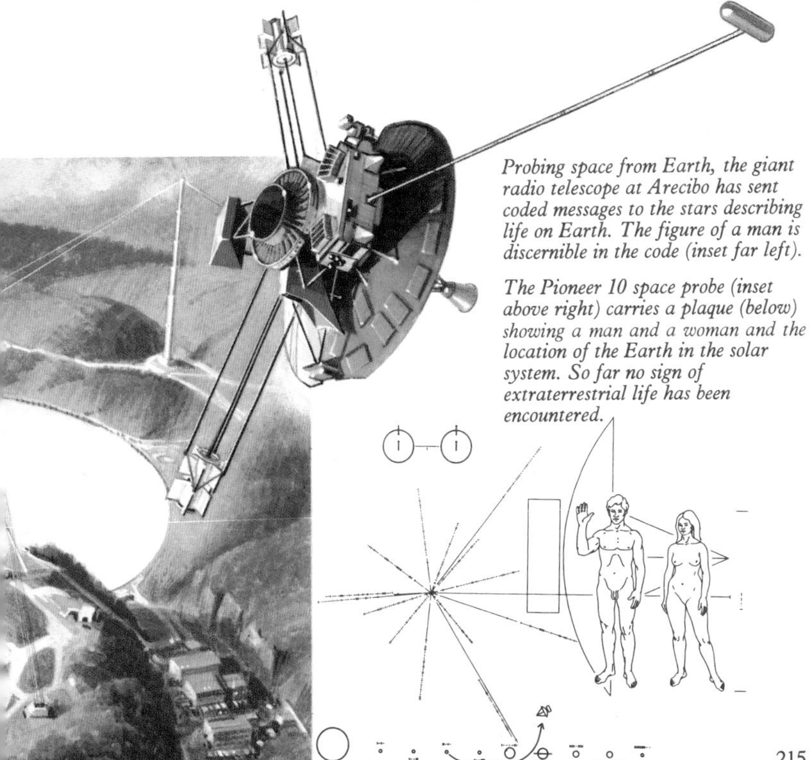

Probing space from Earth, the giant radio telescope at Arecibo has sent coded messages to the stars describing life on Earth. The figure of a man is discernible in the code (inset far left).

The Pioneer 10 space probe (inset above right) carries a plaque (below) showing a man and a woman and the location of the Earth in the solar system. So far no sign of extraterrestrial life has been encountered.

CARIBBEAN SEA
Neth. Antilles
A
B
C
D
E
F
1
2
3
4
5
6
7
8
10°
0°
20°
30°
40°
50°
80°
70°
60°
50°
40°
30°
Barranquilla
Ciénaga
Maracaibo
Cabimas
Maracay
Caracas
Cartagena
Valledupar
Valencia
Barquisimeto
Cumaná
Port of Spain
TRINIDAD
PANAMA
Panama Canal
Panamá City
Montería
VENEZUELA
Ciudad Guayana
Cúcuta
San Cristóbal
San Fernando
Orinoco
Ciudad Bolívar
Gulf of Panamá
Bucaramanga
Georgetown
Medellín
New Amsterdam
Paramaribo
Tunja
GUYANA
Manizales
Pereira
Armenia
Bogotá
Ibague
GUIANA HIGHLANDS
Cayenne
SURINAME
FRENCH GUIANA
Cali
Palmira
Neiva
Boa Vista
ATLANTIC OCEAN
COLOMBIA
Pasto
Macapá
Equator
Quito
ECUADOR
Chimborazo 6272
Guayaquil
Negro
Amazon
Belém
Manaus
São Luís
Cuenca
Iquitos
Amazon
Fortaleza
Marañón
Madeira
Tapajós
Teresina
Piura
BRAZIL
Campina Grande
Chiclayo
Selvas
Caruaru
Trujillo
Chimbote
Huascaran 6768
Rio Branco
Xingu
Tocantins
Araguaia
Maceió
Callao
Lima
Aracaju
PERU
São Francisco
Feira de Santana
Cuzco
Salvador
BOLIVIA
Mato Grosso
Cuiabá
Lake Titicaca
La Paz
Mato Grosso
Brasília
Itabuna
Cochabamba
Goiânia
BRAZILIAN HIGHLANDS
Arequipa
Santa Cruz
Oruro
Paraguay
Sucre
Uberlândia
Governador Valadares
Arica
Lake Poopó
Potosí
Uberaba
Belo Horizonte
Iquique
Atacama Desert
Campo Grande
São José do Rio Prêto
Vitória
Ribeirão Prêto
Juiz de Fora
PARAGUAY
Bauru
Paraná
Concepción
Campinas
Volta Redonda
Petrópolis
Rio de Janeiro
Niterói
Tropic of Capricorn
Antofagasta
Londrina
São Paulo
Santo André
Santos
Salta
Asunción
Foz do Iguaçu
Curitiba
San Miguel del Tucumán
Resistencia
Corrientes
S. Felix
S. Ambrosio (Chile)
Santiago del Estero
Florianópolis
CHILE
ANDES
Santa Mariá
Caxias do Sul
PACIFIC OCEAN
Uruguaiana
Pôrto Alegre
Córdoba
Concordia
Salto
Pelotas
San Juan
Santa Fé
Paysandú
Rio Grande
Rosario
Viña del Mar
Mendoza
URUGUAY
Valparaíso
Aconcagua 6960
Santiago
Buenos Aires
Montevideo
Rancagua
La Plata
Juan Fernández Is. (Chile)
Rio de la Plata
Talca
Pampas
Chillán
Talcahuano
Concepción
ARGENTINA
Mar del Plata
SOUTH ATLANTIC OCEAN
Bahiá Blanca
Temuco
Valdivia
Puerto Montt
Patagonia
Comodoro Rivadavia
miles
0
200
400
600
0
200
400
600
800
1000
kilometres
Stanley
Strait of Magellan
Falkland Islands (U.K.)
Tierra del Fuego
Punta Arenas
Cape Horn

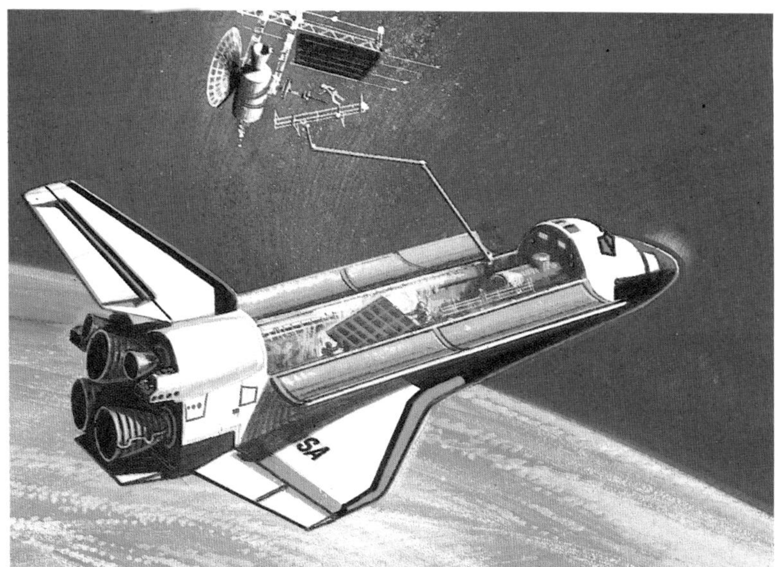

In orbit, the Space Shuttle opens its hatch to launch a satellite by means of its remote-manipulator arm.

Space Shuttle A reusable space plane developed by the United States. It takes off like a rocket, aided by an external fuel tank and two solid fuel boosters, but glides to land on a runway like an aircraft. The Space Shuttle orbiter, the part that actually goes into space, is 37.2 metres long, with a wingspan of 23.8 metres. Most of its body consists of a cargo bay.

The Shuttle program suffered a major setback on 28 January 1986 when the shuttle *Challenger* exploded at lift-off, killing all seven people aboard.

Space station In 1971 the Soviet Union launched its first space station, Salyut I. There followed a whole series of Salyuts in which cosmonauts made marathon space-flights. In 1973 the USA launched the Skylab space station which was abandoned the following year. In the future the Soviet Union is expected to launch larger space stations and to keep them permanently occupied.

Spadefoot toad A small toad, about 7 cm long, with a spade-like growth on its hind feet used for digging. It smells of garlic and screams when attacked, digging itself quickly into the sandy soil where it lives.

Spain Country in SW Europe, occupying most of the Iberian Peninsula. Much of Spain is a high, fairly dry plateau, cold in winter, hot in summer. The coastal beaches are popular with holiday-makers, and tourism is an important industry. Many Spaniards live by farming; they grow wheat, barley, potatoes, olives, fruit and vegetables. Sheep and goats thrive better than cattle in this dry land. Spanish wine is an important export, and industry is developing. Minerals include iron, lead, copper and mercury.

During the 1930s Spain was torn by civil war. After years of dictatorship (1939–75), the monarchy and parliamentary government were restored. Spain successfully negotiated entry to the EEC in 1986. Area: 504,742 km^2; Pop: 38,435,000; Cap: Madrid.

Sparrow Small streaky brown birds with pale underparts that look similar to buntings. Sparrows tend to live in large flocks. The two most common European species are the house and tree sparrow.

Sparrowhawk A bird of prey which hunts by patrolling the edges of woods and hedgerows, seizing any small bird, as well as mice, frogs and insects. The plumage is grey above and white beneath.

Species Smallest group classification of animal or plant. All the individuals in a species can interbreed to produce more of the same kind and normally cannot breed with any other species. Related species are grouped into a genus and when the Latin name of a species is used its genus is always put first. The primrose, for example, is *Primula vulgaris*; its close relative the cowslip is *Primula veris*.

Specific gravity The specific gravity of a substance is its density compared with the density of water at 4°C (39°F). If, for example, a substance is three times as dense as water, it has a specific gravity of 3.

Spectrum The word 'spectrum' used to be applied to the band of rainbow colours produced when white light is passed through a prism or a spectroscope. Now the word usually covers the whole ELECTROMAGNETIC spectrum which includes radio waves, X-rays, ultra-violet rays, infra-red rays and gamma rays.

Sphinx Imaginary creature of Egyptian and Greek myth. The winged Greek sphinx had the body of a lion and the head of a woman. She accosted people and would not let them pass until they had answered a riddle. The Egyptian sphinx had the head of a man and the body of a beast. The Great Sphinx at Giza has the features of the Pharaoh Chephren.

Spices Aromatic plant substances used to flavour food. The most popular include pepper, mustard, cinnamon, cloves, nutmeg, ginger, cumin, coriander and turmeric. In India and the East spices have always been part of the cuisine. The early explorers brought the spices home to Europe and soon a great spice trade began, with merchants chartering ships. Today spices are easy to come by and people take them for granted.

Spiders Group of arachnids whose bodies are divided into two parts. At the front they have two poison fangs, two sensory palps and four pairs of legs. At the back they have a silk gland and spinnerets from which they produce fine, sticky gossamer. Garden spiders and others make spectacular ORB-WEBS to catch their prey. WOLF SPIDERS and bird-eating spiders run after theirs. TRAP-DOOR spiders lie in wait under the ground and crab spiders hide inside flowers. The most dangerous spiders are the American BLACK WIDOW and the Australian FUNNEL-WEB spiders, though their bite is rarely fatal.

Spinning Most natural fibres such as cotton and wool are fairly short. To make a continuous strong yarn, the short fibres have to be gathered and twisted together. This is the spinning process. Different types of spinning frame are used, differing mainly in the way they twist and wind the yarn on the bobbin.

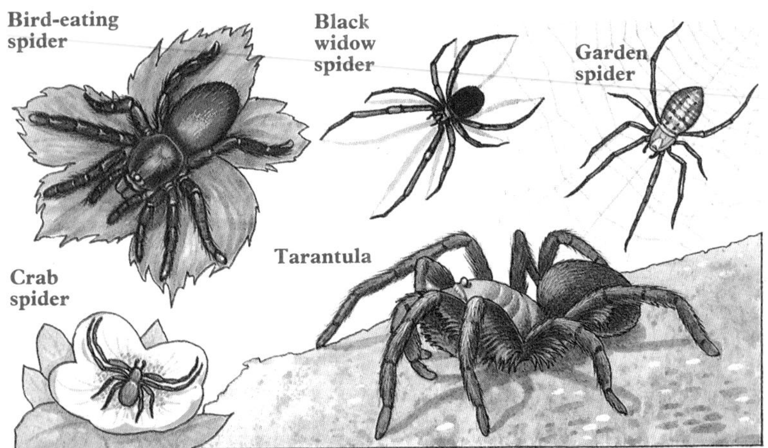

Spiny anteater See **Echidna**

Sponge Simple animals found mainly in warm, shallow seas. Most sponges look like plants but are in fact made up of colonies of tiny animals with sandy or chalky skeletons. Some sponges live singly. They do not move about, and they have neither heads nor limbs. They feed by filtering food particles from the water. Some of the 5000 or so species of sponge live in fresh water.

Spoonbill A large wading bird similar to storks, with long legs and a long flattened bill which ends in a spoon-like tip. The spoonbill uses its bill to hunt for small water creatures, sifting through the mud. Spoonbills are white birds, usually found in swamps and other wet places.

Spore A minute reproductive body that is released by the parent plant and which gives rise, directly or indirectly, to a new individual. Ferns, fungi, and other flowerless plants are scattered far and wide by means of wind-borne spores.

Springbok South African gazelle-like antelope, famous for its stiff-legged leaps into the air when alarmed or simply in play. This is called 'pronking'.

Springtail Primitive wingless insects which get their name from the forked 'spring' at the rear of the body. They can flick this spring downwards and thrust themselves into the air if disturbed. Springtails live mainly among the dead leaves beneath trees.

Spruce Coniferous trees belonging to the pine family. There are about 40 kinds. The Norway spruce is the traditional Christmas tree. The sitka or silver spruce comes from western North America.

Squid Marine cephalopod molluscs related to the octopus and cuttlefish. Squid have eight arms and two long tentacles used to seize prey. They swim rapidly by squirting out jets of water from a siphon tube, and can also hide themselves by giving off a cloud of inky liquid. The largest squids can be 18 metres long.

Squirrel Rodents common to most parts of the world. Some, including the American grey squirrel and the Eurasian red squirrel, are tree-dwellers who make nests called dreys. Others, including marmots, chipmunks and prairie dogs, are ground-livers. In Britain the native red squirrel has virtually been ousted by the grey which was introduced in the 19th century.

Sri Lanka An island state off the SE tip of India, formerly called Ceylon. The landscape is mostly one of rolling plains but there are mountains in the south. The climate is hot, with monsoon rains. Tropical forests cover great areas, and on the hillsides are large plantations of tea. Other crops are rubber, coconuts and cinnamon. Emeralds and rubies are mined. The people of Sri Lanka are Sinhalese and Tamils (from India) and there is conflict between the two. Area: 65,605 km^2; Pop: 15,925,000; Cap: Colombo.

Stalactite An icicle-like growth from the roof of a limestone cavern created by the continuous evaporation of water containing dissolved calcium carbonate. **Stalagmites** are columns of calcium carbonate growing from the floor of a cavern in the same manner.

Stalin, Joseph (1879–1953) Russian revolutionary who assumed power after the death of Lenin in 1924. A ruthless dictator, he rid himself of all his political opponents, and set up a string of forced labour camps that remain to this day. He reorganized the agricultural system on a five year plan basis and led Russia through World War II.

Joseph Stalin

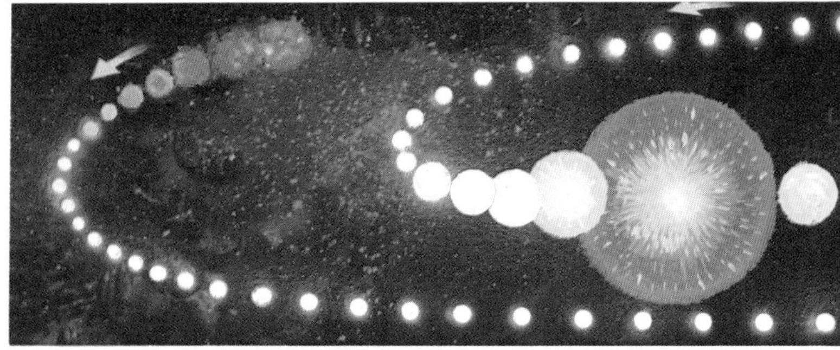

Star A glowing ball of intensely hot gas whose energy is derived from the nuclear fusion of hydrogen atoms to form helium atoms. Stars range in size from giants, 100 times or more the size of the Sun, to dwarfs smaller than the Earth, yet 100,000 times more dense. They also range in colour depending upon their temperature, from bluish-white (the hottest) to red (the coolest). Yellow stars like the Sun are midway between. Two-thirds of all stars have one or more companion stars and many vary in brightness.

Starch Naturally occurring substance produced by plants as a food store, and commonly found in cereals and root vegetables, such as potatoes. Starch is one of the important energy-giving food substances called CARBOHYDRATES. It is also used to stiffen fabrics, and in many industrial processes.

Starfish Named after their star shape, these marine creatures are not fishes at all but echinoderms. They have a series of arms radiating from a central body. Many species have five arms but some have as many as 50. They use the tube-feet on the undersides of their arms to pull apart the shells of oysters and other shellfish on which they feed. If an arm is broken off, the stump can regrow to full size.

Starling A common European bird which forms huge, noisy flocks in the autumn and winter months. At a distance starlings appear black, but close to their feathers gleam with specks of purple and green. On the ground they are easily distinguished because they run, while other songbirds hop. In the past hundred years starlings have taken to living in cities, where they have become a serious pest.

Statistics Facts usually expressed as numbers after analysing a lot of information. For example, if you wanted to know the average height of women in Britain, you could take a random sample of perhaps a hundred women's heights. The average of the hundred would be close to the nation's average. The larger your sample, the closer you are likely to come to the true average.

Steam engine Early steam engines worked with a simple up-and-down movement of a piston in a cylinder. Rods from the piston rotated a wheel. By the early 1800s, steam engines like this started the Industrial Revolution and powered locomotives. Many engines still work on this principle. Modern steam engines are steam TURBINES. In these, the expanding steam spins the blades of a turbine to produce direct rotary movement. A large part of the world's electricity comes from generators powered by steam-driven turbines.

Steel See **Iron**.

Stegosaurus Herbivorous dinosaur of Jurassic period about nine metres long and weighing 1.75 tonnes. A double row of plates ran along its back from its tiny head to its spiked tail. As well as a defence against predators these plates may have conducted heat like radiators.

Stephenson, George (1781–1848) English engineer who invented the steam locomotive (1815). The world's first public passenger train, between Stockton and Darlington in 1825, was drawn by his locomotive *Active* (renamed *Locomotion*). The famous *Rocket* was built for the opening of the Liverpool and Manchester railway in 1830. Stephenson's son **Robert** (1803–59) and nephew **George Robert**

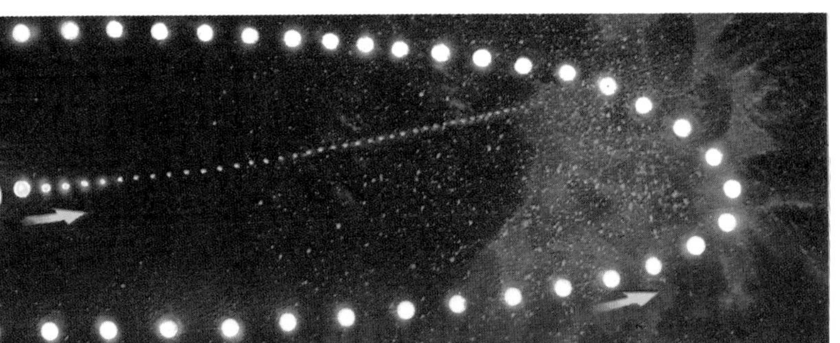

The life history of a star like the sun (above). Born in an interstellar gas cloud, it evolves via stable middle age to become an aged red giant, and finally dies as a white dwarf.

Despite its huge size, Stegosaurus could not have been a very intelligent creature. Its brain was the size of a walnut. With neither wit nor agility, it relied on armour for defence.

(1819–1905) were also notable railway engineers, especially in the construction of railway bridges.

Stevenson, Robert Louis (1850–94) Scottish novelist and poet. Among his most popular novels are: *Treasure Island*, *Kidnapped*, *The Strange Case of Dr Jekyll and Mr Hyde*, and *The Master of Ballantrae*.

Stickleback Small colourful fishes named after the spines on their back, the number of which varies from type to type. Some live in fresh water, others in salty or brackish water. They build nests and the male keeps guard over the young fishes when they hatch.

Stoat Small carnivore related to the weasel found over much of the N hemisphere. It is about 27 cm long with a long tail and short legs. The summer coat is brown, and the winter coat in northern regions is pure white except for a black tip to the tail. The pure white varieties are called ermine and are much prized for their fur.

Stoats

Stockholm Port and capital of Sweden on L. Mälaren and an arm of the Baltic. Industrially, Stockholm developed rapidly during the 19th century and is now a modern, commercial city while retaining the fine medieval buildings of the 'Old Town' adjacent to the Royal Palace. Pop: 649,000.

Stocks and shares When companies need money to develop their business, they sell shares in it. The shareholders are part owners of the company and they benefit when the company's business prospers by an increase in the value of their shares. As well as the value of the shares increasing (or decreasing), the shareholder gets an annual dividend based on the profits the company has made, after allowing for actual costs and future development costs. The number of shares a person owns is known as his stock, and all selling and buying of stock is done through the stock exchange. The first stock exchange was in Belgium in the 16th century. The London stock exchange was established in the 18th century, as was the New York stock exchange on Wall Street.

Stone Age Earliest period of prehistoric man. It is usually divided into the Paleolithic, Mesolithic and Neolithic (Old, Middle and New Stone Age). In the Old Stone Age, which lasted perhaps two million years and ended about 10,000 years ago, the first tool-making human being appeared. Men made simple choppers by chipping flint stones. Mesolithic men made stone axes and arrow heads. In the Neolithic period, village life began, with domestic animals and crops. It ended with the coming of the BRONZE AGE.

Stonehenge Prehistoric monument near Salisbury, England. There are four circles of standing stones, the largest being five metres high and two metres wide. Some were hauled all the way from Wales. Stonehenge dates from between about 2100 BC and 1200 BC; it was rebuilt several times. It probably had some religious purpose, connected with astronomy but no one knows what.

Stork Large birds with long legs and a long neck. They look ungainly in flight, with their necks outstretched and their legs trailing behind them. On the ground they have a slow, graceful gait.

Strauss Family of Austrian musicians. **Johann** the Elder (1804–49) was famed for his Viennese waltzes and was also an able conductor. His son **Johann** the Younger (1825–99) achieved even greater fame with operettas like *Die Fledermaus* and over 150 waltzes, the most famous being *The Blue Danube*. His two brothers, **Josef** and **Eduard**, were also popular conductors and composers.

Strauss, Richard (1864–1949) German composer and conductor who broke new ground with his early work but returned to a more classical style late in his life. His operas include *Salome*, *Elektra* and *Der Rosenkavalier*. He also composed sym-

Stonehenge

phonic poems including *Don Juan* and *Don Quixote*. The moving *Four Last Songs* was his final work.

Stravinsky, Igor (1882–1971) Russian-born composer and pupil of Rimsky-Korsakov. He became a French citizen and then a US citizen in 1945. His music for the ballet *The Rite of Spring* with its strange rhythms and harmonies caused a near riot when first heard in Paris in 1913. Other works include his ballets *The Firebird* and *Petrouchka* and his one opera *The Rake's Progress*.

Stringed instruments Musical instruments which produce sound when their strings are vibrated by being plucked or stroked with a bow. Such instruments include the violin, viola, cello, GUITAR and double bass. Their strings can be made of fibre, metal, animal gut or plastic. Most instruments have a soundboard which amplifies their sound.

Stroboscope An instrument that makes rapidly rotating objects seem to stand still. The stroboscope produces flashes of light timed to synchronize with the rotating object. The eye only sees the object at the instants when it is lit by the flashes. The slower the stroboscope flashes, the slower the rotating machine seems to travel. Stroboscopes are also used to give lighting for high-speed photography.

Stuart, Charles Edward (1720–1788) Also known as Bonnie Prince Charlie and the Young Pretender, he led a rising in 1745 in support of his father, **James Francis Edward Stuart** (1688–1766) the Old Pretender, who held a strong claim to the throne of England. Defeated at Culloden Moor (1746) he escaped to France and died in exile in Rome.

Sturgeon A survivor of a prehistoric group of fishes, which has armour made up of bony plates. It lives at sea but travels up rivers to spawn in fresh water. It grows up to 4 metres long but most individuals are smaller. Eggs from the female form caviar, a great delicacy. Sturgeons are now very rare in western Europe.

Styx In Greek mythology the river flowing round Hades, the underworld.

Submarine Submarines equipped with torpedoes and guns were used effectively against shipping in World Wars I and II. The latest nuclear-powered submarines are the most deadly naval vessels ever built. They can stay at sea for months without refuelling and remain submerged for as long as they wish, beyond the reach of radar detection. And they can fire their guided missiles while submerged at targets over 3000 km away.

Earlier submarines had diesel engines for surface travel and had to charge batteries for underwater power. All submarines have ballast tanks which can be filled with water to make the vessel dive. When they are emptied again, the vessel rises to the surface. As navigating underwater is difficult, submarines now have complex inertial navigation systems.

Sudan Africa's largest country, lying in the NE of the continent. Mostly desert in the north, where the people are Moslem Arabs, Sudan is greener and more fertile in the south, where the people are mostly Christian Blacks. Through the country run the White and Blue Nile Rivers, which join at Khartoum. At one point the Nile forms a vast swamp called the Sudd. Sudan's farmers grow cotton, groundnuts, rice, maize and millet. Area: 2,505,618 km^2; Pop: 21,174,000; Cap: Khartoum.

Suez Canal Major canal connecting the Mediterranean with the Red Sea and the Indian Ocean. It was opened in 1869. The canal was closed from 1967 to 1975 due to the Arab-Israeli war. Length: 163 km.

Sugar Naturally occurring, and generally sweet-tasting carbohydrates, produced by plants during photosynthesis. There are several different types: fructose, found in fruits; sucrose, found in sugar-cane and sugar beet which are commercially grown and refined for the food industry; and glucose, which is found in bread, potatoes and other starchy foods.

Sullivan, Sir Arthur (1842–1900) British composer who is best known for light operas which he wrote together with W.S. Gilbert. Among them are *HMS Pinafore*, *The Pirates of Penzance*, *The Mikado*, *The Gondoliers* and *The Yeomen of the Guard*. Their success has overshadowed his other compositions, which include the oratorio *The Golden Legend*.

Sulphur Non-metallic element that is found around volcanoes. It is yellow, insoluble in water, and burns with a pungent smell. Sulphur is used in the manufacture of matches, gunpowder and, above all, sulphuric acid which is widely used in industry. Chem. symbol S.

Sun Our nearest star, a giant powerhouse in which the conversion of hydrogen atoms to helium atoms by nuclear fusion generates vast amounts of energy. The surface of the Sun is sometimes marked by sunspots, dark patches of cooler gas. It is also swept by storms called flares that fling hot gas into space. Diameter: 1,390,000 km; distance from Earth: 149,000,000 km; temperature: 6000°C (surface), 15,000,000°C (core).

Supersonic flight When an aircraft travels faster than the speed of sound a pressure disturbance builds up just ahead of the plane. This is called a *shock wave* and people on the ground can hear a *sonic boom* as the aircraft crosses the sound barrier.

Surface tension A force that causes liquids to behave as though an elastic film covered their surfaces. It is because of surface tension that drops of liquid take a nearly spherical shape. Surface tension also makes it possible for the surface of water to support carefully-placed needles and in nature the weight of a pondskater. Surface tension is caused by the fact that surface molecules are attracted to the molecules below and beside them more strongly than to the air above the surface. This pulls them together to make a layer that resists being broken.

Surgery An operation to mend faulty or injured parts inside the body. Surgery has been practised since ancient times but the introduction of anaesthetics and antiseptics in the 19th century led to great improvements in techniques. Today, with the advance of microsurgery, it is possible to replace severed limbs and replace vital organs such as the heart.

Surinam Small country in NE South America, part of the Guiana region. Chief products are bauxite (aluminium ore), sugar, fruit and rice. Timber is also important. Area: 163,253 km^2; Pop: 370,000; Cap: Paramaribo.

Surveying The science of determining the relative position of points on the Earth's surface. Surveyors measure horizontal and vertical distances and the angle of one fixed point from another. The results are calculated using TRIGONOMETRY and can be used to prepare maps etc. Aerial surveying is called photogrammetry.

Swallow A graceful, streamlined bird whose arrival in Europe every spring is generally seen as heralding the summer. The birds spend much of their time on the wing catching insects, and rarely land on the ground, preferring to perch on telegraph wires or buildings. They build their nests on, or preferably in, buildings.

Temperatures at the Sun's core (right) are probably about 15,000,000°C.

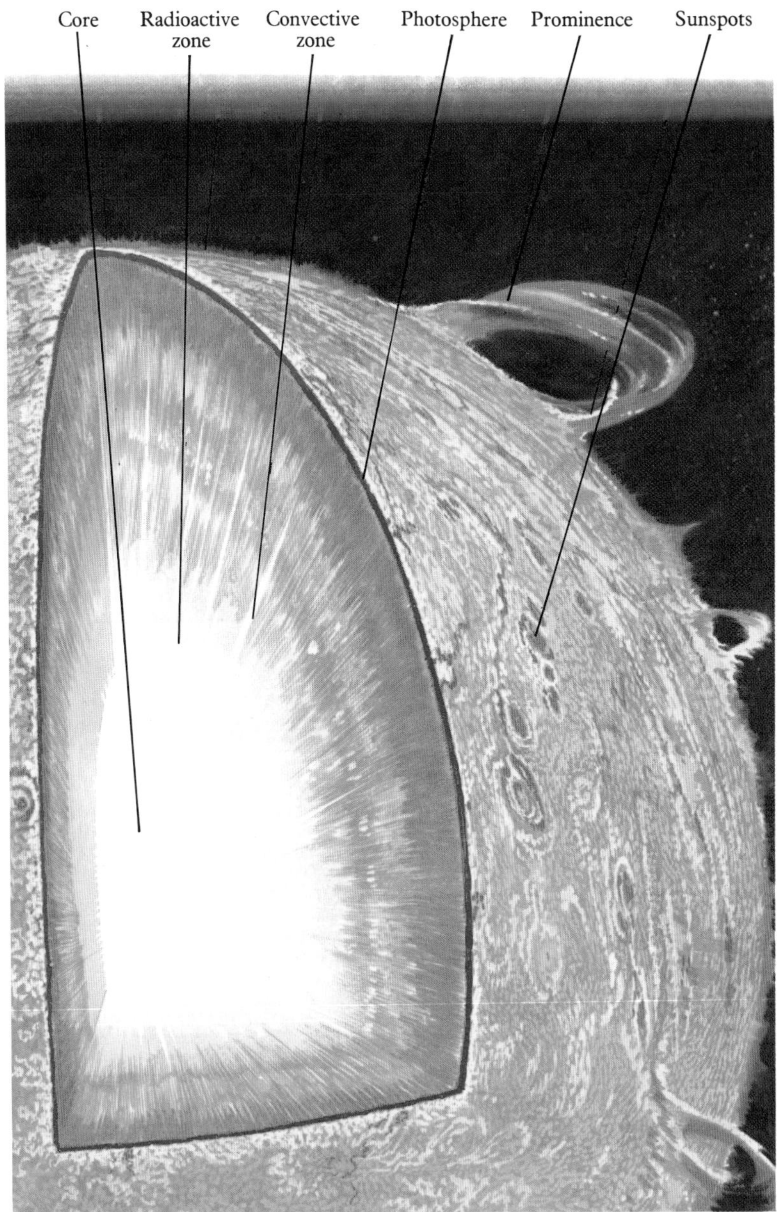
Core
Radioactive zone
Convective zone
Photosphere
Prominence
Sunspots

Swan Large water birds, belonging to the duck family, with elegant long necks. Swans are powerful birds and strong fliers. They have webbed feet for swimming and feed on water plants and animals. The common mute swan and the rarer Bewick's and whooper swans are white. The black swan of Australia is a popular ornamental species. Mute swans are also often seen in parks and water gardens. Pairs mate for life and guard their young, called cygnets, with great care.

Swaziland Country in southern Africa bordered by South Africa and Mozambique. Main crops are sugar, fruits and cotton. Asbestos, coal and iron are mined. Area: 17,362 km^2; Pop: 651,000; Cap: Mbabane.

Sweden Country in N Europe, part of Scandinavia. Much of Sweden has a harsh climate, with cold winters and short summers. Most of the land is not ideal for farming, but cereals, potatoes and root crops are grown. Sweden's wealth lies in its forest, its minerals, and its water power which provides electricity for factories. Manufactured goods, including paper, electrical machinery and vehicles, together with iron ore and wood pulp, are the major exports, and have combined to give Sweden one of the highest standards of living in the world. Area: 450,000 km^2; Pop: 8,335,000; Cap: Stockholm.

Swift Fast-flying, streamlined birds which catch their food on the wing. The common swift has a dark brown plumage with a white throat, and a forked tail. It winters in southern Africa and visits Europe from April to October. Swifts are among the fastest fliers of all birds.

Swift, Jonathan (1667–1745) Irish-born satirical writer who is best known for his *Gulliver's Travels* and *Tale of a Tub*. He was a clergyman from 1694, and became Dean of St Patrick's, Dublin in 1713, after many years in England. He also wrote political pamphlets including the *Drapier's Letters*.

Swimming Pastime and competitive sport, with races from 100 metres to long-distance forming part of the Olympic Games. Various strokes are used in swimming: the fastest is the freestyle crawl, followed by the butterfly, back-stroke and breast-stroke.

Switzerland Small landlocked country in central Europe, enclosed by mountains including the Alpine and Jura ranges. Despite having few resources, Switzerland has become prosperous and is a major financial centre. Tourists come to enjoy its scenery and winter sports. Its factories produce high-quality goods, such as watches, and its valley farms produce dairy products.

Surrounded by countries which have fought many wars, Switzerland has remained at peace. Because of its neutrality international organizations such as the Red Cross and some UN agencies have chosen to work from Switzerland. The people speak German, French, Italian and Romansch. Area: 41,284 km^2; Pop: 6,477,000; Cap: Berne.

Swordfish Two to three-metre long silver and blue fish with a high dorsal fin and elongated sword-like 'beak' that is one-third of its length.

Sycamore A deciduous tree, native to southern and central Europe but now widely distributed further north. It belongs to the maple family and grows up to 35 metres tall. The bark is smooth and grey when young but becomes scaly as it gets older. The fruits consist of two winged seeds joined together.

Sydney Largest city in Australia, situated around Port Jackson Bay. It was founded by the British as a convict settlement in 1788, the first in Australia. Site of the famous Sydney Harbour Bridge and opera house. Pop: 3,281,000 (met area).

Synthetic fibres These are fibres made entirely from chemicals. Nylon, for example, is made from benzene (from coal), nitrogen, oxygen and hydrogen. Chips of the plastic are melted and forced through spinnerets to produce fibres of varying thickness. Fabrics can be made entirely from synthetic fibres or they can be made from mixtures of natural and synthetic yarn to produce material which is crease-resistant and strong.

Syria Country at eastern end of the Mediterranean Sea, bordered by Lebanon, Jordan, Iraq and Turkey. It is a dry land, with only two large rivers, the Orontes and Euphrates. The best farmland is along the coast or where irrigation is possible. Despite its dryness, crops of cereals, fruit, grapes, olives, tobacco and cotton are grown. Textiles is a traditional industry, oil refining a modern one. Area: 185,165 km^2; Pop: 10,154,000; Cap: Damascus.

T

Table tennis Game originally called ping-pong, played indoors. The playing area is a table, with a net across it. The ball is made of celluloid or some similar plastic, and the players use round bats covered with sponge and rubber. Table tennis became popular in the early 1900s, and is now played worldwide. The Chinese are exceptionally good players.

Tadpole The fish-like young of frogs, toads or newts. A tadpole has no legs at first, and swims by waving its tail. Legs gradually develop and the tadpole turns into the adult form and leaves the water. At the same time the animal must change from breathing with gills to breathing air with its lungs.

Tahiti Chief island of French Polynesia, in the Society Islands group. Mountainous island with a fertile coastal belt, and site of admin capital of the group, Papeete.

Taiwan Island off the mainland of China. Since 1949, Taiwan (formerly Formosa) has been the home of the Republic of China. The people grow rice, tea and sugar but live chiefly by working in businesses and factories. Taiwan exports many manufactured goods, from television to textiles. Area: 36,000 km^2; Pop: 18,000,000; Cap: Taipei.

Taj Mahal Building at Agra, India, which some say is the most beautiful building in the world, especially by moonlight. It was built in 1632–53 by the Emperor Shah Jahan as a memorial to his wife, Mumtaz Mahal. The marble surfaces are richly decorated with precious stones.

Tanks Heavily armoured fighting vehicles which run on caterpillar tracks. Tanks were first introduced in World War I and played a major part in the German invasion of France in World War II. There are several types of tank, but they are normally armed with a large shell-firing gun and one or more machine guns.

Tanzania Country in E Africa, including parts of the huge lakes, Victoria, Tanganyika and Malawi-Nyasa, and Africa's highest mountain, Kilimanjaro (5895 metres). The interior highlands are cool and fertile, the coastal plain bordering the Indian Ocean hot and humid. Chief crops are cashew nuts, cloves, tea, oilseeds, cotton, sisal and coffee. Diamonds are mined, and industry and tourism are developing. Area: 945,013 km^2; Pop: 21,048,000; Cap: Dodoma.

Tape recorder A machine capable of recording sound on a plastic tape coated with magnetic iron oxide or chromium oxide. During recording and replay, the tape is made to move past record and playback heads. The heads are electromagnets which become magnetized when electric currents pass through them. In recording, the signals from the microphone magnetize the record head. This magnetizes the iron-oxide particles in the tape. The sound waves are therefore 'fixed' on the tape. In playback, the reverse process takes place.

The Leopard and the M1 tanks will be in service with NATO well into the twenty-first century.

American M1

German Leopard 2

Tapestry Material woven on a loom using coloured threads. Tapestries often form large pictures used for wall-hangings. They were known in the ancient East as well as Greece and Rome, and in the Europe of the Middle Ages were used to decorate large houses and churches. The main home of the art was France. Famous tapestries were made at Arras and at the Gobelins' factory in Paris. The Bayeux Tapestry is not a tapestry at all, but a work of embroidery.

Tapeworm Parasitic worm which lives in the gut of many animals, including humans. The tapeworm fastens itself by hooks or suckers on its head to the gut wall of its host and takes in food through its skin, since it has no mouth. Tapeworms look like long white ribbons, the longest ones being 15 metres in length.

Tapir Stocky pig-like mammal of horse family with short snout. It lives deep in forests of tropical America and SE Asia, and feeds on plants by night.

Tarantula Popular name for any large hairy spider and particularly of the bird-eating spider of S America. This creature is over 20 cm wide. Its bite is fatal to small animals but only painful to humans. The true tarantula is a wolf spider from near Taranto in Italy. When bitten, local people are said to have performed a frenzied dance called a tarantella.

Tarsier Tree-living primates of the Philippines and East Indies with sucker-like discs on its hands that aid climbing. Active at night, the animals have huge eyes and ears.

Tasmania Island off south-eastern Australia and the country's smallest state. It was named Van Diemen's Land in 1642 by the Dutch navigator Abel Tasman, but it was renamed Tasmania in 1856.

Tasmanian wolf Australian dog-like, carnivorous marsupial whose proper name is the *Thylacine*. Almost extinct, a few individuals survive in Tasmania.

Taste See **Senses**

Taxation Money raised by a government in the form of charges on people's income, the goods they buy or the services they use. There are various forms of taxes. Income tax is levied on what a person earns. Value-added tax is charged on goods and services. Customs duties are taxes paid on goods brought into one country from another. By imposing taxes, the government collects money to pay for roads, hospitals, defence, power stations and so on. Rates are a form of local taxation levied on property owners.

Tchaikovsky, Peter Ilyich (1840–93) Russian composer whose emotional music enjoys world-wide popularity. His most famous works include the opera *Eugene Onegin*; the ballets *Swan Lake, Sleeping Beauty* and *The Nutcracker*; as well as orchestral compositions, including his violin concerto, the great fifth and sixth symphonies, his piano concerto No. 1, the *Romeo and Juliet* fantasy and the popular *1812* overture.

The map shows the continually moving plates into which the Earth's crust is cracked.

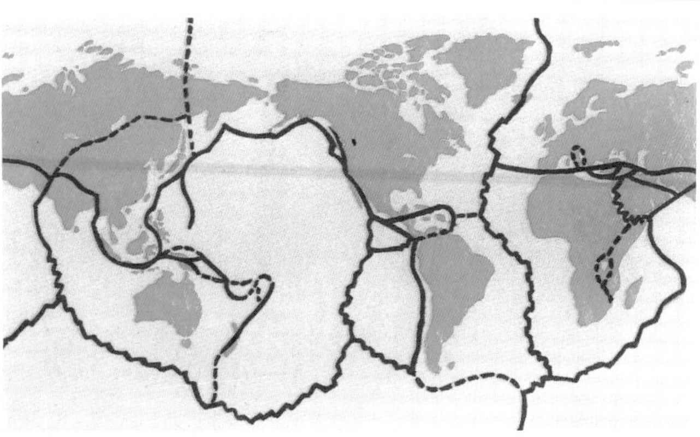

Tea Shrub native to China and cultivated in India, Sri Lanka, Japan and elsewhere in Asia. The young leaves are harvested for use in tea, an aromatic beverage that was introduced to Britain in the 17th century and became the national drink.

Teak Large hardwood tree of southern Asia, growing up to 45 metres tall. Cultivated for its strong, oily timber which is used extensively to make furniture.

Teal Small duck with several species found worldwide. The common teal is the smallest European duck. It lives on lakes and ponds, often moving away from the water to breed.

Tectonic plates Large, rigid sections of the Earth's crust comprising continents, continental shelves and the ocean crust. The plates rest on the dense mantle underlying the crust where convection currents in the semi-fluid rock cause them to move apart or crumple together. Where plate edges move apart (e.g. Mid-Atlantic Ridge) magma rises to plug the gap and creates new rock. Where the plate edges collide (e.g. off the west coast of N and S America) one plate is forced down beneath the other and crustal rock is destroyed by heat. The movement of tectonic plates is responsible for mountain building, earthquakes and volcanoes.

Teeth Teeth are made of a bony substance called dentine, inside which is a small cavity, the pulp cavity, containing nerves and blood vessels. A layer of enamel covers and protects the crown (visible part) of the tooth. The root is embedded in the gum. Different animals have different kinds of teeth, depending on what they eat. Humans have incisors (chisel-shaped teeth) at the front, with stabbing teeth called canines at the sides and grinding teeth, premolars and molars, at the back. Most herbivores have more grinding teeth and carnivores more ripping and cutting teeth.

A section through a molar, one of the grinding teeth at the back of the mouth.

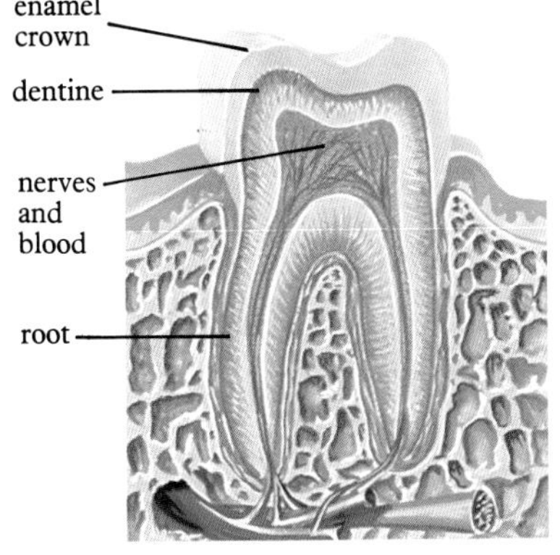

Tehran Capital of Iran, situated on southern slopes of Elburz Mts. It has grown rapidly since World War II into an important modern city. Pop: 4,496,000.

Tel-Aviv-Yafo City and leading financial centre of Israel, situated on the Mediterranean. It was here that the state of Israel was proclaimed in 1948. Pop: 339,000.

Telegraph Means of sending messages in the form of electrical impulses by radio or wire. The first machine built employed a pointer and a dial to indicate the letters transmitted. Samuel Morse later made a device that employed a pen to make a letter code on paper. Today telegraphs are received by machines (teleprinters) in printed form and even pictures can be transmitted on facsimile machines.

Telephone Device invented by Alexander Bell in 1876 for sending messages by wire or radio. The handset is both transmitter and receiver. A metal disc called a diaphragm vibrates as we speak. Behind it is a 'cup' of carbon grains. As varying pressure from the sound waves hits the diaphragm, so the grains are squeezed. An electrical current passing through them becomes weak or strong according to their pressure and exactly copies the voice. At the receiving end the impulses of the current are converted back to speech by means of an electromagnet which causes another diaphragm to vibrate. Millions of telephone cables criss-cross the nations around the world. Increasingly, signals are sent via satellite.

Telescope An instrument that makes distant objects seem nearer. It does this by forming an image of the distant object and then magnifying this image. Telescopes are used mainly by astronomers and there are two main kinds of astronomical telescope. *Refracting* telescopes were invented first. They are basically a tube with a large convex lens at one end and a smaller magnifying lens at the other. The distance between the two lenses can be adjusted to focus the telescope.

The *reflecting* telescope has a large concave mirror at one end which collects the light from the star or planet and reflects it on to a mirror farther up the tube. This second mirror then reflects the light through the eyepiece

Most large astronomical telescopes are of the reflecting type.

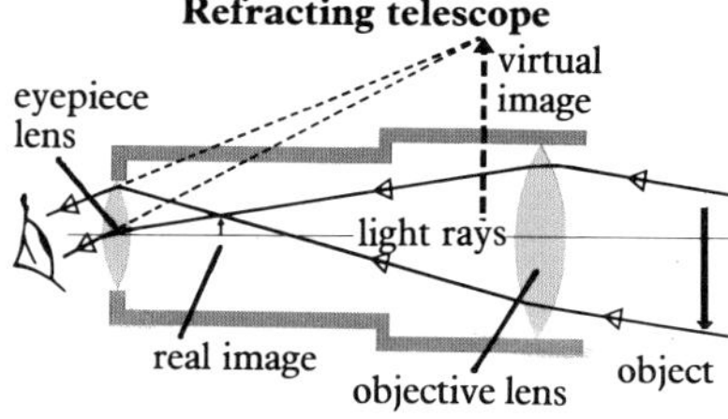

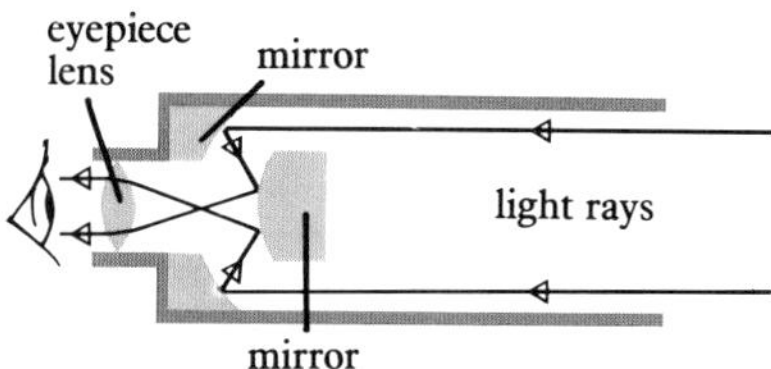

Television A colour television camera produces three separate vision signals, one each for the red, green, and blue light from whatever is being filmed. These signals are sent out as radio waves and are picked up by television aerials. The three signals go into the receiver, which has three electron guns, and these guns scan the screen, one for each colour. The whole screen – the end of a cathode-ray tube – is made up of a mosaic of dots or stripes of phosphor that glow red, green or blue when struck by the electron beams. The beams scan the screen in the same sequence of lines as the camera in the studio, and build up a picture on the screen. A new picture is produced 25 or 30 times a second, so that the image appears to move.

Tell, William Legendary Swiss hero who was forced by Gessler, the Austrian governor, to shoot an apple off the head of his son. Killing Gessler in revenge, he sparked off a revolt which supposedly led to the founding of the 14th-century Swiss Confederation.

Temperature A measure of the 'hotness' of something; not the amount of heat it possesses. A large mass of a substance at a low temperature may have much more heat energy than a small hot mass. There are two main scales of temperature – Celsius (centigrade) and Fahrenheit. In the Celsius scale the boiling point of water is 100° and the freezing point 0°. In the Fahrenheit scale water boils at 212° and freezes at 32°.

Ten Commandments Religious laws given to Moses by God and followed by Jews and Christians alike. Briefly, they forbid: the worship of other gods (1), or idols (2), and profaning the name of God (3). They enjoin: keeping the sabbath (4) and respect for parents (5). They forbid murder (6), adultery (7), theft (8), lying (9) and desire for one's neighbour's goods (10).

Tennis Popular racket game, played both indoors and outdoors, on a court which may be laid out on grass, cement, wood or artificial matting. Also known as lawn tennis, modern tennis developed from an ancient ball game played in the Middle Ages. This game is called real (or royal) tennis, and is still played. There is a court at Hampton Court near London, built by King Henry VIII. Lawn tennis was invented around 1860 in England. In 1877 the first Wimbledon championships (now the most famous in the world) took place.

Tennyson, Alfred, Lord (1809–92) English poet and laureate from 1850. His best known poems include *In Memoriam* (written after the death of his friend Arthur Hallam), *The Charge of the Light Brigade* and *Idylls of the King* which consists of 12 long poems based on the legend of King Arthur.

Termite Tropical insect related to cockroaches (though often called a white ant). Termites live in mud nests that rise as high as six metres from the ground and become rock-hard. Inside is a teeming colony of workers, soldiers, a king and a fat queen who is no more than an egg-laying machine. Termites feed on wood and can swiftly destroy timber.

Tern Seabirds also known as sea swallows because of their pointed wings and forked tails. Terns are smaller than gulls, mostly white or grey, with dark heads. They nest in large colonies on rocks or sand dunes.

Terrapin Mostly aquatic reptile closely related to the tortoise, but distinguished from it by its flatter shell and webbed toes. It always lives in or near water, eating fishes, frogs and other small pond creatures.

Texas Second largest state (after Alaska) and third in population, Texas is the USA's leading mining state and has huge reserves of oil and natural gas. It is also a major farming state, with beef cattle the most valuable source of farming income. Area: 692,402 km²; Pop: 14,229,000; Cap: Austin.

Textiles Woven or knitted fabrics. The first process in textile-making is SPINNING, which turns the fibre into yarn. The yarn is then woven into cloth on a loom or knitted. The traditional materials are wool, silk, cotton and linen, but today many artificial fibres are made from wood, coal and oil.

Thailand Country in SE Asia, formerly called Siam. Thailand is a hilly, forested land with a fertile river valley, the Chao Phraya and, to the east, a drier plateau. Chief crops are rice, maize and rubber. Tin and tungsten are mined, and there is natural gas offshore. The forests yield valuable timber. Thailand is an ancient Buddhist kingdom. Area: 513,961 km²; Pop: 51,724,000; Cap: Bangkok.

Thames Principal river of England, flowing from the Cotswold Hills through London to North Sea. The Thames estuary is a major industrial area. Length: 340 km.

Theatre Place where dramatic or musical performances are given. In the open-air theatres of ancient Greece, the chorus performed on a space called the orchestra. Behind was the skene, where the actors, wearing tragic or comic masks, awaited their cue. The first modern theatres, built in the 16th century, had jutting stages around which the audience sat or stood. Later a frame called a *proscenium arch* was placed around the stage and the audience sat in front. Many modern theatres have returned to being 'in the round', with space for the audience on three sides of the stage.

Theresa, Mother (1919–) Albanian RC nun famed for her work among the poor and dying of Calcutta and for the order of nuns she founded.

Thermometer An instrument for measuring the temperature. Most thermometers consist of a fine glass tube containing a liquid such as coloured alcohol or mercury. As the liquid expands or contracts with the rise or fall of temperature, it moves up or down the tube. Thermometers can be calibrated in either Celsius or Fahrenheit scales.

Thermostat An automatic device that controls temperature. Most thermostats are made of two strips of different metals sandwiched together. One metal expands more than the other when heated. As the temperature increases, the metal that expands more grows longer and pushes the whole strip into a curve. This makes the strip move away from an electric contact, switching off the electricity. When the temperature falls, the reverse process takes place and the electricity is switched on to produce more heat.

Third World Countries which suffer from poverty and lack of industrial development. Since the INDUSTRIAL REVOLUTION the countries of the world have been more sharply divided by wealth. The most prosperous are the manufacturing nations (such as West Germany and Japan) and the two 'super-powers' (USA and USSR). Next come developing nations, such as Brazil, with natural resources that are only just being tapped. At the bottom, in terms of wealth, are the countries of the Third World, where hunger, poverty and disease are serious problems. Third World countries (such as Ethiopia) need help from abroad, particularly in times of drought and famine. Sadly, the gap between rich and poor nations is widening, as the rich nations develop new technologies (such as computers) beyond the means of their poorer neighbours.

Thirty Years' War (1618–48) European war fought mostly in Germany. It began as a conflict between Protestant and Catholic interests but became a political struggle between the two greatest powers, France and the Holy Roman Empire. By the end of the war, the ambitions of the Emperor had been checked and France was on the threshold of her period of greatest glory.

Thistle A large group of flowering plants belonging to the daisy family. Most thistles have very spiny stems and leaves. Their composite flowerheads are usually purple and brush-like. The flower is the emblem of Scotland.

Thomas à Becket, Saint (1118–70) Archbishop of Canterbury from 1162. He resisted Henry II's attempts to extend state control over the Church and in 1164 he fled to France. He later returned and was murdered by Henry's knights in Canterbury Cathedral.

Thrush Common garden birds related to blackbirds and robins. The two most common European species are the song thrush and the mistle thrush.

Thunderstorm A storm associated with towering, anvil-headed cumulonimbus clouds, thunder and lightning and often torrential rain. Thunderstorms are most violent in the tropics, where rapid heating of the land in the morning leads to strong updraughts of moist air in the afternoon and the onset of thunderstorms.

Lightning is a giant spark that reaches from cloud to earth. It occurs when a negative and a positive electric charge meet.

Thylacine See **Tasmanian wolf**

Tibet A region in central Asia known as the 'roof of the world'. It is a barren, windswept plateau averaging 4850 metres above sea level, bounded on all sides by even higher mountain ranges. Hardy crops can be grown in sheltered valleys and the long-haired yak is the chief domestic animal. Since 1951 Tibet has been part of China; its former ruler the Dalai Lama has lived in exile since 1959.

Tick A group of tiny parasites related to mites and spiders. Mammals and birds may be infested with these parasites which suck their blood and also spread disease. Ticks lay their eggs on plants and the young larvae cling on to passing animals.

Tides The regular rise and fall in the level of the sea caused by the gravitational pulls of the Moon and, to a lesser extent, the Sun. When the Sun and Moon are in line their gravitational pulls combine to produce very high (spring) tides. When the Sun

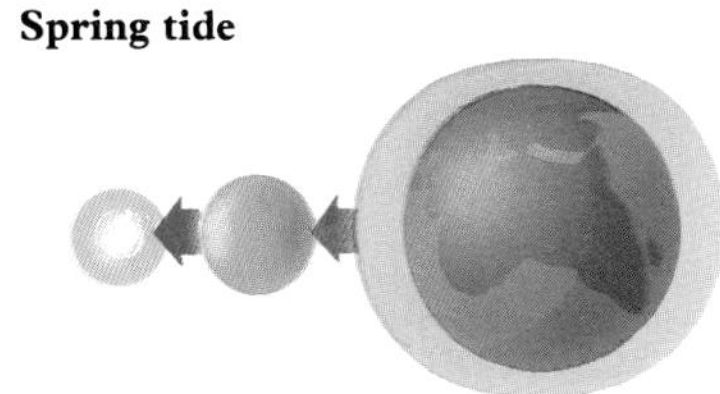

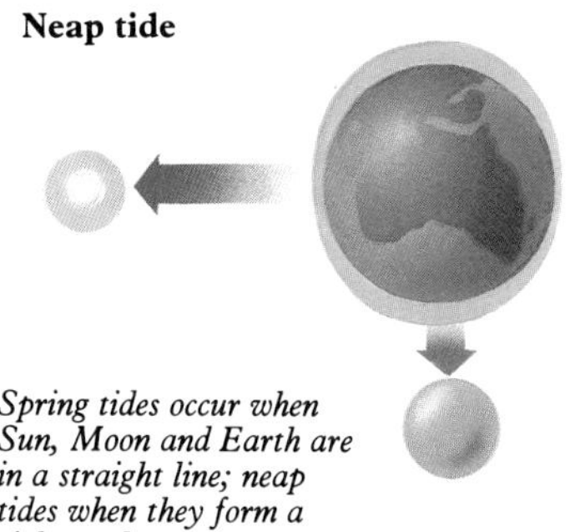

Spring tides occur when Sun, Moon and Earth are in a straight line; neap tides when they form a right angle.

and Moon are pulling at right angles, low (neap) tides occur. There are roughly two tides per day regulated by the rotation of the Earth.

Tiger Large striped Asian cats. The largest, the Siberian tiger, may reach four metres in length but the others are smaller. Powerful animals, they prey on deer, antelopes, cattle and (rarely) humans.

Time zones So that all places will experience 'daytime' as the hours of light and 'night-time' as those of darkness, the Earth is divided into time zones. When you travel from east to west you advance your watch one hour each time you enter a new zone. At the International Date Line the clock time goes back 24 hours – you lose a day – to make up for the difference.

The tiger is the largest and fiercest predator in Asia. It occupies the same ecological niche as the lion in Africa and the jaguar in South and Central America.

Jaguar

Tiger

Lion

Tin Soft, white metal which is unaffected by air and water under normal conditions. It is widely used for plating thin sheet steel (the tinplate of food cans) and in many alloys including solder, bronze and pewter. Chem. symbol Sn (Latin *stannum*).

Tintoretto (1518–94) Venetian painter who concentrated on religious subjects. Many of his canvases are of enormous size and include *The Origin of the Milky Way*.

Tit A family of bright, perky little birds, also called titmice. Some 65 species are found in woodlands and gardens. Tits nest in holes in trees and eat mainly seeds and insects. They hunt together in large flocks after the breeding season and are acrobatic birds, readily hanging upside down from bags of nuts put out for them in gardens.

Titanium Scarce metal which combines lightness and strength with resistance to corrosion. Titanium alloys are used in the construction of aircraft and rockets. Titanium dioxide is a white pigment used in paint. Chem. symbol Ti.

Titian (*c* 1490–1576) Italian Master and head of the Venetian School. His works, influenced by Giorgione, are full of warmth and colour and include *Bacchus and Ariadne* and *Sacred and Profane Love*.

Spadefoot toad

Toad A tailless amphibian related to the frogs. Common toads live in fairly dry places, hiding by day and feeding at night on slugs and other small animals. When alarmed they inflate their bodies to make themselves look bigger.

Tobacco Plant of S and C American origin from which cigarettes, cigars, snuff and pipe tobacco come. It belongs to the nightshade family and its leaves contain an addictive poison called nicotine. It is said to have been introduced into Europe by Sir Walter Raleigh. An important crop in the USA, China, India and USSR, and in Cuba and Jamaica, it is now declining because of the discovery that cigarette smoking can damage health. Smokers have greater risk of developing lung cancer and heart disease than non-smokers.

Tobogganing Winter sport in which people race down icy tracks on sleds or toboggans. The most famous toboggan run is the Cresta Run in Switzerland. The toboggan is called a skeleton, and is ridden head-first. The two other forms of toboggan are the luge (which is ridden feet-first) and the bobsled (which carries two or four riders seated inside a streamlined body). A bobsled can travel at more than 140 km an hour.

Togo Small country in W Africa, sandwiched between Ghana and Benin. The climate is tropical, and rainforest or savanna grasslands cover most of the country. The people are mostly farmers, and cocoa and coffee are the chief crops. Phosphates are the principal export. Area: 55,997 km^2; Pop: 2,927,000; Cap: Lomé.

Tokyo Port and capital of Japan, in central Honshu. Major financial and industrial centre. Owing to its location on marshy ground, expansion of the city requires expensive land reclamation. Pop: 8,494,000.

Tolstoy, Leo (1828–1910) Russian writer, social reformer and moral philosopher. His great novels include *War and Peace* and *Anna Karenina*. An idealistic man, who did not always practise what he preached, Tolstoy offended the government, the Church and his wife. An ardent lover of liberty, he freed the serfs on his estate and started a school for their children. After an extravagant youth, he decided to lead a good and simple life and give away his wealth. Finally at the age of 82 he left home – only to die a few days later.

Tomato Plant of the nightshade family which originated in Central America and was introduced into Europe in the 16th century. The fruit is rich in vitamins A and C, and in iron.

Tonga Country in the Pacific Ocean, also known as the Friendly Islands. Tonga's 169 islands are volcanic or coral in origin. The people grow bananas and coconuts. Copra is the main product, and there is some tourism. Area: 699 km^2; Pop: 105,000; Cap: Nuku'alofa.

Tornado A small but intense storm in which winds of up to 500 km/h whirl around a funnel of low pressure. Tornadoes range in size from a few metres to a kilometre or more across. They occur chiefly in central USA and can cause enormous damage, flattening buildings in their path.

Toronto Canada's second largest city, located on Lake Ontario. Formerly named York, it was renamed Toronto in 1834. Pop: 633,000.

Tortoise Shelled reptile renowned for slowness and longevity. The Giant tortoise of the Galapagos may reach over 1.5 metres in length and live over 150 years. Smaller tortoises from southern Europe and N Africa are popular pets. They need proper care in cool climates and a warm place in which to hibernate. When frightened or resting they withdraw their legs and head into their shell.

Toucan Large boldly coloured S American birds with enormous bills, which probably play a role in courtship. They gather in small flocks in tropical forests and feed on fruit.

Trade unions Organizations of workers formed to seek better pay and conditions, by bargaining with employers. Trade unions began in the 1800s during the INDUSTRIAL REVOLUTION, and helped to spread the ideas of SOCIALISM. Today, many people belong to trade unions: teachers, miners, shop-workers, transport workers and civil servants are just a few examples. If a trade union is in dispute with an employer, it may ask its members to strike.

Transformer Transformers are devices for increasing or decreasing electrical voltage. Most have two separate coils of wire wound around a common iron core. The current to be increased or decreased in voltage goes through the *primary coil*. The new voltage comes from the *secondary coil*. If the secondary coil has more turns than the primary, the voltage is increased. Transformers play an important part in radio and television sets and other electronic apparatus. Large transformers are also used in electric power supply.

Transistor The modern age in electronics began in 1948 when the transistor was invented. It is a device that amplifies minute electric currents and superseded the thermionic valve in radio and television equipment. Transistors are made out of special crystals containing impurities. These are SEMICONDUCTORS such as silicon and germanium. Thousands of transistors can now be incorporated in a tiny wafer of silicon. All the circuitry for a television set or a computer can easily be placed on a few of these 'chips'.

Trapdoor spider Large hairy spiders of various hot regions. They live in a tunnel in the soil, fitted with a silk door. The spider sits below the door, peeping out. When its prey passes it pounces and drags the victim into the tunnel.

Tree A large woody plant with just one main trunk. The largest-living things in the world are trees. There are two main kinds: broad-leaved trees and needle-leaved trees. Broad-leaved trees, such as oaks and elms, have flowers, broad, flat leaves and their seeds are enclosed in a seed case. Nearly all of them are deciduous. Needle-leaved trees are evergreen. They have sharp pointed leaves and cones instead of flowers. Their seeds are 'naked'. They include conifers such as firs and pines.

Treecreeper Small tit-sized birds, brown in colour like the bark of the trees on which they spend their lives. They feed almost entirely on insects which live in tree bark. Treecreepers run up, but not down, tree trunks.

Tree kangaroo Agile tree-dwelling marsupials of Australia and New Guinea, with long, thin, furry tails.

Trigonometry A branch of mathematics that deals with the sides and angles of triangles and how they are related. It is used to measure things which are out of reach such as distances to the stars, the heights of mountains and tall buildings. Trigonometry is useful because it is based on facts that are true of all triangles – they all have three sides and their angles always add up to 180°.

Trilobite Extinct marine shelled arthropods whose bodies are in three lobes. Their FOSSILS are found mostly in Cambrian rocks.

Trinidad and Tobago These two rugged islands form a country in the eastern Caribbean Sea. Their climate is tropical, and fruit, cocoa, coffee and sugar-cane are grown. Oil and asphalt are the chief products. Tourism is also important. Area: 5,128 km²; Pop: 1,167,000; Cap: Port of Spain.

Oak
English elm
Mimosa
Rowan
Silver birch
Beech
Norway spruce
Cedar of Lebanon
Monkey puzzle
Yew
Leyland cypress
Coast redwood

Trojan War Legendary war which is the subject of the *Iliad* by Homer, the 'father' of European literature. The Greeks besiege Troy to regain Helen, wife of one of their leaders, who has been carried off by Paris, son of King Priam of Troy. After ten years, they break into the city by a trick, inside a giant wooden horse.

Trollope, Anthony (1815–82) English novelist who spent his career working for the post office. His 'Barsetshire' novels are the most famous, including *Barchester Towers, Doctor Thorne* and *The Last Chronicle of Barset*, but he also wrote a political series known as 'The Pallisers'.

Tropical cyclones Huge, revolving storms called hurricanes and typhoons in different parts of the world. Winds up to 300 km/h spiral round a central vortex or 'eye' of low pressure. Tropical cyclones bring havoc to islands and low-lying coastlands, partly through the high winds but far more because of the floods they cause.

From above, you can see the calm eye of the hurricane and the whirling vortex of winds around it.

Trotsky, Leon (1879–1940) Russian revolutionary who became commissar for foreign affairs under Lenin. For a time he took a leading role in the conferences at Brest-Litovsk (1917/18), which later ended the war with Germany. But he opposed Stalin's policies and was dismissed from the Communist party in 1927. He went into exile and was assassinated in Mexico.

Trout Fast-swimming fishes of salmon family. Varieties include the sea, brown, and lake trout and the rainbow trout which is native to N America but has been introduced to Europe where it is extensively fished and farmed for food. The sea trout migrates to the sea to feed but returns to fresh water to breed.

Troy Ancient city of Asia Minor in NW Turkey near the Dardanelles. Excavations by archaeologists have found the ruins of several cities at this site. Each was destroyed by fire or earthquake and a new city built on the ruins. Legendary Troy was a mighty city besieged by the Greeks in the TROJAN WAR.

Truffle Member of a group of edible fungi that have underground fruiting bodies shaped like potatoes. Truffles are a highly prized delicacy in cooking.

Tsetse fly African blood-sucking fly which carries a parasitic protozoan (trypanosome). As it sucks the blood it infects its victim with the parasite, causing a disease called nagana in cattle and sleeping sickness in humans.

Tuatara A burrowing lizard-like animal that is the sole living representative of a group of prehistoric reptiles. It can live over a hundred years but survives only on a few islands in the Cook Strait in New Zealand.

Tuna See **Tunny**

Tundra Low-lying treeless plains around the Arctic Ocean in N America, N Europe and Siberia. The ground is frozen to a great depth (permafrost) except for about a metre which thaws in the summer. The swampy surface is covered only with moss and an occasional windswept shrub, except for a few brief weeks when a carpet of flowers blooms.

Tungsten Hard, brittle metal with the highest melting point among metals (3380°C). It is widely used in steel alloys where strength has to be maintained at high temperatures, as in cutting tools. Tungsten wire forms the filaments of electric lamps. Tungsten carbide is one of the hardest substances known and is used for making very tough tools. Chem. symbol W (formerly called wolfram).

Tunisia The smallest country in N Africa, bordered by Algeria and Libya. Its climate is hot and, away from the coast, very dry. There are salt lakes inland, and oases where date palms grow. But the coastal region is fertile, growing olives, fruit, grapes and cereals. Sheep and goats are raised. Area: 163,598 km²; Pop: 7,178,000; Cap: Tunis.

Tunnels There are three main methods of tunnelling. The simplest is called *cut-and-cover*, a method used for many underground and railway tunnels. A cutting is dug from the surface and the tunnel's walls and roof are built before soil is replaced on top. Only shallow tunnels can be dug by this method.

In hard rock, the tunnel is drilled and blasted out by explosives. In softer rocks, tunnel shields are used. These are giant steel tubes, the size of the intended tunnel. The end of the tube is forced into the earth and the earth inside the tube is dug out. The tunnel behind the shield is lined to prevent it falling in.

The largest road tunnel is the 19.3-km St Gotthard Tunnel in Switzerland. The longest railway tunnel was for many years the Simplon between Switzerland and Italy (19.8 km) but this has been eclipsed by the Japanese Shimuzu Tunnel (22.2 km). If underground railways are taken into account the longest tunnel is that on the Northern Line of the London Underground between East Finchley and Morden (28 km).

Tunny (tuna) A large marine food fish. It grows up to two metres long and has a series of very small fins just in front of the tail. Tunny feed mainly on herring, mackerel and garfish.

Turbine Engines in which steam, water or air turn wheels or screws to produce useful power. In hydroelectric power stations, falling water is carried through a pipe to the turbine. As the turbine rotates it drives a generator to produce electricity. Steam turbines are turned by jets of steam. Their main use is to generate electricity in power stations.

Turbot A large flatfish, up to 60 cm long, that has bony platelets on its upper side. It is found on sandy or rocky sea beds and preys largely on other fish.

Turin City situated on R. Po in northern Italy. Centre of automobile, aerospace and textile industries. The shroud in which Christ is said to have been buried is kept in the Renaissance cathedral.

Turkey Large American game bird, reared for its flesh and domesticated by the Aztecs. It has an ugly bare head but fine plumage. Domestic birds weigh up to about 17 kilos and are traditionally served in the USA at Thanksgiving, a festival instituted by early European settlers.

Turkey Bridging two continents, Turkey is composed of a small European area and a much larger Asiatic area. The two parts are linked by a road bridge. Coastal farms produce good crops, for the climate here is warm and sunny. Inland, there are cold dry plains and mountains, where livestock are raised. Industries include mining, textiles and paper manufacturing, and ancient crafts like carpet-weaving remain. Area: 780,516 km²; Pop: 50,207,000; Cap: Ankara.

Turner, Joseph Mallord William (1775–1851) English painter who specialized in land- and seascapes. A master of light and colour, he produced highly original works which include *Dido building Carthage, The Fighting Temeraire* and *Rain.*

Turtle Name given to marine version of tortoise. The turtle's body is encased in a bony shell covered by horny plates (tortoiseshell). Turtles can withdraw their head and legs into the shell.

Turtle

Tutankhamun (1300s BC) Egyptian pharaoh who died at about the age of 18. His tomb and its great treasures, including his funeral mask and solid gold sarcophagus, were discovered by Howard Carter in 1922.

Tuvalu Island country in the W Pacific Ocean. Formerly called the Ellice Islands. Area: 25 km²; Pop: 8,000; Cap: Funafuti.

Twain, Mark (1835–1910) Great American humorist who was a journalist, river pilot and author of the children's classics: *The Adventures of Tom Sawyer, The Adventures of Huckleberry Finn* and *The Prince and the Pauper*, as well as adult books and novels, including *A Connecticut Yankee at King*

Arthur's Court. His real name was Samuel Langhorne Clemens.

Typewriter Keyboard machine that prints letters on to paper when keys are struck. The first commercially produced typewriter was made by Remington in 1874. Since then typewriters have become increasingly sophisticated. In most offices secretaries use electric or electronic typewriters or word processors.

Typhoid Disease transmitted by *Salmonella* bacteria in food and water. It is most common in poorer parts of the world where it is not possible to maintain high standards of sanitation. It causes fever and can be fatal.

Typhoon See **Tropical cyclone**

Tyrannosaurus Ferocious carnivorous dinosaur of Cretaceous period. It had large powerful legs for chasing its prey and a huge head. Its wide jaws contained 25-cm long fangs. Its forearms were very small so it must have used its clawed feet for holding its victim.

U

UFO See **Unidentified Flying Objects**

Uganda Small country in E Africa, bordered by Kenya, Sudan, Zaïre and Tanzania. It has forests, lakes (the largest of which is L. Victoria) and mountains. Uganda is a highland country with fertile soil. Its people are mainly farmers growing coffee, tea, cotton and other crops. But there are also factories and some mining of tin, copper and tungsten. Area: 236,019 km²; Pop: 14,265,000; Cap: Kampala.

Ultrasonics A branch of science concerned with the study and use of sounds higher than those the human ear can detect. Engineers use ultrasound to detect flaws in metals and for drilling holes in brittle substances. It is used in medicine to sterilize instruments and is now widely used to examine babies before birth. From the ultrasonic scan, doctors can tell how old the baby is and whether it is in the right

Only a heavily armed beast like Triceratops would dare attack a Tyrannosaurus.

position. Unlike X-rays, which can be harmful, ultrasonic waves are completely safe.

Ultraviolet radiation A band of invisible electromagnetic waves just below the visible light band of the SPECTRUM. The Sun's radiation is rich in ultraviolet rays, which can be produced artificially by a mercury vapour lamp. Over-exposure to these rays can be dangerous. Many kinds of disease-causing bacteria can be killed by ultraviolet rays.

Ulysses See **Odysseus**

Underground railway In New York, Moscow, London, Paris and many other busy cities the main commuter transport system runs underground. The first underground railway system was built in London and is called the tube.

Unicorn Mythical white horse with a single straight spiralled horn, described in Greek and Roman myth. In the Middle Ages it became a symbol of purity; people believed that only a pure maiden could capture the creature. The unicorn is used in heraldry.

Unidentified Flying Objects (UFOs) have been reported all through human history. Most of the sightings in recent years have been explained as tricks of light, balloons, etc. A few sightings have not been explained and some people think they may be alien spacecraft. No one really knows.

Many UFO sightings are caused by natural phenomena like these saucer-shaped clouds.

Union of Soviet Socialist Republics (USSR) Largest country in the world. About one-quarter is in Europe and three-quarters in Asia. It is more than twice the size of the USA. There are vast desert regions, hot and dry in the south, cold and snow-covered in the north. Huge pine forests or taiga cover vast areas, and to the south, as the climate grows drier, these forests give way to endless grassy plains called steppes.

Because it is so huge, the USSR is not really one country at all. It has over 100 different peoples, each with their own customs, beliefs and histories. Of the 15 separate republics, the largest is the Russian Soviet Federal Socialist Republic, which covers three-quarters of the country. Most of the industries are in the west – the European part of the country. But there are great mineral and other riches in Siberia, and these resources are now being developed.

Russia (as the USSR is still often called by foreigners) was ruled by emperors, or tsars, until 1917. It was a backward country with most people working as serfs (peasant labourers) on large estates. In 1917 there was a communist revolution. Communist rule has improved the life of the Russian people but has given them little freedom. During World War II the USSR was invaded by German armies in 1941 and many millions of people died. Since the 1940s it has become a 'superpower' rivalling the USA. Area: 22,400,464 km^2; Pop: 275,093,000; Cap: Moscow.

Units Things that are chosen as the standard by which other quantities of the same kind are measured. There are units of weight, of volume, of time, and many other things. The metre is a unit of length, made up of 100 centimetres.

United Arab Emirates Country in Arabia, on the Gulf. It is made up of seven small states or emirates: Abu Dhabi, Dubai, Ajman, Sharjah, Umm al-Qaiwain, Fujairah, and Ras al-Khaimah. These were formerly known as the Trucial States.

The United Arab Emirates is rich in oil and its people, who once lived as desert nomads, now prosper on the money earned from selling this oil. Area: 83,593 km^2; Pop: 1,262,000; Cap: Dubai.

United Kingdom Country off western coast of Europe, made up of England,

Scotland, Wales and Northern Ireland (see individual entries). Its full name is the United Kingdom of Great Britain and Northern Ireland. The United Kingdom earns its living by trade, and has done so throughout its history. It was the first country to go through the Industrial Revolution, and its industrial wealth helped create a great overseas empire. By the 1960s, this empire had evolved into a more loose-knit 'family' of nations – the COMMONWEALTH. In 1973 Britain joined the EEC. Area: 244,026 km²; Pop: 56,023,000; Cap: London.

United Nations International organization set up in 1945, to succeed the old League of Nations. The UN was intended to settle future disagreements between nations peacefully. Almost every independent nation, large and small, now belongs to the UN, which meets in New York. Its main bodies are the General Assembly and the smaller Security Council, whose members may veto any decision. There are also a number of UN agencies, such as the Food and Agricultural Organization (FAO) and the World Health Organization (WHO).

United States of America The richest nation in the world, stretching across North America from the Atlantic to the Pacific Ocean. It is a federal republic made up of 50 states, all but two within one boundary. The two are Alaska, which is at the NW tip of North America, and Hawaii, an island group in the Pacific.

The world's fourth largest country, the USA has many different landscapes and climates. Alaska is cold and snow-covered, Florida by contrast is warm and sunny most of the year. There are vast prairies, great rivers, and high mountain ranges. Among the most spectacular sights are the Grand Canyon, Great Lakes, and Niagara Falls. Agriculture is highly developed and mechanized. Cereals, fruit and vegetables are grown; cattle reared; timber cut from the forests. Yet industry is even more valuable than farming. The USA produces half the world's factory goods. It has coal, oil, natural gas and other minerals in abundance. Its people enjoy the highest standard of living in the world.

The first people to settle in what is now the USA were Indians. Later came Europeans, mostly Spanish, French and British. African slaves were brought to work on the Europeans' farms. In 1776 the 13 British colonies in America broke away and declared their independence. Other states joined the union as the new nation grew. The black slaves gained their freedom after the Civil War of 1861–65. Many immigrants came from Europe to seek a new life in the USA. Area: 9,362,399 km²; Pop: 236,690,000; Cap: Washington.

Universe The whole cosmic system consisting of all the galaxies in space. Nobody knows the size of the Universe, but the most distant QUASARS are over 10 thousand million light-years away. Many astronomers believe that all the matter in the Universe was once concentrated in one primeval atom and that an enormous explosion between 10 thousand million and 20 thousand million years ago flung the matter outwards. The Universe has been expanding ever since. This is known as the Big Bang theory.

The Big Bang theory of the origin of the Universe.

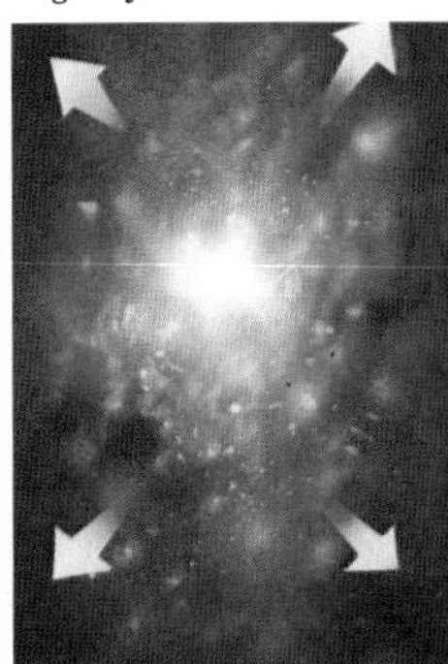

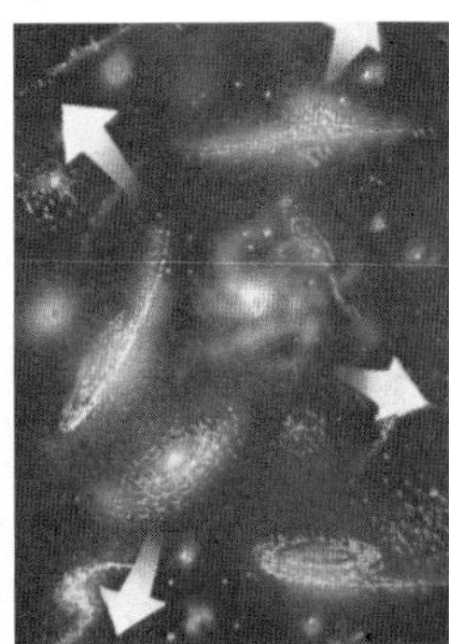

University A place of higher education. The first university was probably Plato's Academy in ancient Greece. The Arabs, too, had universities before the birth of Christ. The first university in Europe was in Bologna in Italy, founded in the 1st century AD, and followed by the University of Paris. Oxford began in the 1100s and Cambridge in the 1200s.

Ural Mountains Mountain range in the USSR, forming a natural boundary between Europe and Asia. They are rich in minerals and supply raw materials to a vast industrial area. Highest peak is Mt Narodnaya (1894 metres).

Uranium Naturally occurring radioactive element. One form, or *isotope*, uranium-235, undergoes *nuclear fission* which, when controlled, is the source of commercial nuclear power. Chem. symbol U.

Uranus The seventh planet in line from the Sun, Uranus appears as a featureless green disc, even to the cameras of the Voyager 2 spacecraft which approached it in 1986. There is a system of faint rings round the planet's equator. Because Uranus is tilted on its side they appear vertical. Diameter: 51,800 km; distance from Sun: 2900 million km; moons: 15.

Uruguay Small country in South America, squeezed between larger neighbours Argentina and Brazil. Uruguay's flat, grassy plains, watered by the Plate and Uruguay Rivers, are ideal for cattle and sheep ranching. Area: 176,202 km^2; Pop: 2,926,000; Cap: Montevideo.

USSR See **Union of Soviet Socialist Republics**

V

Vaccination An inoculation of a harmless form of disease-causing agent, such as a dead bacterium, into a person's blood-stream to induce immunity against future attacks of the disease. The technique was first used by Edward Jenner in 1796 using the cow pox virus to immunize against the more serious chicken pox.

Vacuum A vacuum is a competely empty space, without air or anything else. In practice, this is impossible; even out in space there are a few molecules of hydrogen in every cubic centimetre. A partial vacuum can be created by using vacuum pumps. Partial vacuums have many uses, including electric light bulbs, vacuum flasks, and vacuum cleaners. Sound cannot travel across a vacuum as it needs air molecules for its passage.

Vacuum flask A flask designed to keep things hot or cold by limiting the exchange of heat between the inside of the flask and the outside. It has an inner glass container with another glass container sealed round it. The space between the two glass bottles has the air removed to produce a vacuum. This vacuum slows down the transfer of heat. The facing surfaces of the bottles are also coated with a silvery solution to reflect heat. The outer container is made of plastic or metal.

Valentine's Day Festival of love celebrated on February 14th, the feastday of Saint Valentine, but not connected with the saint. It probably derives from a Roman

The planet Uranus.

feast in honour of Juno, the goddess of women, which took place on February 15.

Vampire Imaginary dead humans who rise from the grave to suck the blood of the living and turn them into vampires. Only a stake driven through the vampire's heart can kill it. The best-known vampire story is that of Dracula by Bram Stoker. His character is based on a real-life Transylvanian count notorious for bloodthirsty cruelty if not for blood-sucking.

Vanadium Scarce metal which is chiefly used in very hard, shock-resistant alloy steels designed for tools and vehicle parts. Chem. symbol V.

Vancouver Port and city in British Columbia, Canada, at mouth of R. Fraser opposite Vancouver I. It is the largest Pacific port in Canada, important for fishing and oil-refining. Pop: 410,000.

Van Dyck, Sir Anthony (1599–1641) Flemish portrait painter who was a pupil of Rubens and settled in England. As court painter his most famous portraits include those of Charles I, his wife Henrietta Maria, and other members of the court.

Vanuatu Island country in the Pacific Ocean, about 800 km west of Fiji. The islands of Vanuatu are hilly and forested, with a warm, damp climate. Crops include coconuts, cocoa and vegetables. Vanuatu was formerly known as the New Hebrides. Area: 14,760 km^2; Pop: 130,000; Cap: Vila.

Vatican City The world's smallest sovereign state, occupying less than 0.5 km^2 of Rome, Italy. It is the spiritual and administrative centre of the Roman Catholic Church and the residence of the pope. The most famous buildings are the basilica of St Peter and the Sistine Chapel.

Velasquez, Diego Rodriguez de Silva y (1599–1660) Spanish artist and court painter to the Royal family of Spain. His best-known works include *The Maids of Honour*, *The Tapestry Weavers* and *Juan de Pareja*.

Velocity The velocity of a moving object changes if either its speed or direction changes. When an object is moving at a constant velocity, it is moving in a straight line at a constant speed. If a car goes round a bend at a constant speed, its *velocity* changes because it has changed direction. Its *speed* remains constant.

Venezuela Country on the north coast of South America. Its wealth comes from oil, found beneath L. Maracaibo. Other minerals include iron ore, bauxite and gold. These natural resources combined with tropical plantation crops, cattle ranching and a wide range of manufacturing industries have made Venezuela the richest country in the continent. Since 1958 it has had the most democratic and progressive government in South America. Area: 911,980 km^2; Pop: 17,279,000; Cap: Caracas.

Venice Port and capital of Venice province, N Italy, built on a group of islands in a lagoon and joined by bridge to the mainland. Its streets are a network of canals and bridges and it is renowned for its splendid architecture and art treasures. Once a powerful trading state, it is now a tourist resort, gradually sinking into the Adriatic. Pop: 362,000.

Venus The second planet in line from the Sun, Venus is much the same size as the Earth. It appears as a bright object in the night sky (the Evening star and Morning star) because it is surrounded by a veil of clouds which brilliantly reflect the Sun's rays. Space probes found the clouds to be sulphuric acid, the atmosphere carbon dioxide, and the surface temperature a furnace-like 475°C. Diameter: 12,100 km; distance from Sun: 108 million km.

Verdi, Giuseppe (1813–1901) Italy's greatest opera composer, who enjoyed tremendous popularity during his lifetime. His best known operas include: *Rigoletto*, *La Traviata*, *Il Trovatore*, *Aida*, *Otello*, and *Falstaff*. He also wrote a celebrated Requiem.

Vermeer, Jan (1632–75) Great Dutch painter who enjoyed considerable success during his own lifetime though he painted fewer than 40 pictures. The best-known include *The Lady Standing at the Virginals* and *Young Woman with a Water Jug*.

Verne, Jules (1828–1905) French writer and father of modern science fiction. His novels include: *Voyage to the Centre of the Earth*, *From the Earth to the Moon*, *Twenty Thousand Leagues under the Sea* and *Around the World in Eighty Days*.

Veronese, Paolo (1528–88) Italian painter famed for his religious subjects. His well-known *Marriage Feast at Cana in Galilee* is in the Louvre.

Versailles Capital of Yvelines dept, France, 18 km SW of Paris. Famous for its magnificent palace, built for Louis XIV, and the two smaller palaces, the Grand

and the Petit Trianon. Site of peace conference after World War I (1919) and signing of Treaty of Versailles. Pop: 95,000.

Vertebrate Any animal with a backbone. Fishes, amphibians, reptiles, birds and mammals are all vertebrates.

Vesuvius Volcano in S Italy, east of the Bay of Naples. Famous for its eruption in AD 79 which buried the cities of Pompeii and Herculaneum. Numerous eruptions have since been recorded. Height: 1186 metres.

Victoria Largest lake in Africa, bordered by Tanzania, Uganda and Kenya. Site of a major fishing industry. Area: 68,000 km^2.

Victoria Falls Large waterfall on Zambezi R., on boundary between Zambia and Zimbabwe. Discovered by Livingstone in 1855 who named the falls after Queen Victoria. Height: 108 metres.

Victoria, Queen (1819–1901) Queen of Great Britain from 1837 and Empress of India from 1876. In 1840 she married her cousin, Prince Albert, and had 9 children. Grief-stricken at his death (1861) she retired from public life for three years. Her long and comparatively peaceful reign saw the expansion of British industry and trade. At her death the British Empire had reached its zenith.

Video recording Video recordings can be made on disc or, more commonly, on tape. A recording head in a video recorder transfers an electronic signal to the tape by altering the magnetism of the tape. The signal is replayed by the reverse process. A picture signal is much more complicated than a sound signal, so it needs more space – video tape is wider than sound tape and the signal is recorded in diagonal strips across the tape.

Vienna Capital of Austria, and port on R. Danube. Historic cultural centre and home of many famous composers. Pop: 1,581,000.

Vietnam Country in SE Asia, bordered by Laos, Kampuchea and China. A long, narrow country, with a sea coast on the east, Vietnam has mountains, forests and fertile river valleys. The Red and Mekong Rivers provide water for rice growing. Rubber and tea are also grown. Industry is mainly in the north, where coal and other minerals are mined.

Vietnam was part of French Indo-China until bitter warfare (1946–54) led to a French withdrawal. Vietnam was divided into North Vietnam (communist) and South Vietnam. More fighting followed, and the USA became heavily involved in helping South Vietnam. However in 1975 the North overran the South, and Vietnam was reunited under communist rule. The southern capital, Saigon, was renamed Ho Chi-Minh City after the North Vietnamese communist leader. Area: 332,500 km^2; Pop: 59,030,000; Cap: Hanoi.

Vikings Scandinavian warriors who began raiding the coasts of Europe in about AD 800. Eventually they settled down with their families in England, northern France, Russia and other parts. The Vikings were extraordinary sailors. They sailed as far as America and the eastern end of the Mediterranean, and set up colonies in uninhabited lands such as Iceland and Greenland.

Virgil (70–19 BC) Roman poet who is best known for his epic poem *The Aeneid* which tells of the voyages of Aeneas after the fall of Troy. He also wrote the *Eclogues* and *Georgics* in praise of rural life.

Virgin Islands Group of islands in West Indies, east of Puerto Rico. The Virgin Is are split into two groups, one belonging to the USA, the other to Britain. Those of the USA were purchased from Denmark in 1917. The islands are a popular tourist resort. Pop: 105,000.

Virus One of many very tiny micro-organisms which can grow and multiply only inside the cells of plants and animals. They convert the cell materials to their own use, and in so doing they interfere with the proper working of the cells and cause disease. All known viruses cause diseases, including influenza (flu), chicken-pox, smallpox, polio, and the common cold. Many plant diseases are also caused by viruses.

Vitamins Substances required in the diet in very small quantities in order for the body to remain healthy. Lack of vitamins may lead to illness. The vitamins are usually known by a letter (vitamin A, vitamin B, etc) and each vitamin is found in a particular range of foods. For example, vitamin C is common in fresh fruits. A lack of vitamin C caused the disease scurvy, common among sailors in the 17th and 18th centuries until their diet was changed to include citrus fruits such as oranges and limes.

Vladivostok Port and city in USSR. Important naval base and chief Pacific port. Pop: 550,000.

Volcano An outlet for hot magma from the Earth's interior. Most volcanoes are situated near the edges of colliding TECTONIC PLATES. Some volcanoes are explosive, spewing ash and gases into the air. Others erupt quietly with runny lava pouring out of the vent.

Vole A small rodent closely related to the lemmings. Voles look similar to mice but have much shorter tails and smaller ears. They live mainly in grasslands and do not hibernate.

Volga River in the USSR, flowing from N of Moscow southwards into Caspian Sea. The Volga is the largest river in Europe and an important industrial and commercial waterway. Length: 3700 km.

Voltaire (1694–1778) Great French author and philosopher who bitterly criticised contemporary French society and was twice imprisoned in the Bastille. He wrote many tragedies including *Zaïre*, satirical novels including *Candide*, and poems.

Vulture Large carrion-eating birds of America, Africa and Asia. They wait in trees or circle in the sky, watching with their sharp eyes for a dead animal. Then they swoop and strip the bones with their hooked bills. The largest vultures are the American condors.

W

Wagner, Richard (1813–83) German composer whose operas and political views aroused much controversy during his lifetime. Wagner wrote his own *librettos* and created a new style of continuous melody using *motifs*. His great music drama *The Ring of the Nibelung*, a 4-opera cycle comprising *The Rhinegold, Siegfried, The Valkyrie,* and *The Twilight of the Gods* was first performed at the Bayreuth theatre he built for performances of his works. His other operas include *Tristan and Isolde, The Mastersingers of Nuremberg* and *Parsifal.*

Wagtail Ground-living birds which walk and run about in a brisk jerky manner, wagging their long tails up and down. They eat insects and build their nests in holes, using holes in old buildings as well as those in rocks.

Wales Part of the United Kingdom, the Principality of Wales is a land of mountains and river valleys, with high rainfall. Sheep are reared on the hillsides, while industry has been traditionally concentrated in the southern valleys. But

The inside of a volcano. The cone-shaped mountain has alternate layers of rock formed from larva and ashes from previous eruptions.

the old industries, such as coal-mining and steel-working, are now in decline. Only 5% of Britain's population live in Wales (in Welsh *Cymru*) and there are few large towns. Tourism is important in both west and north Wales. Wales was once ruled by princes. Today, the sovereign's eldest son bears the title Prince of Wales and Wales is governed as part of the United Kingdom. Area: 21,000 km^2; Pop: 2,791,000; Cap: Cardiff.

Wallaby Small kangaroos of Australia and New Guinea. Some are only the size of hares.

Walrus Bulky seal-like mammals of Arctic coasts. They have leathery skin, whiskers and long tusks, used for scraping up shellfish from the sea bed. Bulls may weigh over a tonne.

Warbler A family of insect-eating birds, many of which are good singers. Warblers are small birds, and many are so similar that only their song and behaviour provide clues to their identity.

Warning coloration A conspicuous colour or pattern exhibited by an animal that is poisonous or distasteful. Experiments have shown that predators soon learn to associate the bold colours with an unpleasant experience, and next time they meet an animal with such colours they leave it alone.

Warsaw Capital of Poland, on R. Vistula. Important industrial and communications centre. During a turbulent history the city has been occupied by Swedish, Prussian, Russian and German armies. In World War II most of the city was razed to the ground. Pop: 1,463,000.

Warsaw Pact Treaty organization set up in 1955. Its members are the USSR, Bulgaria, Czechoslovakia, East Germany, Hungary, Poland and Romania. The treaty calls for military cooperation and allows the USSR to station troops in the other countries belonging to the Pact. The Warsaw Pact is the Communist equivalent of NATO.

Warthog Grotesque-looking wild African pig with a warty skin, upturned tusks and a mane of bristly hair.

Washington DC Capital of USA, on Potomac R. Named after the first American president, George Washington, who chose the location in 1790. Site of White House, the president's residence. Pop: 638,000 (3,061,000 met area).

Washington, George (1732–99) American national hero who successfully led the colonial armies in the American War of Independence. He was elected the first president of the United States in 1789 but declined a third term in 1796.

Wasp A group of insects related to ants and bees, often with striking black and yellow markings that warn other animals that they are not good to eat. Like ants, wasps tend to have narrow 'waists'. Some species are social, living in colonies and building elaborate nests with paper which they make by chewing up wood. Others are solitary. Wasps feed mainly on fruit juices and nectar but they feed their larvae on flesh. Some are parasites, laying their eggs on the bodies of other insects paralyzed by their sting.

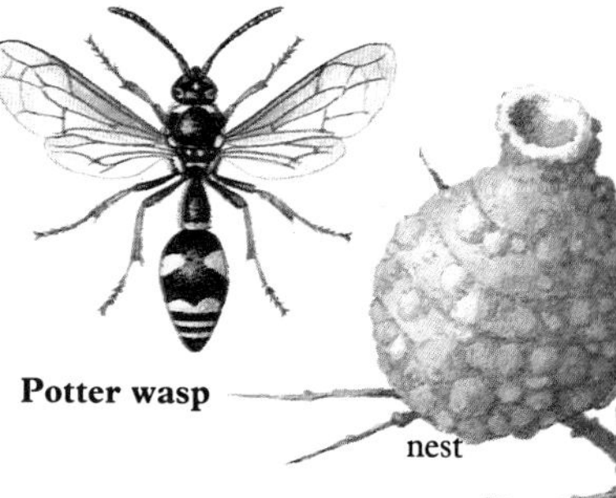

Water This is the most important compound on earth. It exists in three states – solid (ice), liquid and as a vapour. It covers about 70 per cent of the Earth's surface and makes up about 65 per cent of the human body. Water is made up of hydrogen and oxygen, its formula being H_2O. The boiling point of water is 100°C (212°F); its freezing point is 0°C (32°F). Unlike almost any other substance, water expands on freezing so that it floats on liquid water as ice.

Water is turned into vapour by boiling it. Although water boils at 100°C, it does not immediately turn into steam. There is a pause during which the water absorbs more heat without rising in temperature. This heat is called *latent heat*, and it means that steam holds a great amount of latent heat energy. We use this energy to drive engines. Water also has a great ability to dissolve other substances and is known as the 'universal solvent'.

Water beetle Several groups of beetles found in ponds and streams, where they feed on other animals or on algae and rotting plant matter. Many can fly from pond to pond but they spend most of their lives under water. They use their wing cases as air tanks and surface from time to time to take in fresh air. One of the largest is the great diving beetle.

Water boatman A group of aquatic bugs found in ponds, usually in the debris at the bottom where they feed on rotting vegetation. They swim to and from the surface to obtain bubbles of air.

Water buffalo Several kinds of wild oxen, most of which have been domesticated as draught animals. They like to wallow in mud and water so they are ideal for ploughing flooded rice fields. They have large curving horns. The Indian buffalo is the most common but other kinds exist wild in S Asia.

Water cycle A never-ending process of nature in which water from the oceans passes into the atmosphere through evaporation, falls to the ground as rain or snow, and flows back to the sea again through streams and rivers.

Waterfall A 'step' in a river bed over which water tumbles. Waterfalls are often caused by a band of soft rock in the river bed which is eroded more easily than neighbouring hard rock. Often a series of ledges are formed over which the river flows swiftly in *rapids*. The highest falls in the world are the ANGEL FALLS.

Water lily Aquatic flowering plants that are unrelated to the true lilies. Water lilies are found in slow-moving or stagnant water. Their roots lie in the mud at the bottom of the pond, but their broad leaves, borne on long stalks, lie mostly floating on the surface of the water.

Waterloo, Battle of (1815) Final battle of the Napoleonic Wars. Napoleon escaped from captivity on the island of Elba and returned to France, where the army answered his appeal. On 18 June he attacked British and Dutch forces under the Duke of Wellington at Waterloo in Belgium. The arrival of the Prussian army tipped the balance against the French.

Water spider The only spider to spend its entire life under water. It collects air bubbles and carries them down to fill an underwater 'diving bell' made of silk. Inside the bell, the spider rears its young. Water spiders catch other pond animals for food.

Watt, James (1736–1819) Scottish engineer who greatly improved the steam engine invented by Newcomen. His invention was patented in 1769. The watt, a unit of power, was named after him.

A simplified diagram of the water cycle.

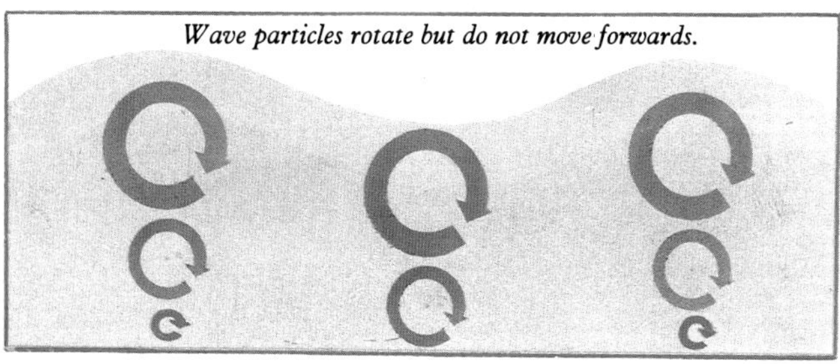
Wave particles rotate but do not move forwards.

Waves Waves travel across the surface of the oceans without taking water along with them. Floating objects merely bob up and down as the waves pass them by. This is why the term 'wave motion' is used to describe many scientific phenomena. Sound waves travel by wave motion of air molecules. Electromagnetic waves – light, radio, etc. – move in the same way.

Weasel Smallest of the carnivores, closely related to the stoat. It is only about 20 cm long with short legs, and has a shorter tail than its cousin, with no black tip. In many areas the coat is brown both winter and summer but in the north of Scandinavia the winter coat is pure white.

Weather The condition of the air around us at a particular time. This includes the temperature, humidity (moistness) and pressure of the air, together with winds, clouds, snow and rainfall. In some parts of the world the weather is much the same day after day. In other places the weather is so variable that it is often difficult to predict even a few hours ahead. The study of weather is the science of METEOROLOGY.

Weather forecasting Information about the weather is collected at weather stations and sent in code to forecast centres. There, with extra information from weather satellites, forecasters analyse the weather and prepare outlook charts to show how it will probably develop in 12 to 24 hours' time. From these charts they prepare written forecasts for radio and television networks.

Weaving Interlacing of yarn on a loom to make fabric. One set of threads (the weft) is passed under and over a set of lengthwise threads (the warp). This is not done like darning but by raising and lowering the warp threads and passing a shuttle between them. The three basic weaves, plain, twill, and satin, produce different effects. Patterns such as tartans and even more intricate ones are produced on a Jacquard loom.

Wedgwood, Josiah (1730–95) Famous English potter. Through improvements in the manufacture of pottery and the use of classical decorations Wedgwood ware achieved world-wide fame.

Weevil A group of small beetles with pointed snouts which infest stores of flour and other food. They also eat plants and some, such as the cotton boll weevil, are pests. More than 40,000 species are known.

Weight-lifting Sport in which competitors test their strength by lifting weights

SOME WORLD WEATHER RECORDS

Highest temperature 57.7°C, Libya, 1922
Lowest temperature: –88.3°C, Vostok, near the South Pole, 1960
Wettest year 1860–61, 9299 mm at Cherrapunji, India
Driest year Most years there is no rain at Calama in the Atacama desert, Chile
Greatest snowfall 31.102 metres, Mt Rainier, United States, 1972
Biggest hailstones 19 cm diameter, Coffeyville, Kansas, United States, 1970
Most thunder 322 days a year from 1916–1919, Bogor Java
Most sunshine 4300 hours a year average, eastern Sahara desert
Strongest wind 371 km/h, Mt Washington, United States, 1934
Most fog 120 days a year, Grand Banks, Newfoundland.

loaded on to iron bars. There are three movements, called snatch, press, and clean-and-jerk. In championship events, lifters are graded by body-weight, and each one is allowed three attempts at each new (and higher) weight. Weight-lifting is a good method of body-building.

Weights and measures These are used to find and describe the weights and sizes of things. The two main measurements are weight and length. From lengths we also get areas and volumes. There are several systems of weights and measures, but the most commonly used throughout the world is the metric system. This is based on the metre, the kilogramme, and the litre. The system using feet, pounds and pints is called the Imperial System. See accompanying conversion table.

Welding The joining together of two pieces of metal by melting them. When the metal cools, the two pieces are one, with a join that should be as strong as any other part. Welders use gas or electricity. In electric welding, a current jumps from a welding rod to the metals being joined and melts them. So-etimes a filler metal is added to the junction. In gas welding, a gas flame is used to melt the metal. The most common welding gas is acetylene mixed with oxygen. Today, the laser is increasingly used in the welding process.

Wellington Port, commercial centre and capital of New Zealand at the southern tip of North Island. Founded in 1840, it succeeded Auckland as the nation's capital in 1865 and grew rapidly, partly on reclaimed land and partly into the surrounding hills. It includes the industrialized Hutt Valley. Pop: 342,000 (met area).

Wellington, Duke of (1769–1852) British soldier and statesman who was victorious in the Peninsular War (1809–13), driving the French out of Spain and later defeating Napoleon I at the Battle of Waterloo (1815). He was Tory prime minister 1828–30.

Wells, (H)erbert (G)eorge (1866–1946) English novelist and historian whose science fiction novels include *The Time Machine* and *The War of the Worlds*. He also wrote *Kipps, The Outline of History* and *Mr Polly*.

Werewolf Superstition in many cultures, and popularized by the film industry, of a man transformed into a wolf by night to prey on human flesh. The legend of wolf-men probably arose from rare cases of a mental illness called *Lycanthropy* whose victims believe themselves to be wild animals and behave like them.

WEIGHTS AND MEASURES

To convert **from** metric, **divide** by the factor shown. To convert **to** metric, **multiply** by the factor.

Length	
millimetres: inches	25.4
centimetres: inches	2.54
metres: feet	0.3048
metres: yards	0.9144
kilometres: miles	1.6093
Area	
square millimetres: square inches	645.16
square centimetres: square inches	6.4516
square centimetres: square feet	929.03
square metres: square feet	0.0929
square metres: square yards	0.8361
square metres: acres	4046.86
hectares: square miles	258.999
hectares: acres	0.4047
square kilometres: square miles	2.59
Volume	
cubic centimetres: cubic inches	16.3871
cubic metres: cubic feet	0.0283
cubic metres: cubic yards	0.7646
Mass	
grams: ounces	28.3495
kilograms: pounds	0.4536
kilograms: stones	6.3503
kilograms: hundredweights	50.8023
kilograms: tons	1016.05
tonnes: tons	1.0160
Capacity	
litres: pints	0.568
litres: quarts	1.137
litres: gallons	4.546

Wesley, John (1703–91) English evangelist who in 50 years travelled over 200,000 miles around the country preaching many thousands of sermons. He was the founder of Methodism and brought his message of salvation through Christ to the very poorest people in the land.

Western Samoa Country in the Pacific Ocean, part of Polynesian island group.

The people live on volcanic islands, mountainous and thick with forest. They farm the fertile lower slopes, growing cocoa and bananas. Coral reefs ring the coast. Tourism is developing. Area: 2841 km²; Pop: 162,000; Cap: Apia.

West Indies Group of islands between N and S America separating the Caribbean from the Atlantic Ocean. For centuries they were European colonies highly prized for sugar and tobacco. Today most are independent island republics.

Whale Marine mammals, amongst them the largest animal that has ever lived, the blue whale, which may grow 30 metres long. Whales' bodies are streamlined with a fluked tail and small flippers, and some are fin-backed. There are two groups: toothed fish-eating whales (including the sperm, killer and bottle-nosed whales, the narwhal, dolphins and porpoises) and baleen whales (including the blue, humpback, finback, and pygmy whales). The latter group feed on plankton strained through a curtain of baleen (whalebone) plates in the mouth.

Wheat A cultivated grass grown in temperate regions as a cereal crop. Main producers include the USA, Canada, the USSR, and China. The grain is ground into flour or meal and used to make foods, especially bread.

Wheel The invention of the wheel some 10,000 years ago in Asia was one of the most important discoveries in human history. It is used to harness energy in devices from windmills to steam turbines, and in machines from simple pulleys to the car wheel and axle.

Whitsun (Pentecost) An important Christian festival held to commemorate the coming of the Holy Ghost to the apostles. It is celebrated seven Sundays after Easter.

Wilberforce, William (1759–1833) English humanitarian and MP whose efforts secured the abolition of the slave trade within the British Empire in 1807, and of the institution itself in 1833, the year of his death.

Wild cat A carnivore that, at a glance, looks like a domestic tabby. It is found in mountain forests from western Asia to southern and central Europe, and in Scotland. It is about 60 cm long and has a thick bushy tail with dark rings. Like its domestic cousin, the wild cat is a solitary animal that prefers to hunt at night.

Wilde, Oscar (1854–1900) Irish dramatist and author who wrote poems, witty comedies, short stories and fairy tales. They include *The Importance of Being Earnest*, *Lady Windermere's Fan*, *The Picture of Dorian Gray* and *The Ballad of Reading Gaol*.

Wildebeest See **Gnu**.

William I (1027–87) The Conqueror. As Duke of Normandy he defeated Harold II of England near Hastings in 1066 and became King of England. A wise and firm ruler, he quelled Saxon revolts and gave much of the land to his Norman courtiers. In 1086 he ordered the first national

A wheelbarrow in use in Ancient China. The wheel was invented in Asia.

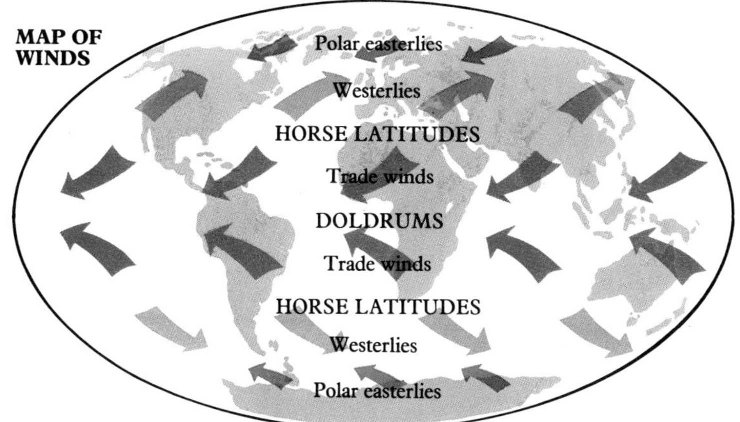

survey of his kingdom to be made; the results are contained in the *Domesday Book*.

William III (1650–1702) King of England, Scotland and Ireland (1689–1702) and Prince of Orange. He married James II's daughter Mary and ruled jointly with her after James's abdication. He is remembered by the Orangemen of Ulster to this day for his merciless defeat of a Catholic force under James at the Battle of the Boyne (1690).

Willow A group of deciduous trees and shrubs, most of which have long, narrow leaves. Willows have single-sexed flowers arranged as catkins, male and female catkins occurring on different trees. Most species like damp soil.

Wind Air blowing from an area of high atmospheric pressure to an area of low pressure. The strength of the wind depends upon the difference between the high and low pressure areas and the distance between them. Winds which blow most often in one direction, e.g. westerlies, are called prevailing winds.

Wind instruments Musical instruments that sound when air is blown through or across them. There are three groups. Keyboard instruments, such as the organ and concertina, are played by bellows. The woodwind group includes the flute and the reed instruments (oboe, bassoon, clarinet, saxophone, bagpipes). Brass wind instruments include the horn, trombone and trumpet.

Wine Alcoholic drink made (usually) from grapes. White wines are made from the juice alone, red wines from the skins and pips as well. The dryness or sweetness of a wine depends on the amount of natural sugar that is turned to alcohol during fermentation. Fermentation is halted in sweet wines so that the sweet taste is retained. Fortified wines like sherry and port have brandy added. Champagne, the best of wines, is fermented twice to produce the characteristic bubbles.

Winkle Several species of small sea snail, also called periwinkles. Most winkles live in water and breathe through gills.

Winnipeg Capital of Manitoba province, Canada, on the Red River to the S of L. Winnipeg. One of the world's major wheat markets. Pop: 560,000.

Wisent See **Bison**

Witchcraft Today, except for a few primitive people, almost nobody believes in witchcraft, the practice of magic and devilry by (mostly) women called witches. Common since ancient times, such occult practices were outlawed by the Romans. Later, witches were said to gather in covens (of 13) using spells, charms and curses to work evil, even transforming themselves into beasts and taking to the air on broomsticks. So-called witches (usually harmless innocents) were persecuted for centuries by the Christian Church and perhaps as many as half a million were put to death, often by burning. The last witchcraft trial in Britain was in 1722.

Wolf Carnivorous dog-like animal which ranges over remote areas of Europe, northern Asia and North America. Wolves live in family groups and work together in packs when hunting large animals.

Wolf spider A group of spiders that hunt by running after their prey, usually insects. They do not spin webs. Most wolf spiders are small and dull coloured. The females carry their eggs around with them, inside silken sacs on their bodies.

Wolsey, Cardinal (1471–1530) The son of a butcher, he gained favour with Henry VIII. He became Archbishop of York in 1514, Cardinal and Chancellor in 1515 and amassed a great fortune. When he failed to obtain Rome's sanction for the King's divorce he was charged with treason but died on the way to London.

Wolverine A carnivore belonging to the weasel family. It lives in northern forests and looks rather like a small bear. It is about 75 cm long with dark brown fur, and is sometimes called the glutton because it eats anything it can find, including carrion. It is even capable of killing reindeer.

Wombat Stocky, burrowing marsupial of southern Australia and Tasmania. It is a nocturnal plant-eater with rodent-like teeth.

Wood A major building material for thousands of years, wood is still vital in the building and furniture industries today. Softwoods, which come from pine, fir and spruce trees, are used for building, for mass-produced furniture and for paper. Hardwoods, which come mostly from broad-leaved trees, and have distinctive colours and grains, are used for furniture. Rosewood, maple, mahogany, oak, beech and chestnut are popular.

Woodlouse The only crustaceans that live permanently on land. Woodlice are often found beneath stones or in damp places indoors. They are scavengers, feeding on rotting plant matter. Some woodlice can roll their armoured bodies into a ball for protection.

Woodpecker A bird renowned for the rat-a-tat noise it makes while hammering into a tree trunk with its chisel-like bill. The birds can climb vertically up tree trunks. With their strong bills they can drill large holes into wood in search of insects or to make their nests. They generally attack trees that are rotten on the inside. They are found in most parts of the world, and are commonest in South America and Southeast Asia.

Woodworm The larva or grub of the furniture beetle. The grubs burrow through wood, sometimes reducing it to sawdust. The holes seen in old timber and furniture are made when the adult beetle bores its way out.

Wool The fleece of sheep and man's traditional insulation from cold. Sheep have been shorn of their wool since ancient times and the wool spun and woven into yarn. Today many artificial fibres 'mimic' wool but the lightness and warmth of the natural fibre is still popular. Leading wool exporters are Australia, New Zealand, USSR and Argentina.

Word processor Sophisticated typewriter with a keyboard linked to a computer, a VDU (visual display unit) and a printer. The operator can make alterations to the words as they appear on the screen, correct mistakes and print the same 'top copy' letter to as many people as he wishes, addressing each one personally. The copy is stored, usually on a floppy disk, so it can be re-used or altered at a later date.

Wordsworth, William (1770–1850) English poet who with his sister Dorothy settled in the Lake District. His best-known works include *The Daffodils*, *The Prelude*, *The Tables Turned*, *Tintern Abbey* and *Ode on the Intimations of Immortality*.

World War I (1914–18) War in which nearly all Europe was involved. The real cause of the war was the mutual fear and rivalry of the great powers, heightened by the aggressive ambitions of Germany. The chief contestants were Britain, France and Russia (the Allies), against Germany and Austria-Hungary (the Central Powers).

Most of the fighting was done by infantry in trenches, dominated by the machine-gun. Thousands of men died to gain a few yards of Belgian mud. It was also the first war in which aeroplanes and submarines played important parts. The entry of the United States against the Germans in 1917 tipped the balance in favour of the Allies.

World War II (1939–45) International conflict fought in Europe, Asia, Africa and on all the world's oceans. The main opponents were the same as in WORLD WAR I, but Germany was allied with Italy and the formidable new power of Japan.

A stretcher party bringing in wounded from the World War I battlefield of Passchendaele. There were half a million casualties.

After several years of brutal and aggressive behaviour by Nazi Germany, Britain and France declared war. The Germans were at first successful, conquering most of Europe. They were eventually halted at Stalingrad, in the Soviet Union, and checked in North Africa by the British and their allies.

When Japan attacked the United States in December 1941, the eventual victory of the Allies was assured, thanks to the huge industrial power of the United States. The war in Europe ended with Germany's surrender in May 1945. Japan surrendered in August after atomic bombs were dropped on Hiroshima and Nagasaki.

Worm A name given to a wide range of long slender animals without legs. They belong to many different groups. Earthworms belong to the group known as annelids or ringed worms, because their bodies are made up of lots of rings or segments. Silk worms and slow worms are not really worms at all: one is a caterpillar and the other a legless lizard.

Wren A tiny brown bird which nearly always keeps its tail cocked up as it scuttles through the undergrowth. Wrens hunt for insects on the ground, but otherwise hide in hedges and bushes.

Wren, Sir Christopher (1632–1723) English architect who, following the Great Fire of London in 1666, was responsible for the rebuilding of St Paul's Cathedral and more than 50 other London churches. He also built Chelsea Hospital, sections of Greenwich Hospital and the Sheldonian theatre in Oxford.

Wrestling One of the most ancient sports, dating back 5000 years at least. The aim in wrestling is to throw, unbalance or subdue your opponent. Blows and punches are not allowed. In modern wrestling there are two styles: Greco-Roman and freestyle or catch-as-catch-can.

Wright, Orville (1871–1948) and **Wilbur** (1867–1912) Brothers who were American aeroplane inventors. In 1903 they made the first powered flight at Kitty Hawk, North Carolina, covering a distance of 260 metres.

X

Xenon A chemical element and one of the rare gases which occurs in minute quantities in the atmosphere. Chem. symbol Xe.

Xerxes I (*c* 519–465 BC) Persian king and son of Darius I (who was defeated at Marathon). To avenge that defeat Xerxes fought the Greeks at Thermopylae and won a resounding victory. He then crushed Athens but in 480 BC his own vast fleet was destroyed at Salamis. He was later murdered by one of his guards.

X-rays A form of electromagnetic waves that can pass through human tissue but are partially blocked by the bones and other parts. This means that X-ray photographs can be taken to show details of the internal organs.

X-rays have many applications in science and industry. They are used to study the crystal structure of substances, to analyse the chemical content of materials, and to find flaws in castings. They are extensively used at airports to search baggage.

Nearly 340,000 men of the British army were evacuated at Dunkirk in World War II after retreating to the coast. An armada of ships crossed the channel to save them but most of their equipment had to be abandoned.

Y

Yachting Small sailing boats called yachts were first built in Holland in the 1600s. One of the oldest yacht races is the America's Cup, first raced for in 1851 and retained by the United States every time until 1983, when Australia won it. There are many classes of yacht; some are large ocean racers, others small craft owned and raced by amateur sailors, purely for fun. Yachting is an Olympic Games event.

Yak Wild oxen of the Himalayas and Tibet, with very shaggy coats and horns which extend sideways. The domesticated yak is a beast of burden and provides milk and hair for cloth.

Yangtze Kiang The longest river in China and Asia, flowing from Tibet into the East China Sea. Major commercial waterway. Length: 5550 km.

Year A solar year is the time taken for the Earth to complete one orbit of the Sun (365 days, 5 hours, 48 minutes and 46 seconds). This is about one-quarter of a day more than the calendar year. The additional time is allowed for by having a leap year of 366 days every four years.

Yeast A group of single-celled fungi that are important in brewing and baking because during respiration they form alcohol and the gas carbon dioxide. The chemical process involved is called fermentation.

Yemen, Arab Republic of (North Yemen) Country in SW Arabia, bordered by South Yemen and Saudi Arabia. A hot, mountainous country with a narrow coastal strip of fertile land. Farmers also grow crops on terraces cut into the hillsides. The chief crops are millet, vegetables, coffee and cotton.

Having no minerals or industries, North Yemen is poor compared with some of its oil-rich neighbours. Area: 195,000 km²; Pop: 5,895,000; Cap: Sana.

Yemen, People's Democratic Republic of (South Yemen) Country in SW Arabia, larger than neighbouring North Yemen but with far fewer people. Away from the coast, the land is barren rocky desert. Yet in the fertile irrigated areas good crops of dates, wheat, millet, cotton and fruit are grown. There is some oil and some fishing. Aden, a key port at the mouth of the Red Sea, was a British base for many years. Area: 332,942 km²; Pop: 2,147,000. Cap: Aden.

Yeti The abominable snowman, a manlike creature believed by some to live in the Himalayas.

Yew A coniferous tree commonly planted as an ornament, particularly in churchyards. It grows to a height of 25 metres and its branches tend to become wide-spreading. The poisonous seeds are borne singly inside bright red, berry-like cups instead of cones. The soft leathery needles are also poisonous.

Yoga Physical exercises associated with meditation designed to help a person reach spiritual discipline by physical discipline. Practised properly by the Hindus.

Yoghurt Nutritious food product that results from the bacterial curdling of milk.

Yokohama Major seaport in Honshu, Japan. Important shipbuilding and manufacturing centre. Badly damaged in 1923 by earthquake. Pop: 2,729,000.

Yom Kippur The Day of Atonement, a day of fasting when Jews ask God's forgiveness. It is the tenth day of the Jewish New Year and may fall in either September or October since the Jewish calendar is based on months of the moon.

Yosemite Falls A series of waterfalls in Yosemite National Park, California, USA and the highest in North America. Height: 740 metres.

Yugoslavia Country in SE Europe. Much of Yugoslavia is mountainous. Many people are farmers growing cereals, tobacco, fruit and olives. Industries include iron and steel, timber and manufacturing. Tourism is also important.

Yugoslavia came into being in 1918 after World War I. It is made up of six states (Bosnia and Hercegovina, Croatia, Macedonia, Montenegro, Serbia and Slovenia). Since 1945 Yugoslavia has had a communist government but has followed an independent path in foreign affairs. Area: 255,785 km^2; Pop: 22,997,000; Cap: Belgrade.

Z

Zaïre Second biggest country in Africa, formerly called the Congo. Much of central Zaïre is hot, wet forest. Elsewhere are savanna grasslands, with mountains and lakes in the east.

Most Zaïrean people work the land growing food and crops such as palm oil, coffee and rubber to sell abroad. The country also has valuable minerals, notably copper. Area: 2,345,000 km^2; Pop: 32,054,000; Cap: Kinshasa.

Zaïre The second longest river in Africa, flowing through Zaïre to the Atlantic coast, forming the boundary with the Congo. Length: 4667 km.

Zambezi River in SE Africa, flowing through Zambia and Mozambique into the Indian Ocean. The Zambezi forms the boundary between Zambia and Zimbabwe. It is separated into three stretches by rapids and the Victoria Falls. Length: 3530 km.

Zambia Landlocked country in SE Africa. Much of the land is high, with a cool, healthy climate. The soil is rather poor and although most Zambians are small farmers, the economy is based on mining. The most valuable mineral is copper. Zambia shares HEP from the Kariba Dam with Zimbabwe. It also shares the Victoria Falls which, like the wildlife in the game parks, attract many visitors. Area: 752,554 km^2; Pop: 6,554,000; Cap: Lusaka.

Zebra African mammal with distinctive stripes related to horses. Grazing animals, they live in small herds and are preyed upon by lions. There are three species: the common (Burchell's), the mountain and Grevy's, the largest.

Zeus In Greek myth the King of the gods. Brought up by shepherds, he battled with the Titans when he was still only a child. He made HADES god of the underworld and POSEIDON god of the sea. (Roman equivalent Jupiter.)

Zimbabwe Country in southern Africa, bordered by Mozambique, South Africa, Botswana and Zambia. Most of Zimbabwe is high savanna grassland. Its farmers grow tobacco, cotton, sugar and cereals and also raise cattle. Copper, nickel, chrome and other minerals are mined. Industry is developing, and uses electricity from the Kariba Dam HEP scheme on the Zambezi River. Tourists visit Zimbabwe to see the wildlife and to view the great Victoria Falls. Area: 390,550 km^2; Pop: 8,383,000; Cap: Harare.

Zinc Bluish-white metal with a brittle crystalline structure. It is coated on steel to prevent rusting, a process known as galvanizing. Brass is an alloy of zinc and copper. Chem. Symbol Zn.

Zodiac The band of 12 constellations across which the Sun appears to move during the course of a year. These are Aries (Ram), Taurus (Bull), Gemini (Twins), Cancer (Crab), Leo (Lion), Virgo (Virgin), Libra (Balance), Scorpio (Scorpion), Sagittarius (Archer), Capricornus (Goat), Aquarius (Water-bearer) and Pisces (Fishes).

Zola, Emile (1840–1902) French novelist who is as well known for his intervention in the Dreyfus case where a soldier had been unjustly convicted, as for his novels. He wrote an open letter beginning *J'accuse* (I accuse) and Dreyfus was given a new trial. He wrote a series of 20 volumes, *Les Rougon-Macquart*, realistically depicting the lives and fortunes of one family, and several controversial novels including *Nana* and *Germinal*.

Zoology Science and study of animal life. Together with botany it forms the science of biology.

Zürich Capital of Zürich canton, Switzerland, situated at NW end of L. Zürich. Largest city in Switzerland and major international centre of banking. Pop: 383,000.